T0366104

E–Business Innovation and Process Management

In Lee
Western Illinois University, USA

A volume in the Advances in
E–Business Research (AEBR)
Book Series

Acquisition Editor:	Kristin Klinger
Senior Managing Editor:	Jennifer Neidig
Managing Editor:	Sara Reed
Assistant Managing Editor:	Sharon Berger
Development Editor:	Kristin Roth
Copy Editor:	Toni Fitzgerald
Typesetter:	Jamie Snavely
Cover Design:	Lisa Tosheff

Published in the United States of America by
    CyberTech Publishing (an imprint of IGI Global)
    701 E. Chocolate Avenue
    Hershey PA 17033
    Tel: 717-533-8845
    Fax: 717-533-8661
    E-mail: cust@igi-global.com
    Web site: http://www.igi-global.com

Library of Congress Cataloging-in-Publication Data

E-business innovation and process management / In Lee, editor.
    p. cm.
  Summary: "This book provides researchers and practitioners with valuable information on advances and developments in emerging e-business models and technologies; it covers a variety of topics, such as e-business models, e-business strategies, online consumer behavior, e-business process modeling and practices, electronic communication adoption and service provider strategies, privacy policies, and implementation issues"--Provided by publisher.
  Includes bibliographical references and index.
  ISBN 978-1-59904-277-0 (hardcover) -- ISBN 978-1-59904-278-9 (softcover) -- ISBN 978-1-59904-279-7 (ebook) 1. Electronic commerce. I. Lee, In, 1958-
  HF5548.32.E17735 2006
  658.8'72--dc22
2006031357

This book is published in the IGI Global book series Advances in E-Business Research (AEBR) Book Series (ISSN: 1935-2700; eISSN: 1935-2719).

British Cataloguing in Publication Data
A Cataloguing in Publication record for this book is available from the British Library.

Advances in E-Business Research (AEBR) Book Series

In Lee (Western Illinois University, USA)

ISSN: 1935-2700
EISSN: 1935-2719

MISSION

Technology has played a vital role in the emergence of e-business and its applications incorporate strategies. These processes have aided in the use of electronic transactions via telecommunications networks for collaborating with business partners, buying and selling of goods and services, and customer service. Research in this field continues to develop into a wide range of topics, including marketing, psychology, information systems, accounting, economics, and computer science.

The **Advances in E-Business Research(AEBR)** series provides multidisciplinary references for researchers and practitioners in this area. Instructors, researchers, and professionals interested in the most up-to-date research on the concepts, issues, applications, and trends in the e-business field will find this collection, or individual books, extremely useful. This collection contains the highest quality academic books that advance understanding of e-business and addresses the challenges faced by researchers and practitioners.

COVERAGE

- E-Business Management
- E-Business Models and Architectures
- E-Business Systems Integration
- E-Business Technology Investment Strategies
- E-CRM
- E-Marketing
- Global E-Business
- Outsourcing and E-Business Technologies
- Semantic Web
- Sustainable E-Business
- Virtual Organization

IGI Global is currently accepting manuscripts for publication within this series. To submit a proposal for a volume in this series, please contact our Acquisition Editors at Acquisitions@igi-global.com or visit: http://www.igi-global.com/publish/.

Titles in this Series

For a list of additional titles in this series, please visit: www.igi-global.com

Interdisciplinary Perspectives on Business Convergence, Computing, and Legality
Himanshu Khurana (NCSA, University of Illinois, USA) and Rashimi Aggarwal (Institute of Management Technology-Ghazibad, India)
Business Science Reference • copyright 2013 • 354pp • H/C (ISBN: 9781466642096) • US $165.00 (our price)

Research and Development in E-Business through Service-Oriented Solutions
Katalin Tarnay (University of Pannonia, Hungary & Budapest University of Technology and Economics, Hungary) Sandor Imre (Budapest University of Technology and Economics, Hungary) and Lai Xu (Bournemouth University, UK)
Business Science Reference • copyright 2013 • 328pp • H/C (ISBN: 9781466641815) • US $185.00 (our price)

Mobile Services Industries, Technologies, and Applications in the Global Economy
In Lee (Western Illinois University, USA)
Information Science Reference • copyright 2013 • 368pp • H/C (ISBN: 9781466619814) • US $190.00 (our price)

Strategic and Pragmatic E-Business Implications for Future Business Practices
Karim Mohammed Rezaul (Glyndwr University, UK)
Business Science Reference • copyright 2012 • 496pp • H/C (ISBN: 9781466616196) • US $185.00 (our price)

Emergent Strategies for E-Business Processes, Services and Implications Advancing Corporate Frameworks
In Lee (Western Illinois University, USA)
Information Science Reference • copyright 2009 • 424pp • H/C (ISBN: 9781605661544) • US $195.00 (our price)

Semantic Web for Business Cases and Applications
Roberto Garcia (University of Lleida, Spain)
Information Science Reference • copyright 2009 • 444pp • H/C (ISBN: 9781605660660) • US $195.00 (our price)

www.igi-global.com

701 E. Chocolate Ave., Hershey, PA 17033
Order online at www.igi-global.com or call 717-533-8845 x100
To place a standing order for titles released in this series,
contact: cust@igi-global.com
Mon-Fri 8:00 am - 5:00 pm (est) or fax 24 hours a day 717-533-8661

E-Business Innovation and Process Management

Table of Contents

Section V: Privacy Policies and Implementation Issues

Preface

With the advent of e-business, organizations have been fundamentally changing the way they do their business. From business operation to managerial control to corporate strategy, e-business has become an integral part in organizations. As e-business evolution continues with emerging technologies and business models, a solid understanding of e-business innovation, process, and strategy proves invaluable for the successful e-business development and management. *E-Business Innovation and Process Management* provides researchers, professionals, and educators with the most current research on e-business trends, technologies, and practices. The book is divided into five segments: Section I, which discusses various e-business models; Section II, which addresses e-business strategies and consumer behavior model; Section III, which discusses e-business process modeling and practices; Section IV, which evaluates various electronic communication adoption and service provider strategies; and Section IV, which addresses privacy policies and implementation issues.

Section I: E-Business Models consists of two chapters. Chapter I, "Different Types of Business-to-Business Integration: Extended Enterprise Integration vs. Market B2B Integration," by Frank Goethals, Jacques Vandenbulcke, Wilfried Lemahieu, and Monique Snoeck, Katholieke Universiteit Leuven (Belgium), argues that there exist two basic forms of business-to-business integration (B2Bi), namely extended enterprise integration and market B2Bi. This chapter clarifies the meaning of both concepts, shows that the difference between both is fundamental, and discusses the consequences of the difference in the realm of Web services development. The importance of coordination and the role of standards are studied for both types of e-business. The authors hope that this chapter clearly shows the foundations of B2Bi and that the chapter as such brings clarity into B2Bi practices.

Chapter II, "E-Business Models in B2B: A Process-Based Categorization and Analysis of Business-to Business Models," by Mahesh S. Raisinghani, TWU (USA), Turan Melemez, Lijie Zou, Chris Paslowski, Irma Kikvidze, Susanne Taha, and Klaus Simons, Purdue University (USA), presents an in-depth study with examples from industry that provides a process-based approach to B2B e-commerce. The authors argue that due to the variety of existing models, it seems difficult to find a widely accepted categorization that can be analysed and assessed. A comparative examination of both the buy-side and the sell-side based on a process-related approach provides extensive insights for further comparative research and evaluation of products/services and models.

Section II: E-Business Strategies and Consumer Behavior Model consists of four chapters. Chapter III, "Drivers of Adoption and Implementation of Internet-Based Marketing Channels," by Jørn Flohr Nielsen, Viggo Høst, and Niels Peter Mols, University of Aarhus (Denmark), analyzes factors influencing manufacturers' adoption and implementation of Internet-based marketing channels based on survey data from Danish, Finnish, and Swedish manufacturers. The adoption is shown to be influenced by market pressure, management support, knowledge of IT, and, in particular, willingness to cannibalize other investments. As the process moves on, political factors become more important. Successful implementation seems mainly to depend on top management support and IT knowledge.

Chapter IV, "Content is King? Interdependencies in Value Networks for Mobile Services," by Uta Wehn de Montalvo, Netherlands Organisation for Applied Scientific Research (The Netherlands), Els van de Kar, Delft University of Technology (The Netherlands), and Carleen Maitland, Pennsylvania State University (USA), investigates interdependencies in value networks for mobile services. This chapter analyzes the role of content and the content providers, respectively, in the process of value creation to bring these mobile services about. In a cross-case comparison, this chapter contrasts the power structures in different value networks for a number of mobile information and entertainment services and identifies similarities and differences in terms of the types of industrial players that assume positions of greater or lesser importance. The position of content providers turns out to be surprisingly weak.

Chapter V, "Buyer-Supplier Relationships in Business-to-Business E-Procurement: Effects of Supply Conditions," by Ravinder Nath, Creighton University (USA), and Rebecca Angeles, University of New Brunswick Fredericton (Canada), investigates the relevance of the resource dependency and relational exchange theories in explaining e-procurement activities of firms. Survey data were gathered from members of the Institute for Supply Management and the Council for Supply Chain Management Professionals (formerly the Council of Logistics Management). Effects of the resource dependency theory variables—supply importance, supply complexity, supply market dynamism, and availability of alternatives—on the information exchange and operational linkages, the relational exchange theory variables, are observed. Study findings show that supply importance and supply complexity primarily predict information exchange and operational linkages.

Chapter VI, "Consumer Factors Affecting Adoption of Internet Banking Services: An Empirical Investigation in Taiwan," by Wen-Jang (Kenny) Jih, Middle Tennessee State University (USA), and Shu-Yeng Wong and Tsung-Bin Chang, Da-Yeh University (Taiwan), empirically examines the effects of consumer-perceived risk, personal involvement, and perception of banks' risk-reduction measures on their willingness to adopt Internet banking services. The results show that more experienced Internet users tend to involve themselves than their less-experienced counterparts in the use of Internet banking services. Adoption willingness is directly affected by the perception of risk-reduction measurements, perceived risks, and personal involvement, and indirectly by familiarity with the Internet technology and Internet banking. Further, adoption willingness is found to be impacted more by the perception of risk-reduction measures than by the perceived risks.

Section III: E-Business Process Modeling and Practices consists of four chapters. Chapter VII, "A Simonian Approach to E-Business Research: A Study in Netchising," by Ye-Sho Chen, Louisiana State University (USA), Guoqing Chen, Tsinghua University (China), and Soushan Wu, Chang-Gung University (Taiwan), draws upon five seemingly unrelated research areas of Herbert Simon (skew distributions, near decomposability, docility, causal and effectual reasoning, and attention management) and proposes a holistic framework of attention-based information systems for firms to frame an enduring competitive strategy in the digital economy. As an ongoing project, the framework is applied to model Netchising, an emerging research topic in global e-business.

Chapter VIII, "Business Process Modeling with the User Requirements Notation," by Michael Weiss, Carleton University (Canada), and Daniel Amyot, University of Ottawa (Canada), demonstrates how the user requirements notation (URN) can be used to model business processes. URN combines goals and scenarios in order to help capture and reason about user requirements prior to detailed design. This chapter illustrates the notation, its use, and its benefits with a supply chain management case study. It then briefly compares this approach to related modeling approaches, namely, use case-driven design, service-oriented architecture analysis, and conceptual value modeling.

Chapter IX, "How E-Services Satisfy Customer Needs: A Software-Aided Reasoning," by Ziv Baida, Jaap Gordijn, and Hans Akkermans, Free University Amsterdam (The Netherlands), and Hanne Sæle and Andrei Z. Morch, SINTEF Energy Research (Norway), outlines an ontological approach that models how companies can electronically offer packages of independent services (service bundles) based on understanding their customers' needs and demands. To enable this scenario, it is necessary that software can reason about customer needs and available service offerings. The proposed approach for tackling this issue applies conceptual modeling and requirements engineering techniques to broadly accepted service management and service marketing concepts, such that software can be developed—based on the service ontology—that designs service bundles for a given set of customer demands. The authors use a running case example from the Norwegian energy sector to demonstrate how they put theory into practice.

Chapter X, "Personalization of Web Services: Concepts, Challenges, and Solutions," by Zakaria Maamar, Zayed University (UAE), Soraya Kouadri Mostéfaoui, Fribourg University (Switzerland), Qusay Mahmoud, Guelph University (Canada), Ghita Kouadri Mostéfaoui, University of Montreal (Canada), and Djamal Benslimane, Claude Bernard Lyon 1 University (France), highlights the need for context in Web services personalization. This personalization aims at accommodating user preferences and needs. Besides user preferences, this chapter argues that the computing resources on which the Web services operate have an impact on their personalization. Indeed, resources schedule the execution requests that originate from multiple Web services. To track this personalization, three types of contexts are devised: user context, Web service context, and resource context. A fourth type of context denoted by security enables protecting the content of each of these three contexts.

Section IV: Electronic Communication Adoption and Service Provider Strategy consists of four chapters. Chapter XI, "Managing Corporate E-Mail Systems: A Contemporary Study," by Aidan Duane, Waterford Institute of Technology (Ireland), and Patrick Finnegan, University College Cork (Ireland), presents a multiple case study investigation of e-mail system monitoring and control. The study examines the interaction between key elements of e-mail control identified by previous researchers and considers the role of such controls at various implementation phases. The findings reveal eight major elements to be particularly important in monitoring and controlling e-mail systems within the organizations studied. These are: (1) form a cross-functional e-mail system management team; (2) implement and regularly update e-mail management software; (3) formulate a detailed and legally sound e-mail policy; (4) engage in structured e-mail system training; (5) create and maintain ongoing awareness of e-mail policy; (6) engage in a process of hybrid feedback and control-based e-mail monitoring; (7) firmly enforce discipline in accordance with the e-mail policy; and (8) conduct regular reviews and updates of the e-mail management program.

Chapter XII, "Predicting Electronic Communication System Adoption: The Influence of Adopter Perceptions of Continuous or Discontinuous Innovation," by Gary Hunter and Steven Taylor, Illinois State University (USA), investigates the factors predicting adoption of electronic communication systems. A contribution of the study is that it focuses on comparing factors predicting initial adoption relative to adoption of an upgrade. Given the importance of upgrade adoption in e-business, it is important to compare the factors predicting initial adoption and upgrade adoption. The study uses a survey-based method to examine the factors influencing the adoption of customer relationship management software (CRM).

Chapter XIII, "Computer Self-Efficacy and the Acceptance of Instant Messenger Technology" by Thomas Stafford, University of Memphis (USA), investigates motivations for instant messaging (IM) use in a technology acceptance framework that seeks to evaluate computer self-efficacy as an antecedent to critical TAM constructs. It is demonstrated that user self-efficacy is mediated in its impact on perceived usefulness of IM technology by the ease with which the technology can be used. This has important implications for managers seeking to promote IM applications, as well as for theorists interested in user efficacy and technology acceptance, with a conclusion that better user training will lead to greater user value in the technology.

Chapter XIV, "User Perceptions of the Usefulness of E-Mail and Instant Messaging," by Philip Houle and Troy Strader, Drake University (USA), and Sridhar Ramaswami, Iowa State University (USA), describes research that explores the impacts of unsolicited traffic on the perceived usefulness of electronic message technologies. Two technologies were explored: e-mail and instant messaging. The hypothesis is that unsolicited message traffic would have negative effects on the perceived usefulness of the technologies. However, the findings did not support this expected result. Users of the technologies appear to cope with the unsolicited traffic in a variety of ways. The implications of results are discussed from the perspective of managers, researchers, marketers, service providers, and public policy makers.

Section V: Privacy Policies and Implementation Issues consists of two chapters. Chapter XV, "Is P3P an Answer to Protecting Information Privacy?," by Noushin Ashrafi and Jean-Pierre Kuilboer, University of Massachusetts Boston (USA), aims at providing a brief explanation of P3P both as a new technology and as a standard. This chapter presents the background on use of technology for privacy protection. It then examines the role of P3P in privacy protection and presents a brief history of how it started. The authors use empirical data on top 500 interactive companies to assess its adoption in the e-commerce environment.

Chapter XVI, "Semi-Automatic Derivation and Application of Personal Privacy Policies," by George Yee and Larry Korba, National Research Council (Canada), shows how personal privacy policies for e-business may be semi-automatically derived and applied. This chapter first examines privacy legislation to derive the contents of a personal privacy policy. It then describes two methods for semi-automatically generating a personal privacy policy, using community consensus to valuate privacy. The chapter concludes by presenting a privacy management model that explains how privacy policies are applied in e-business, followed by a discussion and a review of related works.

Recently, organizations have witnessed rapid improvement in e-business technologies and their deployment as a strategic weapon. The growing importance of e-business and its inevitable effect on organizations presents numerous challenges as well as opportunities for academics and practitioners. Sustained innovation, competitiveness, and market growth occur when e-business enables companies to redesign the business processes, develop new business models, and improve management practices. An outstanding collection of the latest research associated with the emerging e-business technologies and business models, *Advances in E-Business Research: E-Business Innovation and Process Management* provides researchers and practitioners with study findings and insight valuable in advancing the knowledge and practice of all facets of electronic business.

In Lee, PhD
Editor-in-Chief
E-Business Innovation and Process Management

Section I

E-Business Models

Chapter I

Different Types of Business-to-Business Integration:
Extended Enterprise Integration vs. Market B2B Integration

Frank Goethals, Katholieke Universiteit Leuven, Belgium

Jacques Vandenbulcke, Katholieke Universiteit Leuven, Belgium

Wilfried Lemahieu, Katholieke Universiteit Leuven, Belgium

Monique Snoeck, Katholieke Universiteit Leuven, Belgium

Abstract

In this chapter we argue that there exist two basic forms of business-to-business integration (B2Bi), namely extended enterprise integration and market B2Bi. This chapter clarifies the meaning of both concepts, shows that the difference between both is fundamental, and discusses the consequences of the difference in the realm of Web services development. The importance of coordination and the role of standards are studied for both types of e-business. The authors hope this chapter clearly shows the foundations of B2Bi and that the chapter as such brings clarity into B2Bi practices.

Introduction

Information and communication technology (ICT) is becoming more and more prevalent in many businesses. In the past, many information systems have been developed to deliver some specific functionality. Nowadays, one of the tasks of information technology (IT) departments is to integrate existing information systems, not only within the company borders but also across company borders. Also, new information systems are being developed that should deliver cross-company functionality. The human communication processes that are involved in analyzing and designing the business, and in designing, implementing, and maintaining information systems, are affected by the fact that the IT department of one company has to create software to fulfill requirements of people not only in their own company but in *other* companies too. In this context, the term "extended enterprise" is often used. The extended enterprise concept is, however, not unequivocally defined.

This chapter first discusses the concept of the extended enterprise and opposes this form of economic organization to the two other basic forms of economic organization, namely the firm and the market. Next, we derive from organization theory (see, e.g., Hatch, 1997; Morgan, 1996) two basic types of B2Bi, namely extended enterprise integration and market B2Bi. We show that the extended enterprise constitutes a specific context within which information systems are being developed, integrated, and maintained, and that this context allows for/needs specific ways of integration. We discuss the role of standards and coordination for both types of B2Bi.

This chapter is relevant for both researchers and practitioners. Researchers can relate their research to the two types of B2Bi. It is interesting to note that not all ICT innovations are appropriate for both types of B2Bi. For example, the public universal description, discovery, and integration initiative focuses on market B2Bi, not on extended enterprise integration. For practitioners the chapter reveals a number of coordination issues they should be aware of when pursuing B2Bi. For both groups it is interesting that the chapter investigates the role of standards in realizing B2Bi.

The Extended Enterprise vs.
Other Forms of Doing Business

For a long time, two basic forms of economic organization have been recognized: markets on the one hand and hierarchies (firms) on the other. Powell (1990) refers to Ronald Coase as the person who first discussed the firm as a governance structure rather than just as a black box that transforms inputs into outputs. Coase (1937) asserts that firms and markets are alternative means for organizing similar kinds of transactions. Only in the 1970s did proponents of the transaction cost economics act upon Coase's findings. One of these proponents, Williamson (1975, 1985), argues that some transactions are more likely to take place within hierarchically organized firms (Williamson equated *firms* with *hierarchies*) than through a market interface. More specifically, he states that transactions that are to be executed within hierarchically organized firms are likely to involve uncertainty about

Figure 1. The network form of organization as a hybrid of markets and hierarchies

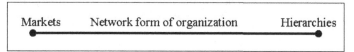

their outcome, recur frequently and require substantial "transaction-specific investments" (of money, time, or energy) that cannot be easily transferred. On the other hand, exchanges that are straightforward, non-repetitive, and require no transaction-specific investments can be expected to take place across a market interface.

> *Organization, or hierarchy, arises when the boundaries of a firm expand to internalize transactions and resource flows that were previously conducted in the marketplace.*
>
> (Powell, 1990, p. 303)

This dichotomous view of markets and hierarchies—as discussed by Williamson (1975)—sees firms as separate from markets and assumes the presence of sharp firm boundaries. These sharp boundaries, however, do not always seem to be present. This is true especially in the case of partnering organizations (extended enterprises, see Figure 1). Transactions between partnering companies can be seen as a hybrid form of economic organization. That is, if transactions are distributed as points along a continuum with discrete market transactions located at one end and the highly centralized firm at the other end, partnering companies fall in between these poles. This is illustrated in Figure 1.

Podolny and Page (1998, p. 59) define a network form of organization as:

> *... any collection of actors (N ≥ 2) that pursue repeated, enduring exchange relations with one another and, at the same time, lack a legitimate organizational authority to arbitrate and resolve disputes that may arise during the exchange.*

The definition of Podolny and Page is very much aimed at identifying the differences between the network form of organization on the one hand, and markets and hierarchies on the other hand: in pure markets companies do not aim at enduring relations, and in hierarchies there is a clearly recognized, legitimate authority that can resolve disputes that arise among actors.

Besides these two characteristics, *some* scholars (e.g., Dore, 1983; Powell, 1990) have argued that network forms of organization also posses another characteristic, namely a distinct ethic or value-orientation on the part of exchange partners. Hirschman (1970) argues that partners are willing to make relationship-specific investments without contractual guarantees protecting those investments, and for Powell the norm of reciprocity is key (1990, pp. 303-304):

> *The parties to a network agree to forego the right to pursue their own interests*
> *at the expense of others ... The 'entangling strings' of reputation, friendship,*
> *interdependence, and altruism become integral parts of the relationship.*

The presence or absence of such a distinct ethic relates to the difference between "collaboration" and "cooperation."

Bowersox, Closs, and Stank (2003) assert that most cooperative engagements between commercial organizations do not represent cross-enterprise collaboration. In their vision:

> *... cross-enterprise collaboration emerges when two or more firms voluntarily*
> *agree to integrate human, financial, or technical resources in an effort to create*
> *a new, more efficient, effective, or relevant business model.*

> (Bowersox et al., 2003, p. 22)

The governance mechanism should thus not be based on command-and-control principles (as in the firm), but should involve a *"voluntary commitment and integration of resources in pursuit of jointly defined goals"* (Bowersox et al., 2003, p. 22). Liedtka (1996) discusses the importance of a 'partnering mindset' as a critical success factor for collaboration.

Podolny and Page (1998, p. 61) state that:

> *... this more trusting ethic is one of the defining elements of a network form of*
> *governance, and the network form of governance is therefore not reducible to a*
> *hybridization of market and hierarchical forms, which, in contrast, are premised*
> *on a more adversarial posture.*

However, they also think that *"it is probably true that a moral community or spirit of goodwill is not a functional necessity for a network form of organization to exist."* They believe that two parties may enter into a long-term *contract* in order to place restrictions on the opportunistic behavior of one another. However, in cases of unexpected changes (thus changes that were not foreseen in the contract) long-term contracts (to bind the parties together) are not likely to allow for the same flexibility and adaptability as a spirit of goodwill (or a norm of reciprocity)[1].

In literature the term "extended enterprise" is often used to refer to the network form of organization. From literature it is, however, unclear whether the concept of the "extended enterprise" requires some kind of *collaborative mindset*. We believe this issue is the reason that two different conceptualizations of the extended enterprise exist in literature. Sometimes the extended enterprise is defined as a *collection* of different enterprises (see, e.g., Petersen & Szegheo, 2000). In other cases the extended enterprise is regarded as one enterprise reaching out to its suppliers, customers, and partners (see, e.g., IFS, 2004). Figure 2 illustrates the issue. The light-grey area contains the elements that are part of the extended enterprise. Company A has a long-term relationship with companies B, C, D, E, and F (and short-term relationships with companies G, H, I, J, K, and L in the market). In the left panel of the figure, the case is illustrated where A collaborates with the other companies. Cross-enter-

Figure 2. Two different conceptualizations of the extended enterprise (Left panel: Collabora-tive extended enterprise; Right panel: Cooperative extended enterprise)

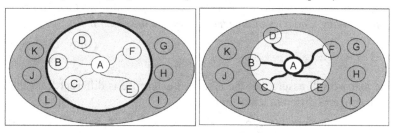

prise collaboration has a major impact on the organizations. Liedtka (1996) stresses that effective collaboration is difficult to achieve in a climate of business as usual, as it relies on qualities that are not present in most organizations. Successful collaboration requires the development of new skills, mindsets, and corporate architectures. Bowersox et al. (2003) argue that cross-enterprise collaboration requires companies to remodel the organizational structures. Cross-enterprise collaboration is thus a far-reaching effort. As such, the ensemble of enterprises forms one "collaborative extended enterprise."

In the right panel of Figure 2 there is no true collaboration among the companies. In that case, company A merely extends the optimization of its business processes to the (public) processes involving companies B, C, D, E, and F, and can as such be called an "extended enterprise." It is worth mentioning that this still requires that companies are on very good terms with each other. They *are* cooperating, which is very different from regarding the counterparty as a party in a (series of) isolated transaction(s) that is done in the marketplace. The cooperation is characterized by a win-win vision, instead of a "what you win, I lose" mindset.

Bowersox et al. (2003) argue that "collaboration" entails more than "cooperation." Therefore we denote the two types of extended enterprises as the "collaborative extended enterprise" (left panel in Figure 2) and the "cooperative extended enterprise" (right panel in Figure 2). In the remainder of this chapter, we use the terms "extended enterprise" and "partnering" (instead of collaborating/cooperating) if we do not need to distinguish between the two types of extended enterprises.

As a conclusion to this discussion, we submit the following definition of the extended enterprise:

> *The extended enterprise is a collection of legal entities (N ≥ 2) that pursue repeated, enduring exchange relations with one another.*

In contrast to the definition of Podolny and Page of the network form laid out above, we do not emphasize the absence of a legitimate organizational authority to arbitrate and resolve disputes. Such authority may be present. Emery and Trist (1965) and Williams (1982) even affirm that:

... to the extent that stakeholders regard each other as potential coproducers of desirable changes in their shared environments, they need to create long-term structures to support and sustain their collective appreciation, a forum for future problem solving, and a regulative framework for the domain.

(Gray, 1989, p. 90)

Please note that we still assure that the extended enterprise is different from the firm by stating that it concerns different legal entities.

Three theories are often cited (see, e.g., Podolny & Page, 1998; Selz, 1999) to explain the presence of the network form of organization, namely *transaction cost economics, principal-agent theory*, and *property rights theory*. These three theories are basic elements in "new institutional economics." Picot, Ripperger, and Wolff (1996) state that one may conclude from new institutional economics that the efficient design of organizations requires the simultaneous consideration of coordinational and motivational aspects. The coordination problem involves the determination of which things should be done, how they should be done, and who should do them. It is also about who makes decisions and with what information. The motivation problem is to make sure that the individuals involved in these processes are willing to do their part. Williamson (1991, p. 283) refers to the balancing of coordination and motivation as follows:

As compared with the market, the hybrid sacrifices incentives in favor of superior coordination among the parts. As compared with the hierarchy, the hybrid sacrifices cooperativeness in favor of greater incentive intensity.

Transaction cost economics approaches the problem of organizational design from a coordination perspective, principal-agent theory and property rights theory from a motivational perspective. In this chapter, we do not discuss these theories in detail. It is, however, interesting to have a look at transaction cost economics.

Transaction cost economics discusses the fact that the cost of organizing a transaction in a market sometimes exceeds the cost of coordinating the transaction in a firm and the other way around. The key here is Coase's law (1937, p. 7), which states that:

A firm will tend to expand until the costs of organizing an extra transaction within the firm become equal to the costs of carrying out the same transaction by means of an exchange on the open market.

Transaction costs consist of ex ante costs (searching for a trading partner, specifying the products to be traded, price and contract negotiations) and ex post costs (late or non-delivery, problems of quality control) (Casson, 1996). Williamson (1991) defines three critical dimensions of transactions: their frequency, the uncertainty to which they are subject, and the type and degree of asset specificity. Although all are important, transaction-cost economics attaches special interest to the last one. A resource is defined as specific to the degree to which it loses its value when being used for other than the original task (Picot et al., 1996). Transaction cost theory recommends the vertical integration of highly specific tasks.

Williamson (1991) extended the initial transaction cost framework (which was based on a discrete choice between markets and hierarchies), and the theory now endorses hybrid forms. He shows that under specific conditions (especially concerning asset specificity), choosing for a network form of organization is appropriate[2]. In the final section of this chapter we will come back to the idea of asset-specificity, then from the point of view of standardization-efforts.

To end the discussion on organization theory, it is important to note that there are two basic levels of business-to-business integration companies envision. As is clear from Figure 2, enterprises that are involved in an extended enterprise setting split their environment in two. First, there is the integration with other enterprises with which a long-term relationship is pursued (and of which the identity is thus not only relevant but of major importance). This way, an extended enterprise is created (be it a collaborative extended enterprise or a cooperative extended enterprise). Secondly, there is a coupling with other organizations with which no long-term relationship is pursued but with short-term benefits (and of which the identity is less relevant). Clearly, doing business with partners requires another approach than doing business with other organizations in the market.

Besides these two basic forms of integration, we note that enterprises need to achieve an internal integration as well, namely an integration of the diverse functions and departments within a legal entity (the firm).

The IT-Enabled Extended Enterprise

Nowadays, enterprises do not only want to use ICT internally (i.e., within their organization) but also in their communication with other organizations. In what follows, we first present three levels of systems integration organizations envision. These are (1) enterprise application integration, (2) extended enterprise integration, and (3) market B2Bi. Next, we discuss coordination problems that arise when developing business-to-business systems. More specifically, our attention goes to issues in the relatively new Web services paradigm. Although this paradigm resolves a number of problems older technologies suffer from, still some problems remain. Finally, we reveal the role of standards in B2B integration and the relationship of standards to the coordination problems.

Fitting Organization, Environment, and ICT

In the previous section, we argued that businesses can be involved in three types of organizational integration. As the business needs to be integrated, ICT systems need to be integrated, too (as is discussed in contingency theory; see, e.g., Borgatti, 2001). Therefore, as companies are confronted with three basic types of integration at organizational level (internal, within the Extended Enterprise, and with the marketplace) we should recognize three levels of IT-integration as well.

Figure 3. Different types of B2B systems integration

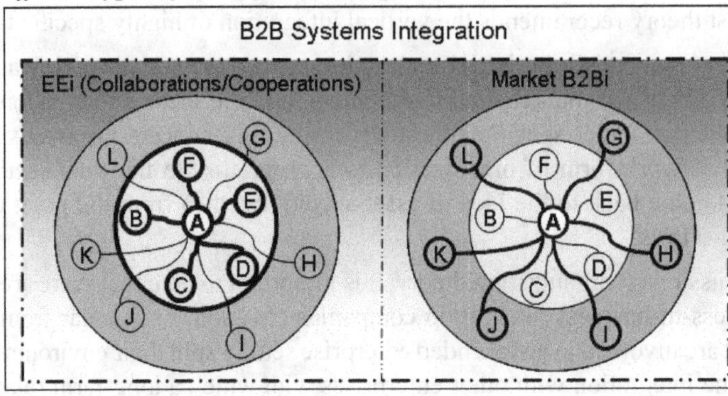

The first type of IT-integration companies should realize is the *internal* integration of the diverse systems within company walls generally referred to as "enterprise application integration" (EAI).

The two other types of IT-integration concern B2Bi, the topic of this chapter. First there is the *extended enterprise integration* (EEi). In the context of the extended enterprise, companies that dispose of capabilities that are useful for each other try to cooperate/collaborate. It is important to note that partnering organizations have decided to do business with each other for an extended period of time. They know the other company can deliver to a certain extent what is needed. A partnership is set up to get more out of the other company than what is already being delivered, and it is recognized that some form of coordination is necessary to realize additional benefits. Partnering enterprises need to find out how they can be of more value to each other. The development of customized software is part of this value adding effort. It is clear that partner-specific IT investments can be made.

Essentially, this is not the case in the other type of B2Bi. This second form of B2Bi we call *market B2Bi*. Companies that do business in the marketplace do not cooperate/collaborate. Basically for each transaction they try to find out who can deliver what is needed. Every time again, companies have the free choice to choose the services from a company (present in the marketplace) that fulfills the needs. Therefore, no thorough coordination among the companies is needed. Of course, service-providing companies try to pick up signals from the market to deliver the services that are useful, and they try to minimize costs, but there is no partnering. This scenario shows the IT integration alternatives. Market Web services have mainly been developed in isolation and may be found through a market mechanism such as the global UDDI (universal description, discovery, and integration) registries. Furthermore, organizations may do business with many other organizations through an electronic marketplace. Figure 3 shows the ideas presented here.

Currently, the boundary between EEi and market B2Bi is vague. These two types of B2Bi actually cover a whole continuum of B2Bi practices (as is also clear from organization theory). With the current state of technology, we believe that Market B2Bi primarily concerns the indirect integration through electronic marketplaces. In the future new Web services standards and semantic Web standards may be developed that enable organizations to dynamically

Figure 4. Two communication gaps in realizing B2B systems

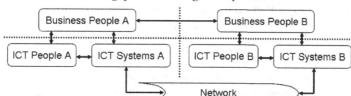

make direct links to other organizations in the marketplace. Unfortunately organizations that want a direct link between their systems nowadays are often forced to work with a long-term relationship because of the inflexibility of IT. This is in contrast to organizations that truly envision a long-term relationship (for example with suppliers of critical, scarce half-finished products). The contemporary "long-term" relationship between enterprises may thus become much shorter if revolutionary dynamic technologies come available. The key differentiating characteristic (extended enterprise or market) is—in our view—the willingness to make partner-specific IT investments, which is related to the *fundamentally desired duration* of the relationship.

Although the boundary between EEi and market B2Bi is vague, the distinction between both is useful. For example, nowadays it is often stated that enterprises should be "flexible" (see, e.g., Spies, 2001). The interpretation of terms like flexibility depends on the integration under consideration. Flexibility in the extended enterprise clearly does not involve the flexible replacement of one collaborating partner by a new collaborating partner. Flexibility here concerns the ease with which processes can be redesigned and new processes can be implemented so as to better deliver the services the customer needs. In market B2Bi flexibility is less on the introduction of new jointly created public business processes but more on the replacement of counterparties in doing standardized transactions. Please note that this does not imply that no standardized processes can be realized in the collaborative extended enterprise. Some standardized processes (namely those that require the sharing of private information) cannot even be expected to take place in the market.

Coordination Problems

The ICT-systems that are used need to be developed first. When developing systems, it is important to know the functional and non-functional requirements of the future user of the system. This is, of course, also the case in a Web services[3] world. However, in actual practice the attention seems to be going much more to *playing* with Web services technology than to using the new technology in *a way interesting* to businesses (Frankel & Parodi, 2002). In realizing Web services that are relevant to the business, many problems may arise.

For example, in Goethals, Vandenbulcke, Lemahieu, Snoeck, De Backer, and Haesen (2004c) the existence of two communication gaps is recognized. First, there is the classic problem of business-ICT alignment that has challenged companies for many years. Secondly, there is a communication gap between the integrating companies. Pollock (2002) states that "*most problems contributing to the high failure rates of integration projects are not technical in nature.*" Pollock points out the importance of semantics in B2Bi. While misunderstandings (and semantic obscurities) within a company may be large, the problems only increase when looking at relationships between different companies. The two gaps are shown as dotted lines in Figure 4.

The work of many people needs to be brought into line in order to realize the required computer systems. The presence of coordination problems in the development of ICT systems was detected a long time ago (see, e.g., Brooks, 1975), and the solution proposed to resolve the problem was to diminish the need for coordination. The "distributed computing" paradigm was expected to do so. An important building block of this paradigm is the idea of "componentized software" (of which the Web services concept is the latest incarnation).

A software component is a coherent composite of objects, necessary for the execution of specific functionality. This composite is callable through an interface. Lindgren (2001, p. 62) states that:

> ... *a component may be very complex internally and be built using class structures and inheritance; but to the rest of the world, the component is only viewed by a clean, external interface that is not interdependent upon other components.*

A loose coupling between components is key to the component model; this model offers the possibility to build a software system by stitching different components together. As components are called through an interface, a Web service can be changed internally without having to change the calling component (that is, if the interface remains the same).

Cooperating components (such as Web services) can thus be developed in isolation. If one component is informed about the interface of another component, it can call this other component. Unfortunately, the fact that components can technically work together if they know each other's interface and know which communication protocol to use works as a trap for systems developers. The distributed computing paradigm did not resolve all coordination problems. There seems to be confusion between "decentralized" and "distributed" computing. That is, in the past there has been a bad coordination between project teams in that projects that should have had shared data or logic became decoupled, resulting in data and software redundancy. The term "distributed computing" has often been (erroneously) used as an excuse for a decentralized free-for-all approach. The term distributed computing actually implies the "*division of a previous whole*" (Cook, 1996, p. 14). According to Cook, the concept of distributed computing is similar to Peter Drucker's management concept of federal decentralization, that is, it requires both strong parts and a strong center.

> *While distributed computing is clearly not a physically centralized approach, it is a logically centralized approach.*
>
> (Cook, 1996, p. 15)

There needs to be a balance between the flexibility of decentralized computing and the coordination advantages of centralization. If components are not being developed from

Figure 5. Different levels of compromise

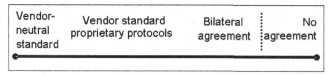

an enterprise-wide point of view, they will not form an integrated complex that fulfills the functional and non-functional requirements.

We end this discussion by linking the above to the two types of B2Bi. As stated, Web services standards allow for the isolated development of software. However, if the necessary functionality and service levels are to be provided by one specific party (i.e., in house or by a partnering company), the development of the Web service cannot be left up to coincidence. Coordination is then necessary, and one should speak about (and live by the rules of) "distributed computing." Practices such as "extended enterprise architecture" could prove indispensable in this context (see Goethals, Snoeck, Lemahieu, & Vandenbulcke, 2006). The functioning of the marketplace is different in that "service consuming" companies can freely choose from a plethora of available services, that is, they "hope" that some functionality will be delivered by an arbitrary party. From the provider's side, the willingness to make counterparty-specific investments is lacking, and only standard, generic Web services will be offered. The identity of the counterparty is less relevant in this case, and no centralized coordination is present. Consequently, the term "decentralized computing" is more applicable.

Achieving the Necessary Coordination in Web Services Development

The question concerning distributed vs. decentralized computing directly shows in a discussion on standards. After all, standards play a big role in integrating systems; they resolve the need for coordination (at the level at which the standard works). The concept of Web services is currently receiving very much attention as a paradigm that allows B2Bi. The biggest strength of this concept is just that it includes a set of ICT standards. Simple object access protocol (SOAP), for example, is a standard way to communicate with Web services.

In building a business-to-business process, companies need to agree on a number of issues. Agreement is not only needed at ICT level but also at business level. Above that, it is important to know how to translate the business agreement into an ICT agreement, and—the other way around—how to use ICT agreements to enable the business.

It is important to recognize the role of standards, their powers, and their threats. It can be very useful to standardize issues—be it business issues or ICT issues—on which it does not make any sense to compete. But of course, *by standardizing some issues, competition shifts to other issues.* Companies want to make a difference somewhere. Standards such as SOAP are very useful and lift the competition to the level of using the standard creatively.

There are different levels of compromise possible among parties (Besen & Farrell, 1994). The levels of agreement on ICT issues are shown in Figure 5. Parties need at least bilateral agreements. An active coordination among the parties is, however, not always necessary. Some issues have already been standardized sufficiently at a higher level (for example at the level of the software vendor). Clearly, companies do not have to discuss on the contents covered by a standard anymore if they both agree to use the same existing standard.

Of course, not everything is being standardized. When it comes to technology, it is only where interoperability is important that standards become required. Features that cause customer dissatisfaction or hinder industry growth[4] evolve into standards, while "customer-useful differentiating features" do not tend to evolve into standards. Furthermore, the demand for standards usually comes from the users and customers of the technology who experience the confusion caused by the lack of standards (Cook, 1996). Employees (be it business or ICT employees) may for example notice that there is no standard terminology for important concepts in their company and that this creates communication problems. Companies then consider creating a "data dictionary" with a standardized vocabulary. At the level of business-to-business relations, companies may suffer from a non-standardized vocabulary too. If one company uses the field "customerno" in its database, and another company uses the field "customernumber," both companies know the same concept but have a different name assigned to the concept. In order to have IT systems of such companies talking to each other, a translation will be necessary (from the standardized vocabulary of one company to the standardized vocabulary of another company).

In choosing which level of agreement (and which standard) to use, it is important to evaluate the opportunities that are being offered by the different levels (and standards at those levels). As such, the presence/absence of network effects should be taken into account when deciding when to use standards. Network effects are based on the concept of positive feedback, that is, the situation in which success generates more success. The value of connecting to a network depends on the number of other people already connected to it (i.e., you can connect to). Network effects do not play in the extended enterprise ("change partners" is a contradiction in terms), but they do play in market B2Bi.

As network effects do play in market B2Bi, only minor investments can be made to replace one counterparty by another. Therefore, market B2Bi Web services are generic, standard services that can be used/are being offered by many counterparties. Human coordination is consequently no issue in market B2Bi (a side effect of which is that the success of market Web services can only be measured by usage statistics). Vendor-neutral standards are required for market B2Bi. This is—of course—closely related to the theory of transaction cost economics, which shows that short-term market relations are characterized by straightforward exchanges and the absence of transaction-specific investments. In standardized (straightforward) practices it is easy to switch counterparties, enabling network effects (which are desired in Market B2Bi).

Transaction cost economics shows that transactions within the extended enterprise are more likely to involve uncertainty about their outcome and rely on transaction-specific investments.

Web services may be developed for use by one specific partner, and fairly complex choreographies of Web services may be built (which are difficult to test). The physical distance

Figure 6. Characteristics of Web services in the extended enterprise compared to market Web services

Characteristic	EEi	Market B2Bi
User of the Web service	'One' user-organization. User needs to be identified before the development begins. Partner-specific investments. Counterparty is fixed.	'Many' using organizations. User need not be identified before the development begins. No counterparty-specific investments. Counterparty is variable.
Devlopment coordination	Coorination is needed. Creativity is possible.	No coordination needed (i.e., standards are used) Only standardized processes.
Measure of success	Statisfaction and acceptance	Usage statistics
Life span	Life span Constituting Companies / Life span Extended Enterprise / Life span EE Web Service	Life span Market B2Bi Web Service / Duration Market B2B Transaction

between user and developer is usually large in a Web services context, but in the case of extended enterprise Web services development coordination is necessary. Therefore, the physical distance will be lowered artificially to enable the development of radically new business practices. While standards are the only option in Market B2Bi, bilateral agreements (even at technology level) may be used in the extended enterprise. Developed Web services can be evaluated by investigating the satisfaction of the users (which are known). These issues are shown in Figure 6.

Conclusion

In this chapter, we have identified three basic types of systems integration, based on organization theory. The extended enterprise was defined as a collection of legal entities ($N \geq 2$) that pursue repeated, enduring exchange relations with one another. It is a form of economic organization that—as such—can be related to two other forms of economic organization, namely markets and hierarchies (firms). Williamson (1991) revealed that under certain conditions, especially pertaining to asset specificity, the network form of organization is appropriate. The concept of extended enterprise integration includes the possibility of making partner-specific IT investments. On the other hand, transactions that are straightforward and require no transaction-specific investments are typically executed in the marketplace, and market B2Bi keeps thus off any investments that are counterparty specific.

Companies can use ICT to automate cross-company communication processes. In order to get the systems working together smoothly, coordination is needed. One way to achieve coordination is through standardization. The standardization of some issues moves competition to other issues. The key is to standardize the issues on which it does not make any sense to compete (e.g., because there are network effects). Clearly, for direct market B2Bi to achieve its full potential, many more standards will need to be developed, eespecially the realization of the semantic web is still in its infancy. Also, much research is required toward the realization of transactions, standard security protocols, an infrastructure to check the reliability of Web services (and their providers), autonomous software agents that use the standards, and so on. Furthermore the capability to creatively use standards is of strategic importance, and it should thus be researched how organizations can acquire this capability.

As IT-systems should align with the business, standards should only be used to the extent that they allow for such business-ICT alignment. Although standards have a role to play in both types of B2Bi, the practice of extended enterprise integration experiences the pros and cons of the freedom to be creative (especially at the level of business processes). If standards are not desirable/available, another form of coordination is needed. The discipline called enterprise architecture is gaining momentum in this context. Basically, an enterprise architecture fulfills the same role as a standard (Cook, 1996): it restricts the choices of people (where needed) in order to make sure everything will fit together well once everything is implemented. Extended enterprise architecture is an important topic for practitioners and researchers. After all, it deals with describing the business and the ICT side of Extended Enterprises, and is thus relatable to standards such as Web Services Description Language (WSDL), Buisiness Process Execution Language (BPEL), and Business Process Modeling

Language (BPML) (see, e.g., Goethals, Vandenbulcke & Lemahieu, 2004a; Goethals et al., 2004c; Goethals et al., 2006).

This chapter is the first one that discusses the two basic types of B2Bi in such detail. This should bring structure and clarity in the B2Bi realm. The chapter can serve as the basis for further research; for example, toward more concrete information systems design and implementation methodologies for both types of B2Bi. While managers and ICT people can design entire systems themselves in an extended enterprise context (and can create tactical and even strategic plans for the total extended enterprise; see Goethals, Vandenbulcke, Lemahieu, & Snoeck, 2004b), they only have to instantiate the generic standards that have been designed by standardization organizations and software vendors to realize market B2Bi.

Acknowledgments

This chapter has been written as part of the SAP-leerstoel-project on extended enterprise Infrastructures at the K.U. Leuven, sponsored by SAP Belgium.

References

Besen, S. M., & Farrell, J. (1994). Choosing how to compete: Strategies and tactics in standardization. *Journal of Economic Perspectives, 8(2),* 117-131.

Borgatti, S. (2001). *Organizational theory: Determinants of structure.* Retrieved March 4, 2004, from http://www.analytictech.com/mb021/orgtheory.htm.

Bowersox, D., Closs, D., & Stank, T. (2003, July/August). How to master cross-enterprise collaboration. *Supply Chain Management Review,* 18-27.

Brooks, F. (1975). *The mythical man-month.* Addison-Wesley.

Casson, M. C. (1996). The firm and the market: Studies in multinational enterprise and the scope of the firm. In M. C. Casson (Ed.), *Critical writings in economics: The theory of the firm* (p. 72). Cheltenham, UK: Edward Elgar Publishing. (Reprinted from Cambridge, MA, 1987.)

Coase, R. (1937). The nature of the firm. *Economica, 4,* 386-405.

Cook, M. (1996). *Building enterprise information architectures.* Prentice-Hall.

Dore, R. (1983). Goodwill and the spirit of market capitalism. *British Journal of Sociology, 34*(459), 82.

Emery, F. E., & Trist, E. L. (1965). The causal texture of organizational environments. *Human Relations, 18,* 21-32.

Frankel, D., & Parodi, J. (2002). *Using model-driven architecture to develop Web services.* IONA Technologies white paper. Retrieved on October 2, 2006, from http://www. iona.com/archwebservice/WSMDA.pdf

Goethals, F., Vandenbulcke, J., & Lemahieu, W. (2004a, March 14-17). *Designing the extended enterprise with the FADEE.* Proceedings of the ACM Symposium on Applied Computing (SAC2004), Nicosia, Cyprus.

Goethals, F., Vandenbulcke, J., Lemahieu, W., & Snoeck, M. (2004b). Structuring the development of inter-organizational systems: WISE (Web Information Systems Engineering). In *Proceedings of 2004 Conference Brisbane Springer* (LNCS Series, 3306, pp. 454-465).

Goethals, F., Snoeck, M., Lemahieu, W., &Vandenbulcke, J. (in press). Management and enterprise architecture click [Special issue]. *Information Systems Frontiers.*

Goethals, F., Vandenbulcke, J., Lemahieu, W., Snoeck, M., De Backer, M., & Haesen, R. (2004c). Communication and enterprise architecture in extended enterprise integration. In *Proceedings of ICEIS 2004 Conference* (Vol. 3, pp. 332-337).

Gray, B. (1989). *Collaborating: Finding common ground for multiparty problems.* San Francisco: Jossey-Bass Publishers.

Hatch, M. J. (1997). *Organization theory, modern symbolic and postmodern perspectives.* Oxford University Press.

Hirschman, A. O. (1970). *Exit, voice, and loyalty: responses to decline in firms, organizations, and states.* Cambridge, MA: Harvard University Press.

IFS. (2004). *Glossary.* Retrieved June 7, 2004, from http://www.ifsworld.com/

Liedtka, J. (1996). Collaborating across lines of business for competitive advantage. *Academy of Management Executive, 10(2),* 20-34.

Lindgren, L. (2001). *Application servers for e-business.* Boca Raton, FL: Auerbach.

Morgan, G. (1996). *Images of organization.* Sage Publications.

Petersen, S., & Szegheo, O. (2000). *A model-based methodology for extended enterprise engineering.* Retrieved June 7, 2004, from http://www.idi.ntnu.no/

Picot, A., Ripperger, T., & Wolff, B. (1996). The fading boundaries of the firm: The role of information and communication technology. *JITE, 152*(1), 65-79.

Podolny, J., Page, K. (1998). Network forms of organization. *ARS, 24,* 57-76.

Pollock, J. (2002). *Dirty little secret: It's a matter of semantics.* Retrieved January 29, 2003, from http://eai.ebizq.net/str/pollock_2a.html, p 12. [registration required]

Powell, W. (1990). Neither market nor hierarchy: Network forms of organization. *Research in Organizational Behavior, 12,* 295-336.

Selz, D. (1999). *Value Webs: Emerging forms of fluid and flexible organizations.* Retrieved October 2, 2003, from http://www.netacademy.org

Shapiro, C., & Varian, H. (1999). *Information rules.* Cambridge: Harvard University Press.

Smith, H., & Fingar, P. (2002). A new path to business process management. *Optimize, 1*(12), 55-61.

Spies, C. M. (2001). *The implementation of business process reengineering in the short-term insurance industry.* Master dissertation, Rand Afrikaans University, Johannesburg,

South Africa. Retrieved June 7, 2004, from http://etd.rau.ac.za/theses/available/etd-03172004-120004/restricted/

Williams, T. A. (1982). *Learning to Manage our Futures*. New York: Wiley.

Williamson, O. E. (1975). *Markets and hierarchies: Analysis and antitrust implications*. New York: Free Press.

Williamson, O. E. (1985). *The economic institutions of capitalism*. New York: Free Press.

Williamson, O. E. (1991). Comparative economic organization: The analysis of discrete structural alternatives. *Administrative Science Quarterly, 36*(2), 269-296.

Endnotes

[1]   Nevertheless, if there are reputational costs from breaking relationships, then a relation that may have originated for some functional reason may persist only for the purpose of preserving reputation, lowering adaptability (Podolny & Page, 1998).

[2]   Picot et al. (1996) show that new developments in ICT have lowered transaction costs (after all, transaction costs include the costs of information and communication required for coordinating activities). They conclude that thanks to new developments in ICT *"many transactions, e.g., which were previously coordinated by hierarchies can now be coordinated by hybrid coordination systems."*

[3]   The idea behind "Web services" is that IT systems can offer services to one another. Currently, these are mostly query services (e.g., the system of a supplier checking the stock at the customer site), but action-based services (such as a customer's system actually placing an order) can also be achieved through Web services.

[4]   This may also be the "software industry," of course..

Chapter II

E-Business Models in B2B:
A Process-Based Categorization and Analysis of Business-to-Business Models

Mahesh Raisinghani, Texas Woman's University, USA

Turan Melemez, Purdue University, USA

Lijie Zou, Purdue University, USA

Chris Paslowski, Purdue University, USA

Irma Kikvidze, Purdue University, USA

Susanne Taha, Purdue University, USA

Klaus Simons, Purdue University, USA

Abstract

The business models in the business-to-business (B2B) e-commerce and their effectiveness have been a major topic of research in the recent years. Due to the variety of existing models, it seems difficult to find a widely accepted categorization that can be analysed and assessed. An in-depth study that provides a process-based approach to B2B e-commerce is presented and illustrated with examples from industry. A comparative examination of both the buy and the sell side based on a process-related approach provides extensive insights for further comparative research and evaluation of products/services and models. Selling services and e-procurement using Web-electronic data interchange (EDI) as sub-models are clarified using real-world examples. Problems and trends in the B2B area form the conclusion of the examination with suggestions for further research.

Introduction

The economic impact of the Internet is like the oil shock in reverse. The jump in oil prices during the 1970s increased inflation and pushed the world into recession. However, the Internet reduces the cost of information. This has positive economic effects, since it makes it easier for buyers and suppliers to compare prices and eliminate the middlemen between firms and customers, lowers transaction costs, and reduces entry barriers. Economists have an interesting argument: the main reason why firms exist is to minimize transaction costs. These reduced transaction and communication costs can lead to both bigger and smaller optimal firm sizes. Smaller firms can buy services cheaply from outside, and this reduces the barriers to entry.

The Internet can link up supply chains, make it easy to place and track orders, and display specifications at the click of a mouse. Hence few companies are willing to miss out on the benefits e-commerce offers. So, it is certain that the Internet reduces costs, increases competition, and improves functioning of the pricing mechanism. The Internet moves the economy closer to the theory of perfect competition, which assumes abundant information, zero transaction costs and no entry barriers. Analysts feel markets should become more efficient as the Internet increases the flow of information between buyers and sellers. This, in turn, should ensure efficient allocation of scarce resources.

E-commerce increases competitive intensity by allowing business customers to consider every available alternative to every offering. Suppliers no longer compete with two or three familiar competitors but with every company in the world that has a web site and a comparable product or service. E-commerce also undermines traditional sources of advantage based on asymmetries of information. In the past, sellers derived some advantage by knowing more than their buyers. Such an advantage came from knowing more about the product, the cost availability of raw materials and components, and the efficiency of their own manufacturing processes. Each step in the supply chain had a lock on its own information, which made each link more defensible but the chain as a whole less efficient.

The Internet does away with much of this privileged access to information, shifting the competitive emphasis away from secrecy and toward transparency and the absolute comparative value of the offering. Distribution and sales channels have always conveyed a certain amount of information back to suppliers. However, bandwidth, precision, ease, speed, and manageability of the information flowing in both directions are orders of magnitude greater on the Internet. The interactive exchange of information, design requirements, component specifications, cost tracking, logistics oversight, service requests and troubleshooting advice permits an unprecedented level of customization. Competition on this level will necessarily become the rule.

As B2B e-commerce becomes one of the most profitable applications for the Internet, we need to understand the implications of the many technological and market changes that will usher in an entirely new way of doing business. The B2B e-commerce revolution includes e-procurement, B2B exchanges, and business infrastructure relationships.

E-procurement involves firms selling supplies, equipment, materials, and services with a streamlined online purchasing function that often eliminates traditional intermediaries, thereby reducing costs and cycle times while offering greater flexibility and responsiveness to changes in demand. Web-based supply chain management networks improve coordination between trading partners by linking a firm's forecasting and production planning systems with its suppliers' and distributors' systems. They can create dramatic savings and quality improvements.

B2B exchanges include various categories of marketspaces, including vertical market portals ("vortals"), hubs, and various types of auctions. A single infomediary (i.e., an industry consortium or a third party) brings together many buyers and sellers within a specific vertical market, such as plastics, steel, or industrial chemicals, charging a commission on all transactions. Hundreds of industry-specific exchanges have now been launched, and more are being developed every day. Some of these "marketspaces" operate with posted pricing models while others employ collaborative negotiated prices, auctions, reverse auctions, Dutch auctions, and other pricing mechanisms. Many are used in spot markets for industrial materials, overstocks, and perishable goods, as well as business services transactions.

More important is the development of entirely new e-business infrastructure industries. Many firms support online activity by facilitating the interaction between various parties in e-commerce as preferred outsourcers for e-business processes. They have become integral to the effective operation of Internet-based activities and may account for the largest source of profits from the future growth of e-commerce. They provide digital content or improve its delivery, bring new customers to Web sites, finance acquisitions, and provide many other services. They include application services providers, adservers, content maximizers, wireless service providers, and payment processors.

There are various categorisations of B2B models. A model is a representation of business concepts that can be validated and checked for rigor and robustness, used to capture and communicate ideas, subjected to what-if-scenarios, and revised as appropriate (Hoque, 2000). A fundamental distinction used by different authors is the categorisation based on the e-business processes applied by the enterprise. Next we examine the various approaches used in business modeling.

Approaches to Business Modeling

Business modeling is a vast area of research and practice, which is gaining increasing importance in the rapid development of e-business and globalisation (Holsapple, 2001). The following are some approaches used in business modeling:

1.   Textual description (e.g., abstract use cases)
2.   Categories and visualization
3.   Simulation approaches
4.   Data/workflow-description programs
5.   Process notation languages (e.g., Unified Modeling Language (UML))

Figure 1. Business model description (partial) as a set of interacting processes (Source: A business model description – The TO-BE-Model; Jaclij, 2002)

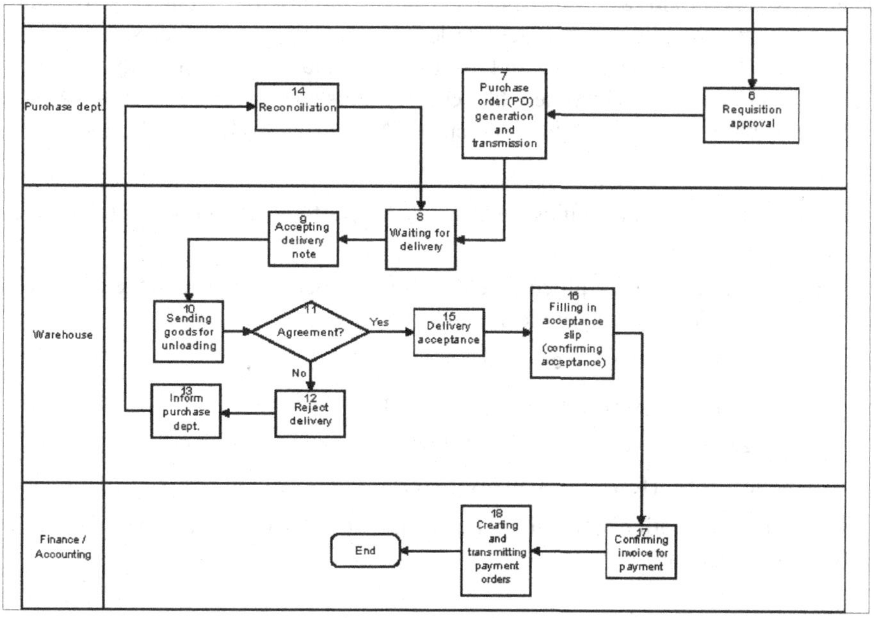

Given the various approaches, the basic commonality is that the main business processes are methodically represented. Hence, the best way to categorize B2B models is based on their main business processes (Dressler 2002; Eriksson & Penker, 2000). Figure 1 illustrates a part of a business model description as a set of interacting processes.

Categorizing B2B Models

The common categorization of B2B models seen in the literature is divisions based on target audience or type of products/services involved in the business processes.

In order to understand this categorization, we have first to observe the two dimensions through which companies obtain the products and services they need (Kaplan & Sawhney, 2000). The first dimension is related to the kind of products and services purchased, and the second relates to the frequency with which companies make their purchases. The products and services can be classified into manufacturing inputs and operating inputs. Manufacturing inputs are raw materials applied in the manufacturing process. Operating inputs are normally low-value products and services, usually commodities (e.g., advertising, utilities, electricity, office supplies), also known as maintenance, repair, and operations (MRO) inputs. In relation to the frequency inputs are acquired, there are both systematic sourcing and spot-market sourcing.

Considering the two dimensions, e-commerce businesses can be placed in one of the categories illustrated in Figure 2.

Another more general and easier-to-remember categorization can be attained by focusing on the processes that these e-business models are designed to facilitate. E-businesses can support the relationship between a company and its customers and suppliers (usually commercial transactions) and with related partners like collaborators and contractors. Thus e-business models can be classified according to its focus (IBM, 2003a; Weill & Vitale, 2001):

- Focus on the process of selling goods and services to other companies (e-commerce sell-side)
- Focus on the process of e-procurement and other processes related to the supply chain management. Various sub-models in this category are as follows:
  o Buyer model (few buyers, many sellers)
  o Marketplace model (many buyers and many sellers)
  o Longer-term relationship model (few buyers and few sellers)
  o Seller model (few sellers, many buyers)
- Focus on collaboration between businesses, partners, and contractors (i.e., e-collaboration, e-engineering)

Figure 2. B2B matrix (Adapted from Kaplan & Sawhney, 2000)

		What the company purchases	
		Operating Inputs	**Manufacturing Inputs**
How the company purchases	**Systematic Sourcing**	**MRO Hubs** (horizontal markets that enable systematic sourcing of operating inputs) Ariba MRO.com …	**Vertical Catalogue Hubs** (enable systematic sourcing of non-commodities manufacturing inputs) Chemdex Verticalnet …
	Spot Sourcing	**Yield Managers** (horizontal markets that enable spot sourcing of operating inputs) Employease Adaction.com …	1) **Vertical Exchange Markets** (enable spot sourcing of commodities manufacturing inputs) e-Steel Altra Energy …

From the B2B perspective, marketplaces represent an e-business model as a combination of the sell- and buy-side processes with many buyers and sellers. E-collaboration will not be analysed in this paper due to its focus on integration of processes rather than the business models. Some examples of the different e-business models for the sell and the buy side are illustrated in the next two sections.

Sell-Side B2B E-Commerce

Sell-side B2B models are involved in selling products or services and are generally catalog based. The goals of B2B sell-side models from the viewpoint of an organization in the retail industry involve the following (IBM, 2003 c):

*   Deliver a superior shopping experience that provides personalized and convenient information to customers
*   Get the most from your marketing efforts by targeting campaigns toward specific customers.
*   Gain new business insights using advanced business analytics.
*   Reach your customers anywhere, anytime across all available channels.
*   Put the right tools in the right hands of the people in your organization.
*   Integrate to achieve greater efficiency and leverage existing investments.
*   Be more agile and responsive than your competitors through a standards-based infrastructure.

Some characteristics of sell-side B2B models are as follows:

*   **Customer registration:** the customer has to provide the login information before being authenticated to use the system. An auditing process is normally followed by application for registration. Accepted users are notified by e-mail or snail mail that includes the authentication information (without passwords).
*   **Displaying new items in the catalog:** An online catalog that provides the information on products and services that are personalized to the potential customer's preferences.
*   **Accepting order entries:** A process to accept orders for goods and services is provided.
*   **Checking order status:** The customer has the ability to check the order status of his/her order and track the shipment process related to the order.
*   **Online payment:** A variety of payment systems and methods are provided, including the associated processes such as validation of the data or credit information.

- **Receive additional information:** Some processes are established to deliver additional information to the customer regarding new products/services and special offers using an e-newsletter and a content management system.

- **Order history/transaction overviews:** Data warehousing and data mining are used to analyze customer profile/ history, frequency of usage of services, number of items bought in different categories, and so forth.

- Complaints and returns are handled through use of a communication center (call center) and/or using a customer relationship management (CRM) system.

Advanced models also include auctions and reverse auctions and value-added services such as calendars, information boards, and archived forums. An example of B2B sell-side is the selling services and provision of payment systems in the financial industry. Efficient processing of transactions that can be completed securely and on time is critical to overall economic performance. Payment systems, however, can create significant exposure and risk for its users. Payment systems comprise networks that link members by routing messages based on rules and procedures for the use of its infrastructure. Key risks include:

- **Credit risk:** The risk that counter-party will not meet an obligation for full value, either when due or at any time thereafter.

- **Liquidity risk:** The risk that counter-party will not settle an obligation for full value when due but at some time thereafter.

Figure 3. Settlement process in CHAPS (Source: Apacs, 2003)

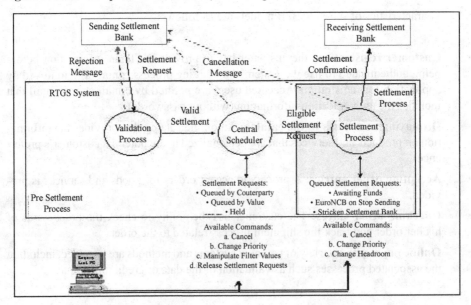

- **Operational risk:** The risk that hardware or software technical issues, human error, or malicious attack will cause a system to break down or malfunction, leading to possible financial losses.
- **Legal risk:** The risk that unexpected interpretation of law or legal uncertainty will leave the payment system or members with unforeseen financial exposures and losses.

The Clearing House Automated Payment System (CHAPS) facing these risks is an electronic transfer system for sending real-time gross settlement and value payments from bank to bank on the same day. It is one of the largest real-time gross settlement systems in the world. CHAPS Clearing Company is a limited company under English law and is owned and controlled by its member banks, which includes the Bank of England. It is the most visible to the public through the use of making same-day payments for house purchases. CHAPS offers its customers an efficient, risk-free, and reliable same-day payment mechanism. Every CHAPS payment is unconditional, irrevocable, and guaranteed. The world's major global payment banks are included in CHAPS membership (Apacs, 2003). Currently there are 21 direct members and more than 400 indirect participants in their clearinghouse. Thus, CHAPS enables banks to utilize their own strategic IT preferences rather than requiring them to use proprietary hardware and software requirements.

The settlement process in CHAPS is illustrated in Figure 3.

The settlement processes within the payment system include the following steps (BIS, 2000):

Figure 4: CHAPS sterling and CHAPS euro clearings combined volumes and values, 1990 to 2001 (Apacs, 2003)

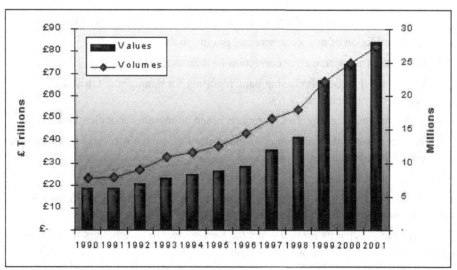

- **Submission:** The details of the payment gets transmitted to the payment system. The payment system conducts various operational processes on the payment, such as validation.

- **Validation by the system:** Payments can be placed in a queue before being accepted for settlement. The payment system applies risk management tests.

- **Acceptance of the settlement:** After the payment has passed all risk management and other tests and the system has determined that it can be settled.

- **Final settlement:** The settlement account of the receiving participant within the payment system has been credited, and settlement is unconditional and irrevocable.

The Bank of England states that the volume and value of payments through U.K. payment systems has increased considerably in recent years. In 1999, it was valued at 100 trillion pounds sterling, that is, more than one hundred times the UK's gross domestic product (GDP). An amount equivalent to about half of UK's GDP flows through its payment systems every business day. The chart in Figure 4 shows a tripling during the 1990s in the nominal value, and a doubling in the real value, of UK payments of CHAPS Sterling, the U.K.'s main high-value payment system (Apacs, 2003).

Another example of B2B sell-side is in the selling products and services area. Premier is a leading healthcare alliance collectively owned by more than 200 independent hospitals and healthcare systems in the United States. Together, they operate or are affiliated with nearly 1,500 hospitals in 50 states and hundreds of other healthcare sites (Premier.com, 2003a).

Hospitals and healthcare systems come together in Premier for the purpose of gaining scale advantages such as the group purchasing of supplies and services and achieving greater operational and clinical effectiveness and efficiency in services essential to healthcare and sharing the risk of developing new resources needed in healthcare's e-commerce capabilities.

The digital company Premier.com provides (Premier Inc., 2003b):

- Electronic purchasing and settlement integrated with the in-house MIS
- Faster activation of new contracts and pricing to the costumers
- Automated transaction error correction for transactions
- Aggregated member purchasing data, reporting for management, historical development of buying behavior
- Real-time, line-item purchasing reports based on member specifications
- Enhanced materials management capabilities that enable members to identify cost-reduction opportunities

Figure 5 illustrates electronic cataloging system (ECS) used for group ordering on Premier.com's e-business model.

Premier tries to provide its group buyers the best pricing from suppliers for products and services, including financing, warranty, training, and trade-in benefits. Value-added sheets (explanation of group buy benefits and savings in simple summary form) and market guides

Figure 5. Premier.com's e-business model

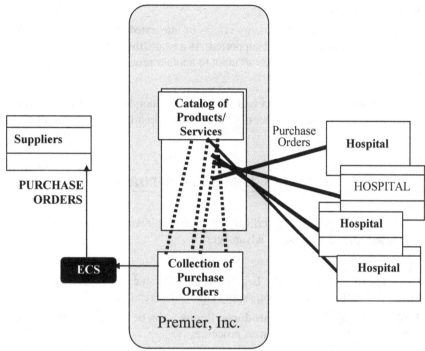

that provide up-to date review of products and services are provided on Premier.com's website (http://www.premierinc.com/frames/index.jsp).

B2B E-Procurement

B2B e-procurement is used not only by participation in a procurement marketplace but also as an enhancement of the existing conventional model. The goals of various e-procurement business models are cost saving through exchanges/marketplaces, direct connection of supply chain via electronic data interchange (EDI), Web-EDI, desktop purchasing, and elimination/reduction of procurement department (Lee, 2001).

The above e-procurement models are normally implemented by e-procurement systems and supplier portals. The major goals in most cases are process and marketing advantages, such as:

- **Availability:** 24/7 availability is provided for a set of services 365 days a year
- **Speed:** Transactions are fulfilled faster, compared to non-electronic transactions

- **Logistics efficiency considerations:** Support for "Just in time delivery" and "Just in sequence delivery"
- **Integration of processes:** Synergy effects of integrated processes can be achieved, and parallelism of processes is supported. As a result, the time between the output of one process to be recognized as an input to another process is significantly reduced.

Due to the integration of processes and systems, the complexity of the e-procurement models increases as businesses further digitally enhance their business with e-procurement facilities.

Process-Based Approach

Since e-business models can be described in very different ways, a description based on a processes-based approach has some advantages:

- **Coverage of various models:** E-business models can easily be described as a set of processes (EDI, e-procurement, supply chain management)
- **Understanding of software products:** Products can be understood easily as a set of functions related to these business processes
- **Comparability:** The capacity of e-business models, systems, and products can be compared in a practical manner

However, when evaluating economic value, more detailed descriptions of the processes are necessary (Holsapple, 2001). Hence, we take a closer look at the categories of processes in e-procurement. Major processes in e-procurement are categorized as follows:

a.   Inquiry/Proposal Processes
b.   Ordering Processes
c.   Delivery Processes
d.   Invoicing/Payment Processes

This image illustrates the EDI processes covered by electronic procurement system (EPS) (Dressler, 2003).

E-procurement systems and supplier portals (e.g., SCM portals) implement some subset of these processes. Enhancement subsets and supersets deliver a characteristic specialty to e-business models in the e-procurement area. The following common processes implemented in e-procurement models are defined and the explanation of their salient points is provided based on existing implementations of procurement systems (IBM, 2002).

a.   Inquiry/Proposal Processes

- **List and categorize products/services that have been requested:** Companies normally list and categorize products according to the relevance of the products/services to main operating business and costs.

- **Send out requests for products/services to suppliers:** The suppliers are divided into different groups of preferred, audited, or not preferred suppliers. The automation of sending "requests for bids" is one part of this process.

- **Build rank according to criteria:** Offers coming in must be compared and organized according to some procurement criteria for the order decision.

- **Communications about question and choice decisions:** Questions of suppliers and requests for additional data must be handled.

- **Archival of communication and results and management of supplier data:** The communication with vendors/suppliers, thee final bids, and the decision must be archived in a database, that is, "no bids" can be deleted and may need to be stored for possible future reactivation.

b.   Ordering Processes

- **Enable need previews:** Suppliers can be informed of future needs of the buying organisation on a daily, weekly or monthly basis. Normally, this includes the functionality of online checking of the need for some parts or products.

- **Communicate the order to supplier/s:** An order can be transmitted online to the supplier using EDI /Web-EDI. Smaller suppliers are also automatically informed via an e-mail, mail, or fax message.

- **Confirm, change or cancel order:** Orders have to be confirmed to supplier/s. Since changes can occur in non-confirmed orders, this process is subject to some transactional constraints. A non-confirmed order has to initiate some escalation process and possibly cancel orders to other supplier/s.

c.   Delivery and shipment

- **Report delivery status, notes and etiquettes:** The delivery status and the attributes of the shipment are transmitted to the buying company. This process also involves transport organisations, where the times of delivery and estimations of arrivals are considered.

- **Announce delivery of goods and inform of delay in delivery:** The supplier or the transportation organisation should inform the buying organization about any delays in delivery since this may impact the entire supply chain.

- **Accept supplier application (for supplier self information):** New suppliers are audited to check if they fulfil the criteria for receiving orders and their credibility, track record, and references are checked and evaluated.

d.   Invoicing/Payment

- **Submit invoice in a secure format:** Invoices must be submitted from the suppliers and transmitted to the buying organisation. This process should meet high security requirements. Digital signatures and public/private key encryption are often used to ensure the uncorrupted transfer of the invoice.

- **Audit and transmit to the billing system:** The invoice is delivered to the accounts payable system/ERP system used by the company that automatically triggers the payment to the supplier based on its business rules.

- **Archive information:** The archival of relevant information in this process according to the needs of financial auditors is mandatory.

E-procurement models normally cover a subset or superset of the above-mentioned processes as services to suppliers. The combination of a set of processes with different business partners is illustrated in the Web-EDI products example of special e-procurement and logistics support.

Scope of the EDI and Web-EDI Models in B2B

EDI is the electronic transfer of business documents such as purchase orders or invoices between computer systems of different enterprises based on an established norm/format such as UN/EDIFACT or ANSI X.12 (Galileo Computing, 2003). EDI has now been used for over 30 years for the exchange of business data (e.g., delivery notes and invoices as mentioned above) between two application systems in a standardized and automated form

Figure 6. Traditional EDI without using Internet technology

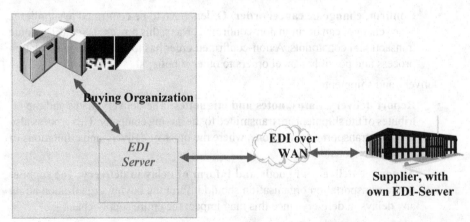

(Emmelhainz, 1993; Dressler, 2003). The benefits associated with traditional EDI include cost reductions induced by rationalization and automation and shorter order processing time (Deutsch, 1994).

Traditional EDI includes converters on both sides of the communication line. Data are normally transferred between enterprises as illustrated in Figure 6. Therefore, on both sides, a translation into formats understandable by different ERP systems such as SAP R/3 or JD-Edwards is to be guaranteed. Because of the early introduction and the market acceptance of EDI systems in the 1980s, different standards exist for the description of EDI data (EDI Comp., 2003).

Beck, Weitzel, and König (2000) state that besides the alleged benefits, EDI is not as widespread as many had expected. Presently only 5% of all companies that could benefit from EDI actually use it (Segev et al., 1997) due to the considerably high costs for implementing EDI systems (Swatman et al., 1997). New developments of innovative EDI solutions such as Web-EDI or XML/EDI avoid the problems of traditional EDI technologies.

Web-EDI

Web-EDI uses technologies and standards such as HTML, Java, CGI, or ASP for electronic data interchange over the Internet (Thomas, 1999). The supplier of a Web-EDI system provides its business partners with a Web site on which they can electronically transact business by means of a conventional web browser that communicates with a Web-EDI server. The target user group for Web-EDI is small and middle-sized business partners who cannot afford their own traditional EDI system due to initial cost and/or ongoing maintenance costs.

Web-EDI systems are transaction-oriented; that is, the processes on the Web-EDI server are steered by business transactions like orders or accounting. The user must complete the authentication and authorization process on the website in order to mail an order or retrieve and print an order. If the user has filled out the corresponding HTML form completely, he can send the data back to the Web-EDI server. The transmission of data by the Web-EDI server is carried to the in-house system of the supplier automatically. The integration of the data into the supplier's system can be carried out by direct correspondence with its import interfaces or its EDI converter.

If a supplier already has a traditional EDI system in use, conventional EDI methods are preferred in order to avoid the additional efforts resulting from conversion into Web-EDI formats. These in-house systems can normally be used with different EDI partners due to the ability of the most EDI products to route information. The Web-EDI server is simply a new data source for the converter. After the data arrives at the converter, the handling of orders is the same as conventional EDI orders, and the translation process is completely transparent to the end user.

Figure 7. Implementation of Web-EDI using Web-EDI server without using traditional EDI

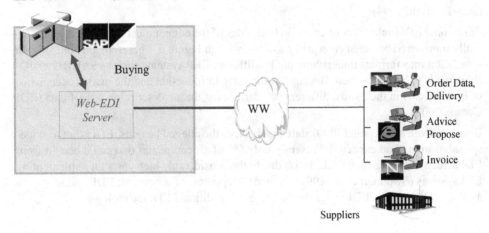

Standards and Architectures

During the early stages of EDI, the respective partners had to bilaterally agree on the communication standards to be used. With the increasing use of EDI, however, this procedure has proven to be too difficult to practice. The Web-EDI standards are mainly driven by different organizations that have relationships with different industries. For example, in Europe the VDA standard of the German Association of the Automotive Industry is one of the commonly accepted descriptions of Web-EDI and is based on the well-known EDIFACT standards. Some Web-EDI software products based on these standards are implemented several hundred times in Europe (see also www.seeburger.de or www.atosorigin.de).

Newer trends and solutions in Web-EDI (IBM, 2003b) ignore the need for EDI and the EDIFACT standard and provide direct ways to connect the ERP-system of an enterprise with a web-EDI portal using a Web-EDI server (see Figure 7).

The trend is that an explicit EDI server with translation to the intermediate format of EDIFACT or ODETTE is considered unnecessary for small- and intermediate-size organizations since an XML-interface performs the same service. Figure 7 illustrates an example describing this model (EDI Comp., 2003b).

E-Procurement Supplier (EPS) Portal in B2B

The following example is the result of a project implemented in the year 2003. The results are collected in an asset and are now in the process of transfer to a standard product.

Figure 8. A screenshot of supplier portal software EPS from IBM

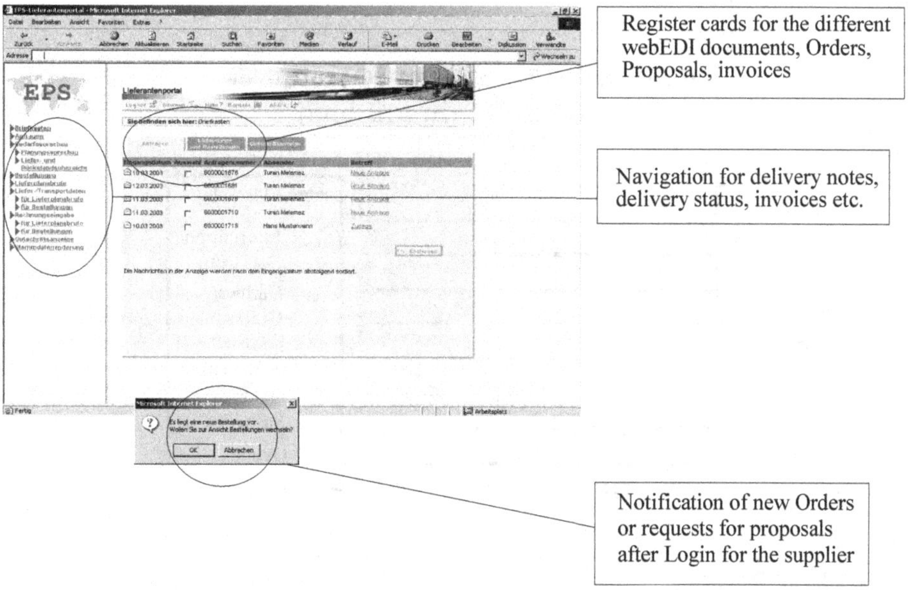

Register cards for the different webEDI documents, Orders, Proposals, invoices

Navigation for delivery notes, delivery status, invoices etc.

Notification of new Orders or requests for proposals after Login for the supplier

Dressler (2003, p. 2) states:

> *The goal of the project was the successful implementation of the supplier portal for e-procurement and supplier collaboration for CLAAS, a leading manufacturer of agricultural engines in Germany with customers around the world. This supplier portal supports sourcing and procurement processes of the company by providing a web-based interface to suppliers and enabling efficient data interchange over the Internet. The implementation approach divided the implementation of the system into three stages with each stage containing a subset of functionalities of the total planned scope of the project.*

The implementation of stage one was based on the results of an analysis of supplier-related processes and the successful development of a process and functional concept for the supplier portal for CLAAS prepared in advance of the implementation. The implementation included installation and configuration of hardware and software, development and implementation of defined functionalities, and deployment and testing of the application.

The processes for order, delivery, proposal, and invoice have been implemented based on the standard described from the VDA (German Association of the Automotive Industry). For a description of the standard for VDA-Web-EDI see www.vda.de.

Figure 8 illustrates a Web page with some of the services offered by the Web-EDI software EPS from IBM, currently sold as an asset in the development stage.

Figure 9. Development of the B2B e-commerce markets according to different researchers (Source: Saucini LLC, 2002)

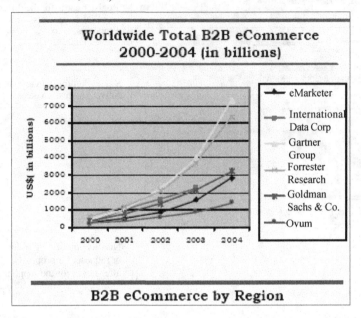

The EPS system represents one of the purest forms of Web-EDI e-business models for B2B. There is no EDI server needed. The data interchange between the Web-EDI-server and the SAP-Systems are transferred via a WebSphere connector using XML (Steinert, 2002). IBM Global Services consultants state that a return on investment for a Web-EDI project using EPS can be achieved in approximately two years on average.

Key Issues and Trends in E-Business

Over the last decade, economic and technological advances have created a period of intense globalization. A single world market is emerging in which the opportunities for global business are enhanced by technical advances. These rapidly evolving new technologies enable companies to reach their customers and trading partners around the world in just seconds, regardless of geographic and/or time distances, political boundaries, and other barriers. The growth of the Internet has intensified the speed of globalization and the need for companies to implement effective global marketing and e-commerce strategies. With non-U.S. B2B e-commerce spending projected to reach $2.8 trillion by 2004 (87% of total e-commerce), global e-commerce is a major growth opportunity for U.S. companies (Saucini, LLC, 2002).

In summary, the key trends are as follows (Lee, 2001):

- E-commerce, and particularly B2B, is still in a rapid growth phase
- The domestic B2B e-commerce opportunity is dwarfed by the international opportunity (European e-commerce revenues will surpass those of North America by 2005)
- Trends in e-commerce adoption are rapidly shifting the buyer base away from the current North American, English language dominance
- Research indicates that B2B buyers are three to four times more likely to buy from an e-commerce site presented in their native language

Analyzing the Effectiveness of B2B

After the fallout of the dot-com companies and some unfulfilled expectations of the "B2B hype," the analysis of the effectiveness of B2B is important as it builds a base for understanding the problems and actual trends in the area. Kaplan and Garciano (2001) state that B2B's key role is that of reducing transaction costs faced by buyers and sellers. They identify the following five ways in which B2B e-commerce can potentially decrease transaction costs and effectively operate in the post dot.com crash era:

1. **By changing or improving processes:** Ariba reduces the costs of purchasing used automobiles by not having to physically ship the product to an auction site.
2. **By changing the marketplace:** For both buyers and sellers it is less costly to search for products over the Internet than having to conduct a physical search.
3. **By changing decisions:** Indirect benefits may arise due to the reduced transaction costs. As transaction costs decline, the buyer might decide to outsource a product as opposed to producing it himself. Furthermore, "better information about future demand through B2B e-commerce may allow a seller to improve its demand forecasts and change its production decisions" (Kaplan & Garciano, 2001, p. 5).
4. **By changing information incompleteness and asymmetries:** The Internet changes the asymmetric information buyers and sellers have about each other and their products, leading to a transformation in the marketspace.
5. **By changing the ability to commit:** By standardizing processes and by providing an electronic trail, the Internet has the potential to increase the ability to commit, thus reducing imperfect commitment costs.

Finally, Kaplan and Garciano (2001) conclude that in order to succeed future B2B business models must include "measurable benefits and charge customers as a function of those benefits." Similarly, if a company cannot secure a customer's commitment when allowing or facilitating price discovery, it is likely to fail since its customers will likely use its services to define a market for the product/service and go elsewhere to complete the transaction.

Key Issues

The concerns in the B2B area are mostly due to the failure of standardization and the special requirements of each business model. According to Lee (2001) most companies face problems in the following areas:

- **Selection of right strategy:** The strategy chosen does not fit the existing strategies or concepts, or lacks in-depth analysis of market impact. The business case is based on unsound assumptions and expectations.

- **Selection of right architecture:** The architecture chosen is not scalable or too difficult to customize to changing needs.

- **Selection of right solution:** The solution chosen is an island/silo-solution, not tested well, and/or not a good fit with the strategy based on the processes used.

- **Integration of procurement systems with legacy systems (or ERP):** Integration is not fully achieved, due to incompatibilities of the different systems. Self-made solutions are not maintainable and lack integration functionalities in changing or heterogeneous IT-infrastructure.

- **Changes in the procurement procedure:** As the introduction of a new system lasts normally more than one year including rollouts, the changes in the environment and the changes introduced with the system need a detailed change of management and risk management plan. The acceptance of new systems from suppliers has to be addressed in early stages of e-procurement ambitions.

- **Change in corporate culture:** The change in corporate culture in transferring processes to paper-free, digital processes can lead to immense cultural discrepancies and problems in the organization and its supply-chain.

An example for the concerns above is the Web-EDI area of e-procurement. The decision to introduce EDI in its classical form is a high risk, given that the products are in a progress of standardization. Extensible Markup Language (XML) and Java 2 Platform, Enterprise Edition (J2EE) will solve the integration problems in the long run (Steinert, 2002). In addition, historical problems such as format compatibility, high entry costs, and maintenance costs are driving the market. The following key trends can be observed:

- **XML-based integration:** XML is a standard document definition and description language that can be used for the integration of different systems. Application servers underlying the most commonplace e-procurement systems support some sort of XML interface to retrieve information from various systems. This trend is observable in the Java-compliant application servers, where the XML-support is built in. Parsers to retrieve objects from XML-streams and functionalities to write XML-documents are in use in most existing application servers, that is, IBM's Websphere or Sun's WebLogic. This XML-approach is furthermore enhanced with the outcome of XML-based databases in the market.

- **Integrated solutions based on applications servers:** The underlying IT-infrastructure can be ignored to a great extent using an application server as an integration platform. The application server builds the connection between the different software systems and hosts the e-business application. This is achievable due to the major advantages of application servers such as high-integration capability, scalability, and ease of deployment of applications.

- **Development of single-server based EDI solutions:** The major drawbacks of multi-server chain solutions in EDI and Web-EDI resulting from different format conversations are more apparent today. These solutions are on the decline, due to the advantages of the Internet technologies in comparison to the proprietary formats and server systems. Newer products using one server are in favor. Often these new products are already planned to work integrated to an ERP-system. This trend is illustrated by SAP's strategy of Web-enabling SAP R/3 and mysap.com products and the announcement of the SAP-compatible Web-EDI application server.

- **Breadth of functions:** Newer products in the market include more functionalities in the request/inquiry area, new payment systems, and e-payment clearinghouse services. One major enhancement recognizable in the new versions of the IBM products, for example, is the addition of logistics and transport processes. The design of the new models for the buy side expands to a three-party action in the e-procurement, increasing the complexity of the models and exponentially adding complexity to the underlying systems. From the managerial viewpoint, the dedication and commitment to use standards is seen as one major method to handle this increasing complexity.

- **Standardization:** Ongoing standardization increases the quality and comparability of some processes. On the other hand, the definition of standards in some industries is restricted to some process chains, resulting from interests of some stakeholders, and are not always reliable since they may be subject to change in a short period of time. For example, the EDI standards in the automotive industry includes only delivery and order-processes, is influenced by existing products in the industry and lacks important features like XML, or payment integration.

These trends can also be concluded with a comparative result of the change in Web-EDI products in the market, and as a result of ongoing standardization (see also www.seeburger.com, and www.atosorigin.com).

Contributions and Implications of this Study

The most important contribution of this study is the representation of a process-based categorization of B2B models and their assessment. This approach can also be used as a benchmark for the evaluation and comparison of other new and upcoming B2B business models and processes based on these models.

The authors assume that similar studies or parts of these are used by consulting companies in approaches to carry out analyses of models and process chains or SWOT analyses. The process-based approach in this cross-sectional study is presented with some selected B2B buy- and sell-side models. A longitudinal study could provide more meaningful and deeper insights.

Future research in this domain could examine:

- **Details of the processes:** Lists introduced in this paper for the B2B fields of buy- and sell-side. A major goal should be to increase the depth for the classification and refinement of existing models: A survey methodology could be used to determine the frequency of these processes used by different B2B models in the marketspace.

- **Expansion of the process:** Lists to other models such as B2B-marketplaces, e-collaboration, or to the extended supply chain. This could widen the universe for classification of B2B models and lead to standardization in the categorization.

- **Establishment of process B2B model arrays:** (Showing models and processes in a table format) for simplified analysis of similarities and differences between models. Such matrices can also be used for fitting software products to different business models or in the support of "Make or Buy" decisions in different stages of organizational readiness.

References

Apacs. (2003). *Selected materials about CHAPS* [company profile, statistics, and traffic analysis]. Retrieved September 4, 2003, from www.apacs.co.uk

Beck, R., & Weitzel, T. (2002). Promises and pitfalls of SME integration. In *Proceedings of the 15th Bled Electronic Commerce Conference e-reality 2002,* Bled, Slovenia.

Beck, R., Weitzel, T., & König, W. (2002). *The myth of Web-EDI.* Paragraph 1, Institute of Information Systems Research Project IT Standards and Network Effects, University of Frankfurt.

BIS. (2000, November). *Summary of G10 report on core principles for systemically important payment systems BIS.* Retrieved September 22, 2003, from http://www.bankofengland.co.uk

BoE. (2000). *Oversight of payment systems.* Retrieved September 22, 2003, from http://www.bankofengland.co.uk/fsr/fsr09art8.pdf

Bouc. (2001, November 21). Realizing inter-portal connectivity through neutral construction hub. In *Proceedings of ICX123 Private Ltd Presentation at Baucon Conference Trends in B2B e-Commerce.*

Curtis, C. (1996, September 9). EDI over the Internet: Let the games begin. *Internetweek,* 627. Retrieved from http://www.techweb.com/se/directlink.cgi?CWK19960909S0076

Deutsch. (1994). Unternehmenserfolg mit EDI: Strategie und realisierung des elektronischen datenaustausche. *Braunschweig.* Translated from German

Dressler, T. (2002). IBM- business consulting services. *Prozesskonzepte Entwurf*, 25 April Köln.

ECB. (2003). *Information guide for credit institutions using TARGET European central bank.* Retrieved July 2003, from http://www.ecb.int/pub/pdf/targetguide_en.pdf, p.15

EDI Comp. (2003a). *EDI competence center.* Retrieved October 19, 2003, from http://141.2.66.122/index.php and http://141.2.66.122/basics.php

EDI Comp. (2003b). *EDI competence center.* Retrieved October 19, 2003, from http://141.2.66.122/ressourcen/links.php

Gallileo Computing. (2003). Retrieved October 16, 2003, from www.gallileocomputing.de and http://www.galileocomputing.de/glossar/gp/anzeige-8474

Hans, E., & Penker, M. (2002). *Business modeling with UML: Business patterns at work.* OMG Press.

Holsapple, C. (2001). *Business modeling: Multidisciplinary approaches, economics, operational and information system perspectives.* Lexington: University of Kentucky College of Business and Economics.

Hoque, F. (2000). E-enterprise: Where to begin. *Applying Principles of Modeling, Knowledgebase and Decision Making Infrastructure*, p. 5.

IBM (2002). *E-business.* (General presentation, IBM Global Services, marketing, papers on best-practices).

IBM. (2003a). *Glossary-short IBM software group.* Retrieved October 15, 2003, from http://www-.ibm.com/software/genservers/portal/library/InfoCenter/wps/glossary.html

IBM. (2003b). *IBM publication.* Retrieved October 17, 2003, from http://www.elink.ibmlink. ibm.com/public/applications/publications/cgibin/pbi.cgi?SSN=03IVQ0014147687640&FNC=TXT

IBM. (2003c). *IBM Publication.* Retrieved October 17, 2003, from http://www.elink.ibmlink. ibm.com/public/applications/publications/cgibin/pbi.cgi?CTY=US&FNC=SRX&PBL=G325-5510#

Jaklicl. (2000). *Evaluation of alternative e-business models by business process simulation modeling.* Ljubljana, Slovenia, University of Ljubljana, Business Informatics Institute, faculty of economics.

Kaplan, S. N., & Garciano, L. (2003). *A framework for analyzing B2B e-commerce.* Retrieved September 29, 2003, from http://gsbwww.uchicago.edu/fac/steven.kaplan/research/frame.pdf on

Lee, J. K. (2001, June 21-22). B2B e-commerce planning. In *Proceedings of PACIS 2001.* Retrieved September 14, 2003, from http://iis.kaist.ac.kr/~jklee/PACIS2003-Plenary-0708-JKLee.ppt

Premier.com. (2003a). *Company profile* (paragraph 3). Retrieved October 22, 2003, from http://www.premierinc.com/frames/index.jsp?pagelocation=/all/newsroom/company_profile/

Premier.com. (2003b). *E-sourcing advantages* (paragraph 1). Retrieved October 22, 2003, from http://www.premierinc.com/frames/index.jsp

Steinert. (2002). *Mails to EDI and Web-EDI*. IBM Global Services, sell and support consulting.

Saucini, L. L. C. (2002). *Global B2B e-commerce trends. 10*(28), 35-36.

Thomas. (1999). *Die neuen EDI-Wege - Ein Überblick. in:* Die neuen EDI-Wege, Referatensammlung zur 14. DIN-Tagung EDI/EDIFACT, Hersg.: Deutsches Institut für Normung e.V. Berlin, p. 1-7- translated from German.

Vogel. (2002). *E-business allgemein*. Sercon GmbH Vertrieb, Präsentation 2002.

Weill, P., & Vitale, M. R. (2001). *Place to space: Migrating to ebusiness models*. Boston: Harvard Business School Press.

Weitzel, et al. (2001). *Electronic business und EDI mit XML*. Heidelberg Press.

Wiesbaden. P. A., Neuburger, R., & Niggl, J. (1993). Electronic data interchange (EDI) und lean management. *Zeitschrift für Führung und Organisation*, 20-25.

Editor's Note

The following reference list contains hyperlinks to World Wide Web pages. Readers who have the ability to access the Web directly from their word processor or are reading the paper on the Web can gain direct access to these linked references. Readers are advised that:

1.   These links existed as of the date of publication but are not guaranteed to be working thereafter.

2.   The contents of Web pages may change over time.

3.   The author(s) of the Web pages, not Idea Group Publishing (IGP), is (are) responsible for the accuracy of their content.

4.   The author(s) of this article, not IGP, is (are) responsible for the accuracy of the URL.

Section II

E-Business Strategies and Consumer Behavior Model

Chapter III

Drivers of Adoption and Implementation of Internet-Based Marketing Channels

Jørn Flohr Nielsen, University of Aarhus, Denmark

Viggo Høst, University of Aarhus, Denmark

Niels Peter Mols, University of Aarhus, Denmark

Abstract

This chapter analyses factors influencing manufacturers' adoption and implementation of Internet-based marketing channels, using models based on marketing channel and organizational innovation theory. Survey data from 1,163 Danish, Finnish, and Swedish manufacturers form the empirical basis for testing the models using LISREL analysis. The results stress that adoption of Internet-based marketing is influenced by willingness to cannibalize, management support, market pressure, and a firm's knowledge of information technology. Willingness to cannibalize mediates the effects of future market orientation, ownership, specialised investments, and management support. This is mainly the case in small firms, as the importance of the various drivers and the adoption pattern vary between size categories. Market-pull factors have relatively more explanatory power in medium-sized and large companies.

Introduction

It is now conventional wisdom that both customers and manufacturers have strong incentives to use Internet-based marketing channels (Alba et al., 1997; O'Cass & Fenech, 2003). It has been argued that the Internet is changing the structure of marketing channels, especially in industries such as retail banking, news media, and music, where an important part of the output is in digital form (Mols, Bukh, & Flohr Nielsen, 1999). However even many small and medium-sized manufacturers have adopted and implemented Internet-based marketing channels, though great differences can be observed in how these firms have actually gone about this.

This chapter examines possible explanations of the adoption and implementation. Some of the drivers of such radical innovations have been identified in previous research. Notably willingness to cannibalize (Chandy & Tellis, 1998) and recent findings in the U.S. stress the importance of the sense-and-respond capabilities of firms in e-business (Srinivasan, Lilien, & Rangaswarny, 2002). As our study is based on a large European sample including several small and medium-sized manufacturers, the intention is to allow more rigorous analyses using structural equation modelling and trace how size may influence the models of adoption. In continuation, the path to successful implementation is explored.

First, the chapter briefly reviews the literature on changes in marketing channels and on organizational innovation. Then it proposes a basic research model for examining the adoption of new channels, and the model and its 11 hypotheses are explained in detail. After describing the methodology, we present the results of our survey of Nordic manufacturers, stressing the role of willingness to cannibalize. Finally, the results and the theoretical and managerial implications are discussed.

Theoretical Background

The Inertia of Marketing Channels

Internet-based marketing channels may radically interfere with the work and communication connected with getting products and services from producer to consumer. However the literature on marketing channels stresses that distribution systems are usually rigid and stable because of persistent inertia. Firms wanting to convert from one type of marketing channel to another often face resistance, conflict, and customer confusion (Anderson, Day, & Rangan, 1997; Weiss & Anderson, 1992). Thus, Stern and Sturdivant (1987) contend that of all marketing decisions facing firms, those that concern the design of distribution systems are the most far reaching, resource demanding, and time consuming. The right investments in distribution channels have traditionally provided long-term protection against competition, and few researchers have been concerned with proposing strategic design principles focussing on the dynamics of marketing channels or on feedback mechanisms that continually monitor the design of distribution channels (for an exception, see Anderson et al., 1997). The economic approach to analyzing marketing channels has been concerned with understanding efficient channels (Bucklin, 1966, 1970; Mallen, 1973). Taking this as a starting point, normative models for the design of customer-driven distribution channels have been proposed (Rangan, Menezes, & Maier, 1992; Stern, El-Ansary, & Coughlan, 1996; Stern & Sturdivant, 1987). For example Bucklin (1966) argues that the starting point for changes in distribution channels is innovations in marketing technology and changes in consumer wants. These start an adaptation process in which the existing channel gravitates toward the new normative channel. The adaptation process is revealed by changes occurring in the functional and institutional structure. However Weiss and Anderson (1992) conclude that many firms do not change their distribution channels in the frictionless way suggested by normative theory, and that the conversion process meets with substantial inertia. Bucklin (1966) also notes that such adaptation is unlikely to happen overnight because of barriers and temporal constraints related to existing distribution channels.

Perspectives on Innovation

Research from various perspectives has helped show how to overcome this inertia. As pointed out by strategic analysts, environmental forces for change, such as proliferation of customer needs and shifts in the balance of channel power (Anderson et al., 1997), may not suffice. As stressed in theories on innovation, these forces must be combined with internal organizational and attitudinal drivers in order to promote innovation (Chandy & Tellis, 1998; Damanpour, 1992; Srinivasan et al., 2002).

Thus several factors have been found to be important for understanding new service and product development (Johne & Storey, 1998), and several of these may be relevant to the introduction of Internet-based marketing channels. However, variables such as specialised investments and willingness to cannibalize are mentioned in only a few studies of new service and product development (for example, Chandy & Tellis, 1998; Easingwood, 1986; Easingwood & Storey, 1995; Chandrashekaran, Mehta, Chandrashekaran, & Grewal, 1999).

Channel-specific investments are investments that have a lower value if they are used for other purposes than in a specific marketing channel. Chandy and Tellis (1998) have argued that specialised investments may be important in explaining willingness to cannibalize. They made willingness to cannibalize a central construct in their framework for explaining product-innovation behavior and argued that specialised investments may make firms reluctant to introduce innovations in their markets. In new projects requiring radically different capabilities, existing capabilities may also serve as barriers to success (Leonard-Barton, 1992). A number of organizational forces, however, may counter the negative effect of specialised investments on the willingness to cannibalize. Using data from three high-tech industries, computer hardware, photonics, and telecommunication, Chandy and Tellis (1998) found a negative relationship between specialised investments and willingness to cannibalize. However, the existence of a product champion and a future market focus had a significant positive influence on the willingness to cannibalize and the ability to innovate.

Model and Hypotheses

As there is no general explanatory theory of innovation, descriptive quasi-theories have had to be developed that fit specific innovations, whose specific antecedents should be identified and measured (Damanpour, 1991; Mohr, 1982, 1987; Pennings & Harianto, 1992). In the case of the adoption of Internet-based marketing channels, it would seem a proper point of departure to categorise this innovation according to the dimensions used in Damanpour's well-proven contingency models (Damanpour, 1996), but this innovation fits Damanpour's scheme poorly. We cannot say whether it is a technical or an administrative innovation because it is both. Neither can we clearly say whether it is a change in product/service or in process because it is a *service innovation* in the sense that it meets an external market need, and a *process innovation* in the sense that workflow may be changed. Furthermore, to understand how the process moves from initiation to adoption, structural explanations and impersonal contingencies such as size are insufficient; attitudinal factors may be the most important in our model, presented in Figure 1.

The variables "future market focus," "ownership," "specialised investments," and "top management support" are all mediated by "willingness to cannibalize" and have a direct effect on the adoption of Internet-based interaction with the customers. We suggest that the other two independent variables, "IT knowledge" and "market pressure," have only a direct effect on the adoption of the new channels. Compared to models of new product development (for example, Chandy Y Tellis, 1998), this model has added variables for ownership, top management support, information technology (IT) knowledge, and market pressure; compared

Figure 1. Model of Internet channel adoption

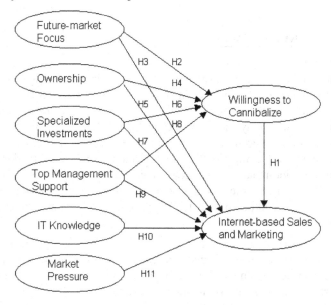

to what is described in the literature on new service and product development (*cf.*, Johne & Storey, 1998), the model has additional variables for matters such as specialised investments, IT knowledge, and willingness to cannibalize. The model is also consistent with the model developed by Srinivasan et al. (2002), who place "technological opportunism," that is, sense-and-respond capabilities, as a central construct in their explanation of e-business adoption. Our model is developed to analyze the path to adoption more specifically.

Willingness to Cannibalize

Willingness to cannibalize has been defined as the extent to which a firm is prepared to reduce the actual or potential value of its investments (Chandy & Tellis, 1998, p. 475). A firm has often invested considerable resources in its marketing channels. Either its salespeople spent considerable time and effort developing close, trusting, and profitable relationships with its distributors, or it has invested in its own marketing channels. A firm that is willing to cannibalize existing marketing channels does not avoid channels that might render employees or existing stores redundant. It does not wait until it is forced by competitors to innovate and introduce new channels but allocates resources in order to handle the new channels and integrate them into the existing organization. As noted by Chandy and Tellis (1998), the willingness to cannibalize current investments is often desirable because it promotes innovation and is necessary for the long-term survival of the firm. It may, however, hurt short-term profit because using new marketing channels may result in old channels becoming unprofitable. The conclusion regarding the willingness to cannibalize is summarized in Hypothesis 1.

H_1:   The greater a firm's willingness to cannibalize, the more likely it will be to adopt Internet-based interaction with its customers.

Future Market Focus

Customer-driven design models take their starting point in existing segments of the market (Stern & Sturdivant, 1987). However in some markets new technology may change the relationship between costs and service output. In such markets, firms that are oriented toward the current market may end up with channels that fail to satisfy the needs and wants of their customers. A future-oriented firm, however, will be interested in future profits, customer segments, and competitors. Future orientation and future-market focus indicate how alert the decision-makers are to new technologies and changes among competitors and customers. A future-market focus is defined as the extent to which a firm emphasizes future customers and competitors relative to current customers and competitors (Chandy & Tellis, 1998, p. 479).

A firm oriented toward the present and the past will be unwilling to cannibalize existing investments, whereas a future-oriented firm expects to do so. A future-oriented firm will be interested in those customers who will be the most attractive a year or more from now, whereas a firm oriented to the past and present will be attached to its customers and focus on serving customers' current needs and wants without preparing for how these needs and wants may develop. This is in accordance with the finding that future-oriented firms are more innovative (Kitchell, 1995) and seem more inclined to adopt e-business (Srinivasan et al., 2002) and suggests the following hypotheses:

H_2: The greater the attention a firm pays to the future, the greater its willingness to cannibalize.

H_3: The greater the attention a firm pays to the future, the more likely it is to adopt Internet-based interaction with its customers.

Ownership of Technological Innovation

Successful implementation of a strategy depends on employee commitment (Noble & Mokwa, 1999). Specific commitment to a strategy or an innovation is almost synonymous with the concept of ownership (Argyris & Kaplan, 1994), or with the concept of user involvement as used in information-systems literature (Barki & Hartwick, 1994). User involvement is seen as the individual user's understanding of the importance, for instance, of an information-system project, and may in turn be established through user participation (Barki & Hartwick, 1994; Ives & Olson, 1984).

Whenever achieved, the inherent feeling of ownership may not merely help in overcoming resistance to change; rather, "owners" may play innovating roles themselves. Some may even become "champions" of technological innovation, by acting as informal transformational leaders contributing to the innovation by actively and enthusiastically promoting its progress (Howell & Higgins, 1990). In information-systems projects users now often take the lead because widespread decentralization has made information technology a powerful business tool in the hands of end-users, including those who are responsible for satisfying customers (Martinson & Chong, 1999).

Though intuitively compelling, the impact on performance of ownership, specific commitment, and user involvement has not been well documented. The reported positive results are often insignificant, and the literature on commitment still makes little comment on the motivational impact of specific commitment (Becker, Billings, Eveleth, & Gilbert, 1996). Even the reported positive impact of user involvement on information-system projects may be questioned because of methodological problems (Ives & Olson, 1984).

In this chapter, "ownership" means employee commitment to the Internet project; ownership is not limited to isolated individuals but may include all the employees working in a firm or on a certain project. It is assumed that a strong feeling of ownership of an Internet project will generally stand in opposition to any personal loyalty to existing marketing channels. The effect of ownership on the adoption of Internet-based interaction with customers may be mediated by the willingness to cannibalize. There may, however, also be a direct effect because innovation is not always expected to cannibalize existing investments or because the cannibalization effect is unimportant.

H₄: The stronger the ownership feeling toward the Internet projects in a company, the greater the company's willingness to cannibalize.

H₅: The stronger the ownership feeling toward the Internet projects in a company, the more likely the company is to adopt Internet-based interaction with its customers.

Specialized Investment

The huge resources invested in existing distribution channels may be channel-specific investments (*cf.*, Williamson, 1996). Many companies have built relationships with various distributors or have opened stores, hired employees, taught them to work with their products and services, and implemented effective organizational routines (Stern et al., 1996; Weiss & Anderson, 1992). All these investments will be of no or lower value if Internet-based marketing channels become the most important channels.

The managers may have developed strong commitment to these investments, which can lead to sub-optimal or irrational decision and to commit new resources to a losing course of action (Staw, 1981). Hence, in order to protect channel-specific investments, managers may end up without ability to pursue courses of action that threaten to cannibalize current investments (Chandrashekaran et al., 1999; Ghemawat, 1991). Based on this we expect:

H₆: The more specific investments a firm has made in a current marketing channel, the less willing it is to cannibalize those investments.

Firms possessing such *specialised* investments will need more time to adapt a sales organization to Internet-based interaction with customers than if existing assets are *general* and *flexible* and easy to adapt to new ways of selling and marketing. Thus some firms may respond that they are highly willing to cannibalize but that relationship ties with existing distributors and existing contracts and investments may slow down the adoption of Internet-based interaction with customers. In line with this Leonard-Barton (1992) argued that development projects imply organizational struggle to maintain, renew, and replace core capabilities because new technologies may both enhance and destroy existing competencies within an industry. She argued that existing values, skills, managerial systems, and technical systems may be inappropriate for some projects and that these sets of knowledge become core rigidities creating problems for projects that require new capabilities. Hence we expect:

H₇: The more specific investments a firm has made in a current marketing channel, the less likely the firm will be to adopt Internet-based interaction with its customers.

Top Management Support

While ownership of technological innovation typically involves "advocates" who may be situated at lower levels in the organization, top management support may be needed to compel or legitimise a change beyond the initiation stage (Argyris & Kaplan, 1994). Leonard-Barton

(1992) also emphasizes the important challenge to make empowered individuals channel their energy towards corporate aims. Hence it seems that for new marketing channels to become a success, it is important that one or more among the management team are ready to play the role of "sponsors" or "orchestrators" (Galbraith, 1982). Managerial support is especially required in the implementation stage when conflict resolution is needed (Damanpour, 1991). Thus the effect of top management support on the adoption of Internet-based marketing channels is likely mediated by the willingness to cannibalize because the trade-off between different marketing channels materializes in the managers' decisions on project financing.

H$_8$:   The greater the support from top management, the greater the willingness to cannibalize.

There is a direct relationship as well, and several studies on innovation have emphasized the relationship between management support and the adoption of innovations (Damanpour, 1991). In their comprehensive review article, Johne and Storey (1998) also identified top management and their provision of a clear corporate vision, resources, and help as among the most important factors for successful development of new services.

The information-system literature identifies top management support as one of the factors that regularly appear as being significantly related to successful information-system imple- mentation (Kwon & Zmud, 1987, pp. 227-251). Recent information-system literature also documents the fact that management climate may influence the use of IT, and that effec- tive innovation management may require the simultaneous use of mechanistic and organic structures (Boynton, Zmud, & Jacobs, 1994). This suggests the following hypothesis:

H$_9$:   The greater the support from top management, the more likely a firm will be to adopt
Internet-based interaction with its customers.

IT Knowledge

Innovations are based on knowledge related to the firms' existing skills, abilities, and routines (Nelson & Winter, 1982). Both radical and incremental innovations are contingent upon the presence of relevant technical knowledge (Dewar & Dutton, 1986; Ettlie, Bridges, O'Keefe, 1984; Pennings & Harianto, 1992). Individual skills and abilities are important for successful change efforts, and technical knowledge resources may be expected to have a positive influ- ence on the implementation of an innovation (Damanpour, 1991; Burke & Litwin, 1992). The more competent a firm is in an area, or the better it masters a specific technology, the easier it will be to apply that technology for various uses in the firm. In accordance with this Wang and Cheung (2004), in their study of e-business adoption by travel agencies in Taiwan, found that IT resources had a significant positive effect on the firms' adoption of e-business. A study by Lin and Lee (2005) also found a significant positive relationship between the level of adoption of e-business systems among the largest companies in Taiwan and the five knowledge variables: training availability, technical expertise, knowledge level, knowledge acquisition, and knowledge application. Based on this, we expect that firms possessing the core capabilities needed for a technological project will be more ready for and have an easier time implementing such a project. Hence we suggest the following hypothesis:

H_{10}:   The more IT knowledge in an organization, the more likely it will be to adopt Internet-based interaction with its customers.

Market Pressure

So far our model only includes internal drivers of innovation, as described in the model developed by Chandy and Tellis (1998). Changes in channel design are also expected to be determined by strong external forces, such as changes in customer needs or shifts in the balance of channel power (Anderson et al., 1997). Technology advances through the competition between technologies promoted by rival organizations and internal change processes are heavily influenced by the context within which they occur (Tushman & Anderson, 1986). The presence of competitors with Internet-based channels may motivate adoption, making willingness or reluctance to cannibalize less important. Thus the pressure from competitors is considered a critical element of the construct "institutional pressure" that has been shown to correlate e-business adoption (Srinivasan et al., 2002). Also Wang and Cheung (2004) found a significant relationship between competitive pressure and the degree to which e-business had been adopted by travel agencies.

H_{11}:   The greater the pressure from competitors using Internet channels, the more likely a firm will be to adopt Internet-based interaction with its customers.

Firm Size

It is questionable to treat organizational size as a simple independent variable. Size is a major indicator of organizational complexity and has been covered in several studies of innovation, but the empirical findings on the size-innovation relationship are inconclusive (Damanpour, 1996; Hage, 1999). Since the seminal work of Schumpeter (1942), a number of researchers have argued for a positive relationship between firm size and ability to innovate because large organizations have more slack, more marketing skills, and more technological knowledge (for example, Chandy & Tellis, 1998; Damanpour, 1992; Dewar & Dutton, 1986; Pavitt, 1990). On the other hand some have stressed that small organizations are more flexible and able to innovate because of the easier availability of cross-functional co-operation (Mintzberg, 1979). Despite some evidence in favour of a positive relationship between size and innovation (Damanpour, 1992), this relationship seems to be moderated when administrative and process innovations are the focus (Damanpour, 1996). Some of the most relevant recent studies found size to be negatively related to innovation (Chandy & Tellis, 1998; Hoest et al., 2001; Srirojanant & Thirkell, 1998). These studies may indicate that managers in smaller businesses were more ambitious concerning the implementation of interactive Web sites. However it is worth noting the weak and insignificant relationship between firm size and e-business adoption found in the study by Srinivasan et al. (2002) and between firm size and product development found in the study by Chandy and Tellis (1998), who controlled for willingness to cannibalize and antecedents to this factor.

In our approach, this is a point of departure. We ignore size as an independent variable *per se*, as suggested by Hage (1999) but explore how the model changes depending on size category. For instance willingness to cannibalize may be less crucial to a large company.

Methods

The survey was conducted between October 1999 and May 2001 by means of a questionnaire mailed to 2,581 manufacturers. The sample consisted of Danish, Finnish, and Swedish manufacturers drawn from a number of different industries and generally having 20 or more employees. The Swedish sample included manufacturers with fewer than 20 employees. The distribution of the sample and the respondents is described in Table 1. No single industrial sector contributed more than a quarter of the respondents. Most of the respondents represented small and medium-sized firms, with 12.2 percent having fewer than 20 employees, 42.5 percent having 20 to 49 employees, and 45.3 percent having 50 or more employees. These figures can be compared with the study by Srinivasan et al. (2002), in which 69.9 percent represent firms with more than 500 employees.

The questionnaire was pre-tested, and key informants were identified using national databases. One questionnaire was sent to the marketing manager of each firm, as we considered

Table 1. Profile of respondents

	Danish			Finnish		Swedish		
	Small firm	Medium-sized firm	Large firm	Small firm	Large/ medium-sized firm	Very small * firm	Small firm	Large/ medium-sized
N	173	150	34	153	174	134	139	138
Seniority, years (Means)	9.5	8.7	6.6	9.7	9.2	12.2	10.8	10.0
Mean-score on "we receive orders through the Internet" **	2.85	2.90	3.18	2.64	2.78	2.24	2.58	2.50

* Only included in analysis of size effects (Table 3); ** Scale: Not considered (1), Considered (2), Planned (3), Under implementation (4), Implemented (5) Successfully implemented (6)

Note: Very small firm (Only Swedish): Fewer than 20 employees. Small: More than 20 and fewer than 50 employees. Medium-sized: More than 49 employees and fewer than 250. Large: More than 249.

this function likely to be most knowledgeable about the central issues of our study. To avoid some of the interpretation problems stressed in the literature on cross-cultural comparative methods (Hui & Triandis, 1985) and to ensure an adequate translation, the questionnaires were formulated in English and Danish and then translated into each of the other Nordic languages. After sending a reminder, we received 1,174 responses, giving an overall response rate of 45 percent.

Following the example of Armstrong and Overton (1977), several tests were made of the Danish sample to ensure that the respondents were representative. Non-respondents were compared to respondents, and respondents answering before receiving a reminder were compared to respondents answering after receiving a reminder. At a one percent level of significance, only one difference was found for any of the questions in the questionnaire, and none were found for the measures of industry type, firm size, and export markets. Together with the acceptable overall response rate, this indicates that non-response bias is not a problem.

Our measures were first developed by scanning the literature and adapting the measures reported to the specific context of our study. The questionnaire was then pre-tested and revised. After the data collection, the measures were purified several times. The coefficient alpha was calculated for each measure, and items with low item-to-total correlations were deleted. Inspection of the measurement part of the LISREL model during confirmatory factor analysis also resulted in the deletion of a few items because their coefficients were considerably below 0.70.

We initially decided to construct two manifest measures (questionnaire items) for each latent variable, except for the "Internet-based marketing and sales" variable, which is based on an index. When more than two items remained for a latent variable, the items with the highest correlation coefficients were summed. This reduced the number of manifest variables (observed variables) to 16. All manifest variables were treated as ordinal-scaled variables. Due to missing values for some of these manifest variables, the application of list-wise deletion reduced the sample size to an effective sample of 420 and 454, respectively, for the small and medium-sized/large company categories. Some of the manifest variables were recoded in order to ensure a reasonable number of answers in each category. The final measures are presented in the Appendix.

Findings

Hypotheses Testing

On average the companies represented in our sample were in the midst of adopting Internet-based communication with their customers, as indicated in Table 1, but large variations were found. To explain variation and to assess our theoretically deduced model, we used path analysis. The data were analyzed by means of LISREL modelling and followed a competing-models strategy (Jöreskog & Sörbom, 1993). First we estimated a model based on data pertaining to small companies, then this model was modified by adding the "market pressure" variable to the model. This procedure was repeated in a sample of medium-sized/large companies.

As input to the estimation of the LISREL models, we estimated the polychoric correlation matrix and the corresponding asymptotic covariance matrix for the 13 manifest variables based on the 420 and 454 observations in the sample of small and medium-sized/large companies, respectively. The LISREL model was then estimated using the generally weighted least squares method (Jöreskog & Sörbom, 1989).

The initially estimated model for the group of small manufacturers is depicted in Figure 2. It consists of both a structural equation model based on latent variables corresponding to the theoretical model from Figure 1 (without the market pressure variable) and measurement models for the latent variables. In the model depicted in Figure 2, the three path coefficients are insignificant (not supporting H3, H5, or H7), but the overall fit of the model is good (Table 2) and the seven path coefficients are significant (supporting H1, H2, H4, H6, H8, H9, and H10). Furthermore, 33 percent of the variation in the latent variable, willingness to cannibalize, and 36 percent of the variation in the latent variable, Internet-based marketing and sales, are explained by the model. Thus this model suggests that future market focus, ownership, and specialised investments have mainly indirect effects, mediated by willingness to cannibalize, on adoption of Internet-based marketing and sales, whereas top management support has both direct and indirect significant effects. IT knowledge has a significant direct impact on adoption of Internet-based sales and marketing. Removing insignificant paths and re-estimating a reduced model only marginally improves the fit of the model and path coefficients. In the next step, the market pressure variable is added and, as shown in Figure 3, the new estimation shows a significant path from market pressure to Internet-based sales and marketing while other coefficients hardly change at all.

Figure 2. Estimated adoption model for small firms

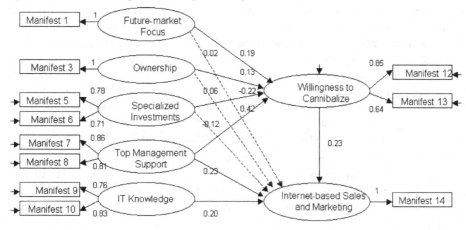

Figure 3. Estimated model for small firms with added market pressure variable

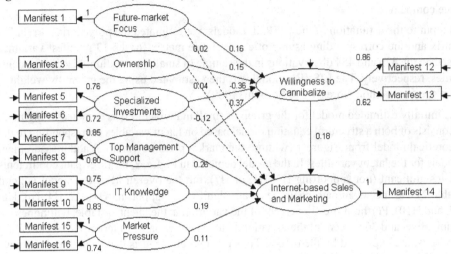

Note: Insignificant paths are indicated by dotted lines. All other arrows between the latent variables
indicate significant paths (p < 0.05, two-tailed test)

When the whole estimation procedure is repeated for the sample of medium-sized and large manufacturers, the coefficients and degrees of path significance change, as shown in Figures 4 and 5, and in Table 2. There are still significant paths (supporting H2, H6, H8, and H11), indicating the general validity of this part of the model, but the mediating role of willingness to cannibalize has changed. This model suggests that future market focus and top management support mainly have indirect effects, mediated by willingness to cannibalize, on adoption of Internet-based marketing and sales, whereas specialised investments has both direct and indirect significant effects. Ownership and especially IT knowledge and market pressure have a significant direct impact on adoption of Internet-based sales and marketing. Adding the market-pressure variable implies a strong direct path from market pressure to the adoption of Internet-based sales and marketing, while ownership and willingness to cannibalize no longer have significant impacts at the 0.05 level. Thirty-one percent of the variation in the latent variable, willingness to cannibalize, and 37 percent of the variation in the variable, Internet-based marketing and sales, are explained by the last model.

Considering their better goodness-of-fit statistics (Table 2), the models that omit market pressure are preferred to the competing models that include market pressure. We should, however, note that market pressure, especially in the case of larger companies, provides a significant supplementary explanation of the early adoption of Internet-based marketing channels.

To sum up, the analyses indicate significant support for *H1* (path from willingness to can-nibalize to adoption of Internet-based sales and marketing channels) except in the last larger firm model. *H2* (path from future orientation to willingness to cannibalize) is significantly

Figure 4. Estimated adoption model for medium-sized large firms

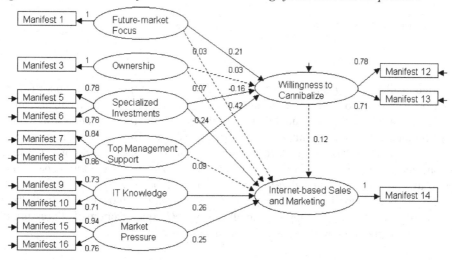

Note: Insignificant paths are indicated by dotted lines. All other arrows between the latent variables indicate significant paths (p < 0.05, two-tailed test)

Figure 5. Estimated model for medium-sized and large firms with market pressure

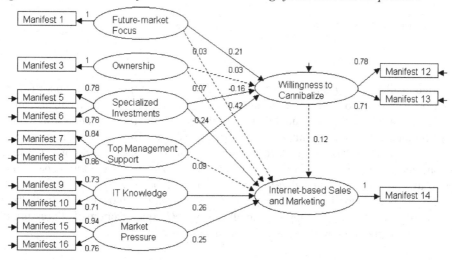

Note: Insignificant paths are indicated by dotted lines. All other arrows between the latent variables indicate significant paths (p < 0.05, two-tailed test)

Table 2. Goodness of fit measures of estimated LISREL models

	Small firms		Medium-sized/large		
	Initial model (Figure 2)	Model with market pressure (Figure 3)	Initial model	(Figure 4)	Model with market pressure (Figure 5)
Sample size	420	420	454		454
Chi-square test statistics	39.03	75.89	43.48		83.89
Degrees of freedom	27	43	27		42
Prob-value	0.063	0.001	0.023		0.0001
Population discrep. function (F_0)	0.0287	0.0785	0.0364		0.0925
Root mean square error of approx. (RMSEA)	0.033	0.043	0.037		0.047
Prob-value for test of RMSEA<0.05	0.906	0.765	0.865		0.616
Expected cross-validation index (ECVI)	0.279	0.410	0.268		0.402
ECVI for saturated model	0.315	0.434	0.291		0.402
Goodness of fit index (GFI)	0.993	0.989	0.993		0.990
Adjusted goodness of fit index (AGFI) Parsimony goodness of fit index (PGFI)	0.984	0.978	0.983		0.977
	0.406	0.468	0.406		0.457
R^2 (Adoption of Internet-based..)	0.36	0.38	0.31		0.37

supported in all models. *H3* (path from future orientation to adoption) is unsupported. *H4* (path from ownership to willingness to cannibalize) is only supported in the small firm models. *H5* (path from ownership to adoption) is only supported in the first larger firm model. *H6* (path from specialized investments to willingness to cannibalize – negative relationship) is supported in all models. *H7* (path from specialized investments to adoption – negative relationship) is only supported in the larger firm models. *H8* (path from top management support to willingness to cannibalize) is supported in all models. *H9* (path from top management support to adoption) is only supported in the small firm models. *H10* (path from IT knowledge to adoption) is supported in all models. *H11* (path from market pressure to adoption) is supported in both a small firm and a larger firm model.

Path to Successful Implementation in Small and Large Firms

There may be a giant step from initiation and adoption of innovations to successful implementation of them. In particular, an Internet-based marketing channel may imply difficult changes in internal procedures before interactive features make it useful to customers.

Table 3. Size and correlations of successful implementation

Relationships		Rank-order correlations #		
Antecedents	Adoption/ Success	Very small firms ## (N>99)	Small/ medium -sized firms (N >439)	Larger firms (N>473)
Level: Adoption of Internet-based sales and marketing				
Future Market Focus	Channel adoption	-0.23**	0.02	0.05
Ownership	Channel adoption	-0.05	0.08*	-0.03
Specialized Investments	Channel adoption	-0.27**	-0.20**	-0.21**
Top Management Support	Channel adoption	0.39**	0.32**	0.23**
IT Knowledge	Channel adoption	0.35**	0.20**	0.19**
Willingness to cannibalize	Channel adoption	0.02	0.25**	0.20**
Market Pressure	Channel adoption	0.15*	0.17**	0.22**
Level: Successful Implementation of Internet-based sales and marketing				
Future Market Focus	Successful Implem	-0.03	-0.00	0.07
Ownership	Successful Implem.	-0.02	0.13**	0.04
Specialized Investments	Successful Implem.	-0.11	-0.13**	-0.07
Top Management Support	Successful Implem.	0.25**	0.20**	0.14**
IT Knowledge	Successful Implem.	0.22**	0.17**	0.21**
Willingness to cannibalize	Successful Implem.	0.01	0.11*	0.10*
Market Pressure	Successful Implem.	0.16	0.02	0.11*

#) *Kendall tau b - coefficients based on grouped variables*
##) *Very small companies: Only Swedish sample*
*: $p < 0.05$
**: $p < 0.01$

Thus, we were interested in the characteristics of those organizations reporting successful implementation of interactive technology.

The correlations found in this explorative part of the analysis indicate that the explanations for success or failure in implementation differ from the explanations for success or failure in initiation and adoption. Willingness to cannibalize seems to be a less-important driver in the final steps toward successful implementation, in which IT knowledge and top management support become dominant factors (Table 3). This is partly in line with the argument that as the process moves on, political factors become more important, whereas more rational decision-making models may explain behaviors that lead to information technology adoption (Cooper & Zmud, 1990).

These findings as well as findings from a related study of Internet banking indicate that the adoption and implementation of Web technologies are complex processes that can be understood as both technology push and demand pull processes, and they are subject to disagreement (Flohr Nielsen, 2006). Conflicts grow out of structural differentiation or specialization and are found at the inter-organizational, inter-departmental, and interpersonal levels. Differences in the willingness to cannibalize do not necessarily develop into manifest conflict, but opinions often differ between key people such as IT and marketing managers. Thus, when identifying a firm's willingness to cannibalize as an important antecedent to early adoption and implementation of Internet-based marketing channels and Internet banking, it must be understood that such willingness reflects an overall attitude that results either from *compromise* between key actors' different attitudes or from the *defeat* of one or more actors.

From an organizational change view this seems to have important implications for practitioners. In planned change processes it has to be taken into account how conflicts are handled. Often it may become necessary to include participative organizational development techniques as well as conflict-handling interventions. When implementation success seems to be very dependent on top management support, it is in line with a recent meta-analysis of information systems implementation (Sharma & Yetton, 2003). This study shows that task interdependence moderates the effect of management support on implementation success. Since the activities connected to sophisticated marketing channels are highly interdependent and cross-functional, it is important that management provides the resources and incentives necessary to accomplish these projects.

However, the capability of organizations to fully exploit their current investments in installed IT is generally an issue involving complex post-adoptive behaviors, and neither prior use, habit, nor feature-centric views have been fully addressed in previous research (Jasperson, Carter, & Zmud, 2005). Because of such deficiencies we can only cautiously suggest that the successful implementation and use of Internet-based marketing may also need interventions that induce members of the organization to engage in learning on these IT-enabled work systems.

Discussion

The major contribution of this study is the formulation and rigorous testing of a model describing the adoption of Internet-based marketing channels, a model including both structural and attitudinal explanatory factors. The results identify knowledge of IT and management support as important drivers of the adoption of Internet-based sales and marketing. Willingness to cannibalize is also an important factor and plays a major role as a mediator of other drivers and barriers, in particular among small firms. Specialized investments in logistical systems, sales and marketing skills, and current operating procedures had a negative effect on willingness to cannibalize. Future market focus and management support, however, increased the willingness to cannibalize, and together these two variables are able not only to neutralize the effects of specialized investments, but together they may be more important determinants of the willingness to cannibalize.

We found that future market focus, ownership, specialised investments, and (partly) management support had only weak direct effects on adoption of Internet-based sales and marketing. This indicates that in cases where the implementation of Internet-based sales and marketing is expected to detract from existing investments in traditional marketing channels, willingness to cannibalize appears to be an important mediating variable. However, in other settings where the innovation seems to have a neutral or even positive effect on the value of present investments, willingness to cannibalize decreases in importance as a mediator. This seems often to be the case in larger companies. This finding is in accordance with Geyskens, Gielens, and Dekimpe (2002), who conclude that powerful firms will experience fewer negative reactions from existing marketing channels because they can use their power to ensure that their distributors will continue to honour their agreements even after the adoption of Internet-based marketing channels.

Our analysis somewhat supports a generalization of the radical innovation model developed by Chandy and Tellis (1998). We found that willingness to cannibalize exerted a significant mediating effect on the adoption of Internet-based marketing channels in a sample covering different countries and different industries. Size seems to play a minor role.

However, the findings also indicate some limitations to this reasoning. First of all, the relationships between the variables in the model are sensitive to size groupings. Willingness to cannibalize has the most explanatory power in small firms, whereas market-pull factors are most important in medium-sized and large firms.

The strength of the relationship between future orientation and willingness to cannibalize may be specific to the particular innovation and industries studied. Kohli and Jaworski (1990) argue that for firms operating in markets where technology is changing rapidly, a market orientation is not as important as in stable industries. In such industries, R&D-driven innovations and a future orientation may be more important than customer-driven innovations. This is probably truer for radical innovation and less so for incremental innovations; in the case of incremental innovations, manufacturers are more likely to benefit from being market oriented.

Commitment to relationship marketing may facilitate the development of interactive Web sites, as indicated in the study of Srirojanant and Thirkell (1998). Our findings, however, stress that one should exercise caution in accepting such statements. Especially in small and medium-sized companies, managers probably have to make uneasy decisions regarding cannibalization and the provision of IT knowledge for successful implementation to be achieved.

The feeling of ownership was only weakly related to willingness to cannibalize or to the adoption of Internet-based sales and marketing. However, ownership and involvement are usually important when either (1) the focal problems are complex and unstructured or (2) user acceptance is crucial. In the case of the introduction of Internet-based marketing channels, the problems may indeed be complex and unstructured, but user acceptance may not be a problem. This is because of the widespread belief that Internet-based communication with customers is inevitable and that all employees will have to accept and learn how to use the new communication medium. Nevertheless in the group of small companies the ownership variable is significantly and positively associated with successful implementation, indicating that the feeling of ownership is indeed important in the later stages of implementation. Another recent study also indicates that the extent of co-ordination is positively related to the Web assimilation (Chatterjee, Grewal, & Sambamurthy, 2002).

Firm size in itself is an explanatory factor that has to be treated with caution, though we cannot deny that firm size may be an advantage. When attitudinal and organizational factors are taken into account, however, the effects of size are weak; other analyses have even shown a negative relationship (Hoest et al., 2001). Our data from three Nordic countries indicate that only when moving from a very small to small firm does early innovation adoption increase, but that with further increases in firm size the effect disappears. Although our findings indicate that large organizations may have an advantage in that they seem able to react earlier to competitors' moves, the problems of differentiation in the case of a large company make it difficult to initiate and implement an innovation that involves important administrative and procedural factors. During implementation processes large firms may be very dependent on proper organizing, for example, by allowing smaller self-contained units to react to changes in their environments.

Conclusion and Implications

The adoption of Internet-based marketing channels is an underdeveloped area of research. This study attempts to model the drivers of and barriers to firms when they want to introduce new Web-based marketing channels. The empirical results suggest that knowledge of information technology, firm size, future market focus, specialised investments, management support, and the willingness to cannibalize old channels for the sake of new ones are all important factors influencing firms' effective introduction of Internet-based sales and marketing channels. Thus, our findings offer some insight into the interplay between structural and attitudinal variables in the initiation and adoption of these channels; in particular, the use of "willingness to cannibalize" as a mediating variable seems to have explanatory power.

This is in line with a study of radical product innovation in high-tech industries (Chandy & Tellis, 1998) and a study of adoption of Internet banking (Flohr Nielsen, 2002). The fact that our study included a broad range of manufacturers and was international in scope allows further generalization on the adoption of the new marketing channels.

Nevertheless, the study is not without limitations. Additional specific analysis of the role of organizational barriers would be a fruitful area for future research, perhaps conducted by using several respondents in each organization. In particular, issues connected to cross-functional co-operation in the late stages of implementation and issues connected to overcoming internationalization barriers need to be examined more thoroughly. Qualitative studies may be needed here as well.

The study, however, does have some important implications. First of all, it should be recognized that the adoption of new marketing channels often involves the painful process of cannibalizing older channels. Especially in the case of smaller organizations wanting to implement Internet-based sales and marketing, managers need employees with knowledge of information technology and the Internet. They also have to cope with the strong organizational inertia established through existing marketing channels. Thus, in smaller organizations, management support is especially important for the implementation of Internet-based sales and marketing. Management support and a future market orientation may counteract the negative effects of specialised investments. Even though specialised investments act as an important barrier, this may be overcome if upper management has a proper focus on the future and demonstrates its commitment and support. The study also has implications for understanding the role of size in these innovations. Small firm size seems to be no obstacle to the adoption of Internet-based marketing channels. In fact, it may be an advantage to be a small firm with only 20 employees, as long as many of these employees possess the necessary knowledge of the Internet and can design and update a Web site. On the other hand, managers in large firms can compensate by investing in knowledge of IT, supporting Internet-based marketing channels, and by being oriented toward future markets.

Acknowledgments

The authors gratefully acknowledge financial support from the Aarhus University Research Foundation and the support of Maria Bengtsson, Håkan Boter, and Sören Kock for their help in providing the Finnish and Swedish data.

References

Alba, J., Lynch, J., Weitz, B., Janiszewski, C., Lutz, R., Sawyer, A. & Wood, S. (1997). Interactive home shopping: Consumer, retailer, and manufacturer incentives to participate in electronic marketplaces. *Journal of Marketing, 61*, 38-53.

Anderson, E., Day, G. S., & Rangan, V.K. (1997). Strategic channel design. *Sloan Management Review 38*(4), 59-69.

Anderson, E., & Weitz, B. (1992). The use of pledges to build and sustain commitment in distribution channels. *Journal of Marketing Research, 29*(1), 18-34.

Argyris, C., & Kaplan, R. S. (1994). Implementing new knowledge: The case of activity-based costing. *Accounting Horizons, 8*(3), 83-105.

Armstrong, J. S., & Overton, T .S. (1977). Estimating non-response bias in mail surveys. *Journal of Marketing Research, 14*(3), 396-402.

Barki, H., & Hartwick, J. (1994). Measuring user participation, user involvement, and user attitude. *MIS Quarterly, 18*(1), 59-82.

Becker, T. E., Billings, R. S., Eveleth, D. M., & Gilbert, N. L. (1996). Foci and bases of employee commitment: Implications for job performance. *Academy of Management Journal, 39*(2), 464-482.

Boynton, A. C., Zmud, R. W., & Jacobs, G. C. (1994). The influence of IT management practice on IT use in large organizations. *MIS Quarterly, 18*(3), 299-318.

Bucklin, L. P. (1966). *A theory of distribution channel structure.* Berkeley, CA: IBER Special Publications.

Bucklin, L. P. (1970), A normative approach to the economics of channel structure in L.P. Bucklin (Ed.), *Vertical marketing systems* (pp. 159-175) Glenview: Scott, Foresman and Company.

Burke, W., & Litwin, G. (1992). A causal model of organizational performance and change. *Journal of Management, 18*, 523-545.

Chandrashekaran, M., Mehta, R., Chandrashekaran, R., & Grewal, R. (1999). Market motives, distinctive capabilities, and domestic inertia: A hybrid model of innovation generation. *Journal of Marketing Research, 36*(February), 95-112.

Chandy, R. K., & Tellis, G. J. (1998). Organizing for radical product innovation: The overlooked role of willingness to cannibalize. *Journal of Marketing Research, 35*(4), 474-487.

Chatterjee, D., Grewal, R., & Sambamurthy, V. (2002). Shaping up for e-commerce: Institutional enablers of the organizational assimilation of Web technologies. *MIS Quarterly, 26*(2), 65-89.

Cooper, R. B., & Zmud, R. W. (1990). Information technology implementation research: A technological diffusion approach. *Management Science, 36*, 123-136.

Damanpour, F. (1991). Organizational innovation: A meta-analysis of effects of determinants and moderators. *Academy of Management Journal, 34*(3), 555-590.

Damanpour, F. (1992). Organizational size and innovation. *Organization Studies, 13*(3), 375-402.

Damanpour, F. (1996). Organizational complexity and innovation: Developing and testing multiple contingency models. *Management Science, 42*(5), 693-716.

Dewar, R. D., & Dutton, J. E. (1986). The adoption of radical and incremental innovations: An empirical analysis. *Management Science, 32*, 1422-1433.

Easingwood, C. (1986). New product development for service companies. *Journal of Product Innovation Management, 3*(4), 264-275.

Easingwood, C., & Storey, C. (1995). The impact of the new product development project on the success of financial services. *Logistics Information Management, 8*(4), 35-40.

Ettlie, J. E., Bridges, W. P. & O'Keefe, R. D. (1984). Organization strategy and structural differences for radical versus incremental innovations. *Management Science, 30,* 682-695.

Flohr Nielsen, J. (2002). Internet technology and customer linking in Nordic banking. *International Journal of Service Industry Management, 13*(5), 475-495.

Flohr Nielsen, J. (2006). Models of change, organizational redesign, and the adoption of Web technologies. In R. M. Burton, B. Eriksen, D. D. Haakonsson, & C. C. Snow (Eds.), *Organization design: The dynamics of adaptation and change (information and organization series).* Boston: Springer Publishers (in press).

Galbraith, J. R. (1982). Designing the innovating organization. *Organizational Dynamics, 11*(Winter), 5-25.

Geyskens, I., Gielens, K., & Dekimpe, M. G. (2002). The market valuation of Internet channel addition. *Journal of Marketing, 66*(April), 102-119.

Ghemewat, P. (1991). Market incumbency and technological inertia. *Marketing Science,* 10(Spring), 161-171.

Greaves, C., Kipling, P., & Wilson, T. D. (1999). Business use of the World Wide Web, with particular reference to UK companies. *International Journal of Information Management, 19*, 449-470.

Hage, J. (1999). Organizational innovation and organizational change. *Annual Review of Sociology, 25*, 597-622.

Hoest, V., Mols, N. P. & Flohr Nielsen, J. (2001). The adoption of Internet based marketing channels. *Homo Oeconomicus, 17*(4), 463-488.

Howell, J. M., & Higgins, C. A. (1990). Champions of technological innovation. *Administrative Science Quarterly, 35*(2), 317-341.

Hui, C. H., & Triandis, H. C. (1985). Measurement in cross-cultural psychology: A review and comparison of strategies. *Journal of Cross-Cultural Psychology, 16*(2), 131-152.

Ives, B., & Olson, M. H. (1984). User involvement and MIS success: A review of research. *Management Science, 30*(3), 586-603.

Jasperson, J., Carter, P. E., & Zmud, R. W. (2005). A comprehensive conceptualization of post-adoptive behaviors associated with information technology enabled work systems. *MIS Quarterly, 29*(3), 525-557.

Johne, A., & Storey, C. (1998). New service development: A review of the literature and annotated bibliography. *European Journal of Marketing, 32*(3/4), 184-251.

Jöreskog, K., & Sörbom, D. (1989*). LISREL 7: user's reference guide.* Chicago: Scientific Software International Inc.

Jöreskog, K., & Sörbom, D. (1993). *LISREL 8: structural equation modelling with the SIMPLIS command language.* Chicago: Scientific Software International Inc.

Kitchell, S. (1995). Corporate culture, environmental adaptation, and innovation adoption. *Journal of the Academy of Marketing Science, 23*(3), 195-205.

Kohli, A. K., & Jaworski, B. J. (1990). Market orientation: The construct, research propositions, and managerial implications. *Journal of Marketing, 54*(2), 1-18.

Kohli, A. K., Jaworski, B. J., & Kumar, A. (1993). MARKOR: A measure of market orientation. *Journal of Marketing Research, 30*(November), 467-477.

Kwon, T. H., & Zmud, R. W. (1987). Unifying the fragmented models of information systems implementation. In R. A. Boland, Jr. & R. A. Hirschheim (Eds.), *Critical issues in information systems research* (pp. 227-251). Chichester, UK: Wiley.

Leonard-Barton, D. (1992). Core capabilities and core rigidities: A paradox in managing new product development [Special issue]. *Strategic Management Journal, 13*, 111-125.

Lin, H. F., & Lee, G. G. (2005). Impact of organizational learning and knowledge management factors on e-business adoption. *Management Decision, 43*(2), 171-188.

Mallen, B. E. (1973). Functional spin-off: A key to anticipating change in distribution structure. *Journal of Marketing, 37*(July), 18-25.

Martinson, M. G., & Chong, P. K. C. (1999). The influence of human factors and specialist involvement on information systems. *Human Relations, 52*(1), 123-152.

Mintzberg, H. (1979). *The structuring of organizations.* Englewood Cliffs, NJ: Prentice Hall.

Mohr, L. R. (1982). *Explaining organizational behaviour: The limits and possibilities of theory and research.* San Francisco: Jossey Bass.

Mohr, L. R. (1987). Innovation theory: An assessment from the vantage point of the new electronic technology in organizations. In J. M. Pennings & A. Buitendam (Eds.), *New technology as organizational innovation: The development and diffusion of microelectronics* (pp. 13-31). Cambridge, MA: Ballinger.

Mols, N. P., Bukh, P. N. D., & Flohr Nielsen, J. (1999). Distribution channel strategies in Danish retail banking. *International Journal of Retail and Distribution Management, 27*(1), 37-47.

Nelson, R. R., & Winter, S. G. (1982). *An evolutionary theory of economic change.* Cambridge, MA: Belknap Press of Harvard University Press.

Noble, C. H., & Mokwa, M. P. (1999). Implementing marketing strategies: Developing and testing a managerial theory. *Journal of Marketing, 63*(3), 57-73.

O'Cass, A., & Fenech, T. (2003). Web retailing adoption: Exploring the nature of Internet users' Web retailing behaviour. *Journal of Retailing and Consumer Services, 10*, 81-94.

Pavitt, K. (1990). What we know about the strategic management of technology. *California Management Review, 23*(3), 17-26.

Pennings, J. M., & Harianto, F. (1992). The diffusion of technological innovation in the commercial banking industry. *Strategic Management Journal, 13*(1), 29-46.

Rangan, V., Menezes, M., & Maier, E. (1992). Channel selection for new industrial products: A framework, method, and application. *Journal of Marketing, 56*(3), 69-82.

Schumpeter, J. A. (1942). *Capitalism, socialism, and democracy.* New York: Harper.

Sharma, R., & Yetton, P. (2003). The contingent effects of management support and task interdependence on successful information systems implementation. *MIS Quarterly, 27*(4), 533-555.

Srinivasan, R., Lilien, G. L., & Rangaswarny, A. (2002). Technological opportunism and radical technology adoption: An application to e-business. *Journal of Marketing, 66*(July), 47-60.

Srirojanant, S., & Thirkell, P. C. (1998). Relationship marketing and its synergy with Web-based technologies. *Journal of Market-Focused Management, 3*(1), 23-46.

Staw, B. M. (1981). The escalation of commitment to a course of action. *Academy of Management Review, 6*(4), 577-587.

Stern, L. W., El-Ansary, A., & Coughlan, A.T. (1996). *Marketing channel*. London: Prentice-Hall.

Stern, L.W., & Sturdivant, F.D. (1987). Customer-driven distribution systems. *Harvard Business Review, 65*(4), 34-41.

Tushman, M. L., & Anderson, P. (1986). Technological discontinuities and organizational environments. *Administrative Science Quarterly, 31*, 439-465.

Wang, S., & Cheung, W. (2004). E-business adoption by travel agencies: Prime candidates for mobile e-business. *International Journal of Electronic Commerce, 8*(3), 43-63

Weiss, A. M., & Anderson, E. (1992). Converting from independent to employee salesforces: The role of perceived switching costs. *Journal of Marketing Research, 29*(1), 101-115.

Williamson, O. E. (1996). *The mechanisms of governance*. New York: Oxford University Press.

Appendix: Measures

Nearly all the items were measured using a five-point Likert-scale, ranging from 1 = totally disagree to 5 = totally agree. The numbers refer to the manifest variables shown in figures.

Future Market Focus (Manifest 1 and 2)

(Adapted from Chandy & Tellis, 1998; Kohli, Jaworski, & Kumar, 1993)

1.   This firm gives more emphasis to customers of the future, relative to current customers

2.   In this industry it is important to be first with new initiatives

     (The last item was removed because confirmatory factor analysis showed a poor coefficient)

Ownership: Internet Ownership/Involvement (Manifest 3 and 4)

3.   We need employees, who will take responsibility for the development of the Internet in this firm (Reversed)

4.   There is a need for more involvement of employees in order to be able to implement the use of the Internet (Reversed)

(The last item was removed because confirmatory factor analysis showed a poor coefficient)

Specialised Investments (Manifest 5 and 6)

(Adapted from Anderson & Weitz, 1992)

5.   Our knowledge of sales and marketing cannot be applied to exploiting the Internet.
6.   Many of our current operating procedures cannot be applied to the new Internet technology.
6.   Our logistical system is badly suited for Internet-based sales and marketing.

Top-Management Support (Manifest 7 and 8)

(See, for example, Noble and Mokwa, 1999)

7.   Top management supports the exploitation of the Internet.
7.   The Internet receives a lot of attention from top management.
8.   The use of the Internet is linked with the rest of the firm's strategy.

IT Knowledge (Manifest 9 and 10)

9.   We possess the necessary knowledge of the Internet.
9.   We have many employees with competencies connected to the Internet.
10.   We can design and update a Web site ourselves.

Willingness to Cannibalize (Manifest 12 and 13)

(Adapted from Chandy & Tellis, 1998)

12.   We are willing to support Internet projects even though they take away sales from existing marketing

channels.
12.   We are willing to sacrifice sales through our existing channel in order to stake on Internet-based sales.
13.   We are willing to pursue a new technology even if it causes existing investments to lose value.

Market Pressure (Manifest 15 and 16)

15.   Our closest competitor has started to use the Internet for marketing and sales.
16.   We are forced to use the Internet as our competitors already do.

Internet-Based Sales and Marketing (Manifest 14)

(Developed with inspiration from Srirojanant & Thirkell, 1998; Greaves, Kipling, & Wilson, 1999)

An index for the adoption of interactive Internet-based communication with customers.

The sum of the scores for the following four items, each measured on a scale from (1) = not considered to (6) = successfully implemented:

Our company uses or plans to use the Internet for the following activities:

- Communications with customers via e-mail
- Receiving orders through our Web site
- Getting feedback from customers through our Web site
- Integrating the Web site with other systems (order processing, logistics, etc.)

Implementation Success

Number of the following items that are reported to have been successfully implemented:

- Communications with customers via e-mail
- Receiving orders through our Web site
- Getting feedback from customers through our Web site
- Integrating the Web site with other systems (order processing, logistics, etc.)

Chapter IV

Content is King?
Interdependencies in Value Networks for Mobile Services

Uta Wehn de Montalvo,
Netherlands Organisation for Applied Scientific Research, The Netherlands

Els van de Kar, Delft University of Technology, The Netherlands

Carleen Maitland, Pennsylvania State University, USA

Abstract

The advent of new electronic platforms is forcing firms from a range of industries to come together in so-called "value networks" for the provision of innovative mobile services. Firms from different industries have widely varying resources, among which content is often praised as being "king." We are particularly interested in the role of content and of the content providers, respectively, in the process of value creation to bring these services about. Therefore, our analysis is aimed at specific types of interdependencies, relating the actors' own and others' resource contributions. To better understand these interdependencies, we draw on theories about firm resources and inter-organisational relations. We analyse the importance and relevance of different resources in a number of case studies of "mobile information and entertainment services," in terms of the actors' resources and contributions to value in the provision of such mobile services. In the cross-case comparison, we contrast the power structures in the different value networks and identify similarities and differences in terms of the types of industrial players that assume positions of greater or lesser importance. This enables us to assess the position of content providers in these mobile services, which turns out to be surprisingly weak. In contrast, intermediaries (service providers) claim a strong position by contributing the service conception and design. We conclude with a discussion of the implications for value network research.

Introduction

The advent of new electronic platforms is forcing firms from a range of industries to come together in so-called "value networks" for the provision of innovative mobile services. Yet the rapid evolution of mobile services has left many issues unresolved. The problems of interest to us include uncertainty with respect to the complex networks that are involved in delivering these services. In environments of increasing electronic interaction, the value chain concept, where materials are moved sequentially down a supply chain, has been replaced by the value network, which is a dynamic network of partnerships and information flows (Bovel & Martha, 2000), changing as customer preferences change. This phenomenon is also taking place in the telecommunications industry (Li & Whalley, 2002; Maitland, Bauer, & Westerveld, 2002; Sabat, 2002). We aim to understand the interdependencies among actors involved in delivering mobile services in general, and mobile information and entertainment services and location-based services in particular in terms of their contribution to value creation. To this end, we adopt a resource-based perspective.

We consider a number of innovative cases of mobile information and entertainment services. Such services involve the delivery of information and entertainment content to a mobile user. Since these services typically require collaboration of a range of actors across different sectors, our analysis encompasses the entire "value network" of firms involved in making the service available. Whilst research on value networks for mobile services could be approached from several angles, including network formation, strategic management, and so forth, here we focus on resources and interdependencies. We investigate the actual constellation of actors: what are their resources, how are they interdependent, and what do they contribute to the value network? Is content really king?

The chapter is structured as follows. We begin with a brief review of relevant literature to provide a basis for our analysis of several mobile information and entertainment services. In particular, we examine the interdependencies among actors in the value networks and how their contribution to value creation determines their strategic position within the network. These tools are then used to analyse each of the five case studies of specific services. In the cross-case analysis, we collate and discuss the findings from the cases, paying particular attention to the role of content and the position of content providers. We conclude with the implications of our research for the literature on value networks and point to further areas of research.

Theoretical Context

A fundamental aspect of a value network is that it accomplishes the directed utilisation of resources in the provision of a product or service. In the following subsections, we derive a basis for our analysis of interdependencies in mobile information and entertainment services. The aim is to arrive at an analytical tool that can be used to understand the interdependencies among actors involved in delivering such services in terms of their contribution to value creation. This will provide important insights into the configuration and dynamics of actors in value networks and the extent to which these value networks depend on content providers to succeed.

We begin with a definition of resources and, given the context of value networks, we include a discussion of the resource-based view and its links to strategic alliances. Next we look at interactions among organisations in inter-organisational relations and, more specifically, value networks for the provision of mobile services. Finally, we consider different classes of interdependencies, focusing on the strategic position of firms within the value network and not within the market. We will argue that the configuration of actors is based on their resource-based contribution to value. We conclude this section with a summary of the analytical tools to be employed in the analysis of the case studies.

Resources

In this section, we first consider the concept of resources in detail in order to arrive at a definition/classification of resources for the analysis of interdependencies.

Definition of Resources

Resources have been studied from many perspectives, and the concept can be conceived very broadly to include almost everything in an organisational (capital, labour, infrastructure, technology, knowledge, processes, routines, capabilities) and inter-organisational setting (relationships, etc.). Hoskinson, Hitt, Wan, and Yiu (1999) review a range of studies by researchers from different disciplines that analyse resources giving rise to competitive advantage.

With our focus on the role of resources as they relate to interdependencies in a network of actors, we find the distinction between *tangible* and *intangible* resources (Itami & Roehl, 1987; Wernerfelt, 1984) most useful. Haanæs and Fjeldstad (2000) identify tangible resources as concrete and tradeable, factories, technology, capital, raw material, and land, and intangible resources as difficult to transfer, skills, knowledge, relationships, culture, reputation, and competencies. Essentially, this distinction parallels the two types of resources, *property-based* resources and *knowledge-based* resources, identified by Miller and Shamsie (1996). Building on this distinction, Das and Teng (2000) have identified three salient *characteristics* of resources in the resource-based literature and arrive at a matrix of resources that illustrates specific kinds of resources in each category. The basis for this classification is the reasoning that alliances need to be formed in order to obtain resources

Table 1. Typical resources (Source: Based on Das & Teng, 2000, p. 42; Porter, 1991)

Resource characteristics	Resource type	
	Property-based resources	Knowledge-based resources
Imperfect mobility	Human resources	Organisational resources (e.g., culture, reputation, relationships)
Imperfect imitability	Patents, contracts, copyrights, trademarks, and registered designs	Technological and managerial resources, skills
Imperfect substitutability	Physical resources	Technological and managerial resources, skills

featuring imperfect mobility, imitability, and substitutability. Imperfect mobility refers to the difficulty and cost of moving certain resources from one firm to another and obtaining them from the owner. Imperfect imitability and imperfect substitutability imply the difficulty of obtaining similar resources elsewhere. Complementing this with the external assets identified by Porter (1991) (reputation and relationships), we arrive at the following illustration of resources (see Table 1).

Resources, Strategic Alliances, and Value Networks

Resources have been considered in a range of different literatures, and they play a particularly central role in the resource-based view (RBV) of the firm and in the resource-dependence literature. More recently, links have been established between the RBV literature and the role of resources in strategic alliances (Erasmus, 2004; Das & Teng, 2000). We consult these to arrive at a definition (classification scheme) of resources for our analysis of interdependencies in value networks of mobile information and entertainment services.

The focus of the resource-based view (RBV) is the resources possessed by the firm. The RBV stresses value maximisation through the integration of resources. Successful firms are those firms that are able to acquire and maintain valuable idiosyncratic resources for competitive advantages (Oliver, 1997).

The resource-based view has been applied mainly to the individual firm to analyse various resources possessed by the firm but increasingly also in strategy research. Recently, the resource-based view has also been linked to a network perspective, specifically by considering the resource-based view in the context of strategic alliances (see, for example, a review of studies by Das & Teng, 2000):

> ... the resource-based view suggests that the rationale for alliances is the value-creation potential of firm resources that are pooled together.

> (Das & Teng, 2000, p. 56)

The application of the resource-based view to research on strategic alliances provides the link with value network research in focus here. Strategic alliances can be regarded as a category of inter-organisational relations and networks. The common premise is that it is precisely the complementarity of resources that necessitates the formation and evolution of both, strategic alliances and value networks, and that none of the actors can make all the necessary components available for product development or service provision.

The resource-based logic suggests that the competitive advantage of alliances is based on the effective integration of partner firms' valuable resources.

(Das & Teng, 2000, p. 48)

A resource-based perspective of the actors therefore provides a relevant basis to examine interdependence in the value network. From a resource-based perspective, paraphrasing Das and Teng (1998) on strategic alliances, *value networks are about combining resources that an individual firm cannot provide all on its own, yet are critical for the provision of a mobile service.*

Interdependencies

It has long been argued that all firms are embedded in one or more networks in which they collaborate with others to create value and in order to service the markets (Granovetter, 1985). Network boundaries are not easily defined because mostly there is no overarching purpose for the interactions. As noted in Maitland, van de Kar, and de Montalvo (2003a, 2003b), this is different for so-called value networks where the boundaries of the network can be more clearly distinguished by identifying the actors involved in the provision of a specific service. In a value network, the interaction among actors is goal-directed (i.e., the provision of a service) and cannot be assumed to be influenced merely by the individual actors' intention to influence each other. Value networks imply interdependencies (which may differ in their form and extent) among the organisations involved in it. Our analysis is aimed at specific relationships and interdependencies within the value network, i.e., the actors' own and others' resources, rather than in terms of products, markets, and competitors. Gadde, Huemer, and Håkansson (2003) have argued that each actor has a unique position in the network that is perceived differently by the different actors in the network because all have different relationships. We are interested in a more "objective assessment" of the different actors' positions within the value network on the basis of the resources and their relevance or importance to value creation in a given network.

In social systems and social interactions, interdependence exists when one actor does not entirely control all of the conditions necessary for the achievement of an action or for obtaining the outcome desired from the action. ... Interdependence characterizes the relationship between the agents creating an outcome, not the outcome itself.

(Pfeffer & Salancik, 1978, p. 40)

Theories on strategic management and resource dependence have often regarded interdependencies among organisations as inherently negative. Emphasis is therefore placed on how to manage interdependencies, on the implication of different coordination mechanisms (e.g., Ebers, 1999) and on strategies to restructure the conditions of interdependence (e.g., Mintzberg, 1979, 1983; Nassimbeni, 1998). In order to analyse dependencies in industrial networks, Håkansson (1987; Håkansson & Waluszewski, 2002) presents a "network model" inspired by strategic management theory with three dimensions: (1) actors, (2) activities, and (3) resources whereby actors perform activities and control resources. Activities are used to change other resources in different ways. These three elements are assumed to be related to each other as networks, that is, actors related to other actors, activities related to other activities, and resources related to other resources. In addition, these "networks" are closely connected in an "overall" network. The interdependence between various relationships in the network implies that a certain actor's change in behaviour also influences the position of other actors (Axelsson, 1987).

The distinctions and relations of the dimensions in this network can provide a basis for our analysis of interdependencies in value networks and the process of value creation. Activities within the value network bring together different types of actors and resources and create (different) relationships of (inter)dependency.

Several forces are identified binding the three networks together (actor network, activities network, and resource network (Håkansson, 1987)): (1) functional interdependence (actors, activities, and resources as a system that is functionally related), (2) power structure (actor power based on activities and resources), (3) knowledge structure (activities' design and resource use bound together by actors' knowledge), and (4) time-related structure (network as a product of its history). For our analysis of the strategic position of actors within the value network in terms of their contribution to value creation, the second type (power structure) is of greatest interest for our analysis. Actor power is assumed to be based on the activities and resources of a particular actor. In particular, we argue, that actor power stems from the characteristics (degree of mobility, imitability, and substitutability) of the resources. To typify the power "structure" among the actors in a value network, we propose a distinction between *essential*, *network-specific*, and *generic* resource contributions to value creation, ranging from greater to lesser relevance to value creation in the network and based on resource characteristics. We define **essential** resources as resources that are indispensable to the value network and the service it provides. These resources cannot be replaced without affecting the existence of the service, and they are highly immobile, difficult to imitate or substitute. **Network-specific** resources are crucial for the service that the value network provides, yet their replacement would be possible without affecting the service directly. They are fairly mobile, able to be imitated or substituted. **Generic** resources are required for the provision of the service, but they are so general that they could be replaced fairly easily without impacting the service. They are reasonably mobile, imitable, or substitutable.

This distinction provides a basis to define different partner types in the value network:

> ... *structural, contributing,* and *supporting* partners (ranging from greater to lesser actor power depending on the kind of resources they contribute), thus identifying the nature of interdependencies in a given network and the strategic position of actors within the network.
>
> (Ballon & Hawkins, 2003)

Summary and Conclusion on Theoretical Framework

Summarising the above discussion, this section provides a brief overview of the key concepts and their definitions that will be used in the subsequent analysis of mobile information and entertainment services. In order to "unpack" interdependencies in value networks for the provision of mobile information and entertainment services, we adopt Håkansson's distinction of networks of actors, of activities, and of resources as a functionally related system.

To capture the importance or relevance of different resources to value creation in a given network, we have proposed a distinction between *essential, network-specific,* and *generic* resource contributions to the value network. Each of these contributions may be in the form of tangible (property-based) or intangible (knowledge-based) resources. For our analysis, the matrix in Table 2 will be used to "map out" the different resources in a given value network and their relevance or importance to it. In each case study, we consider the actors and their resource contribution to the network.

Given our interest in resources from an interdependency perspective, our focus is not on all possible resources a partner may possess. Rather, we consider resources of partners in terms of their contribution to the value network, that is, to the provision of the specific service. With this approach we are also able to counter criticisms of the resource-based view (e.g., Foss, 1998) by looking beyond the individual resource and considering how resources are clustered and how they relate; in this case, in the provision of a mobile service provided by a value network.

The distinction of different resource contributions provides a basis to label different partner types in each value network: structural partners provide essential resources, contributing partners add network-specific resources, and supporting partners contribute generic resources to the process of value creation. This allows us to identify the nature of resource-based interdependencies in a given network and the strategic position of actors within the network. At this level of analysis, it will be possible to carry out a cross-case comparison of power structures in different value networks and identify similarities and differences in terms of the types of industrial players that assume positions of greater or lesser importance.

Table 2. Partner types and resource contributions in a value network

Partner type	Resource contribution to value network		Actor
structural	**essential**	*tangible*	
		intangible	
contributing	**network-specific**	*tangible*	
		intangible	
supporting	**generic**	*tangible*	
		intangible	

Case Studies: Interdependencies in Value Networks for Mobile Information and Entertainment Services

This section presents the analysis of the case studies of five mobile information and entertainment services. First, we set out the scope of the empirical research with a brief introduction and definition of mobile information and entertainment services, followed by an outline of the methods used and an overview of the five services that were selected as case studies. Then, each service is introduced and analysed in turn. The findings of the cases are collated and discussed in the cross-case analysis.

Mobile Information and Entertainment Services

The mobile services discussed in this research are limited to mobile information and entertainment services. As depicted in Figure 1, mobile information and entertainment services (category 2) are a subset of the broader category of mobile services (category 1), which are simply services made available to mobile users independent of the type of network (GPS, public switched mobile network, etc.). As defined here, mobile information and entertainment services require a connection to a network, which is in turn connected to the Internet. Currently, the dominant mode of access is through the mobile telecommunications network infrastructure connected to the fixed public switched network.

We define "mobile information and entertainment services" as *the delivery of information and entertainment from specially formatted content sources (e.g., Internet sites, SMS, MMS) via the mobile telecommunication network to a mobile user.* The terms "value added services in mobile commerce" and "mobile information and entertainment services" are often used

Figure 1. Mobile information and entertainment services domain

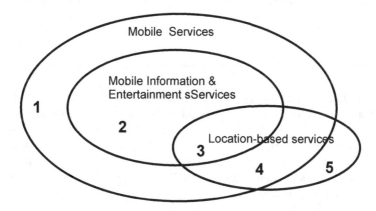

synonymously. What is important is that parties other than the network operator are involved to make the service available to customers.

In this research we also consider information and entertainment services that are based on location information. The use of location information has the potential to enable a whole range of new services and requires the involvement of a new kind of actor such as geographical information system (GIS) suppliers. In general *location-based services* can be offered through the mobile telecommunications network (category 3), independent of this network (4), and also in a fixed environment (5). Of interest to this research are services offered in the domain of category 2 (mobile information and entertainment services) and category 3 (location-based mobile services) offered over the mobile telecommunications network.

Method

Within the context of mobile information and entertainment services, five services were selected as case studies. The services were offered to end-users in three different European countries: Netherlands, Germany, and Sweden. To understand the service network composition and the dynamic among actors in terms of interdependencies and resources, interviews were held during the summer and fall of 2002. For each service, depending on the network size, interviews were held at between two and five firms. At each firm the interviewees were typically managers in charge of the relationship with the external partners associated with the particular service. Data from interviews were also supplemented with information gathered from company Web sites as well as through industry reports and in some cases other academic literature. The scope of the five service networks was defined by their relationship to end-customers. Services for which end-users were charged were chosen. In the appendix, we first present a table with an overview of the cases. Then a completed matrix (based on Table 2) is shown for each of the five services in Tables 5-9.

Case Studies

In this section each service is introduced and analysed in turn. The findings of the cases are collated and discussed in the cross-case analysis. First the two non-location based services are discussed.

My Babes

My Babes is a Dutch i-mode service that allows a customer unlimited access to a variety of genres of erotic content for a monthly subscription. Customers can view photos in different categories (topless, bikini, etc.), access games (Stripjack and HotOrNot) and store their favorite photos in a photo album for easy reference. The actors are KPN Mobile, iMedia, and Internet-based raw content suppliers. iMedia is a media firm that purchases content through market-based transactions with Internet firms and then modifies the content to meet the standards for the i-mode service.

Analysis of the My Babes Case

The i-mode cases have many of the resource contributions in common. The network operator contributes a large number of the essential resources (see Table 5). The operator takes care of the network, platform, billing, marketing, and partner network concept and is involved with customer support. This is all part of the i-mode concept. Another element of the i-mode concept is that the operator controls a procedure to enforce content quality management. Thus the resource contribution of the content suppliers is influenced through this relationship. In the MyBabes case, iMedia acts as an intermediary, which developed the specific service concept. In the i-mode model, intermediaries propose services to the i-mode staff, and they are approved or rejected. One of the items they are judged on is feasibility, and hence they must have their downstream partners identified. Once the service is accepted, the intermediary is responsible for developing the content to the specifications of the operator, which may change according to demand and feedback from consumers. This ongoing content development, which is a network-specific resource, places iMedia in the contributing partner role. In this role the firm must contend with an abundant supply of pornographic material (raw content) and provides the value-added service of matching the raw content to the tastes of the i-mode target market as well as editing the content so that it can be considered 'erotic' rather than pornographic. The intermediary also handles customer support problems. While the operator handles problems related to the data access service, iMedia is responsible for any problems specifically related to the service. In this capacity iMedia functions as a supporting partner. Also appearing as a supporting partner are the raw content suppliers, which are left to supplying the generic resources. In the case of myBabes the generic content is a class of pornographic images that can be easily transformed into erotic content, which does not contain depictions of sexual acts. This content tends to be of higher quality (settings, models, etc.), and therefore the intermediary requires a raw content supplier who can discriminate pornographic content quality. Despite this caveat, this function is in demand across a number of industries and hence is considered a generic resource. Thus this case presents a clear picture of a dominant network operator and an intermediary that appears as a structural partner but also plays contributing and supporting roles. The raw content suppliers are supporting and can be easily replaced, as did occur after only four months of operation.

Radio538

The Radio 538 ringtune case is also a Dutch i-mode service. A monthly subscription to the Radio 538 ringtunes service allows customers to download five ringtones from a variety of categories: music, voices and sounds. Radio 538 branded their service as "ringtunes" to distinguish the service from other "ringtone" services on the KPN Mobile i-mode portal. The i-mode handset, manufactured by NEC, allows customers to store a total of 13 polyphonic (16-chord) ringtones. Radio538 is a Dutch media firm that owns and operates a popular radio station. The ringtones are developed by several means that include the participation of the Radio538 DJs, Tutch and Jingle Hell, which turns popular music into ringtones. Permission to use the popular songs for ringtones is obtained through a copyright clearinghouse, BumaStemra, and the software that makes the ringtones available via the i-mode service is provided by Faith.

Analysis of the Radio538 Case

Like the MyBabes case, the network operator contributes a large number of resources. However, there are quite a few differences with the former case related to the other actors. In the Radio538 case the partner type identification is not so clear. Many actors are involved in content development with each actor offering their own very specific contribution. There is a strong intermediary, Tutch, responsible for the service conception and design and ringtune application provision. Tutch, however, is invisible in the market, since the well-known media firm radio station Radio 538 provides the branding. KPN Mobile wanted to pursue a relationship with Radio538 because it has access to the targeted customers. Initially the ringtones made by Radio538 were expected to match the tastes of the target market; subsequently the diversity provided by the DJs' ringtones added to their popularity. However there were other motives for pursuing a relationship with Radio538 given Radio538's national radio coverage and hence national brand recognition in the iMode target market. The media company Radio 538 also develops content, since they decide which songs are considered hits and will be the source for ringtones; facilitate DJs to register remarkable pronunciations for ringtones; and produce sounds for ringtones. The DJs and the music makers are the providers of the generic content that is turned into ringtones by another intermediary, Jingle Hell. Customers are supported by the network operator as well as by the first intermediary, Tutch, depending on the kind of question they have. Often customers first address the media firm Radio 538, and subsequently they are invisibly transferred to Tutch. Because of the nature of the service, other specialized resources are also involved, like software for ringtones and a copyright clearinghouse. In this case the handset provider is explicitly mentioned as a contributing partner, since not all handsets have the capability of storing the 13 polyphonic ringtones. The handset provider was involved in the process of service development.

In sum, this case presents a picture of a core triangle consisting of a dominant network operator, an intermediary that appears as a structural partner but also plays contributing and supporting roles, and a media firm classified as a structural partner for providing the brand. The raw content suppliers are supporting and only indirectly involved by producing hit songs, voices, and sounds, which all can be easily replaced.

Case 3: Finder

Finder is a location-based i-mode service offered by E-Plus in Germany. The service enables the consumer to find the nearest hotel, restaurant, taxi, or ATM. The content and geographical information are updated on a regular basis and stored in databases on the application platform. When a customer sends a request for information to the application platform, its position information is combined with the content and geographical information, and the customer receives the desired information. Actors include the operator E-Plus and Webraska, a worldwide provider of location-based services and telematics software solutions. Webraska also serves as the intermediary between E-Plus and the content providers together with the geographical information provider. Cell Point provides the positioning equipment.

Analysis of the Finder Case

In this third i-mode case the analysis of the resource contributions shows again the same list of resources of the operator. Since this is a location-based service, the operator, E-Plus, contributes also the resource for the user positioning. The operator is again here the structural partner in the network that cannot be replaced. The intermediary Webraska is another structural partner. Webraska is a specialist in location-based applications and is involved in the primary process of real-time geocoding the requested information. Webraska intermediary aggregates the content provided by five other intermediaries who develop content. Besides interesting content, Webraska also needs to update geographical information to create a location-based system (LBS). Webraska chose *Navtech* because they are a major player in digital maps in the U.S. and Europe. Webraska develops the location-based application and controls essential as well as network-specific resources, like in the other i-mode cases. E-Plus maintains contact with the customer. The customer is probably not even aware of a company called Webraska. If a customer finds an error in the information they send this information to E-Plus and E-Plus forwards it to Webraska.

To conclude, the i-mode cases show a similar pattern of a dominant network operator, an intermediary that appears as a structural partner but also plays contributing and supporting roles, and one or two other structural or contributing partners. The raw content suppliers are only supporting, and all can be easily replaced.

Case 4: LBS Directory[b]

The LBS directory service is a location-based service offered via WAP and SMS. It offers directory-type location information for ATMs, taxis, cinema, hotels, restaurants, events, emergency pharmacies, and fastfood. The service is produced in two steps. First, the content is aggregated, aligned technically (in terms of file formats), geo-coded, checked for quality assurance and then transferred at regular intervals to the operator in an ongoing process. The second step consists of the actual provision of the service, i.e. receiving a service request from the user, positioning the user, matching the request with appropriate content and passing the response, with routing information, back to the user. These two levels of implementation are a result of the service design and implementation that was driven by the operator. Actors consist of the operator, an intermediary, and a group of content providers specifically chosen to provide pre-determined content categories.

Analysis of the LBS Directory Case

The analysis of the resource contributions in this case indicates a noticeably large number of essential resources all being contributed by one actor, the network operator (see Table 8). This is due to its intention to learn as much as possible about the different aspects of providing a location-based service.

The operator is the structural partner in the network that cannot be replaced without the service ceasing to exist. He conceived the service, designed the network in terms of partners and roles, and, as service provider of the LBS directory, provides the branding of the service.

The LBS directory is marketed as a service of this operator so that the identity of the other actors in the network is almost entirely hidden from the customers (information about their involvement in the service is available on the Internet). In essence, the operator carries out all the activities that imply some form of customer contact: billing, marketing, and customer support and service provision. Other essential contributions of the operator are the provision of the network on which the service runs and the user positioning.

The intermediary controls several network-specific and generic resources, appearing as both a contributing and a supporting partner. This position is due to the intermediary's explicit strategy to provide generic resources (i.e., finalized content and content development) that are typically supplied to the value network by the supporting partners but for which no adequate content provider could be identified in the market. Thus, in the long run, the intermediary could replace at least some of the content providers and add to its own importance in the network.

As a contributing partner, it has established the service-specific portfolio of content partners for the network, and it constitutes the single point of contact for both the network operator and the content providers. Content quality management implies a range of checks and procedures to align and standardise the content from different sources, such as completeness of required fields, spell checking, and address correction. Regardless of existing geocodes in the content databases, all content is geocoded according to one standard (i.e., the points/events of interests are enhanced with the X/Y coordinates of their actual geographical location). Finally, the intermediary also provides technical customer support for queries about the LBS directory. These queries are passed on to the intermediary by the operator, while the solution or response from the intermediary is passed to the customer via the operator. Other resources contributed to the LBS directory are related to its technical competence; for example, working with the database formats preferred by the operator and aligning content from a diverse range of content providers that are able to submit their input in whatever format suits them.

Essentially, the content providers are supporting partners in this value network, left to supply generic resources, for example content in specific categories. Each of them develops and then provides one type of content (in which they are typically market leader) to the content aggregator (the intermediary). The content they produce can be used and sold in a range of projects so no technical adjustments are required to their content that may imply extra costs.

In sum, this presents a clear picture of the relative position of the different actors in this network, showing a dominant network operator as the sole structural partner, the intermediary as both a contributing and a supporting partner, and the content providers as supporting partners. All partner types in this network base their position on both tangible and intangible resources.

Case 5: Botfighter

Botfighter is the world's first location-based mobile game that uses mobile positioning information from an operator's network and is played using a standard GSM phone with SMS capabilities. On a Web site, the player designs a robot, which will be used to carry out a mission. The mission, which is obtained through the phone or Web site, involves another player, either a friend or one who is randomly assigned. Information concerning the location of the opponent is provided through the robot's radar system (the mobile handset). Botfighter's service network includes both companies and end-users, who provide content via the game's Web site. The service was conceived by It's Alive!, which maintains the game and organizes the Web site and the geographical information. The game, along with other Telia content, is hosted on a platform by Mobilaris. Ericsson provides the positioning equipment.

Analysis of the Botfighter Case

Overall a mixed picture of the relative position of different actors in this value network arises (see Table 9). Essential resource contributions are made by a number of different actors that seem to form a core of structural partners to produce the service: Telia, It's Alive!, Ericsson, and Mobilaris. Telia provides the infrastructure, marketing, and branding as well as customer support. It integrates the various technologies that are necessary to offer the service to the end-customer and also contributes the billing relation. Whilst service idea was proposed by It's Alive, Telia conceived the value network design and allocated revenue streams to the other actors within the network. At the start of the project, the cooperation between the two companies was intensive addressing technical issues, graphical interface for the Web presence, and integration aspects.

It's Alive appears at all levels, contributing essential, network-specific, and generic resources. Its essential contributions consist of the game service conception and design and the application provision. It also maintains the Web site and the application, which are network-specific resource contributions. Furthermore, the finalized content (e.g., missions) provided by It's Alive is a supporting resource. It's Alive! has its own GIS data provider (Cartesia) and integrates the GIS data into the Botfighter Web site. While It's Alive did not use the GIS server from Telia at the time of the empirical research, discussions were planned about whether It's Alive may use Telia's GIS server. For Telia, this would mean consistency in terms of recognizable maps across its service offerings. Its'Alive!'s function as an intermediary between network operator and other partners (typically content providers) is less apparent than in the other cases. There is only one "formal" content provider (Cartesia) aside from the end-users who can act as informal content providers via the Web site.

Whilst the Botfighter application could be fully integrated into the network of Telia, Telia decided to run the application on a platform that can be used as middleware. This service management platform, bridging end-user services and the complexity of the mobile network infrastructure, is provided by Mobilaris. Mobilaris only has a relationship with Telia to provide the platform. The lack of a formal relationship between Mobilaris and It's Alive, despite the fact that the Botfighter application needs to be programmed according to the API (Application Protocol Interface) of Mobilaris, is striking and suggests that Telia wants to exert control over the interaction of its value network partners.

Ericsson provides the positioning technology to offer a location-based service. This mobile positioning system (MPS) enables the whereabouts of mobile phones to be made known to providers of location-based services. It is the outcome of a joint venture between Telia and Ericsson called Team Positioning that was established with the aim of providing Telia with the best possible system for services based on GSM-based positioning. As such it constitutes an essential resource contribution to the Botfighter value network. By participating in this value network, Ericsson is able to learn from a network operator and its end-customer requirements in order to enhance the MPS. The obtained know-how provides insight and arguments for it when selling its product to other network operators. The generic resource contributions by Cartesia, that is, the geographical data that is built into the Botfighter Web site, and Genuity, that is, hosting the Botfighter Web site, are easily substituted. An unusual actor in this network is the user of the game whose involvement via the Web site, that is, to design the robot, means that he supplies raw content. Nevertheless users can be replaced easily if they choose to opt out of the game.

Summary of Findings: Cross-Case Analysis

To summarise the findings from the individual cases and to assist with the cross-case analysis, Table 3 provides an overview of the partners in the different cases. In all cases, a network operator and an intermediary can be distinguished that contribute a variety of resources, although the intermediary function is less apparent in the Botfighter case. In addition a content supplier, as a raw content supplier or as a supplier of adapted content, is present in all cases. Besides those three kinds of partners, different case-specific partners appear.

As far as network operators are concerned, they appear as structural partners in all five cases. Natsuno (2003) argued that that the decisive difference between Japan, the U.S., and Europe is that neither of the latter two had a telecommunications provider like DoCoMo with the will to grow a new business and service based on a comprehensive view of the ecosystem. It seems that Europe started to follow the example of Japan.

In four out of our five cases, the intermediaries appear as structural partners. The crucial resource that allows them to claim such a strong position in their respective network is service conception and design. The only case where the intermediary does not control this resource is the LBS directory, where the network operator initiated the service and kept hold of the service design.

Furthermore the cross-case comparison reveals that the "same" resource, for example, customer support, can vary in importance in the different networks. The implication is that the possession of a particular resource—with the exception of the possession of the network—does not necessarily propel the actor into a specific position within the network. It is the composition of resources that is important. With respect to the distinction between tangible and intangible resources, we observe that in several cases (Botfighter, Finder, Radio538) the supporting partners are limited to providing tangible resources whereas the contributing and structural partners in all cases are, with a few exceptions, providing tangible and intangible resources. While intangible resources are particularly immobile, difficult to imitate or substitute, these partners base their position in the value network on the combination of both tangible and intangible resource contributions.

The position of the content providers in our value networks for mobile information and entertainment services is, perhaps surprisingly, of lesser importance. These services are designed to deliver content and, therefore, content could have been expected to show up as an essential resource. However, content providers never appear as structural partners that can easily assert their place in the network. In our cases content providers are either contrib-

Table 3. Cross-case findings

	My Babes i-mode case	Radio538 i-mode case	Finder lbs i-mode case	Botfighter lbs game	LBS directory
Structural partner(s) [essential resources]	**Network Operator** *Platform Provision* *Billing* *Marketing* *Content quality* *Partner network concept* *Customer support* **Intermediary** *Service conception & design*	**Network Operator** *Platform Provision* *Billing* *Marketing* *Content quality* *Partner network concept* *Customer support* **Intermediary 1** *Service conception & design* *Application provision* **Media** *Branding*	**Network Operator** *Platform provider* *Billing* *Marketing* *Content quality* *Partner network concept* *Customer support* **Intermediary 1** *Service conception & design* *Application provision* *Real time geocoding*	**Network Operator** *Billing* *Partner network concept* **Intermediary** *Service Conception & design* *Application Provision* **Platform provider** **Positioning & equipment vendor**	**Network Operator** *Platform Provision* *Billing* *Marketing* *Customer support* *GIS application* *User positioning* *Partner network concept* *Service conception & design* *Branding*
Contributing partner(s) [network-specific resources]	**Intermediary** *Finalised content* *Content development*	**Intermediary 1** *Finalised content* **Media** *Content development* **Intermediary 2** *Content development* **Handset provider**	**Intermediary 1** *Content aggregation* **Intermediary 2** *Finalised content* *Content development* **GIS Provider** **Handset provider**	**Intermediary** *Application maintenance* *Web site maintenance*	**Intermediary** *Batch geo-coding* *Content quality* *Portfolio management* *Technical support* *Single point of contact* *Content aggregation*
Supporting partner(s) [generic resources]	**Intermediary** *Customer support* **Raw content suppliers**	**Intermediary 1** *Customer support* **Raw content suppliers** **Hardware and Software suppliers** **Legal right clearing**	**Intermediary 1** *Customer support* **Raw content suppliers** **Positioning Equipment Vendor**	**Intermediary** *Finalised content* **Content Quality** **GI Provider** **Web hoster**	**Intermediary** *Finalised content* *Content quality* **Content suppliers** *Finalised content* *Content quality*

uting or supporting partners that can be replaced fairly easily in their respective networks. Considering the type of content involved, this is of such a generic nature (in the case of MyBabes and Radio538, raw content that is developed and finalized by other partners), it is mainly supporting and complementing the functionality of the service (e.g., information supporting the search and find functions for the Finder, LBS Directory, and Botfighter cases, the application for which is run by other partners) rather than constituting a unique service element in its own right that it could be easily provided by a different party without affecting the function or quality of the overall mobile service. So it is both substitutable (because other content providers of such generic content could be easily found) and imitable (because the content is not so unique that it is protected by tight copyright provisions).

Conclusion

"Content is king" was the adagio when convergence among telecommunication and media industries seemed inevitable not so long ago. However, analysis of the case studies in this paper shows that this period is gone. The mobile services examined in this paper are offered jointly by a network operator, an intermediary, and one or more content providers. The network operator is the structural partner who controls the value network. The intermediary plays an important role in coordinating the production of specific services on the network, with resources like application provision, geocoding, and content aggregation. The service concept further enhances their position in their network. In everyday life, the intermediary is referred to as service or application provider. And the content provider? The activities related to content show a dispersion of effort in which content supply alone can be divided among many actors. But more essential ones, such as content development, are contributed by other actors, typically the intermediaries. We conclude that the content providers are not even princes or princesses; content provision of *generic* content alone (which is highly imitable and substitutable) does not propel them into a strong position in the value network. This confirms our proposition that actor power stems from the characteristics (degree of mobility, imitability, and substitutability) of the resources.

This does not imply, however, that content *per se* will always fall into the generic resource category. More advanced mobile information and, especially, entertainment services are coming to the market now, offering video streams and downloads and TV via the Universal Mobile Telecom System (UMTS) network. Examples of services that are difficult to substitutable are those produced by especially skilled professionals and requiring dedicated platforms, for example, high-quality video criticisms of theater and sport events.

Exclusive, that is, rights-protected, content (e.g., exclusive live coverage of Eurodivision football competitions via Internet Protocol Television by Versatel in the Netherlands in the fixed environment) clearly falls into the property-based resource type category, which is characterized by imperfect imitability. The more unimitable the content offered in the mobile environment becomes, the more we can expect that the content providers will be confirmed in the critical position—assuming the role of a structural partner rather than a supporting one—that they are so often praised for. Then it will be difficult, if not impossible, to substitute them easily.

While it may appear obvious that the network operators have a strong position in the value network, this is due largely to their external-facing orientation. Even in the case where the intermediary would act as the dominant structural partner, it may still appear that the operator is in this position. Thus, the theoretical framework constructed in this paper provides a basis for a detailed analysis and, as such, it presents a valuable tool that extends the view beyond mere network operator dominance to confirm and categorize the resource-based "status" of all actors involved in such value networks, based on their contributions to the service. Moreover, this framework serves as a useful tool for comparing and contrasting different value networks for mobile services in terms of their resource-based configuration and dynamics among actors.

We also note that the findings of the analysis presented in this paper are limited to the current market situation and that in the future the positions of the various partners may change. Therefore, analyses such as the one presented here should be performed from time to time to assess the extent to which any changes have occurred.

References

Axelsson, B. (1987). Supplier management and technological development. In H. Håkansson (Ed.), *Industrial and technological development – A network approach* (pp. 128-176). London: Croom Helm.

Appelman, J.H. (2004). (2004). *Governance of global interorganizational tourism networks.* Unpublished doctoral dissertation, Erasmus Research Institute, The Netherlands.

Ballon, P., & Hawkins, R. (2003). From business models to value networks. *TNO/STB working paper* (December), Schoemakerstraat 97, 2600JA Delft, NL.

Bovel, D., & Martha, J. (2000). From supply chain to value net. *Journal of Business Strategy, 20*(4) 24-29.

Das, T. K., & Teng, B. S. (1998). Resource and risk management in the strategic alliance making process. *Journal of Management, 24*(1), 21-42.

Das, T. K., & Teng, B. S. (2000). A resource-based theory of strategic alliances. *Journal of Management, 26*(1), 31-61.

Ebers, M. (1999). The dynamics of inter-organizational relationships. In S.B. Andrews & D. Knoke (Eds.), *Network in and around organization. Research in the sociology of organizations* (pp. 16, 31-56). Stamford, Connecticut: Jai Press Inc.

Foss, N. (1998). The resource-based perspective: An assessment and diagnosis of problems. *Scandinavian Journal of Management, 14*(3), 133-149.

Gadde, L. E., Huemer, L., & Håkansson, H. (2003). Strategizing in industrial networks. *Industrial Marketing Management, 32*, 357-364.

Granovetter, M. (1985). Economic action and social structure: A theory of embeddedness. *American Journal of Sociology, 9*(3), 481-510.

Haanæs, K., & Fjeldstad, O. (2000). Linking intangible resources and competition. *European Management Journal, 18*(1), 52-62.

Håkansson, H. (Ed.). (1987). *Industrial and technological development: A network approach.* London: Croom Helm.

Håkansson, H., & Waluszewski, A. (2002). *Managing technological development: IKEA, the environment and technology.* London: Routledge.

Hoskisson, R., Hitt, M., Wan, W., & Yiu, D. (1999). Theory and research in strategic management: Swings of a pendulum. *Journal of Management, 25*(3), 417-456.

Itami, H., & Roehl, T. (1987). *Mobilizing invisible assets.* Cambridge, MA: Harvard University Press.

Kar van de, E. A. M., Maitland, C., Wehn de Montalvo, U., & Bouwman, H. (2003, September 30-October 3). Design guidelines for mobile Information and entertainment services, based on the Radio538 ringtunes i-mode service case study. In N. Sadeh (Ed.), In *Proceedings of the Fifth International Conference on Electronic Commerce.* Pittsburgh, PA.

Li, F., & Whalley, J. (2002). Deconstruction of the telecommunications industry: From value chains to value networks. *Telecommunications Policy, 26*, 451-472.

Maitland, C., Bauer, J., & Westerveld, R. (2002). The European market for mobile data: evolving value chains and industry structure. *Telecommunications Policy, 26*, 485-504.

Maitland, C., Kar van de, E. A. M., & Wehn de Montalvo, U. (2003b, June 9-11). Network formation for mobile information and entertainment services. In *Proceedings of 16th Bled Electronic Commerce Conference,* Bled, Slovenia.

Maitland, C., Kar van de, E.A.M., Wehn de Montalvo, U., & Bouwman, H. (2003a). Mobile information and entertainment services: Business models and service network. In *Proceedings of The Second International Conference on Mobile Business.* Vienna, Austria.

Miller, D., & Shamsie, J. (1996). The resource-based view of the firm in two environments: The Hollywood film studios from 1936 to 1965. *Academy of Management Journal. 39*, 519-543.

Mintzberg, H. (1979). *The structuring of organizations: A synthesis of research.* London: Prentice-Hall.

Mintzberg, H. (1983). *Power in and around organizations.* London: Prentice Hall.

Nassimbeni, G. (1998). Network structures and co-ordination mechanisms: A taxonomy. *International Journal of Operations & Production Management, 18*(6), 538-554.

Natsuno, T. (2003). *The I-mode wireless ecosystem.* West Sussex, UK: John Wiley & Sons.

Oliver, C. (1997). Sustainable competitive advantage: Combining institutional and resource-based views. *Strategic Management Journal, 18*(9), 697-713.

Pfeffer, J., & Salancik, G.R. (1978). *The external control of organizations: A resource dependence perspective.* New York: Harper & Row, Publisher.

Piccinelli, G., Di Vitantonio, G., & Mokrushion, L. (2001). Dynamic service aggregation in electronic marketplaces. *Computer Networks, 37*(2), 95-109

Porter, M. (1991). Towards a dynamic theory of strategy. *Strategic Management Journal, 12*, 95-117.

Sabat, H. (2002). The evolving mobile wireless value chain and market structure. *Telecommunications Policy, 26*, 505-535.

Wernerfelt, B. (1984). A resource-based view of the firm. *Strategic Management Journal. 5*, 171-180.

Endnotes

[a]   An earlier version of this chapter was published as Wehn de Montalvo, U., Kar van de, E.A.M. and Maitland, C. Resource-based interdependencies in value networks for mobile e-services. *International Journal of E-Business Research, Special Issue on e-Services, 1*(3), July-September, 1-20.

[b]   Fictitious service name; case is anonymous.

Appendix

Table 4. Overview of MIES case studies

	General MIES		Location-based MIES		
Service	i-mode MyBabes	i-mode Radio 538	i-mode Finder	LBS directory	Botfighter
Content	Erotic pictures and games	Ringtones	Find-the-nearest	Find-the-nearest	Multi-actor game
# interviews (# firms)	2 (2)	3 (3)	6 (4)	6 (4)	5 (5)
Country	The Netherlands	The Netherlands	Germany	confidential	Sweden
Network	GPRS	GPRS	GPRS	GSM and GPRS	GSM and GPRS
Device	i-Mode handset (NEC)	i-Mode handset (NEC)	i-Mode handset (NEC)	Any mobile phone	Any mobile phone Web site
Interface	cHTML	cHTML	cHTML	WAP and SMS	SMS

Table 5. MyBabes overview of partner types and contributions to the network

Partner type	Resource contribution to value network		KPN Mobile	iMedia	Internet sites
Structural	essential	tangible	Network provision, Platform provision Billing provision		
		intangible	Marketing, i-mode concept, quality management, customer support	Service conception & design	
Contributing	network-specific	tangible		Finalised content	
		intangible		Content development	
Supporting	generic	tangible			Raw content
		intangible		Customer support	

Table 6. Radio538 overview of partner types and contributions to the network

Partner type	Resource contribution to value network		KPN Mobile	Tutch	Radio538	Jingle Hell	DJs/ Music makers	Faith	NEC (Toshiba)	Yamaha	BUMA Stemra
Structural	essential	*tangible*	Network provision, platform provision, billing provision	Application provision							
		intangible	Marketing, i-mode concept, quality management, customer support	Service conception & design	Branding						
Contributing	network-specific	*tangible*		Finalised content					Handsets		
		intangible			Content development	Content development					
Supporting	generic	*tangible*					Raw content	Ringtune software		Handset chips for ringtunes	
		intangible		Customer support							Legal right issues

Table 7. Finder overview of partner types and contributions to the network

Partner type	Resource contribution to value network		E-Plus	Webraska	Schober, varta, foot-food, taxi, fovium	Navtech	NEC, Toshiba	Cell point	Schober intern. and other raw content prov.
Structural	essential	tangible	Network provision, platform provision, billing provision, user positioning	Application provision, real time content geocoding					
		intangible	Marketing, i-mode concept, quality management, customer support	Service conception & design					
Contributing	network-specific	tangible		Content provision/ aggregation	Finalised content	Geographic information provision	Handsets		
		intangible			Content development				
Supporting	generic	tangible						Positioning equipment	Raw content
		intangible	Customer support						

Table 8. Botfighter partner types and contributions to the network

Partner type	Resource contribution to value network		Telia	It's Alive!	Mobilaris	Ericsson	Cartesia	Genuity	User
Structural	essential	*tangible*	Value network design, network provision, user positioning, billing provision	Application provision	Platform provider	Positioning vendor, equipment provider			
Structural	essential	*intangible*	Branding, marketing, customer support	Service conception & design					
Contributing	network-specific	*tangible*		Application maintenance, Web site maintenance					
Contributing	network-specific	*intangible*							
Supporting	generic	*tangible*		Finalised Content			GI provider	Web hosting	Raw content
Supporting	generic	*intangible*		Content quality management					

Table 9. LBS Directory resource contributions to the network per actor

Partner type	Resource contribution to value network		Company X	Company Y	Companies A - F
Structural	essential	*tangible*	Network, user position information, billing provision, marketing, customer support facility, GIS application, LBS directory application, middleware platform, financial resources for manpower & knowledge development		
		intangible	Service conception & design, value network design, branding		
Contributing	network-specific	*tangible*		Portfolio of content partners	
		intangible		Geo-coding of content in batch process, quality management, technical support, Technical competence, single point of contact for NO & CPs	
Supporting	generic	*tangible*		Finalised content	Finalised content
		intangible		Content development	Content development

Chapter V

Buyer-Supplier Relationships in Business-to-Business E-Procurement:
Effects of Supply Conditions

Ravinder Nath, Creighton University, USA

Rebecca Angeles, University of New Brunswick Fredericton, Canada

Abstract

This study explores the resource dependency and relational exchange theories to understand firms' participation in e-procurement and seeks to determine the degree to which the resource dependency theory variables—supply importance, supply complexity, supply market dynamism, and availability of alternatives—affect information exchange and operational linkages, the relational exchange theory variables. Data was gathered from the Institute for Supply Management and the Council of Logistics Management members using the survey technique. Supply importance and supply complexity primarily predict information exchange and operational linkages. Study findings reconfirm the important impact of environmental and market uncertainty on firm responses as echoed in past studies.

Introduction

Procurement typically accounts for the largest expense item in a firm's cost structure (Computer Sciences Corporation, 2002). Reducing procurement costs, therefore, has always been a high priority for all organizations. Many firms have turned to e-procurement—using the Internet and Web technologies to facilitate buyer-seller transactions. A well-designed e-procurement system provides benefits that go beyond cost savings. In a study of the experiences of North American and European firms and evaluations of 40 e-sourcing solution providers, the Aberdeen Group (Aberdeen Group, 2002) found that successful e-procurement adopters negotiated about an average of a 14.3 percent reduction in goods and services costs; cut sourcing cycles in half; reduced sourcing administrative costs by 60 percent; and shortened time-to-market cycles by 10 to 15 percent. Cecere and D'Aquila (2005) reported that the procurement and sourcing market grew by 14 percent to $2 billion in 2004. Sourcing business applications are expected to exhibit a stronger showing in 2005, when the market is projected to grow at 10 percent.

Cost reduction is obviously an important factor in favor of buyer-supplier coupling vis-à-vis e-procurement. However, several business trends are creating momentum toward the adoption of more efficient forms of procurement initiatives such as e-procurement. First businesses are increasingly outsourcing not only manufacturing but also other business processes as well. In a study of 162 manufacturing and service firms around the world, A.T. Kearney (2000) found that 52 percent of the firms planned to entrust most, if not all, of their engineering and design work to suppliers, while 40 percent planned to outsource manufacturing. Firms are continuing to shift away from highly vertically integrated models of production toward virtual partnering with suppliers and outside contracted manufacturers (Stephens, Inc., 2001). The transition to leaner operating models has resulted in suppliers or contracted manufacturers providing most of the "value" of original equipment manufacturers' (OEM) products. Second many manufacturers may mandate the use of electronic procurement by its customers, as studies have shown that manufacturers' savings accrue in proportion to the number of customers joining the e-procurement system (Raghunathan, 1999). Also large customer firms are more likely to require the use of some means of electronic procurement among their suppliers, especially so if these large firms intend to maintain relationships with just a few highly selected suppliers (Min & Galle, 1999). Bartels, Pohlmann, Ross, Martorelli, and Hudson (2005) reported that the number of firms outsourcing business processes related to the procurement of indirect materials or maintenance, repair, and operating (MRO) expense items to service providers has doubled from a year ago, even if the overall level of e-procurement adoption still remains low. This move appears to be a transitional solution to allow firms to cut costs on the purchasing of indirect goods as they sharpen their internal expertise in sourcing and purchasing direct goods.

Given these trends, it behooves procurement professionals of any sized firm to understand how procurement operates under different electronic environments into which one might find one's firm inextricably and inevitably drawn. Moreover, they need to anticipate the very likely possibility of and plan ahead for participating in any one of these electronic procurement environments whether or not it is instigated by their own proactive choice.

The resource dependency theory (Pfeffer & Salancik, 1978; Ulrich & Barney, 1984) purports that organizations view the environment as the source of valued resources they need to survive in the marketplace. Therefore, firms must enter into relationships with other firms that can supply them with the materials and services they need (Turner, LeMay, Hartley, & Wood, 2000). A key part of this relationship entails connecting electronically with valued suppliers. Major factors that further affect the buyer-seller relationships include supply characteristics such as its importance to buyer, supply complexity, market dynamism, and availability of alternative supplies (Cannon & Perreault, 1999). These are the four resource dependency variables used in this study. In many cases, these characteristics exacerbate a firm's dependence on the supplier and lead it toward new behaviors. What ensues, then, is the introduction of cooperative or collaborative organizational behavior rather than just transaction-based contacts. Heide (1994) elaborates on these ideas further by extending them with the suggestion that firms reduce uncertainty by creating formal or semiformal relationships with other firms.

The relational exchange theory refers to the process of forming relationships among marketing channel members characterized by the following attributes: bilateral information exchange, role integrity, mutuality, solidarity, flexibility, harmonious conflict resolution, and a long-term orientation (Dwyer, Schurr, & Oh, 1987; Ganesan, 1994; Kaufmann & Dant, 1992; Kaufmann & Stern, 1988; Macneil, 1980). With increasing exposure to strategic business alliance partners, participating members (or firms) are protected by shared norms and values that seek to minimize, if not completely eliminate, opportunistic behaviors. "Role integrity," in particular, encourages mutual expectation of mutual sharing of information, frequent interactions among participating firms at different levels, intensive coordination, and honest dealings with each other. Cannon and Perreault (1999) use the concepts of "information exchange" and "operational linkages" in their study of buyer-seller interactions. Recent literature reviews indicate the importance of electronic business application system linkages between and among buyer and seller trading partners, which would be the equivalent of the concept of "operational linkages" in the context of this study (den Hengst, & Henk, 2002; Elmuti, 2002; Gallear & Ghobadian, 2004; Halley & Nollet, 2002) and information exchanges between them (Gallear & Ghobadian, 2004; Kanakamedala, Ramsdell, & Roche, 2003; Vijay & Keah, 2002). In their recent work on measuring important supply chain management concepts, Min and Mentzer (2004) included the concepts "information sharing" (i.e., information exchange) and "process integration" (i.e., operational linkages) in their model as two of several supply chain management (SCM) concepts that enhanced supply chain performance.

The resource dependency theory has been used extensively through time in trying to explain firm adoption of certain kinds of information technology solutions. The following studies in the review of the literature indicate the importance of the resource dependency theory in explaining different aspects of the purchasing transactions between buyers and sellers. In the area of buyer and supplier relationships, Rinehart, Eckert, Handfield, and Page (2004) used resource dependency as the theoretical basis for explaining the perceived dependence of buyers on suppliers, which is one of several attributes in their extensive study of long-term, business-to-business transactions among firms. Their framework for buyer-seller relationship classification could be used to develop negotiation strategies and boundary-spanning strategies with their trading partners. As of late, in the area of logistics, Zacharia and Mentzer (2004) used the resource dependency theory in showing that environmental uncertainty leads to increased adoption of a variety of information technologies to improve the quality of logistics decision making. On the other hand, way back in 1993, Handfield used the theory to explain why firms implemented just-in-time (JIT) purchasing with their suppliers in order to reduce inventory levels, reduce inspection, and produce better products. In addition, the movement to JIT purchasing is characterized by greater information sharing by the firm with fewer suppliers.

Much closer to the subject of e-procurement, a few important studies have been conducted recently that help clarify selected aspects of the practice. Curiously, the element of environmental uncertainty plays an important part in the conceptual frameworks of these studies. Kaufmann and Mohtadi (2004) focused on information technology adoption behavior of firms in the presence of transaction costs, agency costs, and information uncertainty covering both the demand side and supply side of purchasing. Based on these factors, the investigators predict the type of procurement platform a firm ultimately chooses from three options: open platform procurement systems, proprietary platform procurement systems, or hybrid platforms. They found the coexistence of both proprietary and open platforms. Firm size appears to matter. Large firms tended to implement more expensive procurement solutions, such as proprietary electronic data interchange (EDI), in order to gain greater supply-side certainty. On the other hand, smaller firms adopt less-costly procurement systems such as open platform procurement systems that entail greater supply uncertainties.

One other study released two years earlier (Lee, 2002) also focused on product uncertainty, both in the demand and supply sides, and the design of appropriate supply chain strategies to deal with these types of products. The author is arguing that a firm's product strategy should be appropriate to the nature of the product whether the product has a stable demand and reliable source of supply or a highly unpredictable demand and unreliable source of supply. He also argues that the Internet is a powerful enabler of technologies that can support both types of products. Supply-side risks refer to aspects like an "evolving" supply process where the manufacturing process and the underlying technology are still under development or rapidly changing. It also means the supply base may be limited in number and level of experience as a result of both of these situations. The author offers extensive information exchange—starting with the product development stage and proceeding through the product's mature and end-of-life product life cycle stages—to be an effective means of mitigating supply-side uncertainty. Billington, Lee, and Tang (1998) illustrate how buyers share product rollover plans with suppliers to reduce the risks involved in product transitions. Johnson and Lee (2000) detailed how the use of "product data management" software by vendors such as Agile Software has helped firms such as WebTV, Flextronics, and Pair-Gain exchange product content information with their suppliers to minimize the risk of failures during times of product changes and transitions. Collaborative product design with suppliers is now actively supported in consortium-based exchanges such as Covisint, e2open, and Exostar (Lee, 2002).

In another study, Subramaniam and Shaw (2002) created a framework to quantify and measure the value of business-to-business (B2B) e-commerce systems and identify the factors that determine their value. The framework was tested using the case study method and was applied to one site, a large manufacturer of heavy equipment in the midwestern part of the U.S. The firm had just implemented a Web-based e-procurement system and had moved from the experimental to the enterprise-wide adoption stage. The management of the firm wanted to validate the benefits the firm experienced in order to motivate its internal system users and suppliers. Management also wanted to know the factors that directly impacted the delivery of the benefits so that it could redesign its subsequent deployment strategies.

They discovered that the value of Web-based e-procurement was most strongly determined by process characteristics, organization of business units, and attributes of the "extended enterprise." A key finding is the importance of the integration of firm's e-procurement system with those of their suppliers. This is clearly relevant to the construct of "operational linkages" that is used in this study.

Given this state of the current body of knowledge on e-procurement, the intent of this study is to contribute to the literature by focusing on selected resource dependency and relational exchange constructs to understand the firms' motivation for engaging in e-procurement. Also, there exists considerable anecdotal evidence that buyer-supplier relationships continue to transform by virtue of technological innovations, complex supply chains, global sourcing, and shorter time-to-market pressures. E-procurement is one such innovation that is having considerable impact on the how buyers and sellers interact and the type of information they exchange. It can be argued that, to some extent, the nature and degree of the buyer-seller interface are dependent on the characteristics of the product/service that they exchange. There is a paucity of empirical studies that examine the relationships between supply traits and the nature of buyer-seller coupling vis-à-vis e-procurement. In light of the lack of empirical research in this arena, the purpose of this study is to examine the fidelity of the association between supply characteristics—supply importance, supply complexity, supply market dynamism, and availability of alternatives—and "information exchange" and "operational linkages" between buyers and sellers in an e-procurement environment. This is accomplished by collecting data using a questionnaire instrument from supply chain managers.

Operationalization of Key Constructs

The constructs used in this study are adapted from the work of Cannon and Perreault (1999). These researchers analyzed the relationship profiles of more than 400 buyer-seller relationships across many industries. However, the focus of their study is not on e-procurement per se. In the following discussion, we discuss and operationalize supply importance, supply complexity, supply market dynamism, availability of alternatives, information exchange, and operational linkages constructs within the e-procurement environment.

Supply Importance

According to Cannon and Perreault (1999), "supply importance" is defined as "...the buying firm's perception of the financial and strategic significance of a particular supply ..." (p. 444). In the manufacturing sector, "direct goods" are generally considered more critical to the production process than are "indirect goods" or "maintenance and repair" items (Pfeffer & Nowak, 1976). Consequently, the level of dependence of a firm upon another firm is contingent on the criticality or "essentiality" of the resources needed by the first firm (Jacobs, 1974). In this study, respondents are first requested to identify a major product/service acquired via e-procurement and a major vendor of this product/service. Then, the respondents rate the following statement using a seven-point scale anchored by two pairs: unimportant-important and low priority-high priority.

"Compared to other purchases your firm makes, this product/service is ... "

Supply Complexity

Supply complexity is related to the nature of the product itself (Cannon & Perreault, 1999). A product could be "simple" or "complex" or "non-technical" or "technical." The more complex or technical a product is, the more difficult it is for the buying firm to evaluate purchase choices or alternatives prior to the actual purchase itself, and the harder it is to ascertain a supplier's performance after the purchase. In short, the complexity of needed products or resources leads to ambiguity and risk in the purchasing experience. In this study, supply complexity is measured by asking the study participants the same question as was used to measure supply importance, except the anchors used are: simple-complex and technical/non-technical.

Supply Market Dynamism

Achrol and Stern (1988) and Aldrich (1979) define supply market dynamism as the degree of variability in a firm's supply market. A number of market factors can account for this variability: rapidly changing technology, frequent price and product changes, and inconsistency in vendor support or services. Obviously, fluctuations in these dimensions could increase market risk and uncertainty for the firm.

In this study supply market dynamism is measured by asking study participants to respond to the question: *"How significant are changes [in each market factor] for this product/service?"* across five factors: pricing; product features and specs; vendor support services; technology used by suppliers; and product availability. A seven-point Likert scale is used (1 = minor; 7 = major) for each of the five factors.

Availability of Alternatives

Availability of alternative supplies is defined as "… the degree to which a buying firm has alternate sources of supply to meet a need …" (Cannon & Perreault, 1999, p. 444). Achrol and Stern (1988), Jacobs (1974), and Cook (1977) extend the idea further by purporting that organizations form cooperative relationships in the marketplace due to specialization and scarcity. Firms engage in exchange relationships to deal with environmental uncertainty and, thus, reduce resource scarcity.

Availability of alternatives is measured through the following four items:

* This vendor supply market is very competitive.

- Other vendors could provide what we get from our best supplier of this major product/service.
- Our best supplier of the product/service has a monopoly for what it sells.
- No other vendor has this best supplier's capabilities.

Again, each item is measured using a seven-point (1 = strongly disagree; 7 = strongly agree) Likert scale.

Information Exchange

Information exchange is defined as the expectation of open sharing of information that may be useful to all firms participating in the partnership (Cannon & Perreault, 1999). In many cases, firms are expected to share important, even proprietary, information that will best serve the interests of network members. This may lead to involving trusted partners in the early stages of product design, unlocking important databases and sharing cost information, and distributing supply and demand forecasts, among others. Truman (2000) invokes the open systems theory in reiterating the need for a firm to exchange information with elements in the environment in order to ensure its survival. Aldrich and Mindlin (1978) identify physical resources and information as the "two currencies" that firms must be able to exchange with the task environment.

In a research project conducted by the Center for Advanced Purchasing Studies, 52 firms with extensive supply chain management practices responded to both interviews and surveys around key topics involving supply chain integration. A number of findings were directly related to the concept of "information exchange" (Fawcett & Magnan, 2001, p. 7). Study respondents considered "frequent and real communication," "a willingness to share information across functions and between organizations," and "establish information systems capable of sharing real time accurate and relevant information" as the top desirable ways of improving interfirm communication in a supply chain. Increasing investments in different forms of information technologies directly impacts both of these suggestions. The most sought-after technologies are intranets and extranets in enabling the exchange of information like accurate forecasts and actual production schedules, two of the most desired types of information that firms thought should be exchanged. Database and data mining technologies were also in high demand among the firms. A surprising number of customers still use fax machines and the telephone to place orders with suppliers.

Management information systems (MIS) literature has a solid base of research findings supporting the essentiality of sharing information in interorganizational systems (IOS) (Barrett & Konsynski, 1982). Strategic advantage in the marketplace could be obtained by sharing key information between firms (Konsynski & McFarlan, 1990). Henderson (1990) and Konsynski and McFarlan (1990) further reiterate the closer relationships that come about as a result of more frequent and relevant information exchanges among high-performance partners.

The body of research on electronic data interchange (EDI) has firmly demonstrated that critical information is the lifeblood of these types of IOS systems, which have spawned cooperative systems between and among electronic network participants (Chatfield & Yetton, 2000):

As a cooperative relationship develops, value adding joint economic action, such as JIT production systems between the automaker and the supplier, such joint action requires firms to share proprietary information, such as production schedules, quality-control data, and inventory levels to support joint problem solving. Typically, such information sharing includes internal systems integration between EDI with corporate database and other strategic information systems to support joint economic action. ... At a minimum level, the initiator would have limited access to the adopter's corporate database, requiring systems integration by the adopter of EDI with its internal IS applications. At a higher level, both the initiator and a selective set of adopters would have access to each other's corporate databases. What matters here is that information flows are bidirectional and information sharing is reciprocal. This pattern of information sharing across businesses underlies the early conceptual frameworks of value creation through IOS ...

(pp. 201-202)

Significant returns and strategic marketplace advantage await willing EDI network participants that will allow extensive information interchange that originates from the deepest levels of their operational information systems. Lee and Kim (1999) found that information sharing contributed to the partnership quality of firms participating in outsourcing arrangements. Information exchange is measured using the following three items:

* We both share relevant information (product/cost information).
* We include each other in product development meetings.
* We always share supply and demand forecasts.

Each item is measured using a seven-point Likert scale (1 = strongly disagree; 7 = strongly agree).

Operational Linkages

Operational linkages are defined as the extent to which the systems, procedures, and routines of the buying and selling firms have been linked to facilitate operations (Cannon & Perreault, 1999). With such operational linkages, activities and processes between and among the firms enable the flow of information, goods, or services.

The recent focus on supply chain integration has lent the concept of "operational linkages" renewed significance considering the current challenges in the marketplace reflecting competition among "value webs" and not just individual firms.

Supply chain management is the collaborative effort of multiple channel members to design, implement, and manage seamless value-added processes to meet the real needs of customers. The development and integration of people and

technological resources as well as of materials, information, and financial flows
underlie successful supply chain integration... (Fawcett & Magnan, 2001)

A number of forces are driving channel collaboration through supply chain integration: (1) more demanding customers requiring greater supplier responsiveness; (2) competitive global rivals imposing cost pressures and cutting profit margins; (3) increasing pressure to focus on core competencies; (4) preempting competition by allying with channel partners; and (5) increasing levels of merger activities that has led to the reconfiguration of channel power (Fawcett & Magnan, 2001). In a research project conducted by the Center for Advanced Purchasing Studies, 52 firms with extensive supply chain management practices responded to both interviews and surveys around key topics involving supply chain integration. A number of findings were directly related to the concept of "operational linkages." The "technology barrier" in the form of inadequate information systems was cited as the most pervasive barrier to supply chain integration. Supply chain integration relies most fundamentally on the ability of participating firms to establish electronic/digital linkages that work and allow them to exchange critical operational information. Many firms still run dated in-house proprietary systems that have made the creation of interorganizational linkages difficult. While the "open systems" platform and the use of middleware and extensible markup language-based tools are supposed to solve this problem, firms that still support networked systems without these newer capabilities have not overcome systems compatibility issues. Supply chain integration, for instance, requires that extensive databases be combined with open-systems data exchange mechanisms in order to enable operational linkages among firms in conducting collaboration activities such as collaborative planning, forecasting, and replenishment (CPFR), advanced planning and scheduling, product lifecycle management, and joint product design and development. When such operational linkages could not be established and made to work, links in the "information chain" are broken and extra inventory or time are needed to be built into the system to make up for the added variance (Fawcett & Magnan, 2001). The study respondents identified the following as the "bridges" that must be built to overcome the technology barrier: (1) use electronic data interchange linkages; (2) use cross-functional business processes; (3) use common operating procedures; and (4) use enterprise resource planning (ERP) and supply chain management (SCM) software. These suggestions directly impact the quality of "operational linkages" between and among value chain participants. There is evidence that the firms participating in the study are trying to address the technology barrier to operational linkages. More than 50 percent of the respondent firms have made significant investments in ERP systems, application-specific systems (e.g., requisitioning systems, catalogs, accounting records, etc.), and web-based communication platforms. Despite these investments, respondents noted the inadequacy of upstream (i.e., linkages with suppliers) and downstream (i.e., linkages with customers) electronic connections due to dated information systems of participating trading partners. Also, it is very important to customer firms to have spend visibility in order for them to understand spend volume per category and commodity and per supplier (Center for Advanced Purchasing Studies, 2005). It is necessary for both customer and supplier firms to have digital linkages that allow the tracking of data covering these spend visibility indices.

Recent e-procurement practices show indications of a more proactive participation of supplier firms in SCM integration initiatives specifically involving indirect or maintenance, repair, and operating goods (Center for Advanced Purchasing Studies, 2005). For instance, in the case of Chevron, a number of the firm's key suppliers create operational linkages with their customers in order to: (1) manage and own inventory on and off site; (2) assist in cross-location inventory sharing; (3) participate in surplus asset inventory recovery (refurbishment, re-use, sales); and (4) participate in on-site consignment of stock items in company warehouses.

There are also a few welcome signs, however, that there is, in fact, forward movement. In another research project involving firms implementing e-sourcing initiatives, it was found that leading customer and supplier firms are using a variety of electronic technologies to enable electronic operational linkages. The three types of tools are: (1) transactional tools to enable sourcing and procurement transactions through such functionalities as solicitation, auction/bidding, catalog ordering, invoicing, e-funds transfer, etc.; (2) communication and analytical tools to support price and cost analysis applications, global reference databases, contract repositories, etc.; and (3) collaboration tools to enable interactive product or service planning, design, and development. Some customer firms use supplier portals to enable their suppliers to gain access to systems and information in the conduct of, say, collaborative forecasting and demand planning (Flynn, 2004).

Another challenge for implementing effective operational linkages is the integration of e-procurement systems with key business applications such as ERP and SCM. In their study Bendoly and Schoenherr (2005) found that firms that achieved considerable cost savings from the e-procurement of indirect or MRO goods depended highly on the use of ERP systems, and the length of use of these systems was a key factor in achieving their cost savings goals.

At a much earlier phase of supply chain integration, interfirm integration was accomplished primarily through EDI. The EDI literature citations supporting information exchange reinforce the need for electronic operational linkages. Chatfield and Bjorn-Andersen (1997) reported how electronic operational linkages enabled the transformation of Japan Airlines' (JAL) traditional value chain into a more responsive virtual value chain supported by relationship-specific assets, such as common network platforms and software applications, that delivered significant performance results:

> *The more than 130 JAL Group firms have long-established relationships with JAL as suppliers on the value chain, outsourcing vendors, or joint-venture partners. A proprietary EDI was initially developed to network JAL and the JAL Group firms electronically in order to improve their coordination efficiency in managing large-scale interdependent business activities and communications between the various relationships: supplier value chain logistics for procurement and just-in-time delivery, outsourcing service functions, and joint-venture operations. EDI provides JAL and the companies in the value chain with timely and accurate information (e.g., flight schedules, purchase orders, cost structures), which is essential for JAL to manage the complex value chain logistics required by flying operations, including procurement and just-in-time delivery of aircraft fuel, aircraft repair parts, cabin food catering, and other customer requirements. In addition, EDI provides JAL and outsourcing vendors at home and overseas with timely and accurate maintenance records. Furthermore, systems integration of CRS with EDI enables JAL and joint venture partners*

to share business information required for optimal scheduling and high-yield operations of integrated tour packages, as well as efficient handling of domestic and international cargo. (pp. 25-26)

It is often necessary for participants in an EDI network to undertake major changes through business process reengineering and, therefore, alter their operational linkages significantly in order to allow network participants to optimize the benefits from EDI systems (Hart & Saunders, 1998; Riggins & Mukhopadhyay, 1994). Premkumar, Ramamurthy, and Nilakanta (1994) argue that EDI network participants need to overcome constraints like incompatible systems, standards, and work procedures—all inhibitors in creating smooth operational linkages as they strive to integrate EDI increasingly with their other information systems applications to realize EDI's true potential.

The concept of operational linkages is captured by using the following three items:

- Our business activities are closely linked with those of this major supplier in e-procurement.
- This supplier's systems involved in e-procurement are essential to our operations.
- Some of our operations are closely connected with this supplier's systems.

Once again, each item is measured using a seven-point Likert scale (1 = strongly disagree; 7 = strongly agree).

Research Methodology and Results

A questionnaire instrument was developed to gather data for this research study. The operationalization of the major variables focused upon in this study was replicated from the Cannon and Perreault (1999) study instrument, which has been pretested on at least 400 supplier-buyer firm partnerships. Modifications were made in the wording of the items to make them appropriate to the e-procurement context of the study. The questionnaire contained additional items besides the ones used in this study. These included e-procurement benefits and success factors, barriers to e-procurement implementation, and several demographical variables. This instrument was pre-tested with several procurement managers and, consequently, refined by incorporating their feedback.

A cover letter, a copy of the questionnaire, and a postage-paid return envelope were mailed to a random sample of 7,000 procurement managers and professionals listed in the roster of the Institute for Supply Management and the Council of Supply Chain Management Professionals (then called the Council of Logistics Management). A total of 225 completed questionnaires were received. This represents a response rate of 3.21 percent. Of the returned questionnaires, only 185 were useable as the rest contained significant missing data. One main reason for the low response rate is that the questionnaires were mailed to 7,000 randomly

Table 1. Profiles of firms

Size (# employees)	Yes (n = 74)	No (n = 85)
Less than 200	21.0%	21.0%
200-1000	19.7%	35.3%
1001-5000	27.6%	28.2%
5001-10000	6.6%	7.0%
Over 10000	25.0%	7.0%
Average Firm size:	9,474	3,720
Type of Firm		
Manufacturing	41.7%	46.4%
Services	58.3%	53.7%

Note: The number of firms does not add to 185 because of missing data.

selected managers without their prior permission. Also several targeted firms, upon receiving the questionnaire, informed us of their policy of not completing unsolicited surveys.

Firm Profiles

Out of the 185 firms, 74 (40 percent) reported actually having experience with e-procurement. Firms using e-procurement were significantly larger, as indicated by the average number of employees (9,474 versus 3,720). Nearly 25 percent of these firms had more than 10,000 employees while this figure was only 7 percent for firms without e-procurement (see Table 1). Also, there was a higher proportion of service firms as compared to manufacturing firms in both groups. For firms with e-procurement experience, service firms constituted nearly 58 percent of the sample, whereas for firms with no e-procurement experience, this percentage was about 54 percent.

Regression Analysis

Table 2 shows the items comprising the four supply characteristics—supply importance (SI), supply complexity (SC), supply market dynamism (SMD), and availability of alternatives (AA), and the two buyer-seller coupling factors—information exchange (IE) and operational linkages (OL). The scores for the supply characteristics and the coupling factors were

Table 2. Factor items and mean (standard deviation) of the factors

<table>
<tr><td>

Supply importance (SI):

Compared to other purchases your firm makes, this product/service is:
- Unimportant-important
- Low priority-high priority

</td><td>4.76(1.65)</td></tr>
<tr><td>

Supply complexity (SC):

Compared to other purchases your firm makes, this product/service is:
- Simple-complex
- Non-technical-technical

</td><td>3.74(1.72)</td></tr>
<tr><td>

Supply market dynamism (SMD):

How significant are changes for this product/service across the following traits?
- Pricing
- Product features and specs
- Vendor support services
- Technology used by suppliers
- Product availability

</td><td>4.74(1.32)</td></tr>
<tr><td>

Availability of alternatives (AA):

This vendor supply market is very competitive
- Other vendors could provide what we get from our best supplier of this major product/service
- Our best supplier of the product/service has a monopoly for what it sells*
- No other vendor has this best supplier's capabilities*

</td><td>5.24(1.24)</td></tr>
<tr><td>

Information-exchange (IE):
- We both share relevant information (product/cost information)
- We include each other in product development meetings
- We always share supply and demand forecasts

</td><td>3.50(1.73)</td></tr>
<tr><td>

Operational linkages (OL):
- Our business activities are closely linked with those of this major supplier in e-procurement
- This supplier's systems involved in e-procurement are essential to our operations
- Some of our operations are closely connected with this supplier's systems

</td><td>3.52(1.31)</td></tr>
</table>

* *Items reverse-coded for analysis.*

Note: Items for SI and SC are measured using a seven-point scale anchored by each pair; SMD items are measured using a 7-point scale (1 = minor; 7 = major); AA, IE and OL items are measured using a seven-point scale (1 = Strongly Disagree; 7 = Strongly Agree).

Table 3. Correlations among factors

	SI	SC	SMD	AA	IE	OL
SI	1.00					
SC	0.58*	1.00				
SMD	0.43*	0.41*	1.00			
AA	-0.22**	-0.35*	-0.25**	1.00		
IE	0.32*	0.37*	0.26**	-0.02	1.00	
OL	0.33*	0.22**	0.25*	-0.19	0.53*	1.00

*Significant at the .01 level.
**Significant at the .05 level.

obtained by averaging items for each factor. The table also shows the mean and standard deviation of each of the six factors.

Table 3 shows the inter-correlations among the six factors. Note that SI, SC, and SMD all have a significantly negative correlation with AA. This shows that simple, non-technical, and lower-priority products/services tend to be more easily available and the suppliers do not have a virtual monopoly. Further note that, as expected, IE and OL exhibit a positive significant correlation with each other since enhanced buyer-seller operational linkages require a high degree of information exchange.

Next, in order to explore the relationship between the four supply factors—SI, SC, SMD, and AA—and IE, a statistical model using the ordinary least squares (OLS) regression method with IE as the dependent variable and SI, SC, SMD, and AA as the predictor variables is specified and estimated. Table 4 reports the regression results. The estimated regression model is statistically significant at the 1 percent significance level (F = 5.109; p = 0.001). Note that out of the four independent variables, only SC (supply complexity) is statistically significantly (p = 0.006) with a positive sign for the regression coefficient (+ 0.394). Note that the two items that comprise the variable SC relate to the complexity and technical nature of the product and/or service provided by the supplier. To gain additional insights vis-à-vis these items, a regression model with IE as the dependent variable and the two items as independent variables was developed. This model explained nearly 26 percent of the variation in IE. Also, both items (complexity, and technical) were found to be statistically significant at the .05 level. This shows that products/services that are complex and technical in nature require an increased level of e-procurement information exchange between buyers and sellers.

Similarly, when regression analysis was conducted using OL as the dependent variable and the four supply factors as independent variables, SI turned out to be the only significant variable (p = 0.062) at the 0.10 level of significance. Once again, to gain additional insights, when the two items that form SI (product/service importance and priority of product/service) were regressed against OL, only the importance of the product was found to be significant (p = .04) at the .05 level. The priority level of the product/service was not significant (p = .744). This

Table 4. Regression results

Dependent variable: IE			
Variable	Coefficient	t-value	p
Constant	1.638	1.271	0.208
SI	0.133	0.929	0.356
SC	0.394	2.829	0.006
SMD	-0.012	-0.077	0.939
AA	-0.036	-0.226	0.822
$R^2 = 0.23$			

p represents the observed probability value

Dependent variable: OL			
Variable	Coefficient	t-value	p
Constant	2.622	2.528	0.014
SI	0.218	1.899	0.062
SC	-0.024	-0.219	0.827
SMD	0.122	0.950	0.345
AA	-0.118	-0.921	0.360
$R^2 = 0.14$			

p represents the observed probability value.

is reasonable as an important product is assigned high priority leading to a high degree of correlation between the two variables (correlation = +0.88; p < .01).

Managerial Implications of Findings

This research study shows that supply importance and supply complexity are the key variables that significantly predict the relational exchange theory variables. Specifically, the importance of the product/service to the buyer is pivotal to determining the extent to which the buyer will link its relevant business activities and systems with those of the supplier. Also, the degree of buyer-seller information exchange via the e-procurement processes is, to a large degree, influenced by the complexity and technical nature of the product/service.

Shared information may include product/cost information, supply/demand forecasts, and product development collaboration information. These results within the e-procurement perspective reconfirm findings of past studies within the supply chain management context and reiterate both the theoretical and practical impact of market uncertainty on the purchasing organization and the appropriate responses to that condition.

This study also contributes to the creation of knowledge by clarifying that supply complexity is different from supply importance. A product or service could be complex but need not be a high-priority item. The concept of product complexity is important nowadays when firms are looking more toward mass customization and collaborative product design involving customers. The customization aspect naturally leads to more unstructured encounters between the buyer and supplier firms, which would require more extensive information exchanges, which may or may not be supported by electronic-based operational linkages. Prior to collaborative commerce systems, for instance, product design communications between buyer and supplier firms were augmented with increased face-to-face contact or phone/fax exchanges.

This study's findings bode well for the next stage of e-procurement. The initial participation of most firms in e-procurement involves the purchase of indirect goods or services. This is a lower-risk approach, as the firm goes through the learning curve of deploying this application. Once the firm has gone beyond the experimentation stage and has successfully implemented e-procurement throughout the enterprise, it is, then, appropriate for it to move to the electronic procurement of higher-value goods such as strategic direct materials or services.

The mitigating influence particularly of Internet-enabled technologies finds its place at this juncture, giving way to what are now called business-to-business systems (Warkentin, 2002). A wide range of options are now available to firms to enable e-procurement with the availability of low-cost Web interface designs and the ubiquity of the Internet as an interconnectivity facility, thus affording them advantages such as flat pricing for information communication, inexpensive access, public key encryption standards to protect EDI transactions, and the emergence of new business models and new forms of interaction and collaboration between buyers and sellers.

New complex functions such as collaborative planning, forecasting, and replenishment; negotiation and decision support; and the procurement and asset management of highly technical and customizable products present new challenges in ensuring information exchange and setting up electronic operational linkages between buyers and sellers. New electronic environments that support sell-side systems, buy-side systems, and neutral e-marketplaces involve the need to assemble data from a wide variety of sources into a single electronic catalog, for instance, as well as the management of that information. The creation of electronic operational linkages is complicated by the lack of widely adopted data standards and business procedures (Granada Research, 1999). Even with use of extensible markup language (XML), the problem has not disappeared because of existing disagreements on the semantics of data structure and exchange processes (Shim, Pendyala, Sundaram, & Gao, 2000). Integration issues involving firms' legacy systems also pose serious technical and business process reengineering challenges, all affecting the firm's ability to set up operational linkages with trading partners.

No matter how challenging these technical infrastructure issues are and will be, business-to-business systems supporting e-procurement are now here to stay. Working out reasonable strategies to pursue information exchange and electronic operational linkages will remain fundamental requirements of participating in a marketplace where the supply dynamics will be introducing increasing levels of uncertainty.

References

Aberdeen Group. (2002). *Making e-sourcing strategic: From tactical technology to core business strategy.* Boston: Author.

Achrol, R. S., & Stern, L. W. (1988). Environmental determinants of decision-making uncertainty in marketing channels. *Journal of Marketing Research, 25,* 36-50.

Aldrich, H. F. (1979). *Organizations and environments.* Englewood Cliffs: Prentice Hall.

Aldrich, H. E., & Mindlin, S. (1978). *Uncertainty and dependence: Two perspectives on environment. Organizations and environment.* Beverly Hills, CA: Sage Publications.

Barrett, S., & Konsynski, B. (1982). Inter-organization information sharing systems. *MIS Quarterly, Special Issue,* 93-105.

Bartels, A., Pohlmann, T., Ross, C. F., Martorelli, W., & Hudson, M. (2005, July 29). *The mixed procurement BPO opportunity.* Retrieved January 21, 2006, from http://www.forrester.com/Research/Document/Excerpt/0,7211,37335,00.html

Bendoly, E., & Schoenherr, T. (2005). ERP system and implementation-process benefits implications for B2B e-procurement. *International Journal of Operations & Production Management, 25*(4), 304-319.

Billington, C., Lee, H. L., & Tang, C. S. (1998). Product rollover: Process, strategies, and opportunities. *Sloan Management Review, 2*(2), 24-34.

Cannon, J.P., & Perreault, Jr., W.D. (1999). Buyer-seller relationships in business markets. *Journal of Marketing Research, 36*(4), 439-460.

Cecere, L., & D'Aquila, M. (2005, August 19). *The procurement and sourcing applications report,* 2004-2009. Retrieved January 21, 2005, from http://www.amrresearch.com/Content/View.asp?pmillid=18490

Center for Advanced Purchasing Studies. (2004, September). *Developing and implementing e-sourcing strategy* (Critical Issues Report). Flynn, A. E. Retrieved January 22, 2006, from http://www.capsresearch.org/publications/pdfs-protected/cir082004.pdf

Center for Advanced Purchasing Studies. (2005, January). *Supply base rationalization* (Critical issues report). Duffy, R. Retrieved January 22, 2006, from http://www.capsresearch.org/publications/pdfs-protected/cir012005.pdf

Center for Advanced Purchasing Studies. (2005, August). *Critical issues report: optimizing MRO inventory management.* Ashenbaum, B. Retrieved January 22, 2006, from http://www.capsresearch.org/publications/pdfs-protected/cir082005.pdf

Chatfield, A. T., & Bjorn-Andersen, N. (1997). The impact of IOS-enabled business process change on business outcomes: Transformation of the value chain of Japan airlines. *Journal of Management Information Systems, 14*(1), 13-40.

Chatfield, A. T., & Yetton, P. (2000). Strategic payoff from EDI as a function of EDI embeddedness. *Journal of Management Information Systems, 16*(4), 195-224.

Computer Sciences Corporation. (2002). *Achieving bottom line results in a flat economy: Leveraging procurement business services.* El Segundo, CA: Author.

Cook, K. (1977). Exchange and power in networks of interorganizational relationships. *Sociological Quarterly, 18*, 62-82.

Den Hengst, M., & Henk, S. G. (2002). The Impact of electronic commerce on interorganizational coordination: A framework from theory applied to the container-transport industry. *International Journal of Electronic Commerce, 6*(4), 73-91.

Downing, C. E., Field, J. M., & Ritzman, L. P. (2003). The value of outsourcing: A field study. *Information Systems Management, 20*(1), 86-90.

Dwyer. F., Schurr, R., & Oh, S. (1987). Output sector munificence effects on the internal political economy of marketing channels. *Journal of Marketing, 24*, 347-358.

Elmuti, D. (2002). The perceived impact of supply chain management on organizational effectiveness. *Journal of Supply Chain Management, 38*(3), 49-57.

Fawcett, S. E., & Magnan, G. M. (2001). Achieving world-class supply chain alignment. *Center for Advanced Purchasing Studies.* Retrieved January 25, 2006, from http://www.capsresearch.org/publications/pdfs-protected/fawcett2001.pdf

Gallear, D., & Ghobadian, A. (2004). Study of supply-chain purchasing strategy. *Logistics & Transport Focus, 6*(1), 52-54.

Ganesan, S. (1994). Determinants of long-term orientation in buyer-seller relationships. *Journal of Marketing, 58*, 1-19.

Granada Research. (1999). *E-catalog '99: business-to-business electronic catalogs, technology report.* Half Moon Bay, CA: Author.

Halley, A., & Nollet, J. (2002). The supply chain: The weak link for some preferred suppliers? *Journal of Supply Chain Management, 38*(3), 39-47.

Handfield, R. B. (1993). A resource dependence perspective of Just-in-Time purchasing. *Journal of Operations Management, 11*(3), 289-311.

Hart, P., & Saunders, C. (1998). Emerging electronic partnerships: antecedents and dimensions of EDI use from the supplier's perspective. *Journal of Management Information Systems, 14*(4), 87-111.

Heide, J. (1994). Interorganizational governance in marketing channels. *Journal of Marketing, 58*, 71-85.

Henderson, J. C. (1990). Plugging into strategic partnerships: The critical IS connection. *Sloan Management Review, 30*(3), 7-18.

Jacobs, D. (1974). Dependency and vulnerability: An exchange approach to the control of organizations. *Administrative Science Quarterly, 19*, 45-59.

Johnson, E., & Lee, H. (2000). Agile Software--I Want My WebTV. *Stanford Global Supply Chain Management Forum Case* (Paper# 1-0074), January 3, SGSCMF-001-2000.

Kanakamedala, K. B., Ramsdell, G., & Roche, P.J. (2003). The promise of purchasing software. *McKinsey Quarterly, 4*, 20-23.

Kaufmann, P. J., & Dant, R. (1992). The dimensions of commercial exchange. *Marketing Letters, 3,* 171-185.

Kaufmann, R. J., & Mohtadi, H. (2004). Proprietary and open systems adoption in e-procurement: A risk-augmented transaction cost perspective. *Journal of Management Information Systems, 21*(1), 137-166.

Kaufmann, P .J., & Stern, L. W. (1988). Relational exchange norms, perceptions of unfairness, and retained hostility in commercial litigation. *Journal of Conflict Resolution, 32,* 534-552.

Kearney, A.T. (2000). *Assessment on excellence in procurement.* Chicago: Author.

Konsynski, B. R., & McFarlan, F. W. (1990). Information partnerships: Shared data, shared scale. *Harvard Business Review, 68*(5), 114-120.

Lee, H. L. (2002). Aligning supply chain strategies with product uncertainties. *California Management Review, 44*(3), 105-119.

Lee, J. N., & Kim, Y. G. (1999). Effect of partnership quality on IS outsourcing: Conceptual framework and empirical validation. *Journal of Management Information Systems, 15*(4), 29-61.

Macneil, I. R. (1980). *The New social contract.* New Haven, CT: Yale University Press.

Min, H., & Galle, W. P. (1999). Electronic commerce usage in business-to-business purchasing. *International Journal of Operations & Production Management, 19*(9), 909-921.

Min, S., & Mentzer, J. T. (2004). Developing and measuring supply chain management concepts. *Journal of Business Logistics, 25*(1), 63-99.

Pfeffer, J., & Nowak, P. (1976). Joint ventures and interorganizational interdependence. *Administrative Science Quarterly, 21,* 398-418.

Pfeffer, J., & Salancik, G. R. (1978). *The external control of organizations: A resource dependence approach.* New York: Harper and Row Publishers.

Premkumar, G., Ramamurthy, K., & Nilakanta, S. (1994). Implementation of electronic data interchange: An innovation diffusion perspective. *Journal of Management Information Systems, 11*(2), 157-186.

Raghunathan, S. (1999). Interorganizational collaborative forecasting and replenishment systems and supply chain implications. *Decision Sciences, 30*(4), 1053-1071.

Riggins, F. J., & Mukhopadhyay, T. (1994). Interdependent benefits from interorganizational systems: Opportunities for business partner reengineering. *Journal of Management Information Systems, 11*(2), 37-57.

Rinehart, L. M., Eckert, J. A., Handfield, R. B., & Page, T. J., Jr. (2004). An assessment of supplier-customer relationships. *Journal of Business Logistics, 25* (1), 25-62.

Shim, S. S. Y., Pendyala, V. S., Sundaram, M., & Gao, S. J. Z. (2000). Business-to-business e-commerce frameworks. *IEEE Computer, 33*(10) 40-47.

Stephens Inc. (2001, January 30). *Strategic sourcing: Applications to turn direct materials procurement into a competitive advantage* (Internet research industry report). Boston.

Subramaniam, C., & Shaw, M. J. (2002). A study of the value and impact of B2B e-commerce: The case of Web-based procurement. *International Journal of Electronic Commerce, 6*(4), 19-40.

Truman, G. E. (2000). Integration in electronic exchange environments. *Journal of Management Information Systems, 17*(1), 209-244.

Turner, G. B., LeMay, S. A., Hartley, M., & Wood, C. M. (2000). Interdependence and cooperation in industrial buyer-supplier relationships. *Journal of Marketing Theory and Practice, 8*(1), 16-24.

Ulrich, D., & Barney, J. B. (1984). Perspectives in organizations: Resource dependence, efficiency, and population. *Academy of Management Review, 9*, 471-481.

Vijay, R. K., & Keah, C. T. (2002). Supplier selection and assessment: Their impact on business performance. *Journal of Supply Chain Management, 38*(4), 11-21.

Warkentin, M. (2002). *Business-to-business electronic commerce.* Hershey, PA: Idea Group Publishing.

Zacharia, Z. G., & Mentzer, J. T. (2004). Logistics salience in a changing environment. *Journal of Business Logistics, 25*(1), 187-210.

Chapter VI

Consumer Factors Affecting Adoption of Internet Banking Services:
An Empirical Investigation in Taiwan

Wen-Jang Jih, Middle Tennessee State University, USA

Shu-Yeng Wong, Da-Yeh University, Taiwan

Tsung-Bin Chang, Da-Yeh University, Taiwan

Abstract

Banking is often regarded as an information-intensive industry. From the information process point of view, banking services primarily involve creation, processing, storage, and distribution of financial information. Although most of these services can be conveniently handled via Internet-based information technologies, adoption of Internet banking has been less than optimal. Existing research has revealed that this convenience may be offset, to varying degrees, by customer-perceived risk associated with transacting in the wide-open cyberworld. A key challenge for online bankers is to maintain a secure information infra-

structure that effectively manages the perceived risk factors. This research examines usages of Internet banking services, investigates the nature and sources of customers' perceived risks, and tests hypotheses with regard to impacts of perceived risks on Internet banking adoption. Using primary data collected in Taiwan, the study finds significant relationships among involvement, familiarity, perceived risks, perception of measures for reducing perceived risks, and customer willingness to adopt Internet banking services. The findings have significant implications for practice and research in Internet banking.

Introduction

Once touted as a disruptive technology, the Internet has been expected to bring about fundamental paradigm changes in the business arena. Following the rapid bursting of e-commerce bubbles in the spring of 2000, however, many companies have been driven to the pessimistic end of the expectation continuum. Recent successes of e-commerce companies such as eBay and Amazon have demonstrated that Internet technology should be viewed as a critical building block and a powerful enabler in developing a flexible and efficient information infrastructure for innovative business strategies (Porter, 2001). The two unique features of Internet technology, rich information content and global reach, can be cleverly leveraged to develop innovative operations that effectively achieve cost reduction, quality improvement, time compression, and customer service enhancement, all at the same time. The Internet-centric technological infrastructure and the customer-centric business strategy have actually become two tightly coupled aspects of companies' pursuit of sustainable competitive advantage.

The impact of Internet technology is especially obvious in the banking industry. Being information-intensive in nature, virtually every component of the banking business' value chain can benefit from innovative utilization of Internet technology. From the bank's point of view, potential benefits promised by Internet banking include lower operational cost, shorter turnaround time, real-time managerial information, smoother communications within the organization, more convenient interactions with prospective as well as existing customers, and provision of value-added services such as access to professional knowledge in financial management (Nielsen, 2002; Sathye, 1999). Recognizing the strategic value of the Internet, all of the 120 largest banks in the U.S. offer their customers the ability to access a variety of banking services (Pyun, Scruggs, & Nam, 2002). The global banking industry is now facing a fundamental paradigm challenge catalyzed by the advancement of Internet technology.

For banking customers, Internet banking allows for convenient access to a variety of banking services without limitations of time and space experienced with the traditional mode of banking. However, studies reveal that concerns about transaction integrity, information security, and information privacy keep more customers from switching their banking preferences or increasing their level of participation. One trade information source, the Online Banking Report, reports that 20 percent of Internet users now access online banking services, a total that will reach 33 percent by 2006. By 2010, more than 55 million households will use online banking and e-payment services (www.epaynews.com). However the report also reveals that 85 percent of U.S. bank customers have security/privacy concerns over online transactions, though 45 percent of them do find online financial transactions more convenient. In an interview study conducted in the United Kingdom, White and Nteli (2004) found that Internet banking customers are still concerned about the security issues, despite conscious efforts to cope with these issues by the banks. These concerns, often referred to as "perceived risks" in academic literature, along with perception of risk-reduction measures, familiarity with the Internet, and online banking involvement, must be addressed in a proper manner in order for Internet banking to progress to a more mature level of adoption.

The research reported in this chapter was conducted in order to better understand the roles of perceived risk and other related factors in customers' adoption of Internet banking services. The remainder of the chapter is structured as follows. The next section reviews the literature related to perceived risk, risk-reduction measures, involvement, and familiarity. This is followed by a description of the research methodology. The results of data analysis are reported in the subsequent section. The last section discusses major research findings, implications for management practitioners, and suggestions for future research.

Literature Review

Perceived Risk and Risk-Reduction Measures

The concept of risk dates back to as early as the 1920s (Knight, 1921). Bauer (1964) first pioneered the concept of customer-perceived risk associated with such phenomena as information seeking, brand loyalty, opinion leaders, reference groups, and pre-purchase deliberations. The role of perceived risk in the business arena is actively examined in consumer behavior researches. In Rao and Farley (1987) and Srinivasan and Ratchford (1991), for example, perceived risk was used as an explanatory variable. Bettman (1973), Cunningham (1967), Sheth and Venkatesan (1968), and Stone and Gronhaung (1993) viewed perceived risk as a determinant of consumers' intended and actual purchasing behavior. Dowling and Staelin (1994) constructed a descriptive model to depict how perceived risk affected consumers' information search behavior and their risk-modification strategies. Based on the result of a controlled experiment, Dowling and Staelin concluded that:

> ... product-specific perceived risk significantly affected the intensity of the intended use of risk-modification strategies and that there appeared to be an acceptable value below which this product-specific risk has little effect on intended behavior.
>
> (p. 132)

Cox (1967) examined the cause of perceived risk and contended that consumer behaviors were goal-driven and perceived risk arose when the consumer recognized that the goal of consumption might not be met by the behavior. Jacoby and Kaplan (1972) identified five dimensions of perceived risk: financial risk, functional or performance risk, physical risk, social risk, and psychological risk. Their study reported that these five dimensions of perceived risk were capable of explaining 74 percent of variance in the research data. A study conducted by Stone and Gronhaung (1993) found that, when the dimension of time risk was added to the list mentioned above, the percentage of explained variance increased to 88.8%. In an exploratory study of consumer acceptance of Internet banking services in a Turkish bank using a structured-undisguised questionnaire, Polatoglu and Ekin (2001) also found that perceived risk was one of the major factors affecting consumer adoption, as well as customer satisfaction, of Internet banking services.

Perceived risk usually arises from uncertainty. Consumers' purchasing decisions often are characterized by the uncertainty associated with the consequence of the decisions. Taylor (1974) proposed a theory to portray how purchasing decisions created anxiety resulting from uncertainty, and, in an effort to reduce uncertainty and undesirable consequences, how consumers formulated strategies to cope with the perceived risks. His theory identified two general strategies for reducing perceived risks: enhancement of certainty level associated with the consumption behavior through information gathering and reduction of purchasing frequency in order to reduce possible loss. Through a series of in-depth interviews with two consumers, Cox (1967) identified five ways to reduce uncertainty: (1) rely on own experience and others' experience, (2) search for relevant information, (3) Take preventive measures such as purchasing only quality products, (4) purchase familiar brands, and (5) never opt for cheap products.

The relationship between perceived risks and measures for risk reduction was examined in several previous consumer behavior researches. For example, Cunningham's study (1967) found that consumers' satisfactory experience could reduce perceived risks, leading to enhanced brand loyalty. Hirch, Dornoff, and Keman's research (1972) concluded that consumers preferred shopping in trustworthy stores in order to reduce perceived risks. Terence and William's research (1982) confirmed the value of trusted third parties for reduction of perceived risks. The significance and efficiency of information searching for risk reduction were stressed by Sheth and Venkatesan (1968) and Roselius (1967). Other measures for reducing perceived risks include word of mouth (Arndt, 1967), brand loyalty, in-store browsing, and store image (Derbaix, 1983). Based on these consumer behavior researches, this study postulates that perceived risk might play a significant role in bank customers' adoption of Internet banking, given the information-intensive nature of the banking services.

Personal Involvement

The concept of personal involvement has been examined in three marketing research areas: advertising, products, and purchasing decisions. Zaichkowsky (1986) conducted a comprehensive literature review of these researches and proposed a framework to conceptualize involvement in terms of its antecedents and possible impacts on various aspects of consumer behavior. Of the three research directions identified in her framework, the involvement with products and the involvement with purchasing decisions were relevant to the investigation of Internet banking adoption. Three possible results of involvement with products (relative importance of the product area, perceived differences in product attributes, and preference of a particular brand) and four possible results of involvement with purchasing decisions (influence of price on brand choice, amount of information search, time spent deliberating alternatives, and type of decision rule used in choice) were suggested in the framework. The definition given by Zaichkowsky (1985) of involvement was general enough to be applicable to the inquiry of Internet banking adoption:

> ... *a person's perceived relevance of the object based on inherent needs, value, and interests.*

(p. 342)

Other aspects of personal involvement defined in existing researches include information relevance, attention, interest, information processing, motivation, and response to stimulus (Krugman, 1965; Laczniak, Muehling, & Grossbart, 1989; Mitchell, 1992). For example, in the advertising area, involvement was found to affect consumers' level of attention, information processing, comprehension, decision-making, and responses to advertising (Celsi & Olson, 1988; Maheswaren & Meyers-Levy, 1990).

The role of involvement in Internet shopping was examined in an experiment conducted by Balabanis and Reynolds (2001) to measure its impact on the length of time a consumer spent on a web site and on the consumer's attitude toward a Web site. This study found that highly involved consumers spent less time on a Web site than uninvolved consumers, suggesting that the "stickiness" (visit duration) of a Web site should not be viewed as the only indicator of the Web site's effectiveness. The study failed to confirm the result of an earlier study conducted by Butler and Peppard (1998), which found that involvement was an important element of Internet purchasing behavior. It would appear that, although involvement may play an important role in consumers' purchasing behavior, it doesn't do so in isolation. Instead it is likely to work with a variety of factors (e.g., Web site features and content) in a nonlinear fashion in affecting consumers' online purchasing decision.

Familiarity

The concept of familiarity is an important variable in advertising and consumer psychology. Campbell and Keller (2003), for instance, conducted two experiments to confirm the moderating influence of brand familiarity on the effect of communication message repetition. In Balabanis & Reynolds' study (2001), experiment participants' Internet knowledge and Internet experience were correlated with their Web site visit durations and with their attitudes toward the visited Web sites. No significant correlation between Internet knowledge and site duration was found in the study. Internet knowledge was found, however, to correlate significantly with one of the two Web sites used for the study but not with the other one.

A different result, however, was reported by other researchers. Since Internet banking is a relatively new phenomenon, according to the concept of new product life cycle, it seems reasonable to hypothesize that the degree of familiarity with the use of Internet technology might contribute to customers' adoption of Internet banking at the early stage of innovation diffusion. This reasoning was confirmed by the studies conducted by Chou (1997) and Lin (2000). Both studies found that the degree of familiarity with the Web-based interface significantly affected consumers' shopping behavior on the Web. Motivated by these inconsistent findings, our study was designed to examine the effect of familiarity with Internet on perceived risk, risk-reduction measures, and adoption of Internet banking services.

Research Objective and Conceptual Framework

In light of the prior research results, and considering the fact that Internet banking usage is still in the early stage of the users' learning curve, we postulated the existence of correlation relationships between involvement, familiarity, perceived risk, risk-reduction measures, and adoption willingness. From the customers' standpoint, a higher degree of familiarity with Internet technology ought to encourage the use of Internet banking service and vice versa. The more one is personally involved in the use of Internet banking, the more he/she would be able to appreciate the function of various risk-reduction measures taken by the bank and/or the customer. This same reasoning seems to hold true for the relationship between personal involvement and perceived risk. As for the relationship between perceived risk and perception of risk-reduction measures, we assumed that the more risk-conscious customers would be more sensitive to risk-reduction measures. Finally, with the understanding that customers' adoption depends on a multitude of organizational as well as technological factors, we assumed that customers' perceived risk, perception of risk-reduction measures, familiarity with Internet technology, and personal involvement play a significant role in affecting their adoption of Internet banking services.

Drawing from research in consumer behavior and Internet shopping, this research was undertaken in order to obtain more understanding about the significant factors promoting usage of Internet banking services. Specifically, the primary objective of this study was

Figure 1. Conceptual framework for the research

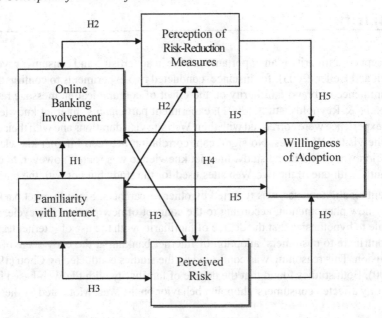

to explore the impacts of perceived risks, perception of risk-reduction measures, personal involvement in Internet banking services, and users' familiarity with Internet technology on the willingness to use the services. This research objective was fulfilled through the testing of the following five research hypotheses, formulated on the basis of the relevant literature and our understanding of current Internet banking practices.

H1: Personal involvement in Internet banking is not significantly correlated with familiarity with Internet technology.

H2: Perception of risk-reduction measures is not significantly correlated with personal involvement in Internet banking and familiarity with Internet technology.

H3: Perceived risk is not significantly correlated with personal involvement in Internet banking and familiarity with Internet technology.

H4: No significant relationship exists between perceived risk and perception of risk-reduction measures associated with usage of Internet banking services.

H5: Adoption of Internet banking services is not significantly influenced by perceived risk, perception of risk-reduction measures, personal involvement in Internet banking, and familiarity with Internet technology.

The research hypotheses are graphically depicted in Figure 1.

Research Methodology

Data Collection and Data Analysis

Primary data were collected from current and prospective customers of Internet banking services in Taiwan, where electronic commerce has been a major thrust in economic, educational, and public sectors (Jih, 2002, 2003, 2004). Online banking based on Internet technology was recognized as an important approach to enhancing banks' competitiveness years before the Internet was commercialized. In October 1984, the Ministry of Finance launched a finance information service center to implement an inter-bank information network. This service center was expanded in 1998 to leverage Internet features and incorporate additional support from both the private sector and other public sectors. The Internet banking service center is now known as the Financial Information Service Co., Ltd. (http://www.fisc.com.tw/). Currently this system is used by all domestic banks to serve their online customers, with some user interface features customized to reflect individual bank's distinct business strategy.

In order to collect primary research data from consumers, a five-point Likert Scale self-reported questionnaire was developed to measure perceived risks, perception of risk-reduction measures, personal involvement, and willingness of adoption of Internet banking services. Ho and Ng (1994) identified two basic approaches used to measure the concept of perceived risk, the uncertainty-consequences approach and the risk-component approach. This study adopted the risk-component approach to design the questions for perceived risk. Data about familiarity with Internet technology and the respondents' demographical characteristics were gathered using nominal scale questions. Two online data collection methods were employed simultaneously to increase the number of responses: in addition to the hyper-link button for the questionnaire placed at a preeminent location on the participating banks' homepages, the questionnaire was also posted on several major Internet bulletin boards to invite voluntary participation in the study.

Several statistical analysis techniques were employed to analyze the research data. Demographic data such as gender, age, education, and occupation were tallied using frequency analysis. Principal components analysis and varimax rotation in factor analysis were conducted to extract latent factors of personal involvement, perceived risks, and perception of risk-reduction measures. The Cronbach's α value for each of these dimensions resulting from factor analysis was obtained as the reliability measure. Canonical correlation analysis was then conducted to evaluate the correlations between sets of research variables. Multiple regression analysis was used to determine the impact of all of the independent variables on the primary dependent variable, that is, customers' willingness to adopt Internet banking.

Research Results

Sample Characteristics

Of the 538 people responding to the survey, 377 respondents were male (70%) and 161 respondents were female (30%). The most predominant age group was from 20 to 39, representing 72.8% of the total respondents. Almost 90% of the respondents had a college

Table 1. Factor analysis for personal involvement in Internet banking services

Question items	Factor 1 Concern involvement	Factor 2 Dependency involvement
Internet banking is significant for me.	.84	.32
I am concerned about development of Internet banking.	.83	.21
I am interested in services offered by Internet banking.	.83	.24
Variations of Internet banking functions affect my usage habit.	.15	.86
I am becoming more and more dependent on Internet banking.	.33	.77
I need to use Internet banking.	.45	.65
Internet banking has become a necessity for me.	.49	.55
Eigenvalues	2.76	2.55
Percentage of explained variance	30.63	28.30
Accumulated explained variance	30.63	58.93

degree. With regard to occupation, the first four largest groups were business consulting and brokerage, information and computer, student, and manufacturing. The marital status was somewhat split between those who were married and those unmarried. There were 2% (8 people) who did not report their marital status.

Results of Factor Analysis for Research Variables

Multiple question items designed to measure each of the research variables from different perspectives were first analyzed by principal component analysis to extract the latent variables (factors) among observed variables. The variance maximizing (Varimax) rotation procedure was applied to the resulted principal components to "obtain a more interpretable set of factor loading" (Nunnally, 1978, p. 370). Only the question items with loading factors greater than 0.40 were included in the factors. The Kaiser-Meyer-Olkin (KMO) and Barlett's test were also conducted to evaluate the appropriateness of the factor analysis. The factorability of the intercorrelation matrix was determined by the Kaiser-Meyer-Olkin (KMO) measure of sampling adequacy. The KMO measure should be greater than 0.5 for a satisfactory factor analysis to proceed. A significant result of the Bartlett's Test of Sphericity serves to confirm the significant correlations between question items.

Two factors were produced for personal involvement, concern involvement, and dependency involvement, with 58.93% of accumulated explained variance (Table 1). Concern involvement consisted of three items with loading factors greater than .40, and dependency involvement consists of four items with loading factors greater than .40. The KMO measure for this analysis was .90, an indication that the set of questions for personal involvement was appropriate for factor analysis. This appropriateness was also confirmed by the significant result of the Bartlett's Test of Sphericity ($\chi^2 = 2552.62$, $p < .001$). The reliability indicators of the two factors as measured by Cronbach's α were 0.86 for concern involvement and 0.85 for dependency involvement. The combined Cronbach's α for the research construct "personal involvement" was 0.89, much greater than the minimum level (0.7) considered appropriate for exploratory studies (Nunnally, 1978).

A similar analysis for perceived risk produced five principal components with an accumulated explained variance of 63.94%: time risk (F_1), functional risk (F_2), financial risk (F_3), social risk (F_4), and physical risk (F_5) (Table 2). The KMO measure was 0.88, and the Bartlett Test of Sphericity was significant ($\chi^2 = 5898.80$, $p < .001$), both indicating the appropriateness of

Table 2. Result of factor analysis for perceived risks

Perceived risk items	F_1 Time risk	F_2 Functional risk	F_3 Financial risk	F_4 Social risk	F_5 Physical risk
Much time is required to search for bank services	.80	.24	.01	.11	.09
Much time is required in learning to use online banking services	.73	.14	-.05	.24	.19
Much time is required to complete an online banking transaction	.68	.30	.07	.27	.05

Table 2. continued

Much time is required to deal with bank personnel in order to correct a mistake	.60	.16	.29	.05	-.13
Inability to conduct online banking transactions due to uncontrollable factors	.52	-.18	.22	.28	.15
Lack of understanding of online banking operations	.51	.47	.05	-.10	.28
Concern about recording errors for transactions completed outside regular business hours that get posted the next business day	.14	.70	.18	.27	.18
Concern about misunderstanding of service functions	.09	.64	.40	.10	.04
Online banking services are too complicated to use comfortably	.36	.63	.05	-.02	.29
Lack of warning regarding system changes	.11	.63	.42	.19	-.03
Concern about potential problems with transfer and payment made outside the business hours	.51	.55	.14	.31	-.04
Concern about insufficient protection	.23	.53	.46	.20	-.02
Probable financial loss caused by virus attacks	.07	.20	.87	.02	.08
Probable financial loss caused by stolen password	.08	.20	.86	.00	.07
Probable financial loss due to insufficient security measures	.08	.18	.82	.03	.08
Complaints from friends and relatives for enthusiasm with online banking	.16	.15	-.11	.84	.10
Neglecting spending time with family and friends	.19	.01	-.05	.80	.14
Strained spouse relationship due to the fact that online banking eases personal holding	.02	.24	.07	.65	.26
Being teased by family and friends as focus of news report headlines	.20	.34	.25	.55	-.00
Strained employer-employee relationship caused by employee engaging in online investing at work hours	.22	.01	.16	.48	.22
Physical discomfort such as eye sore and muscle pain	.16	.11	.12	.25	.84
Health threat caused by CRT radiation	.07	.14	.08	.34	.80
Eigenvalues	3.20	3.06	3.04	2.97	1.79
Explained variance in percentage	14.56	13.91	13.82	13.50	8.15
Accumulated variance in percentage	14.56	28.47	42.29	55.79	63.94

Table 3. Result of factor analysis for perception of risk-reduction measures

Banks' risk-reduction measures	F_1	F_2	F_3	F_4	F_5	F_6	F_7
Shortening online process time with enhanced hardware and software	.81	.17	.24	.13	.05	.08	.01
Shortening online processing time through user interface improvement	.78	.15	.20	.20	.08	.11	.03
Shortening search time via better menu design	.78	.12	.17	.22	.09	.00	.06
Providing alternative transaction modes to cope with unexpected events	.73	.16	.09	.16	.15	.09	.06
Providing confirmation information for transactions to be posted on the next business day	.67	.26	.13	.19	.11	.28	-.05
Cultivate customer trust via advertisements on convenience and security features of online banking	.60	.20	-.02	.17	.19	.15	.24
Implementing tight control over customer information to reduce ethical concern	.59	.32	.20	.35	.08	.08	-.07
Implement basic security mechanisms to ensure data and transaction security	.15	.81	.12	.15	.09	.05	.09
Use encryption and digital certificate to further strengthen data and transaction security	.04	.74	.06	.15	.06	.08	.19
Involving a certification center as the trusted third party	.26	.68	.28	.11	.16	.15	-.04
Implement multi-layered security mechanisms	.28	.67	.26	.11	.07	.17	.03
Subjecting online banking transactions to governmental scrutiny	.30	.57	.17	.01	.18	.08	-.02
Providing online facility to allow customers to set their own transfer amount limit	.20	.10	.73	.07	.13	.11	.02
Encouraging customers to save transaction information for later verification	.02	.16	.66	.14	.07	.24	.08
Providing online facility to allow customers to designate target accounts for transfer	.29	.17	.65	.02	.13	.05	.16
Reminding customers to frequently change their passwords	.18	.23	.63	-.00	.17	.02	.27
Shortening user exposure to radiation via simplified user interface design	.34	.13	.11	.80	.11	.08	.08
Providing friendly user interface to reduce physical discomfort	.35	.12	.11	.78	.09	.07	.12
Providing clear and relevant information to reduce eye sore	.26	.09	.07	.77	.15	.09	.16
Using online banking from prestigious banks	.09	.13	.14	.16	.86	.12	.10
Using online banking from large banks	.11	.14	.20	.25	.78	.16	.14

Table 3. continued

Using online banking from dependable banks	.31	.32	.24	.00	.65	.19	.06
Providing comprehensive transaction protection measures	.36	.45	.16	-.01	.46	.14	-.03
Mailing confirmation message to customers for each completed transaction	.10	.13	.08	.07	.06	.79	.26
Mailing monthly statement to customers	.20	.16	.18	.07	.26	.72	.12
Providing online help for each online functional feature	.32	.20	.38	.19	.17	.57	-.00
Providing news update in a timely manner	.38	.18	.43	.20	.15	.49	-.02
Basing adoption decision on discussions with relatives/friends	-.03	.06	.17	.00	.01	.13	.80
Learning about values of online banking from relatives/friends	.05	-.02	.23	.07	.07	.11	.76
Actively recommending online banking to relatives/friends	.14	.10	-.09	.33	.15	.04	.60
Eigenvalues	4.86	3.49	2.79	2.55	2.47	2.23	1.95
Explained variance	15.69	11.27	9.00	8.22	7.98	7.19	6.30

factor analysis for the instrument. The Cronbach's α value for the perceived risk was 0.90, an indication of a high reliability of the data collection instrument for this research variable.

Seven factors were obtained for risk-reduction measures, with an accumulated explained variance of 65.65%: reduction of non-financial risk (F_1), reduction of financial risk (F_2), use of self-initiated protection features (F_3), reduction of physical risk (F_4), image and reputation (F_5), reduction of functional risk (F_6), and social interactions (F_7) (Table 3). Both the KMO measure (0.93) and the result of Bartlett Test of Sphericity (χ^2 = 9115.24, p < .001) indicated the appropriateness of factor analysis for this variable. The Cronbach's α value for risk reduction measures was 0.93.

Only one principal component was extracted out of the five questions for the research variable Willingness to Adopt Internet Banking Services, with the eigenvalue of 3.61 and explained variance of 72.16%. The Cronbach's α value was 0.90. Its KMO measure was .87. The Bartlett Test of Sphericity value was significant (χ^2 = 1727.57, p < .001). These validation data demonstrated the appropriateness of factor analysis for this research construct.

Testing of Hypotheses 1–4: Canonical Correlation Analysis

Since each part of the research constructs in the hypotheses 1–4 was represented by multiple variables, canonical correlation analysis was employed to test the correlation relationship between the research constructs. Four canonical analyses were conducted to evaluate the correlation relationships between familiarity with Internet technology, personal involvement

Table 4. Canonical correlation analysis between familiarity and involvement

Familiarity	Canonical variate	Involvement	Canonical variate
	χ_1		η_1
Length of Internet usage in years	.38	Concern involvement	.94
Amount of time of Internet usage per week	.36	Dependency involvement	.89
Importance of Internet in daily life	.99		
Extracted variance	41.82	Extracted variance	83.15
Redundancy	5.07		
Canonical correlation (ρ)	.35*	Redundancy	10.09
ρ^2	.12		

*: $p < .001$

Table 5. Canonical correlation analysis between involvement, familiarity, and perception of risk-reduction measures

Involvement and familiarity	Canonical variate		Perception of risk-reduction measure	Canonical variate	
	$\chi1$	$\chi2$		$\eta1$	$\eta2$
Concern involvement	-.88	.29	Reduction of non-financial risk	-.64	-.11
Dependency involvement	-.69	-.07	Reduction of functional risk	-.80	.20
Length of Internet usage in years	-.15	-.71	Use of self-initiated protective features	-.64	.09
Amount of time of Internet usage per week	-.53	-.62	Reduction of physical risk	-.26	.56
Importance of Internet in daily life	-.53	-.50	Public image and reputation	-.74	.49
% of extracted variance	36.55	24.54	Reduction of functional risk	-.36	.27
% of redundancy	4.54	1.18	Reducing risk through social interactions	.02	.44
Canonical correlation (ρ)	.35**	.22*	% of Extracted variance	31.44	12.49
ρ^2	.12	.05	% of redundancy	3.91	.60

*: $p < .01$

**: $p < .001$

in Internet banking services, perceived risk, and perception of risk-reduction measures associated with Internet banking usage.

The canonical correlation coefficient (ρ) between familiarity with Internet technology and personal involvement in Internet banking services, as shown on Table 4, was 0.35 ($p < .001$). This result indicated that the people who were more familiar with Internet technology tended to involve themselves more in the use of Internet banking services. Hypothesis 1 (H1), personal involvement in Internet banking, is not significantly correlated with familiarity with Internet technology and was rejected.

When familiarity and involvement were treated as the independent variables and the perception of risk-reduction measures was treated as the dependent variable in the canonical analysis, two pairs of canonical variates were produced (Table 5). The first pair correlated low concern involvement, low dependency involvement, infrequent use of Internet, and low importance of Internet in daily life with the composition of low levels of all but one dimension of perceived risk-reduction measures. When expressed in positive terms, the relationship suggested that those who were familiar with Internet technology and also involved themselves more in Internet banking services tended to agree on the value of taking a variety of measures to reduce perceived risk. Similarly, the second pair of the canonical variate indicated that those who did not use Internet frequently relied more on public image of bank reputation and social interactions in their effort to reduce perceived risks. Based on these results, the second hypothesis 2 (H2), perception of risk-reduction measures is not significantly correlated with personal involvement in Internet banking and familiarity with Internet technology, was rejected.

Table 6. Canonical correlation analysis between involvement, familiarity, and perceived risks

Involvement and familiarity	Canonical variate		Perceived risks	Canonical variate	
	$\chi 1$	$\chi 2$		$\eta 1$	$\eta 2$
Concern involvement	-.63	.51	Time risk	.85	.03
Dependency involvement	-.86	-.09	Functional risk	.84	-.02
Length of Internet usage in years	-.44	.47	Financial risk	.55	.42
Amount of time of Internet usage per week	-.02	.59	Social risk	.67	-.69
Importance of Internet in daily life	-.06	.40	Physical risk	.22	-.53
% of extracted variance	26.60	19.53	% of Extracted variance	44.04	18.73
% of redundancy	2.12	.66			
Canonical correlation (ρ)	.28**	.18*	% of redundancy	3.52	.63
ρ^2	.08	.03			

*: $p < .05$

**: $p < .001$

Table 7. Results of canonical analysis between perceived risks and perception of risk-reduction measures

Risk-reduction measures	Canonical variates					Perceived risks	Canonical variates				
	χ1	χ2	χ3	χ4	χ5		η1	η2	η3	η4	η5
Reduction of non-financial risks	.31	-.53	-.26	-.24	.68	Time risk	-.30	-.70	-.46	.22	.40
Reduction of financial risks	.27	-.58	.08	-.70	-.03	Functional risk	-.27	-.90	.06	.21	-.27
Provision of use of self-initiated protective features measures	.21	-.56	.25	-.40	.32	Financial risk	.12	-.77	.20	-.60	.02
Reduction of physical risks	-.19	-.31	-.61	-.55	.34	Social risk	-.93	-.32	.13	-.08	.15
Image and reputation	.20	-.62	.20	-.31	.11	Physical risk	-.56	-.23	-.58	-.35	-.41
Reduction of functional risks	.07	-.97	-.22	.03	.01	Percentage of variance extracted	20.90	40.81	12.18	11.64	8.47
Social interactions	-.75	-.47	.27	-.19	.33	Redundancy	4.86	4.83	.65	.43	.13
Percentage of variance extracted	12.17	36.65	9.43	15.97	11.37	Canonical correlation(ρ)	.43***	.34***	.23***	.19**	.12*
Redundancy	2.20	4.34	.50	.59	.17	ρ²	.18	.12	.05	.04	.02

*: $p < .05$ **: $p < .01$ ***: $p < .001$

As shown in Table 6, the analysis with perceived risk as the dependent variable and both involvement and familiarity as the independent variables also resulted in two pairs of canonical variates, with canonical correlations 0.28 and 0.18, respectively. Both were significant at the 0.05 significance level. The first pair of the canonical variate correlated low dependency involvement (canonical loading -0.86), low concern involvement (canonical loading -0.63), and less number of years using Internet (canonical loading -0.44) with high dimensions of perceived risk: time risk (canonical loading 0.85), functional risk (canonical loading 0.84), social risk (canonical loading 0.67), and financial risk (canonical loading 0.55). This result indicated that the people with lower levels of personal involvement with Internet banking services appeared to perceive higher levels of risk associated with the use of Internet banking services.

The items in the second canonical variate that had significant canonical loadings were concern involvement (0.51), number of years using Internet (0.47), weekly usage of Internet (0.59) and importance of Internet in daily life (0.40) on the one side, and social risk (-0.69), physical risk (-0.53), and financial risk (0.42) on the other side of the canonical equation. This relationship essentially suggested that the more familiar people were with Internet technology, the less they perceived the existence of social risk and physical risk. Frequent users of Internet technology, however, tended to perceive greater financial risk associated with usage of Internet banking services. These results rejected the third hypothesis, H3: perceived risk is not significantly correlated with personal involvement in Internet banking and familiarity with Internet technology.

Since perception of risk-reduction measures reflected respondents' opinion of how risks may be reduced and perceived risk measured their perception of the existence of possible risks associated with usage of Internet banking services, it is logical to assume the existence of significant correlation between these two variables. The results of canonical correlation analysis between these two sets of variables were summarized in Table 7. Five pairs of significant canonical variates were extracted. The first pair suggested that those who relied more on social interactions for evaluation of Internet banking were also more in agreement on existence of social risk. The other pairs of variates indicated that those who agreed on reduction of functional risk tended to perceive the existence of functional risk, financial risk, and time risk (second pair), those who understood the significance of risk-reduction measures for physical risk appeared to be more in agreement on the existence of physical risk (third pair), those who did not have much knowledge about how to reduce financial risk did not perceive existence of financial risk (fourth pair), and those who knew more about measures for reducing non-financial risks did significantly perceive the existence of time risk but appeared to pay less attention to physical risk (fifth pair). The canonical correlations of the first three pairs passed the level of significance 0.001. The fourth pair passed the level of significance 0.01. And the fifth passed the level of significance 0.05. Based on these results, the fourth hypothesis (H4), no significant relationship exists between perceived risk and perception of risk-reduction measures associated with usage of Internet banking services, was rejected.

Testing of Hypothesis H5: Multiple Regression Analysis

Multiple regression analysis was employed to evaluate the impact of all independent variables on customers' willingness to adopt Internet banking services. Five variables were found to have regression coefficients passing the level of significance 0.05 or smaller. The standardized regression equation is expressed as follows:

Adoption = 0.385 * Dependency involvement
 + 0.226 * Concern involvement
 + 0.178 * Reduction of non-financial risk
 + 0.175 * Social interaction
 - 0.171 * Functional risk

The percentage of explained variance (R^2) was 48 percent. The result of analysis of variance confirmed the appropriateness of the regression model (F = 97.93, p < 0.001).

The results of data analysis provided evidence to reject all five of the hypotheses formulated by this study. Stated in the alternative form, significant correlation relationships appeared to exist between familiarity with Internet technology, personal involvement with Internet banking services, risks perceived to exist in Internet banking, and measures perceived to be effective in dealing with these risks. In addition, these factors collectively affected user willingness to adopt Internet banking services. The results of hypothesis testing are summarized as follows:

H1: Personal involvement in Internet banking is not significantly correlated with familiarity with Internet technology. (Rejected)

H2: Perception of risk-reduction measures is not significantly correlated with personal involvement in Internet banking and familiarity with Internet technology. (Rejected)

H3: Perceived risk is not significantly correlated with personal involvement in Internet banking and familiarity with Internet technology. (Rejected)

H4: No significant relationship exists between perceived risk and perception of risk-reduction measures associated with usage of Internet banking services. (Rejected)

H5: Adoption of Internet banking services is not significantly influenced by perceived risk, perception of risk-reduction measures, personal involvement in Internet banking, and familiarity with Internet technology. (Rejected)

Discussion and Conclusion

As reported in Scruggs and Nam (2002), much potential of Internet banking has yet to be tapped even in such progressive markets as the U.S., Japan, and Europe due to a variety of non-technological factors. The banks in Taiwan, like their counterparts in the areas where

Internet usage is as pervasive or even more so, are looking to Internet technology as a strategic vehicle for strategic transformation of their core businesses. The progress has been less than satisfactory, however, despite aggressive promotional efforts undertaken by the banks over the years. A major obstacle has appeared to be customers' perception of risk associated with transacting over the Internet. An in-depth understanding of risk-related issues would require a systematic review of perceived risk and risk-reduction activities from both banks' and customers' perspectives in a particular legal and cultural context.

We conducted an empirical study to examine how customers' familiarity with Internet technology, personal involvement in the Internet banking services, perception of risk associated with the use of Internet banking, and perception of risk-reduction measures correlated with each other, using canonical correlation analysis. We evaluated the impact of these aforementioned variables on customers' willingness to adopt Internet banking services using multiple regression analysis. We also conducted a structural modeling analysis to test a causal model to shed more light on the impacting factors of adoption willingness. Our results showed that more experienced Internet technology users were more likely to involve themselves than their less experienced counterparts in Internet banking services. Both perceived risk and perception of risk-reduction measures were affected by familiarity with Internet technology and personal involvement in Internet banking services. Customers' perception of effectiveness of risk-reduction measures taken by both banks and customers was found to be significantly correlated with their perceived risks. Adoption willingness was directly affected by perception of risk-reduction measures, perceived risks, and both levels of personal involvement (concern involvement and dependency involvement), and indirectly affected by an important measure of Internet familiarity (importance of Internet in daily life). This was witnessed from its significant correlation with both levels of involvement and the fact that both levels of involvement in turn were significant contributors to adoption willingness. It is also worth noting that dependency involvement not only directly impacted adoption willingness but also contributed its impact indirectly through perceived risk. Similarly, concern involvement exhibited a direct impact on adoption willingness and an indirect impact through perceived risk and perception of risk-reduction measures. Comparatively, adoption willingness was impacted more by dependency involvement than concern involvement and more by perception of risk-reduction measures than perceived risk.

When contrasted with existing research in Internet banking, our research provided its contribution in the following four ways. First, the positive correlation between familiarity and involvement confirmed Chou's (1997) and Lin's (2000) studies as applied to the context of Internet banking. Second, whereas Chou's study (1997) treated involvement as a single-dimensional construct and classified it into three discrete levels (high, medium, and low), our research identified two distinct sub-constructs for involvement. The two involvement sub-constructs were positively correlated with each other and were both found to contribute to adoption willingness in different ways. Third, we provided a closer examination of the role of risk, both from the perceived risk and from the risk-reduction measures' points of view rather than treating it as a single construct. A closer look at risk enabled a more in-depth analysis of its impact on customers' behavior, such as adoption of Internet banking services. Fourth, by using both multiple regression analysis and structural analysis to examine the impact of risk-related factors on adoption willingness, our study revealed the consumer behavioral aspect of Internet banking adoption from two levels of abstraction: whereas the multiple regression analysis identified the sub-constructs as impacting factors, the structural analysis established the causal model at a higher (or construct) level. Examining impacting factors of technology adoption at multiple abstraction levels enabled interpretations that complement each other.

Three implications can be derived for functional managers and information system professionals. First, as customers' satisfactory experience in using Internet banking increases, so does their level of involvement with and dependency on the convenient services. The high level of involvement generally leads to reduced perception of risks and increased willingness of adoption. Banks must properly allocate resources to ensure delivery of satisfactory services on a continual basis in order to enhance customer loyalty. Second, customers' perception of the effectiveness of risk-reduction measures positively affects both perceived risk and adoption willingness. The importance of perception of risk-reduction measures for both perceived risk and adoption willingness suggests the business value of customer communications and education. As Internet users learn more about risk-reduction measures, they are more likely to become and remain real customers. Third, involvement, risk and risk-reduction measures are all multidimensional issues and are correlated with each other in nature. A comprehensive program, managerial as well as technological, must be implemented to identify major factors and cater to the intricate nature of the interactions between these relevant variables in a systematic manner. Provision of quality information, decision support knowledge, a responsive inquiry mechanism, and friendly user interface, for example, can provide attractive value-added services and, thereby, encourage wider and deeper adoption of Internet banking services.

Limitations and Future Research

The limitation of this study is twofold. First of all the research data may be biased since it was gathered from Web site links and bulletin boards. Secondly the validity of the research data may be limited by the casualness of some people filling out the questionnaire. Readers are cautioned when assessing the generalization of this study's findings.

Three directions are suggested for future research in Internet banking. In light of the importance of operational knowledge about risk control, Internet banking service providers should provide a Web-based user interface that facilitates user learning. A friendly user interface in this regard must balance between information complexity and ease of navigation. An interface design that utilizes a novel interactive animation may encourage deeper exploration without the perception of being overwhelmed with information. Another research direction involves viewing risk perception as a component of trust management. As an essential element of Internet-enabled business models, trust encompasses a variety of managerial and technological issues. A systematic understanding of risk perception in the broader context of trust management will establish a clearer link with overall business strategy. Thirdly replicating the study in areas other than Taiwan would provide a more solid basis to generalize the findings reported in this paper. Consumers' cognitive activities are constrained by the cultural environment. A cross-cultural examination of the research data gathered from different societies would provide insights into the impact of cultural difference on the findings reported in this chapter.

References

Arndt, J. (1967). Perceived risk, sociometric integration, and word of mouth in the adoption of new food product. In D.F. Cox (Ed.), *Risk taking and information handling in consumer behavior* (pp. 289-316). Boston: Harvard University Press.

Balabanis, G., & Reynolds, N. L. (2001). Consumer attitudes towards multi-channel retailers' web sites: The role of involvement, brand attitude, Internet knowledge and visit duration. *Journal of Business Strategies, 18*(2), 105-131.

Bauer, R. A. (1964). Consumer behavior as risk taking. In *Proceedings of Dynamic Marketing for a Changing World, American Marketing Association* (pp. 389-398).

Bettman, J.R. (1973). Perceived risk and its components: A model and empirical test. *Journal of Marketing Research, 10*(2) 184-190.

Butler, P., & Peppard, J. (1998) Consumer purchasing on the internet: Processes and prospects. *European Management Journal 16*(5), 600-610.

Campbell, M. C., & Keller, K. L. (2003). Brand familiarity and advertising repetition effects. *Journal of Consumer Research 30*(2), 292-304.

Celsi, R., & Olson, J. C. (1988). The role of involvement in attention and comprehension process. *Journal of Consumer Research, 15*(2), 210-224.

Chou, J. H. (1997). *Effects of security on Internet banking customers' perceived risk and willingness of adoption.* Unpublished master's thesis, National Taiwan University.

Cox, D. F. (1967). Risk handling in consumer behavior-an intensive study of two cases. In D. F. Cox (Ed.), *Risk taking and information handling in consumer behavior* (pp. 34-81). Boston: Harvard University Press.

Cunningham, S. M. (1967). The major dimension of perceived risk. In Donald F. Cox (Ed.), *Risk taking and information handling in consumer behavior* (pp. 82-108). Boston: Harvard University Press.

Derbaix, C. (1983). Perceived risk and relievers: An empirical investigation. *Journal of Economic Psychology, 4*(1) 19-38.

Dowling, G. R. & Staelin, R. (1994). A model of perceived risk and intended risk-handling activity. *Journal of Consumer Research, 21*, 119-134.

Hirsch, R. D., Dornoff, R. S., & Kernan, J. B. (1972). Perceived risk and store selection. *Journal of Marketing Research, 9*, 434-439.

Ho, S. S. M., & Ng, V. T. F. (1994). Customers' risk perceptions of electronic payment systems. *The International Journal of Bank Marketing, 12*(8), 26-38.

Jacoby, J., & Kaplan, L. (1972). The components of perceived risk. In *Proceedings of 3rd Annual Conference, Association for Consumer Research* (pp. 382-393).

Jih, W. J. K. (2002). Effects of electronic commerce implementations in Taiwan. *Journal of Computer Information Systems, 42*(3), 68-76.

Jih, W. J. (2003). Simulating real world experience using accumulative system development projects. *Journal of Information Systems Education, 14*(2), 181-192.

Jih, W. J., & Lee, S. F. (2004). Exploring relationships between motivating factors and life styles of cellular phone users. *Journal of Computer Information Systems, 54*(2), 65-73.

Knight, F. (1921). *Risk, uncertainty and profit*. New York: Harper & Row.

Krugman, H. E. (1965). *The impact of television advertising: Learning without involvement. Public Opinion Quarterly, 29,* 49-356.

Laczniak, R. N., Muehling, D. D., & Grossbart, S. (1989). Manipulating message involvement in advertising research. *Journal of Advertising, 18,* 28-38.

Lin, J. I. (2000). *Effects of risk-reduction strategies on Internet shopping: A controlled experiment*. Unpublished master's thesis. National Central University, Taiwan.

Maheswaren, D., & Meyers-Levy, J. (1990). The influence of message framing and involvement. *Journal of Marketing Research, 27,* 361-367.

Mitchell, V. W. (1992). Understanding consumer's behavior: Can perceived risk theory help. *Management Decision, 30,* 26-31.

Nielsen, J. F. (2002). Internet technology and customer linking in Nordic banking, Internal *Journal of Service Banking, 13*(2), 475-496.

Nunnally, J. C. (1978). *Psychometric theory* (2nd ed.). McGraw-Hill.

Polatoglu, V. N., & Ekin, S. (2001). An empirical investigation of the Turkish consumers' acceptance of Internet banking service. *The International Journal of Bank Marketing, 2001, 19*(4/5), 156-166.

Porter, M. E.(2001). Strategy and the Internet. *Harvard Business Review, 79*(3), 63-78.

Pyun, C.S., Scruggs, L., & Nam, K. (2002). Internet Banking in the U.S., Japan, and Europe. *Multinational Business Review, 10*(2), 73-81.

Rao, S., & Farley, J. U. (1987). Effects of environmental perceptions and cognitive complexity on search and information processing. *Psychology and Marketing, 4*(4), 287-302.

Roselius, T. (1967). Consumer rankings of risk-reduction methods. *Journal of Marketing, 35,* 56-61.

Sathye, M. (1999). Adoption of Internet banking by Australian consumers: An empirical investigation. *The International Journal of Bank Marketing, 17*(7), 324-339.

Sheth, J. N., & Venkatesan, M. (1968). Risk-reduction processes in repetitive consumer behavior. *Journal of Marketing Research, 5,* 307-310.

Srinavasan, N., & Ratchford, B.T. (1991). An empirical test of a model of extended search for automobiles. *Journal of Consumer Research, 18,* 233-242.

Stone, R. N., & Gronhaung, K. (1993). Perceived risk: Further considerations for the marketing discipline. *European Journal of Marketing, 38,* 54-60.

Taylor, J. W. (1974). The role of risk in consumer behavior. *Journal of Marketing, 38,* 54-60.

Terence, A. S., & William, O. B. (1982). Warranty and other extrinsic cue effects on consumers' risk perceptions. *Journal of Consumer Research, 10,* 38-46.

White, H., & Nteli, F. (2004). Internet banking in the UK: Why are there not more customers? *Journal of Financial Services Marketing, 9*(1), 49-56.

Zaichkowsky, I. J. (1985). Measuring the involvement construct. *Journal of Consumer Research, 17*, 341-352.

Zaichkowsky, I. J. (1986). Conceptualizing involvement. *Journal of Advertising Research, 15*, 4-14.

Section III

E-Business Process Modeling and Practices

Chapter VII

A Simonian Approach to E-Business Research:
A Study in Netchising

Ye-Sho Chen, Louisiana State University, USA

Guoqing Chen, Tsinghua University, China

Soushan Wu, Chang-Gung University, Taiwan

Abstract

The third industrial revolution, combining Internet technology with globalization, produces an increasingly complicated e-business environment. It is no wonder that skew distributions, a striking empirical regularity in the hypercompetitive digital economy, have attracted the attention of many researchers recently. Herbert Simon had studied similar regularities in the industrial economy and developed empirically grounded explanatory theories to help guide strategic decision making in the evolutionary processes of organizations in this area little-known to many. In this chapter, we draw upon five seemingly unrelated research areas of Simon (skew distributions, near decomposability, docility, causal and effectual reasoning, and attention management) and propose a holistic framework of attention-based information systems for firms to frame an enduring competitive strategy in the digital economy. As an ongoing project, the framework is applied to model Netchising, an emerging research topic in global e-business.

Introduction

The third industrial revolution, combining Internet technology with globalization, produces increasingly complicated e-business issues and opportunities. Tackling those new challenges requires multifarious skills, which are becoming inextricably interwoven. In his last public speech, Herbert Simon (2000, p. 751)—Nobel laureate in economics in 1978—pointed out that we have "very little experience" to deal with those challenges:

> *Current developments in electronics, notably the development of the World Wide Web and e-markets, and the enhanced abilities of organizations to manage geographically dispersed activities, provide new opportunities of unknown magnitude for coordination at a distance. Today, we have very little experience with these new developments, both in their current forms and their potential.*

As an attempt to tackle those complicated e-business issues and opportunities, Simon drafted four papers (2002a, 2002b, 2002c, 2002d) documenting his views of how modern organizations ought to do in the digital economy to survive and thrive. It turns out that the four drafts were the last "four unpublished manuscripts by Herbert A. Simon" (Dosi & Teece, 2002, p. 581). Examining the four papers closely, one may find that they were based on Simon's decades of research in the following four areas (with key papers/books referenced) of strategic decision making:

1.   Organizational evolution and near decomposability (Sarasvathy & Simon, 2000; Simon, 1962, 1995; Simon & Ando, 1961);

2.   Organizational identification, docility, and causal reasoning (Simon, 1953, 1991, 1992, 1993b, 1993c, 1997a, 1997b);

3.   Entrepreneurship and effectual reasoning (Sarasvathy & Simon, 2000); and

4.   Attention management and information systems (Simon, 1947, 1971, 1988, 1996, 1997c, 2002e).

Like many of Simon's pioneering research works, the four areas lay out as a groundbreaking source of inspiration for e-business researchers seeking to address the new challenges of issues and opportunities. There are rich treasures hidden in Simon's thought processes. Instead of reinventing the wheel, it makes much sense to draw upon Simon's research works and develop theories to advance our understanding of e-business economy. Specifically, we first review Simon's perspective on business research based on the first three areas above. Following it is the review of Simon's perspective on information systems research. Strategic implications of Simon's perspectives for e-business research are then discussed. Finally, we conclude the chapter with an ongoing Netchising project, which combines the power of the Inter*net* for global demand-and-supply processes and international fran*chising* arrangements for local responsiveness (Davenport, 2000). The intent is to illustrate how Simon's thought processes are useful for addressing issues and opportunities in an emerging global e-business research area.

The Simonian Approach to Business Research

Simon's view of business research was guided by the following empirically grounded process of scientific discovery (Simon, 1977a):

1.   Start with the analysis of empirical data, not theories;
2.   Make simple generations that approximately summaries striking features of the empirical data;
3.   Manipulate the influential variables to seek for limiting conditions that will improve the approximation;
4.   Conduct simple mechanisms to explain the simple generalizations;
5.   Propose explanatory theories that go beyond the simple generalizations and make experiments.

As an illustrative example of how the discovery process works, let us consider Simon's perspective on how businesses compete.

Skew Distributions in Business Competition

Start with the Analysis of Empirical Data, not Theories

What kinds of data can we get regarding business competition? An immediate answer may be market shares of the competitors. Consider Table 1. There is a growing trend of technology firms using franchising as the global growth strategy. For example, *Entrepreneur* magazine—well known for its Franchise 500 listing—in 2001 recognized the growth of these companies by giving them their own category with three areas: Internet businesses, tech training, and miscellaneous tech businesses. With that increasing demand, companies like Computertots/Computer Explorers are teaching home users (including children) to businesspeople how to get the most out of computers. For people who are already computer and Web savvy, companies like WSI Internet provide global Internet-based business applications and solutions, while franchises such as Computer Troubleshooters handle computer services and support. At the time of this writing, 38 companies (Table 1) are listed on its Web site (Entrepreneur.com, 2006).

Make simple generations that approximately summarize striking features of the empirical data.

In the rapidly changing global, digital economy, the cycle of winning and losing and asset redistribution intensifies as the speed of information exchange increases. As a result the sizes and performances of business firms increasingly resemble skew distributions. That is a few businesses, such as eBay and Amazon, dominate the market while a large number of smaller companies struggle to survive. This is true in the franchising industry, as can be evidenced from the constant up-and-down ranking of the Franchise 500 by Entrepreneur.

Table 1. Growth pattern of 38 technology franchises

Company	Founded	Franchising since	Number of franchisee and company-owned units in year							
			1999	2000	2001	2002	2003	2004	2005	2006
WSI Internet	1995	1996			695	925	1237	1674	2489 (49%)	
Cartridge World	1997	1997			98	176	346	564	941 (67%)	
Computer Troubleshooters	1997	1997				149	248	368	445 (21%)	445
Geeks On Call America	1999	2001				51	77	181	271 (50%)	303
New Horizons Computer Learning Centers Inc.	1982	1992			311	286	270	258	259 (0%)	
Wireless Zone	1988	1989			132	149	157	227	249 (10%)	
Island Ink-Jet Systems Inc.	1995	2000			37	92	206	206	234 (14%)	
InstantFX	2004	2004				0	0	0	157	
Expetec	1992	1996			44	64	40	134	156 (16%)	
CM IT Solutions	1994	1998			52	53	83	114	117 (3%)	
Computer Renaissance	1988	1993			119	84	94	94	101 (7%)	
Computertots/ Computer Explorers	1983	1988			96	100	82	94	101 (7%)	
Rescuecom	1997	1998			11	39	51	80	97 (21%)	
Wireless Toyz	1995	2001			13	17	27	36	86 (139%)	
Friendly Computers	1992	1999			4	12	27	57	70 (23%)	
CompuChild	1994	2001			16	52	43	49	56 (14%)	
Data Doctors	1988	2002			4	8	19	46	47 (2%)	
Concerto Networks Inc.	2002	2003					1	33	43 (30%)	
Computer Medics of America Inc.	2000	2003						18	35 (94%)	
Caboodle Cartridge	2003	2004					1	4	32 (700%)	

Table 1. continued

Rapid Refill Ink	2002	2004					27	31 (15%)
Soft-Temps Worldwide	1999	2002				15	26	29 (12%)
Fast-teks On-site Computer Services	2003	2004				1	1	21 (2000%)
Team Logic IT	2004	2005						8
PC Kidz	2001	2005		1	2	4	5	6 (20%)
Cartridge Depot	2004	2004					1	4 (300%)
Audio/Video Handyman	2003	2005				1	1	3 (200%)
Weboffice	2004	2005					0	2
Debugit Computer Services	2000	2005						1
Wireless Dimensions	2002	2002			145	139	139	
Netspace	1996	2000	10	33	45	85	45	
Computer Builders Warehouse	1990	1999	7	9	10	14	15	
Discount Imaging Franchise Corp.	1995	1998		6	7	10	11	
Nextwave Computers	1999	2003				1	9	
Screenz Computing Centers	1996	2004	2	2	2	3	3	
Support On-Site Computer Services	1997	1998	2	2	3			
Fourth R								
Quick Internet								
							Total units in 2005	6091

Data obtained from Entrepreneur.com in January 2006 (the numbers in the parentheses in the 2005 column are the percentages of growth of units from 2004 to 2005) com. Using the 2005 data shown in Table 1, Figure 1 indicates that the first seven companies alone (WSI Internet, Cartridge World, Computer Troubleshooters, Geeks On Call America, New Horizons Computer Learning Centers, Wireless Zone, and Island Ink-Jet Systems Inc.), or about 24% of franchise companies in 2005, produce roughly 80% of franchise units in the industry. This is a highly skew phenomenon. The most outstanding one is a full-service Internet consultancy franchise, WSI Internet. Despite the recent dot-com bust, WSI Internet—founded in 1995 and starting franchising in 1996—has 2,489 franchise units in more than 87 countries on six continents. As such, it is often called the "#1 Internet Franchise."

Manipulate the Influential Variables to Seek for Limiting Conditions that will Improve the Approximation

Examining the data in Table 1 closely, one may find that there are at least two influential variables driving the data of franchise units, the growth rate of *existing* firms, and the entry rate of *new* firms. Taking the 2004 and 2005 data as an example, the numbers in the parentheses in the 2005 column are the percentages of growth of units from 2004 to 2005. As we can see, in general, most of companies have high growth rates. Evidently high growth rates of exiting firms over several years will trigger high entry rates of new firms. Table 1 shows that five new technology franchise firms (Concerto Networks, Caboodle Cartridge, Fast-teks On-site Computer Services, Audio/Video Handyman, and Nextwave Computers) enter into the industry in 2003, one new firm (Cartridge Depot) in 2004, and two new firms (Weboffice and Debugit Computer Services) in 2005.

Figure 1. Cumulative distribution of technology businesses using franchising as the growth strategy in 2005

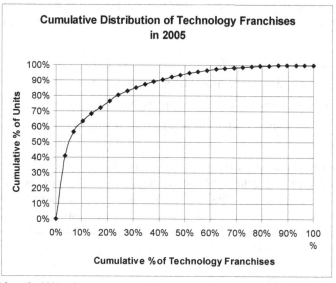

Data obtained from the 2005 column in Table 1

Conduct Simple Mechanisms to Explain the Simple Generalizations

In Simon's first theory of the skew distributions phenomenon (Simon & Bonini, 1958), it is stated that the firm grows based on the following assumptions of influential variables (the growth rate of *existing* firms and the entry rate of *new* firms), where f(n,k) is the number of different firms that have exactly the size of n at the time k:

1.   Gibrat's Law (1931) of Growth of Existing Firms: the probability that the growth opportunity at the (k+1)-st time is taken up by a firm that has the size of n is proportional to $n \times$ f(n,t), that is, to the total number of sizes of all the firms that have exactly the size of n;

2.   Entry of New Firms: there is a constant probability, α, that at the (k+1)-st time the growth opportunity is taken up by a new firm; that is, a firm that has not occurred in the first k time periods.

Based on the two assumptions, it can be proven (Simon, 1955) that f(n) = ρB(n,ρ+1), n = 1,2,3,...., where $\rho > 0$ and f(n) is the frequency of firms with size of n; B(n,ρ+1) is the beta function with parameters n and ρ+1. The distribution explains fairly well most of the skew distributions phenomenon.

Propose Explanatory Theories that go beyond the Simple Generalizations and Make Experiments

Further empirically grounded refinements of the simple mechanism above were collected in a monograph by Ijiri and Simon (1977). The monograph is composed of 11 papers of Simon and his colleagues published from 1955 to 1977. Four major explanatory theories in the monograph that go beyond the simple generations of data are shown below:

1.   Decreasing entry rate of new firms (Simon & Van Wormer, 1963)

2.   Autocorrelated growth of the firm (Ijiri & Simon, 1964)

3.   Growth of the industry and competition in the industry (Ijiri & Simon, 1967)

4.   Mergers and acquisitions in the industry (Ijiri & Simon, 1971, 1974)

A very important aspect of Simon's scientific discovery process is that a good theory shall be able to be replicated and tested through experiments so that it will have meaningful implications for practitioners. In terms of business competition, the explanatory theories enlisted above shall have practical implications for strategic policy decision-making. In addition the implications can be tested experimentally through, for example, computers, before they are executed. In the next three sections we show how Simon related the third theory above (Ijiri & Simon, 1967) to business competition and how computational experimentations can be developed to test the theory.

Organizational Evolution and near Decomposability

The explanatory model proposed by Ijiri and Simon in 1967 decomposed the growth rates of firms into an industry-wide factor and a factor peculiar to an individual firm. The model assumptions were empirically supported by the growth rates of large U.S. firms from 1958 to 1962. An interesting phenomenon of the data was observed (Ijiri & Simon, 1967, pp. 354-355):

> ... a firm that doubled its share of market ... in the first 4 years could be expected, on the average, to increase its share of market by about 28 percent in the second 4-year period. ... Rapidly growing firms 'regress' relatively rapidly to the average growth rate of the economy.

This rapid regression is especially true in today's global economy. For example in the franchising industry one can see the constant up-and-down ranking of franchise businesses from the industry benchmarking sources such as the annual report of Franchise 500 by Entrepreneur.com. Simon's (1993a) explanation of the "regress" phenomenon is based on the evolutionary theory of organizations (Nelson, 1991; Nelson & Winter, 1982).

In the evolutionary processes of natural selection, organizations need to design an enduring architecture of near decomposability capable of adapting to the changing environment and gaining fitness in the evolution (Simon, 1962, 1995, 1996, 2002a; Simon & Ando, 1961). A nearly decomposable system consists of a set of interconnected subsystems with the following properties (Simon, 1996):

1. the interactions within any subsystem are strong and rapid; on the other hand;

2. the interactions among the subsystems are weak and slow, but not negligible;

3. the short-term behavior of each subsystem is approximately independent of the short-term behavior of the other subsystems; and

4. the long-term behavior of each subsystem depends in only an aggregate way on the behavior of the other subsystems.

In order to design a nearly decomposable organization, one needs to shift the evolutionary view from market activities outside of the firms to human activities inside the firms, that is, from a market economy to an organizational economy (Simon, 1991, 2000). The following abstract of Simon's strategic management paper (1993a, p.131) summarizes nicely how a firm shall do in an organizational economy:

> A business firm's 'niche' or comparative advantage typically has a half-life of years rather than decades. Strategic planning must assure a stream of new ideas that allow the firm to find new sources of comparative advantage. Strategic planning must focus attention on the initial stages of the decision-making processes—opportunities and occasions for choice, and the design of new action

*strategies for products, marketing, and financing. Product identification and
alternative generation are crucial components of strategy. Strategic thinking
must permeate the entire organization. Effective identification of employees
with the organization's strategy requires their exposure to the basic postulates
that underlie strategic plans.*

After a detailed study of the abstract and the content of the paper, Augier and Sarasvathy
(2004) identify three key thought processes of Simon on how to design a nearly decomposable organization: biological evolution, cognition, and design. The first two processes are
briefly reviewed in the next two subsections, and the design process is reviewed in the next
section on information systems

Biological Evolution, Organizational Identification, Docility, and Causal Reasoning

Human decision-making behaviors in biological evolution have played a major role in Simon's
decades of prolific research publication. A most well-known example is his Nobel-winning
contributions on bounded rationality and satisficing (Simon, 1982, 1997c). In the area of
organizational economy, we may find the evolutionary trait of human decision-making
behaviors in what Simon called organizational identification or organizational loyalty.

Organizational identification, according to Simon, is:

*... a powerful altruistic force conditioning both participants' goals and the
cognitive models they form of their situations.*

(1993b, p. 160)

On the subject of altruism, Simon wrote:

*... human beings are capable only of very approximate and bounded rational-
ity. Because of bounded rationality, docility contributes to the fitness of human
beings in evolutionary competition. By 'docility' I mean the tendency to depend
on suggestions, recommendations, persuasion, and information obtained through
social channels as a major basis of choice.*

(1993b, p. 156)

Furthermore,

*... people exhibit a very large measure of docility. ... because of docility, social
evolution often induces altruistic behavior in individuals that has net advantage*

for average fitness in the society. Altruism includes influencing others to behave altruistically.

(1993b, p. 157)

Augier and Sarasvathy (2004) argue that docility, altruism, and organizational identification are the drivers behind Simon's strategic thinking in the abstract above: identification of opportunities, generation of alternatives, and design of new action strategies.

Following the principles of scientific discovery (Simon, 1977a) described earlier, Simon spent several decades formalizing the influencing processes of altruism and organizational identification. The study can be traced back to his early work of causal ordering in the 1950s (Simon, 1953), which seeks to:

... explore questions of causality ... predict the effects of manipulating exogenous policy instruments after (known) alterations have occurred in the mechanisms of the system under study.

(Simon, 1997c, p. 3)

This causal reasoning study of cause-effect relationships of influencing reached its peak in the 1990s, when Simon and his doctoral student Yumi Iwasaki (Iwasaki & Simon, 1994) linked causal reasoning with near-decomposability by:

... showing how the presence of near-decomposability permits the links within single system components to be represented statically in the causal analysis, while the between-component links are represented dynamically.

(Simon, 1997c, p. 5)

Cognition, Entrepreneurship, and Effectual Reasoning

In addition to organizational identification, another aspect of human behaviors in biological evolution Simon believed to be important is individual cognition and its ability to shape the social and cultural norms. As is shown in the last sentence of the quoted abstract above, those selected individuals with the exposure to the strategic plans of the firms might challenge the basic assumptions underlying the strategy. As such, a new stream of ideas producing new sources of comparative advantage may be realized.

In the study of entrepreneurship, Simon and his colleagues (Sarasvathy & Simon, 2000) developed the theory of effectuation, the reasoning processes entrepreneurs use to shape the uncertain future by creating and growing enduring firms. Contrary to the causal reasoning most of us are accustomed to (i.e., having *effects* as given and focusing on selecting *means* to achieve those effects), entrepreneurs deploy effectual reasoning by utilizing the *means* available to them and selecting between possible *effects* that can be created with the available means (Sarasvathy, 2001).

Taking the advice of Simon to link effectual reasoning to near decomposability, Sarasvathy, a former doctoral student of Simon, found that effectual reasoning processes:

> *... seek to expand the choice set from a narrow sliver of highly localized possibilities to increasingly complex and enduring opportunities fabricated in a contingent fashion over time.*
>
> (Sarasvathy, 2003, p. 208)

Effectuation processes create near-decomposable systems by exploiting *locality* and *contingency* in the design (Sarasvathy, 2003). There are three basic principles in the effectual reasoning processes (Sarasvathy, 2003): (1) affordable loss rather than expected returns; (2) business partnership rather than engaging competition; and (3) contingencies leveraging rather than avoiding them.

The Simonian Approach to Information Systems Research

Simon's research on information systems can be classified into two categories: (1) public policies relating to computers and electronic communications (Simon, 1977b, 2000); and (2) effects of the computer and the new information technology on organizations and management (Simon, 1971, 1988, 1997c, 2002d). In this section, we review what Simon believed to be the major issue that information systems researchers need to focus on, that is, attention management. In the information-rich world, Simon wrote a famous quote:

> *... a wealth of information creates a poverty of attention.*
>
> (Simon, 1971, p. 173)

The scarcity of attention is due to (1) the major constraint of 24 hours per day we have, during which all of the day's work has to be done; and (2) the seriality of the human mind in processing the information (Simon, 2002d). Simon's information systems solution to attention management goes hand in hand with his business research perspective .

Near Decomposability, Communication, and Silence

As was indicated earlier, near decomposability is an organizational design goal, since it provides an enduring architecture in the evolutionary environment. A nearly decomposable system consists of a set of interconnected subsystems with a high density of interactions among the elements within a subsystem and a low density of interactions between the subsystems (Simon, 1996). Thus, information systems supporting a nearly decomposable organization shall encompass a theory of highly communicative talk within subsystems and a theory of nearly isolative silence between subsystems (Simon, 2002d).

Attention Conservation and Causal Reasoning

Our next design goal is to have an information system that can:

> *... perform an attention-conserving function in two ways: (1) it can receive and store information that would otherwise have to be received by other systems, and (2) it can transform or filter input information into output that demands fewer hours of attention than the input.*

> (Simon, 1971, p. 176)

One major challenge of the design is that much of the information useful to the decision makers (such as customers, competitors, the industry, and trends in the national and global economy) originates from outside of the company instead of inside (Simon, 1988). Causal reasoning techniques such as online analytical processing, data mining (Simon, 2002d), and text mining are helpful for achieving the attention-conserving design goal.

Organizational Identification, Docility, and Knowledge Management

Although modern causal reasoning techniques with the aid of computational power are helpful for identifying and formalizing routine procedures in an organization, there is a limit to those techniques in the process of pursuing an intelligent organization (March, 1999). In their well-known book *The Social Life of Information*, Brown and Duguid (2002) argue that it is a human (not technology) question that improves organizational intelligence. In the words of Simon, the details of the human question lie in docility, altruism, and organizational identification. Thus, the third design goal is to have an information system that helps create and share the working knowledge residing in the docile channels of the social networks within and without the organization.

Contingencies Leveraging and Effectual Reasoning

In today's market-driven and global economy, change is a constant. During the course of social exchanges in social networks, changes (often coming in the form of contingencies) can be detected. The idea of effectual reasoning is to leverage the contingencies by creating timely products or services through strategic partnership and cost reduction. See Wang (2001a, 2001b) for examples of how he used effectual reasoning to develop Formosa Plastics Group, a Taiwan-based multinational conglomerate). Thus, the fourth information system design goal is to empower members in the organization to perform effectual reasoning of the changes in the context of the business environment.

Value Creation and Innovation

With the above-mentioned four kinds of information systems (nearly decomposable networked organizations, causal reasoning, knowledge management, and effectual reasoning) laid out as the foundation, the empowered workers along with Simon's docility and altruism of organizational identification can concentrate on creating innovation through value-added products or services to shape the future (Simon, 2002c). The last design goal is to have an information system that helps the workers generate, evaluate, and implement value-added solutions.

Gates' Digital Nervous System: An Attention-Based Information System Design

We now integrate the five components discussed above with respect to Gates' digital nervous system (DNS) (Gates, 1999, pp. xvii-xviii). A DNS, consisting of three components (empowerment and collaboration, business intelligence and knowledge management, and timely high business value creation and implementation), is:

> ... the corporate, digital equivalent of the human nervous system, providing a well-integrated flow of information to the right part of the organization at the right time." Further a DNS "consists of the digital processes that enable a company to perceive and react to its environment, to sense competitor challenges and customer needs, and to organize timely responses," and it "requires a combination of hardware and software; it's distinguished from a mere network of computers by the accuracy, immediacy, and richness of the information it brings to knowledge workers and the insight and collaboration made possible by the information.

(Gates, 1999, pp. xvii-xviii)

Comparing closely Gates' definition of DNS and Simon's view of attention management (Simon, 1971, 1988, 2002d), we may conclude that an attention-based information system is simply one that is able to detect changes in the business environment and respond timely to the changes to produce profitable results. Figure 2 shows such an attention-based information system with six phases:

1. Managing the content of the networked organization with workers empowered by information technologies to do collaborative activities. Two issues need to be addressed here: First, is the organization nearly decomposable so that it will endure in the

Figure 2. An attention-based information system design framework

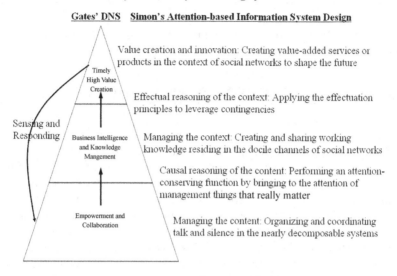

Gates' DNS   Simon's Attention-based Information System Design

Value creation and innovation: Creating value-added services or products in the context of social networks to shape the future

Timely High Value Creation

Effectual reasoning of the context: Applying the effectuation principles to leverage contingencies

Sensing and Responding

Business Intelligence and Knowledge Mangement

Managing the context: Creating and sharing working knowledge residing in the docile channels of social networks

Causal reasoning of the content: Performing an attention-conserving function by bringing to the attention of management things that really matter

Empowerment and Collaboration

Managing the content: Organizing and coordinating talk and silence in the nearly decomposable systems

competitive, evolutionary environment? Second, how to manage the communication channels of the organization for effective coordinative talk and silence?

2.   Causal reasoning of the content of the networked, nearly-decomposable organization by performing an attention-conserving function to bring to the attention of management to things really matter.

3.   Managing the context of the organization by creating and sharing working knowledge residing in docile social channels of the networked organization. This corresponds to Gates' business intelligence and knowledge management component of DNS building, which focuses on linking existing operations in the environmental context of business into knowledge management systems.

4.   Effectual reasoning of the context of the organization by applying the effectuation principles to leverage contingencies occurring in the business environment.

5.   Value creation and innovation by creating value-added services or products in the social networks context of the organization to shape the future. This corresponds to Gates' high business value creation and implementation component, which focuses on selecting timely projects with greatest rewards.

6.   Sensing and responding by incorporating the created value into the operational, transactional environment to empower the knowledge workers to do collaborative activities.

Implications for E-Business Research

The attention-based information system framework proposed in Figure 2 creates many e-business research opportunities, which are discussed in this section.

Managing the Content of Networked Organizations

In the recent literature of networked organizations, there are abundant publications on the observations of striking empirical regularities (Barabasi, 2003; Buchanan, 2002; Dorogovtsev & Mendes, 2003; Watts, 2003). For example, complex and interconnected social networks exhibit hubs and connectors (Barabasi, 2003). That is, few hubs have many nodes connected and, on the other hand, many hubs have few connectors. This skew distributions empirical phenomena has indeed excited the research community in networked organizations. Various models have been proposed, such as the scale-free power law (Barabasi & Bonabeau, 2003) to explain this "new" striking empirical behavior in the complex (social or Internet) networks. Ijiri and Simon's 1977 monograph can provide us insights and foresights on how to tackle these new research opportunities in the networked, digital economy (see Okoli, Chen, & Chong, 2002; Chen, Chong, & Chen, 2001, for some recent examples).

Following the research process trace of Simon on skew distributions, an important e-business research topic is how to design a nearly decomposable networked organization. After all, the skew distributions are just the properties of the evolutionary system. A special class of networked organizations, franchising, is gaining people's attention in the global and digital economy. A franchising organization is nearly decomposable since it has a franchisor headquarters integrating and coordinating with a set of interconnected franchisee subsystems satisfying with the following properties of near decomposability:

1.   the interactions within any franchisee subsystem are strong and rapid;
2.   the interactions (either through face-to-face or Intranet) among the franchisee subsystems are weak and slow, but not negligible;
3.   the short-term behavior of each franchisee subsystem is approximately independent of the short-term behavior of the other subsystems; and
4.   the long-term behavior of each franchisee subsystem depends in only an aggregate (perhaps through the policy making process at the headquarters) way on the behavior of the other franchisee subsystems.

The next important e-business research topic is how to coordinate talk and silence in the nearly-decomposable networked organization. One design strategy is based on the Customer Service Life Cycle (CSLC) model developed by Ives and his colleagues (Ives & Learmonth, 1984; Ives & Mason, 1990). The model can be developed to harness the Internet to serve the needs of customers (including workers and partners of the organization) at four major stages: requirements, acquisition, ownership, and renewal/retirement (Ives, 1999). For example, Chen, Chong, and Justis (2002) recently applied the CSLC approach to managing the franchisor/franchisee relationship in franchised organizations using the Internet.

Causal Reasoning of the Content of Networked Organizations

Lately causal ordering and related topics of causal reasoning have attracted much attention (Glymour & Cooper, 1999; Pearl 2001; Spirtes, Glymour, & Scheines, 2001). Recent development of computational theory of causality (such as TETRAD Project at Carnegie Mellon University) allows a firm to make causal predictions of various new e-business policy and action changes before they are actually implemented. Here are some examples of causal predictions:

1. What will a change in product prices do to the growth of the firm?
2. What will a deduction or increase of marketing promotion do to the total monthly sales?
3. What will a change in rewarding bonuses do to the renewal of the loyal customers?
4. What will a change in compensation packages do to the retention of the experienced employees?
5. What are the legal ramifications when the policies of hiring new employees are changed?

With the advancement of the Internet, computational experimentations can even be shifted to customers for new products or services innovation (Thomke, 2003).

Managing the Context of Networked Organizations

A major question in context management is how the organization can effectively create, share, learn, and manage its context knowledge of social networks in serving the customers and working with partners and suppliers. Since the context of the business environment is ever changing, having knowledgeable workers who can sense, interpret, and respond to the changes is indeed a must for any organization. An important e-business research area related to context management is communities of practice (Wenger, McDermott, & Snyder, 2002) in which knowledge management and communal learning are of major concern (see Wu, Yang, & Wu, 2004) for a recent example of SARS crisis management in a big general hospital in Taiwan). Technological tools supporting communal learning in the communities include social network analysis (Wasserman & Faust, 1994), context mapping, storytelling, mentoring, and after-action reviews tools (Allee, 2002).

Effectual Reasoning of the Context of Networked Organizations

Based on the Effection.org Web site, five areas e-business researchers can benefit from using effectual reasoning to leverage the contingences occurred in the context of the business:

1. Cognition, psychological aspects of human in designing new ways to achieve imagined ends utilizing given means;
2. Ethics, moral aspects in the process of effectual reasoning;
3. Entrepreneurial opportunities, demand-side artifacts as the driver for effectual reasoning;
4. Risk management, risk and its management in using effectual reasoning; and
5. Strategy, leadership issues of deploying effectual reasoning.

Value-Added Innovation of Networked Organizations

Allee (1999) proposes a whole-system view of value that can be served as the idea generator for new value-added products or services innovation. The view includes six dynamic and interdependencies value drivers: human competence, internal structures, business relationships, social citizenship, environmental health, and corporate identity. E-business researchers may expand, refine, and utilize the value drivers to help companies manage their social capital (Cohen & Prusak, 2001).

Sensing and Responding by Networked Organizations

Once the value-added innovation is created, it becomes part of the business rules of the enterprise that can be embedded in the transactional databases to empower the knowledge workers in the networked, operational environment (Chen, Gabriela, & Chong, 1992). This cycle of sensing and responding will continue as the networked organizations adapt to the changing environment.

Netchising: An Illustrative Example

Netchising Defined

Despite the abundance of literature in e-business deployment today, doing business on the Internet is still mostly a "domestic phenomenon" of the developed countries and not yet a global phenomenon (Davenport, 2000). As globalization is unavoidable, there is an urgent need to converge e-business development perspectives from developed to developing countries. International franchising (Justis & Judd, 2003) has been shown to be an effective strategy to transfer technology and emerging markets from developed into developing countries. Franchising is:

> *... a business opportunity by which the owner (producer or distributor) of a service or a trademarked product grants exclusive rights to an individual for the local distribution and/or sale of the service or product, and in return receives a payment or royalty and conformance to quality standards. The individual or business granting the business rights is called the franchisor, and the individual or business granted the right to operate in accordance with the chosen method to produce or sell the product or service is called the franchisee.*

(Justis & Judd, 2003)

Netchising, integrating the power of the Inter*net* for global integration and international fran*chising* for local socialization, is a global e-business growth strategy gaining its popularity. New technology companies (such as those shown in Table 1) understand the importance of Netchising as a global e-business growth strategy. Non-technology conventional companies can also benefit from using the Netchising strategy for global e-business growth. For example, Chen, Justis, and Yang (2004) used Eastman Kodak's Netchising strategy to show how a multinational company may conduct business in developing countries such as China successfully. In the following six subsections, we show how the attention-based information system can be developed for companies interested in using Netchising as a global growth model for e-business. Note that using the three-stage terms defined above, the first three subsections correspond to learning stage and the last three subsections correspond to innovation stage.

Managing the Content in Netchising

There are three major elements in the content of a franchised organization (Chen, Justis, and Chong, 2002; Chen, Zhang, & Justis, 2005a):

1. The activities of the franchisor at the headquarters and with business units, prospective franchisees, suppliers, and government.
2. The activities of the franchisee at his/her franchised outlet and with customers, franchisor headquarters, suppliers, and government.
3. The relationship development between the franchisor and the franchisees.

Using the CSLC model, a franchise system can Web empower (Chen, 2003; Chen, Chong, & Justis, 2002; Chen, Justis, & Wu, 2006b) the franchisor, the franchisees, and the associated parties to manage the talk and silence in doing their activities, developing relationship, and transforming the franchise system into an Edge company (Baker, 2001), that is, concentrating at least 80% of its resources on the touchpoints with its customers and suppliers. Application service providers specializing in certain industries in franchising can be adopted to make the learning process more efficient (Chen, Ford, Justis, & Chong, 2001; Yao, Wohl, Watson, & Chen, 2003).

Causal Reasoning of the Content in Netchising

Besides Web empowering the users for doing their content works, a well-designed CSLC-based Internet strategy shall also collect, use, renew, store, retrieve, transmit, and share the organizational data needed to do the collaborative work in different phases of the CSLC model. For example, business intelligence (Chen, Justis, & Watson, 2000) and data/text mining (Chen, Justis, & Chong, 2004; Chen et al., 2005b; Zhang, Chen, & Pawlowski, 2003) can be used to analyze the volume of data generated in the course of managing the content of the franchise system. In conjunction with the analytical results, recent development of computational causality (for example, the Causality Lab and TETRAD Project at Carnegie Mellon University) allows a firm to make causal predictions of various new business policy and action changes before they are actually implemented. Here are some examples of causal predictions:

1.   What will a change in initial fees do to the franchise development?

2.   What will a deduction or increase of royalty rates do to the total monthly sales?

3.   What will a change in rewarding bonuses do to the renewal of the professional franchisees?

4.   What will a change in compensation packages do to the retention of the experienced employees?

5.   What are the legal ramifications when the policies of recruiting prospective franchisees or hiring new employees are changed?

Managing the Context in Netchising

Lying behind the causal reasoning of the content are the working knowledge profiles of the franchise firm. Knowledge is defended as:

> ... *a justified personal belief that increases an individual's capacity to take effective action.*
>
> (Alavi & Leidner, 1999, p. 5)

Knowledge becomes "working" when the action produces results. When the knowledge is working, the personal belief becomes much more strengthened, intensified, and justified. As such, the individual's capacity is increased and better results are obtained. A working knowledge profile consists of the detailed cause-effect relationships of the personal belief. Typical examples of working knowledge profiles in franchise firms include "How To Find

A Good Location For Business" and "How To Recruit A Good Franchisee" (Chen, Hammerstein, & Justis, 2002).

Working knowledge is incrementally developed by the franchisor through five stages (Justis & Judd, 2003): (1) beginner, learning how to do the operations at the franchisee outlet; (2) novice, practicing how to do the operations at the franchisee outlet; (3) advanced, doing the operations at the franchisee outlet; (4) master, teaching others how to do the operations at the franchisee outlet; and (5) professional, becoming the best that you can be. This spiral-up cycle of working knowledge development of effectual and causal reasoning is very important in the context of franchising. At a higher stage of the franchise development, most of the problems in the previous stages have been dealt with. However, more complicated and challenging questions will arise as the franchise system continues the expansion. This is especially true when the franchise system reaches the stage of professional, when many unforeseen and difficult problems could happen all of sudden. Bud Hadfield (1995, p. 156), the founder of Kwik Kopy franchise and the International Center of Entrepreneurial Development, said it the best: "The more the company grows, the more it will be tested."

In order to understand how the franchisees learn in the franchise system, one needs to know the important concept of the franchisee life cycle (Schreuder, Krige, & Parker, 2000): (1) the courting phase, in which both the franchisee and the franchisor are excited with the relationship and will try very hard to maintain it; (2) the "we" phase, in which the relationship starts to deteriorate, but the franchisee still values the relationship; (3) the "me" phase, in which the franchisee starts to question the reasons for payment-related issues with the attitude that the success so far is purely of his/her own work; (4) the rebel phase, in which the franchisee starts to challenge the restrictions being placed upon; (5) the renewal phase, in which the franchisee realizes the "win-win" solution is to continue teaming up with the franchisor to grow the system. Similar to the franchisor, the working knowledge learning process of the franchisee is incrementally developed through the following five stages of the spiral-up cycle: (1) beginner in the courting phase; (2) novice in the "we"-phase; (3) advanced in the "me"-phase; (4) master in the rebel phase (since the rebel ones tend to be those who know the system well and are capable of influencing others to follow them); and (5) professional in the renewal phase.

The effectiveness of the franchisee learning cycle relies heavily on how the working knowledge is shared in the process of influencing others (Chen, Seidman, & Justis, 2005). In franchising, social influencing is closely studied as it is considered vital for building the good franchisor/franchisee "family" relationship (Justis & Judd, 2003). The process of influencing others consists of five steps (Justis & Vincent, 2001): (1) knowledge, proven abilities to solve business problems in the franchise environment; (2) attitude, positive and constructive ways of presenting and sharing the working knowledge; (3) motivation, providing incentives for learning or teaching the working knowledge; (4) individual behavior, understanding and leveraging the strengths of the participants to learn and enhance the working knowledge; and (5) group behavior, finding the best collaborative way to collect, dissimilate, and manage the hard-earned working knowledge. Thus, working knowledge is the base of the franchise "family" relationship. The franchisor/franchisee "family" relationship is enlarged and expanded as the franchisee incrementally learns the working knowledge through the influencing of the franchisor and the fellow franchisees.

Effectual Reasoning of the Context in Netchising

There is a three-stage process (Chen, Justis, & Yang, 2004) to create an enduring franchising firm: (1) startup stage, in which the franchisor as an entrepreneur creates a new business by effectuation processes; (2) learning stage, in which both the franchisor and the franchisees strive to learn and improve the causation processes between the available means and the targeted goal; and (3) innovation stage, in which both the franchisor and the franchisees work as professional entrepreneurs to create new business ventures by using effectuation processes. Working knowledge creation and sharing processes discussed above are to bring everyone in the franchise system to a high level understanding of the context so that effectual (and social) reasoning of the tangible and intangible social exchanges can be effectively conducted (Chen, Yuan, & Dai, 2004). As such, the three-stage process of creating an enduring franchise can be realized. This collaborative effectual reasoning process will become more productive with the aid of the institutionalization of the working knowledge repository of the franchise. A framework of the Internet strategy to support the three-stage effectual and causal reasoning processes of an enduring Netchising firm can be developed with two dimensions (Chen, Justis, & Yang, 2004).

The first dimension is the franchisee life cycle (Schreuder et al., 2000), consisting of (1) the courting phase; (2) the "we" phase; (3) the "me" phase; (4) the rebel phase; and (5) the renewal phase. The second dimension is the demand-and-supply value chain, consisting of customers, franchisee outlet, franchisor headquarters, suppliers and partners, and franchise community. The foundation of the framework is the causal and effectual reasoning processes of the franchise system. Various Internet technologies can be used to implement the framework. For example, (1) an intranet-based curriculum of working knowledge profiles can be designed for the users to effectively learn the causation processes at various parts of the demand-and-supply value chain; and (2) an artificial-intelligence-based knowledge management system connecting to various partners through extranet will empower the professional franchisees to work with the franchisor to continuously improve the business processes and create innovative opportunities for the system (Chen, Chong, & Justis, 2000).

Value-Added Innovation in Netchising

The continuous desire of effectual reasoning is the major driver enabling the franchise system to develop dynamic capabilities and value-creating strategies. One example of effectual reasoning is asset leveraging through the value networks of the franchise system (Chen et al., 2006a). The asset here is referring to the working knowledge profiles residing in the knowledge repository of the franchise system. Those profiles, continuously being improved, provide the foundation for the asset leveraging, especially when the franchisor or the franchisee has reached the professional stage. For example, consider value-added innovation of the following three working knowledge profiles:

1.   **Site profile.** Consider McDonald's real estate business Franchise Realty Corporation, a result of site selection asset leveraging. It's the real moneymaking engine at

McDonald's, as is evidenced from the 1974 speech of founder Ray Kroc at the University of Texas at Austin:

Ladies and gentlemen, I'm not in the hamburger business. My business is real estate.

(Kiyosaki, 2000, p. 85)

Ray Kroc commented further:

What converted McDonald's into a money machine had nothing to do with Ray Kroc or the McDonald brothers or even the popularity of McDonald's hamburgers, French fries, and milk shakes. Rather, McDonald's made its money on real estate ... .

(Love, 1995, p. 152)

McDonald's makes money out of real estate by leasing properties from landlords and then subleasing the stores to the franchisees who then focus on expanding the business without worrying about finding good locations for the growth. This moneymaking real estate strategy is what separates McDonald's from other fast-food chains (David, 2003).

2.   **Franchisee profile.** In the process of recruiting experienced and hard-working franchisees, Subway founder Fred DeLuca found a very unique and difficult problem facing the prospective franchisees, that is, getting a loan from banks to invest on Subway's franchise. DeLuca (2000) then set up the micro investment lending enterprise (MILE) program to lend money to those qualified people to start their own small businesses. The MILE program shows how a professional franchisor can leverage the franchisee profile by turning problems into opportunities.

3.   Event management profile. Take the International Center for Entrepreneurial Development (ICED) as an example. To find a location to house the training programs and related activities for the variety of franchises is a big challenge to ICED. ICED has developed its own training center and learned how to host large conference events for its franchisees over the years. As part of leveraging its assets, ICED created a very profitable new line of services through the Northwest Forest Conference Center, catering and housing training and meeting events for companies as well as weddings, receptions, banquets, and reunions for individuals.

Sensing and Responding in Netchising

Explicit knowledge of the new value creation can be coded into the franchise operational system. How-to tutorials can be loaded to the intranet-based knowledge repository for the franchise-wide access (Chen, Chong, & Justis, 2000). Implicit knowledge, on the other hand, typically resides in the heads of the participants and can't be easily captured and formalized. Digital coaching technologies can be used to harvest and disseminate the implicit working knowledge to the associates in the story-telling social environment (Chen et al., 2005). Adapting the franchise system to the changing business environment through continuous sensing and responding is vital to the success of the company. This is especially true when the franchise goes global to emerging markets such as China (Chen, Chen, & Justis, 2001; Chen, Chen, & Chen, 2002).

Conclusion

Strategic decision making, in the words of Herbert Simon, is:

> ... a chapter in the topic of decision making under uncertainty—in fact, massive and unending uncertainty.

> (1993a, p. 134)

In the rapidly changing digital economy, the cycle of winning and losing intensifies as the speed of information exchange increases. As a result, the sizes and performances of firms increasingly resemble skew distributions; that is, a few businesses, such as Amazon and eBay, dominate the market while a large number of smaller companies struggle to survive. The e-business research is indeed within the framework of decision making under "massive and unending uncertainty." It is thus more necessary than ever to find explanatory theories of e-business to describe, model, and predict the emerging issues and opportunities of the hypercompetitive digital economy.

Little known by many, Simon had studied similar skew phenomena in the industrial economy and developed empirically grounded explanatory theories to help guide strategic decision making in the evolutionary processes of organizations. In this chapter, we tied together five seemingly unrelated topics of Simon and his colleagues (skew distributions, near decomposability, causal reasoning, effectual reasoning, and attention management) and provided a holistic framework of attention-based information systems for researchers to address issues and opportunities in e-business. The framework, related to Gates' digital nervous system (1999), consists of five components as shown in Figure 2: managing the content, causal reasoning of the content, managing the context, effectual reasoning of the context, and value creation and innovation. To illustrate how the attention-based information system works, we plan to apply the framework to a new emerging e-business research area titled netchising.

Despite the abundance of literature in e-business deployment today, doing business on the Internet is still mostly a "domestic phenomenon" of the developed countries and not yet a global phenomenon (Davenport, 2000). As globalization is unavoidable, there is an urgent need to converge e-business development perspectives from developed to developing countries. International franchising (Justis & Judd, 2003) has been shown to be an effective strategy to transfer technology and emerging markets from developed into developing countries. Netchising, integrating the power of the Internet for global integration and franchise networking for local socialization, is a global e-business growth strategy gaining its popularity.

New technology companies (such as those shown in Table 1) understand the importance of netchising as a global e-business growth strategy. Non-technology conventional companies can also benefit from using the netchising strategy for global e-business growth. An ongoing project is being conducted to show how the attention-based information system framework proposed in this paper can be developed for companies interested in using netchising as a global growth model for e-business.

References

Alavi, M., & Leidner, D. E. (1999). Knowledge management systems: Issues, challenges, and benefits. *Communications of the Association for Information Systems, 1*(February), 1-37.

Allee, V. (1999). The art and practice of being a revolutionary. *Journal of Knowledge Management, 3*(2), 121-132.

Allee, V. (2002). *The future of knowledge: Increasing prosperity through value networks.* Butterworth-Heinemann.

Augier, M., & Sarasvathy, S. (2004). Integrating evolution, cognition and design: Extending Simonian perspectives to strategic organization. *Strategic Organization, 2*(2), 169-204.

Baker, V. (2001). *The edge economy: Give up control, gain revenue.* Retrieved on September 1, 2005, from www.gartnerg2.com/research/rpt-0501-0039.asp

Barabasi, A. (2003). *Linked: How everything is connected to everything else and what it means.* Plume.

Barabasi, A., & Bonabeau, E. (2003, May). Scale-free networks. *Scientific American, 288*(5), 60-69.

Brown, J. S., & Duguid, P. (2002). *The social life of information.* Cambridge, MA: Harvard Business School Press.

Buchanan, M. (2002). *Nexus: Small worlds and the groundbreaking science of networks.* W.W. Norton & Company.

Chen, Y. (2003). Information systems and e-business in franchising. In R. Justis & R. Judd (Eds.), *Franchising* (3rd ed.) (pp.12-1~12-9). DAME Publishing.

Chen, Y., Chen, P. P., & Chen, G. (2002, May 23-26). Global e-business, franchising, and multi-language entity-relationship diagrams. In *Proceedings of the International Conference on E-Business*, Beijing, China.

Chen, Y., Chen, G., & Justis, R. T. (2001, July 4-6). Franchising as an ebusiness growth strategy in China. In *Proceedings of Asian eBiz Workshop*, Beijing, China.

Chen, J., Chong, P .P., & Chen, Y. (2001). Decision criteria consolidation: A theoretical foundation of Pareto principle to Michael Porter's competitive forces. *Journal of Organizational Computing and Electronic Commerce, 11*(1), 1-14.

Chen, Y., Chong, P. P., & Justis, R. T. (2000). An Intranet-based knowledge repository: A structure for learning organization in franchising. *Human Systems Management, 19*, 277-284.

Chen, Y., Chong, P. P., & Justis, R. T. (2002, February 8-10). E-business strategy in franchising: A customer-service-life-cycle approach. In *Proceedings of the 16ᵗʰ Annual International Society of Franchising Conference*, Orlando, FL.

Chen, Y., Ford, C., Justis, R. T., & Chong, P. P. (2001, February 24-25). Application service providers (ASP) in franchising: Opportunities and issues. In *Proceedings of the 15ᵗʰ Annual International Society of Franchising Conference*, Las Vegas, NV.

Chen, Y., Gabriela, S., & Chong, P. P. (1992). Visualizing business rules in corporate databases. *Industrial Management & Data Systems, 2*(7), 3-8.

Chen, Y., Hammerstein, S., & Justis, R. T. (2002, April 5-6). Knowledge, learning, and capabilities in franchise organizations. In *Proceedings of the 3ʳᵈ European Conference on Organizational Knowledge, Learning, and Capabilities,* Athens, Greece.

Chen, Y., Justis, R. T., & Chong, P. P. (2002). Franchising and information technology: A framework. In S. Burgess (Ed.), *Managing information technology in small business: Challenges and solutions* (pp. 118-139), Hershey, PA: Idea Group Publishing.

Chen, Y., Justis, R. T., & Chong, P.P. (2004). Data mining in franchise organizations. In H. R. Nemati & C. D. Barko (Eds.), *Organizational Data mining: Leveraging enterprise data resources for optimal performance* (pp. 217-229) Hershey PA: Idea Group Publishing.

Chen, Y., Justis, R., & Watson, E. (2000). Web-enabled data warehousing. In M. Shaw, R. Blanning, T. Strader, & A. Whinston (Eds.), *Handbook of electronic commerce* (pp. 501-520). Springer-Verlag.

Chen, Y., Justis, R., & Wu, S. (2006a, February 24-26). Value networks in franchise organizations: A study in the senior care industry. In *Proceedings of the 20ᵗʰ Annual International Society of Franchising Conference*, Palm Springs, CA.

Chen, Y., Justis, R., & Wu, S. (2006b, May 15-17). Managing supply chains in the senior care industry: A customer-service-life-cycle approach. In *Proceedings of the International Conference on Information Systems, Logistics and Supply Chain*, Lyon, France.

Chen, Y., Justis, R. T., & Yang, H. L. (2004, March 5-7). Global e-Business, international franchising, and theory of netchising: A research alliance of East and West. In *Proceedings of the 18ᵗʰ Annual International Society of Franchising Conference*, Las Vegas, NV.

Chen, Y., Seidman, W., & Justis, R. (2005, May 20-22). Strategy and docility in franchise organizations. In *Proceedings of the 19ᵗʰ Annual International Society of Franchising Conference*, London.

Chen, Y., Yuan, W., & Dai, W. (2004, December 12-15). *Strategy and nearly decomposable systems: A study in franchise organizations.* International Symposium on "IT/IS Issues in Asia-Pacific Region, Co-sponsored by ICIS-2004, Washington, DC.

Chen, Y., Zhang, B., & Justis, R. T. (2005a). Franchising and information technology. In *Encyclopedia of Information Science and Technology* (Vol. 1, pp. 1218-1225).

Chen, Y., Zhang, B., & Justis, R. T. (2005b). Data mining in franchise organizations. *Encyclopedia of Information Science and Technology* (pp. 714-722).

Cohen, D., & Prusak, L. (2001). *In good company: How social capital makes organizations work*. Cambridge, MA: Harvard Business School Press.

Davenport, T. (2000). E-commerce goes global. *CIO Magazine, 13*(20), 52-54.

David, G. (n.d.). Can Mcdonald's cook again? *Fortune Magazine*, March 30.

DeLuca, F. (2000) *Start small, finish big*. Warner Business Books.

Dorogovtsev, S. N., & Mendes, J. F. F. (2003). *Evolution of networks: From biological nets to the Internet and WWW*. London: Oxford University Press.

Dosi, G., & Teece, D. J. (2002). Introduction to four unpublished manuscripts by Herbert A. Simon. *Industrial and Corporate Change, 11*(3), 581.

Entrepreneur.com. (2006). *Tech products*. Retrieved January 20, 2006, from http://entrepreneur.com/franzone/cats/0,6587,12-12-1-TECH,00.html.

Gates, W. (1999). *Business @ the speed of thought*. Warner Books.

Gibrat, R. (1931). *Les inegabtes economiqaes*. Paris: Libraire du Recueil Sirey.

Glymour, C., & Cooper, G. F. (1999). *Computation, causation, and discovery*. AAAI Press/ MIT Press.

Hadfield, B. (1995). *Wealth within reach*. Cypress Publishing.

Ijiri, Y., & Simon, H.A. (1964). Business firm growth and size. *American Economic Review, 54*, 77-89.

Ijiri, Y., & Simon, H.A. (1967). A model of business firm growth. *Econometrica, 35*, 348-355.

Ijiri, Y., & Simon, H.A. (1971). Effects of mergers and acquisitions on business firm concentration. *Journal of Political Economy, 79*, 314-322.

Ijiri, Y., & Simon, H.A. (1974). Interpretations of departures from the Pareto curve firm-size distributions. *Journal of Political Economy, 82*, 315-331.

Ijiri, Y., & Simon, H.A. (1977). *Skew distributions and the sizes of business firms*. North-Holland.

Ives, B. (1999). *Customer service life cycle*. Retrieved January 20, 2006, from isds.bus.lsu.edu/cvoc/Projects/cslc/html

Ives, B., & Learmonth, G. P. (1984). The information system as a competitive weapon. *Communications of the AC, 27*(12), 1193-1201.

Ives, B., & Mason, R. O. (1990). Can information technology revitalize your customer service? *Academy of Management Executive, 4*(4), 52- 69.

Iwasaki, Y., & Simon, H. A. (1994). Causality and model abstraction. *Artificial Intelligence, 67*, 143-194.

Justis, R. T., & Judd, R. J. (2003). *Franchising* (3rd ed.). DAME Publishing.

Justis, R.T., & Vincent, W. S. (2001). *Achieving wealth through franchising*, Adams Media Corporation.

Kiyosaki, R.T., & Sharon L.L. (2000). *Rich dad, poor dad* (p. 85). Warner Business Books.

Love, J.F. (1995). *McDonalds: Behind the arches* (p. 152). Bantam.

March, J. (1999). *The pursuit of organizational intelligence*. Blackwell Business Press.

Nelson, R. R. (1991). Why do firms differ, and how does it matter? *Strategic Management Journal, 12*, 61-74.

Nelson, R. R., & Winter, S.G. (1982). *An evolutionary theory of economic change*. Cambridge, MA: Harvard University Press.

Okoli, C., Chen, Y., & Chong, P. P. (2002, December 15-18). Strategic growth of firms in the digital economy: Simulation and research proposal. In *Proceedings of the International Conference on Information Systems*, Barcelona, Spain.

Pearl, J. (2001). *Causality: Models, reasoning, and inference*. Cambridge: Cambridge University Press.

Sarasvathy, S. D. (2001). Causation and effectuation: Toward a theoretical shift from economic inevitability to entrepreneurial contingency. *Academy of Management Review, 26*(2), 243-288.

Sarasvathy, S. D. (2003). Entrepreneurship as a science of the artificial. *Journal of Economic Psychology, 24*(2), 203-220.

Sarasvathy, S. D., & Simon, H. A. (2000). *Effectuation, near decomposability, and the growth of entrepreneurial firms*. Paper presented at the First Annual Technology Entrepreneurship Research Policy Conference, University of Maryland, College Park.

Schreuder, A. N., Krige, L., & Parker, E. (2000, February 19-20). The franchisee lifecycle concept: A new paradigm in managing the franchisee-franchisor relationship. In *Proceedings of the 14th annual International Society of Franchising Conference*, San Diego, CA.

Simon, H. A. (1947). *Administrative behavior: A study of decision-making processes in administrative organizations*. Chicago: Macmillan.

Simon, H. A. (1953). Causal ordering and identifiability. In W.C. Hood & T.C. Koopmans (Eds.), *Studies in econometric methods* (pp.49-74). New York: Wiley.

Simon, H. A. (1955). On a class of skew distribution functions. *Biometrika, 42*, 425-440.

Simon, H. A. (1962). The architecture of complexity. In *Proceedings of the American Philosophical Society, 106*, 467-482.

Simon, H. A. (1971). Designing organizations for an information rich world. In M. Greeberger (Ed.), *Computers, communications, and the public interest* (pp. 38-52). Baltimore: The Johns Hopkins Press.

Simon, H. A. (1977a). On judging the plausibility of theories. In H. A. Simon (Ed.), *Models of discovery* (pp. 25-45). Holland.

Simon, H. A. (1977b). *The new science of management decision* (revised ed.). Englewood Cliffs, NJ: Prentice Hall.

Simon, H. A. (1982). *Models of bounded rationality (vols. 1 & 2)*. Cambridge, MA: The MIT Press.

Simon, H. A. (1988). Managing in an information-rich world. In Y.K. Shetty & V.M. Buehler (Eds.), *Competing through productivity and quality* (pp. 45-54). Cambridge, MA: Productivity Press.

Simon, H. A. (1991). Organizations and markets. *Journal of Economic Perspectives, 5,* 25-44.

Simon, H. A. (1992). Altruism and economics. *Eastern Economic Journal, 18*(1), 73-83.

Simon, H. A. (1993a). Strategy and organizational evolution. *Strategic Management Journal, 14,* 131-142.

Simon, H. A. (1993b). Altruism and economics. *American Economic Review, 83*(2), 156-161.

Simon, H. A. (1993c). A mechanism for social selection and successful altruism. *Science, 250*(4988), 1665-1668.

Simon, H. A. (1995). Near decomposability and complexity: How a mind resides in a brain. In H. Morowitz & J. Singer (Eds.), *The mind, the brain, and complex adaptive systems* (pp. 25-43). Addison- Wesley.

Simon, H. A. (1996). *Sciences of the artificial* (3ʳᵈ ed). Cambridge, MA: MIT Press.

Simon, H. A. (1997a). *An empirically based microeconomics.* New York; Melbourne: Cambridge University Press.

Simon, H. A. (1997b). *Administrative behavior* (4ᵗʰ ed.). New York: Macmillan.

Simon, H.A. (1997c). *Models of bounded rationality (vol. 3).* Cambridge, MA: The MIT Press.

Simon, H.A. (2000). Public administration in today's world of organizations and markets. *Political Science & Politics, 33*(4), 749-756.

Simon, H. A. (2002a). Near decomposability and the speed of evolution. *Industrial and Corporate Change, 11*(3), 587-599.

Simon, H. A. (2002b). We and they: The human urge to identify with groups. *Industrial and Corporate Change, 11*(3), 607-610.

Simon, H. A. (2002c). Forecasting the future or shaping it? *Industrial and Corporate Change, 11*(3), 601-605.

Simon, H.A. (2002d). Organizing and coordinating talk and silence in organizations. *Industrial and Corporate Change, 11*(3), 611-618.

Simon, H.A. (2002e). Organization theory in the age of computers and electronic communication networks. In M. Augier & J.G. March (Eds.), *The economics of choice, change, and organization: Essays in memory of Richard M. Cyert* (pp. 404-418). Edward Elgar.

Simon, H. A., & Ando, A. (1961). Aggregation of variables in dynamic systems. *Econometrica, 29*(2), 111-138.

Simon, H. A., & Bonini, C. P. (1958). The size distribution of business firms. *American Economic Review, 48,* 607-617.

Simon, H.A., & Van Wormer T.A. (1963). Some Monte Carlo estimates of the Yule distribution. *Behavior Science, 1*(8), 203-210.

Spirtes, P., Glymour, C., & Scheines, R. (2001). *Causation, prediction, and search* (2nd ed.). Cambridge, MA: MIT Press.

Thomke, S. H. (2003). *Experimentation matters*. Cambridge, MA: Harvard Business School Press.

Wang, Y. C. (2001a). *Collective talks of Y.C. Wang (vols. 1-4)*. Formosa Plastic Publishing.

Wang, Y. C. (2001b). *Social structure change and some conceptual idea for Taiwan*. Formosa Plastic Publishing.

Wasserman, S., & Faust, K. (1994). *Social network analysis*. Cambridge: Cambridge University Press.

Watts, D. J. (2003). *Six degrees: The science of a connected age*. W.W. Norton & Company.

Wenger, E., McDermott, R., & Snyder, W.M. (2002). *Cultivating communities of practice: A guide to managing knowledge*. Cambridge, MA: Harvard Business School Press.

Wu, D., Yang, L. C., & Wu, S. S. (2004). Crisis management of SARS in a hospital. *Journal of Safety Research, 35*(3), 345-349.

Yao, Y., Wohl, M., Watson, E., & Chen, Y. (2003). Customers' decision to adopt application service provider and applications service providers' business strategy in the hospital industry: A research framework [Special issue]. *Journal of Information Technology Cases and Applications,* 40-60.

Zhang, B., Chen, Y., & Pawlowski, S. (2003, August 4-6). Online data mining in franchising supply chain Management: A case study in apparel industry. In *Proceedings of the Americas Conference of Information Systems*, Tampa, FL.

Chapter VIII

Business Process Modeling with the User Requirements Notation

Michael Weiss, Carleton University, Canada

Daniel Amyot, University of Ottawa, Canada

Abstract

This chapter demonstrates how the user requirements notation (URN) can be used to model business processes. URN combines goals and scenarios in order to help capture and reason user requirements prior to detailed design. In terms of application areas, this emerging standard targets reactive systems in general, with a particular focus on telecommunications systems and services. This chapter argues that the URN can also be applied to business process modeling. To this end, it illustrates the notation, its use, and its benefits with a supply chain management case study. It then briefly compares this approach to related modeling approaches, namely, use case-driven design, service-oriented architecture analysis, and conceptual value modeling. The authors believe that a URN-based approach will provide usable and useful tools to assist researchers and practitioners with the modeling, analysis, integration, and evolution of existing and emerging business processes.

Introduction

Business process modeling (BPM) is a structured method for describing and analyzing opportunities of improving the business objectives of stakeholders, including providers and customers. BPM usually involves identifying the roles of users involved in the process, and the definition of activities (often described as workflows or services) that contribute to the satisfaction of well-defined business goals. Approaches for BPM are business-centric rather than technology-centric, although connections to designs and implementations (for example, via mappings to workflow engines or Web services) are also desirable.

BPM approaches need to address the well-known "W5 questions:" *Why* do this activity? *What* should this activity be precisely? *Who* is involved in this activity? *Where* and *when* should this activity be performed? Additionally, a business process model should enable ways of (formally) analyzing the processes and goal satisfaction. Finally, business process models should be understandable to various stakeholders, including customers.

Several years ago, the standardization sector of the International Telecommunications Union initiated work toward the creation of a *user requirements notation* (URN) in the Z.150 series of recommendations (ITU-T, 2003). The purpose of URN is to support, prior to detailed design, the modeling and analysis of user requirements in the form of goals and scenarios, in a formal way. URN is generally suitable for describing most types of reactive and distributed systems, with a particular focus on telecommunications systems and services. The applications range from goal modeling and requirements description to high-level design. An overview of URN with a tutorial example from the wireless communication domain is presented in Amyot (2003). Annex A also includes a summary of the notation.

URN has concepts for the specification of behavior, structure, goals, and non-functional requirements, which are all relevant for business process modeling. URN is in fact composed of two complementary notations, which build on previous work. The first one is GRL, *the goal-oriented requirement language* (URN Focus Group, 2003a). For the last decade goal-oriented modeling has been a very active field in the requirements engineering community (Yu & Mylopoulos, 1998). One well-established language is the NFR (non-functional requirements) framework, published in Chung, Nixon, Yu, and Mylopoulos (2000). GRL includes some of the most interesting concepts found in the NFR framework and complements them with agent modeling concepts from the i* framework (Yu, 1997). GRL captures business or system goals, alternative means of achieving goals, and the rationale for goals and alternatives. The notation is applicable to non-functional as well as functional requirements.

The second part of URN is the *use case map* (UCM) notation, described in URN Focus Group (2003b). The UCM notation was first defined by Buhr and his colleagues (Buhr, 1998; Buhr & Casselman, 1996) to depict emerging behavioral scenarios during the high-level design of distributed object-oriented reactive systems. It was later considered appropriate as a notation for describing operational requirements and services. A UCM model depicts scenarios as causal flows of responsibilities that can be superimposed on underlying structures of components. UCM *responsibilities* are scenario activities representing something to be performed (operation, action, task, function, etc.). Responsibilities can potentially be allocated to components, which are generic enough to represent software entities (e.g., objects, processes, databases, or servers) as well as non-software entities (e.g., actors or hardware resources).

Through an illustrative example, we will argue that URN presents suitable and useful features for modeling and analyzing business processes, and that it satisfies the goals of a BPM language. Our example is based on a WS-I (Web services interoperability) case study (WS-I, 2003a). This document describes usage scenarios defining the use of Web services in structured interactions and identifying basic interoperability requirements. It is sufficiently rich in order to exercise the various features of URN, but, at the same time, it is a simplified model of a supply chain management system that can be understood in its entirety.

In this chapter, we first give an overview of the supply chain management case study as well as of the corresponding UCM model we constructed. Then we discuss how URN models can be used to analyze architectural changes. Service provisioning relationships for mapping the business process model to Web services are then explored, before looking at paths to detailed service design and validation. We finally discuss related work and present our conclusions.

Supply Chain Management:
Overview and UCM Model

In this section we describe how a UCM model can be constructed based on given use cases. We first give an overview of the high-level requirements, followed by a subsection for each use case. It should be noted that we are not mapping each use case to a separate map in the UCM model. Instead, we create a single so-called *root* map that incorporates the other maps through a hierarchical abstraction mechanism. The UCM model presented here was created with the UCMNAV tool (UCM User Group, 2003).

Overview of High-Level Requirements

The WS-I case study (WS-I, 2003a) provides a high-level definition of a supply chain management system for consumer electronic goods. The requirements are specified in the form of a use case model integrating high-level functional requirements, a set of simplifying assumptions, and a set of use cases and activity diagrams. Non-functional requirements of the nature considered by URN are not specified.

There are five high-level functional requirements in this system:

- Retailer offers consumer electronic goods to Consumers.
- Retailer needs to manage stock levels in Warehouses.
- Retailer must restock a good from the respective Manufacturer's inventory, if its stock level falls below a certain threshold.
- Manufacturer must execute a production run to build the finished goods, if a good is not in stock. (Ordering from suppliers is not modeled.)

- Use cases contain logging calls to a Monitoring System to monitor services from a single monitoring service.

These requirements already explicitly specify a set of five actors (in sans serif). We therefore take these actors as given, although we can still reason about whether some of those actors can be made internal actors (e.g., the warehouses could be considered a part of the retailer). However, in a typical application of URN, one of the tasks would be to identify this set of actors from informal requirements or from the UCM model, that is, by considering how the responsibilities we have discovered should be allocated to components.

This system is interesting because it incorporates features of business-to-consumer (B2C, e.g., between retailer and the consumers) and business-to-business (B2B, e.g., between the retailer and the manufacturer). These two business models also imply different communication needs (e.g., asynchronous communication in B2B vs. typically synchronous communication in B2C).

The WS-I case study specifies eight use cases, and we will map six of them to URN: (1) *Purchase Goods*, (2) *Source Goods*, (3) *Replenish Stock*, (4) *Supply Finished Goods*, (5) *Manufacture Finished Goods*, and (7) *Log Events*. The *Run And Configure Demo* use case (6, not mapped) addresses one of the goals of the WS-I case study, namely, to demonstrate the interoperability of different vendors' Web services implementations. However, our objective here is to model the business process in a representative supply chain management system, and the demonstration aspects are outside of our scope. The *View Events* use case (8, not mapped) describes a management functionality that has been removed for space reasons.

Use Case 1: Purchase Goods

This use case gives a high-level overview of the business process as a whole, which includes submitting and fulfilling orders. This corresponds to the root UCM shown in Figure 1. A consumer visiting the retailer Web site expresses her intent to purchase goods by submitting

Figure 1. BusinessProcess root map

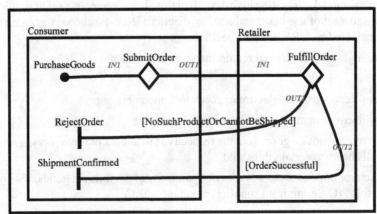

an order. The retailer system replies by fulfilling the order. There are two possible outcomes: RejectOrder and ShipmentConfirmed. The [NoSuchProductOrCannotBeShipped] path is taken if any of the products in the order do not exist (in this case the whole order is rejected) or none of the items can be shipped. In the [OrderSuccessful] path, a shipping confirmation is returned with a list of items shipped, indicating the quantity shipped for each.

In the UCM notation (see Figure 19), scenarios are initiated at *start points*, represented as filled circles, and terminate at *end points*, shown as bars. *Paths* show the causal relationships between start and end points. Generic *components* are shown as rectangles, and they are responsible for the various activities (called *responsibilities* and indicated by X's on a path) allocated to them. Labels for *guarding conditions* are shown between square brackets. Diamonds are used to represent *stubs*, which are containers for submaps called *plug-ins*. Stubs have named input and output segments (e.g., *IN1* and *OUT1* in Figure 1) that are bound to start and end points in a plug-in, hence ensuring the continuation of a scenario from a parent map to a submap and to the parent map again.

Figure 2. SubmitOrder submap

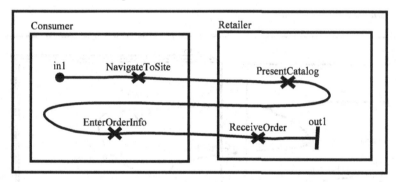

Figure 3. FulfillOrder submap

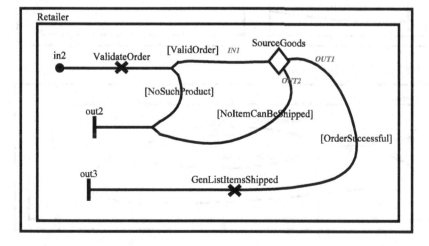

The BusinessProcess root map contains two stubs, each of which with one submap: SubmitOrder and FulfillOrder. In SubmitOrder the consumer navigates to the shopping site, and the system responds with the product catalog. The consumer then enters the order information and submits the order. This submap is shown in Figure 2. In FulfillOrder, shown in Figure 3, the retailer checks with its warehouses whether they can supply the items in the order (assuming the requested product exists), and asks them to ship the items. This use case incorporates the *Source Goods* use case, described in the next section.

Use Case 2: Source Goods

In this use case, the retailer tries to locate the ordered goods in its warehouses. If the requested quantity of a given item is available, the retailer requests its shipment. Otherwise, it will record that the item could not be shipped. (As stated in the requirements, requests can only be fulfilled in full. Stocks from multiple warehouses cannot be combined.) The use case results in a list of the line items that each warehouse will ship and accordingly adjusted inventory levels.

Figure 4. SourceGoods submap

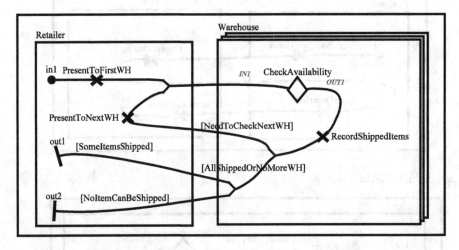

Figure 5. CheckAvailability submap

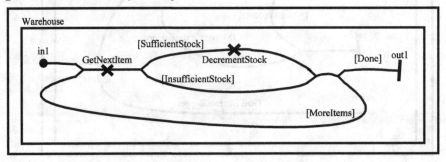

The submap corresponding to this use case is shown in Figure 4. It is important to note that in the UCM model we do not need to map each use case separately, but we can integrate several of them in the same diagram. The complexity of the resulting model can be reduced through hierarchical abstraction as provided by stubs and plug-ins.

The CheckAvailability submap in Figure 5 shows the iteration through the list of items presented to an individual warehouse. Whenever an item is available, the ordered quantity is decremented from the warehouse inventory.

In the next section, we will "attach" the UCM for the *Replenish Stock* use case (discussed in the next subsection) to this submap in order to express that stock replenishment is triggered asynchronously whenever the stock level for a particular item gets below a given threshold after decrementing the stock. We will also discuss an alternative approach and compare both approaches using architectural change analysis.

Use Case 3: Replenish Stock

The warehouse orders goods from manufacturers to replenish its own stock for a given product. The submap for this use case is shown in Figure 6. This map is interesting as it demonstrates the use of parallelism with a UCM *AND-fork*. Upon receiving and validating the order, the selected manufacturer immediately acknowledges the receipt of the order before it starts processing the request (first of two parallel branches, which ends in AckToWH). The reason for this is that the manufacturer may need to produce the requested goods before it can supply them if it has insufficient inventory of the product (second parallel branch).

As soon as the manufacturer has shipped the finished product, it sends a shipping notice to the warehouse (Shipping). In response the warehouse updates its inventory and acknowledges

Figure 6. ReplenishStock submap

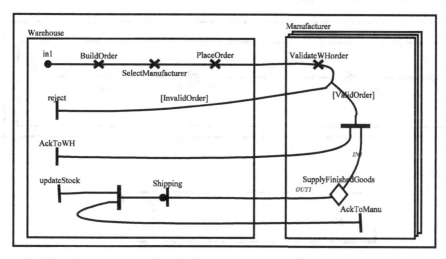

the receipt of the shipping notice to the manufacturer (AckToManu). Again, an AND-fork is used to indicate that these responsibilities are performed in parallel.

Use Case 4: Supply Finished Goods

The manufacturer receives a purchase order from a warehouse. The manufacturer may either be able to satisfy the request with the inventory at hand or may need to manufacture the requested goods. (As stated, these orders only contain a single line item.) The submap for this use case is shown in Figure 7. It makes use of a dynamic stub to represent the optional step of manufacturing finished goods, with two plug-ins as detailed in the submaps for ManufactureFinishedGoods (Figure 8 and Figure 9).

From the context (the ReplenishStock submap), it is clear that we do not need to validate the order again at the beginning of this submap. However, if SupplyFinishedGoods was turned into a service at a later stage, we would also need to check the input and reject purchase orders as necessary. As a general principle, services should, therefore, not make any assumptions about the context in which they will be invoked, for example, whether their input is correct.

Use Case 5: Manufacture Finished Goods

For this use case, two plug-ins (used in the stub of Figure 7) are required. The first one is a simple pass through and is selected when the manufacturer holds sufficient inventory of the product (Figure 8). With no component specified, this plug-in can be reused more easily in other stubs. The second plug-in describes how the finished goods are produced when the

Figure 7. SupplyFinishedGoods submap

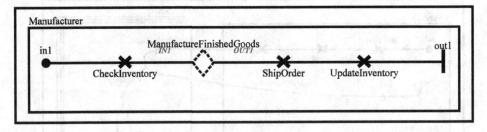

Figure 8. Default submap

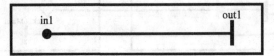

Figure 9. ManufactureFinishedGoods submap

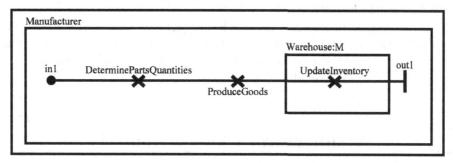

inventory is insufficient. First, the required parts and quantities are determined, then the good is assembled and the manufacturer's inventory is updated (Figure 9). The dynamic stub defines the condition under which each plug-in will be selected (also known as selection policy). These conditions will be formalized in the subsection presenting scenario definitions.

Note that the manufacturer has its own warehouse where it stores its inventory. The inventory is considered insufficient when its level falls below a minimum threshold or the quantity ordered is larger than the current level. A manufacturer is assumed to be able to produce any items requested but not beyond a maximum inventory level.

Use Case 7: Log Events

This use case is concerned with logging events relating to the execution of the other use cases. Events can be logged for any number of reasons, including debugging, maintenance, or non-repudiation. The corresponding UCM is found in Fig. 10. One shortcoming of any scenario-based notation is that logging the execution of a scenario is difficult to model. Of course one could insert a LogEvents stub after each responsibility that we want to log, but that would make the diagrams clumsy. Logging is best modeled as an *aspect* of a responsi-

Figure 10. LogEvents submap

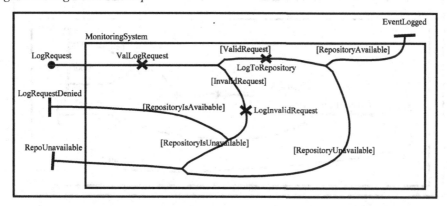

bility that is executed whenever the responsibility is performed. Other examples of aspects are encryption (e.g., to model that messages are sent in encrypted form) and billing.

When Figure 10 shows a submap, it needs to be interpreted as a plug-in that is (logically) inserted after each responsibility that we want to log in any of the other maps (LogRequest would be triggered in passing). In this use case, the event may actually not be logged if the request is invalid or if the repository is unavailable.

Architectural Change Analysis

One of the benefits of URN is the ability to reason about architectural changes. In this section we will look at several examples where URN allows us to consider different types of trade-offs: functional, non-functional, and structural.

Triggered vs. Periodic Replenishment of Stock

In the presentation of the UCMs, we have not discussed under which circumstances the ReplenishStock scenario (Figure 6) is executed. We consider two architectural alternatives: the scenario can be triggered as a result of decrementing the stock level in the CheckAvailability submap (Figure 5), or it can be executed periodically. This is a functional trade-off, since the alternatives realize two functionally different ways of implementing the same requirement.

To implement the first alternative, we can extend the CheckAvailability submap by "touching" it with a path leading to a Replenishment stub. This means that the path is to be executed asynchronously (i.e., in parallel) once the DecrementStock responsibility has been performed. By making Replenishment a dynamic stub, we can specify a selection policy

Figure 11. Alternative 1: Triggered replenishment

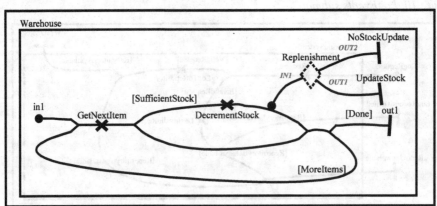

Figure 12. Alternative 2: Periodic replenishment

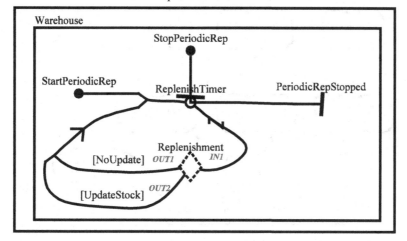

to decide whether the stock needs to be replenished or not. The necessary changes are indicated in Figure 11.

The architectural alternative to triggered replenishment is to replenish the stock periodically. This does not require any changes to CheckAvailability and can be accomplished by a new root map for periodic replenishment shown in Figure 12. This map contains a timer, represented with a clock symbol. ReplenishTimer is reset when the StopPeriodicRep scenario reaches it in time; otherwise this timer expires and the time-out path (squiggly line) is taken.

The choice between these alternatives involves a trade-off between availability and maintainability and manageability. The GRL model in Figure 13 provides details of the trade-off. It represents the two architectural alternatives as *tasks* (hexagons) and the three non-functional requirements as *softgoals* (clouds) to be achieved. In GRL, model elements can contribute to each other, and this is shown with arrows. Contributions can be positive or negative, as well as sufficient or insufficient (see the legend in Figure 18).

Our definitions of the non-functional requirements used in this model and subsequent ones are provided in Table 1.

Table 1. Definition of non-functional requirements in the BPM context

NFR	Definition
Availability	Ability to handle requests (e.g., in terms of the number of fulfilled orders)
Maintainability	Ability to evolve the system and to fix errors
Manageability	Ability to monitor system performance and adjust parameters
Performance	Speed of performing business functions
Scalability	Ability to grow the system (e.g., number of users)
Security	Identification, secrecy, integrity, access control, and audit

Figure 13. GRL model to compare between triggered and periodic replenishment

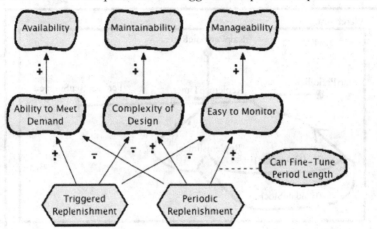

The model in Figure 13 states that, using triggered replenishment, a warehouse can detect more quickly that inventory levels are getting low than when using periodic replenishment. Consequently, we will be able to keep up with higher-than-anticipated demand (up to the limit of the manufacturer's capacity to produce, of course). When using periodic replenishment, we check inventory levels only when triggered by a timer, and the length of the period affects how soon we can respond to changes in demand beyond what we had anticipated when setting the length of the period. On the other hand, the first alternative leads to a more complex design, because we need to distribute the checks for inventory levels wherever the level can change. In the second alternative, the checking logic is centralized, and we do not need know at what points in the business process the inventory level changes. Although setting the length of the period appropriately makes the configuration of the system slightly more difficult, this disadvantage is more than offset by the greater ease with which the system can be managed in the second alternative, which allows us to monitor the inventory levels and adjust the length of the period as necessary.

The reasons we just provided for giving a contribution link a particular weight can also be expressed directly in the diagram in the form of *beliefs*, shown as ellipses. For example we have justified why Periodic Replenishment makes inventory levels Easy to Monitor in Figure 13. Another stakeholder could have a different opinion on this contribution, and her belief could also be added to the model, hence documenting arguments and rationales until agreement is reached. It is often a judgment call on what level of detail to present in the diagram, as its main reason is to summarize the reasoning succinctly and to enable trade-offs in a given context. We therefore do not want to overload the diagram with additional annotations.

Note that the decision regarding triggered or periodic replenishment is not done in the absolute for either one of the alternatives. Which alternative is chosen depends on the context, that is, the priorities of the user (which NFRs are most important). For instance, if our goal was a more maintainable design, periodic replenishment would be the preferred solution, albeit at lower availability. Diagrammatically we can include the context in the GRL model via a goal such as "*total satisfaction*" and indicate the importance of each existing top-level softgoal through an appropriate contribution link (e.g., make or some).

Local Logging vs. Using a Centralized Logging Service

The requirements specified the use of a centralized logging service. However whether to log locally or centrally is often a (non-functional) trade-off faced by an architect. There are benefits and liabilities to either architecture, and they are summarized in Figure 14. In this case, a trade-off is made between performance, on one hand, and manageability and maintainability, on the other. Logging, independently of how it is implemented, improves traceability, and, therefore, maintainability. However local logging results in multiple logs, and filtering those logs for errors or unusual behavior will be harder than if a central logging service is used. Thus, on one hand, central logging leads to a more manageable system. On the other hand, however, central logging will lower performance because of the network overhead.

In addition to the contributions of each architectural alternative, this diagram also shows the results of propagating the effect of choosing one of the alternatives. Evaluations of GRL graphs show the impact of qualitative decisions on high-level softgoals. A tool like OME (Yu & Liu, 2000) can automatically propagate the labels assigned to leaf nodes of the graph. The GRL propagation algorithm discussed in URN User Group (2003a) and supported by OME is inspired from Chung et al. (2000). Propagation is usually bottom-up and takes into consideration three parameters, whose notations are presented in Figure 18:

- Contributions and correlations (positive or negative, sufficient or not)
- Degrees of satisfaction (satisfied or denied, weakly or fully)

Figure 14. GRL model to compare between local and central logging

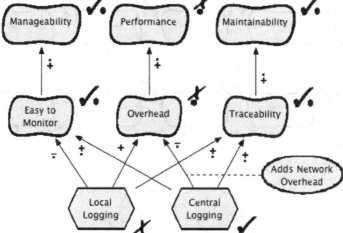

- Composition operators (AND, OR)

Evaluating GRL models usually provides more complete answers than using simple benefits/drawbacks tables or criteria evaluation matrices. One could also use numerical values and functions instead of qualitative (fuzzy) values, although the latter ones are often more appropriate in the early development stages.

As we can see in Figure 14, choosing central logging positively affects manageability and maintainability (weakly satisfied), and negatively affects performance (weakly denied). A similar model for the other alternative would lead to opposite results. In general many combinations of tasks and softgoals can be evaluated, and the results are not always so clear.

Modeling Warehouses as Internal Components

Our final example illustrates a structural trade-off. In addition to allocating responsibilities to UCM components in different ways, we can also nest components within other components. Such nesting then implies that those components are tightly coupled and that the nested component is not visible to top-level components. An example of this in the supply chain management case study is how we model warehouses.

Figure 15. GRL model to compare between top-level and internal actors

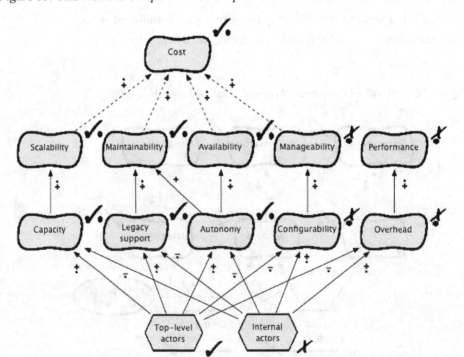

Both alternatives have already been illustrated previously. While the submap in Figure 4 models the retailer's warehouses as top-level components, the manufacturer's warehouse is modeled as a nested component in Figure 9. The trade-offs between these alternatives are summarized in Figure 15. As shown, modeling warehouses as top-level actors trades off maintainability, scalability, and availability for performance and manageability.

This alternative improves maintainability, because of its support for legacy solutions (e.g., warehouses developed within different business units) and autonomy, as it allows for the warehouse service to be provided by a third party (e.g., FedEx). If internalized, the warehouses would need to adopt a common operating platform and/or database schema. It increases scalability as it allows the system's capacity to grow by adding more warehouses. In the other alternative a single retailer database may quickly become a bottleneck.

Availability is higher when representing warehouses as independent entities, since there is no single point of failure. If one of the warehouses fails, the others can continue operating. However, since all requests to warehouses will be remote, there is a messaging overhead that reduces performance. Manageability is also decreased since each warehouse needs to be configured separately. As a side-effect (represented with dashed arrows called *correlations*) of improved maintainability, scalability, availability, and at the expense of reduced manageability, the overall (minimized) cost is positively affected.

Such a structural change also has an impact on the organization of the business. When warehouses are treated as top-level components, the functionality of the warehouse could be outsourced to a fulfillment partner such as FedEx or UPS. These companies have evolved the services they provide beyond just fulfillment and delivery services and can also manage the warehouses of their customers, and even aggregate suppliers' components in transit. The use of URN for reasoning about such organizational issues and its application to business model design and evolution is further explored in Weiss and Amyot (2005).

Service Provisioning Relationships

In this section we are concerned with deriving service provisioning relationships between components from the UCM model. The goal of this step is to map the business process model to a Web services architecture. We define a *service* as a collection of related operations implemented by a component. The component that implements a service is known as *service provider* and components that invoke the service as *service users*. An analysis of the UCM model provides us with potential operations that can then be grouped into services. Note that our definition of the term service abstracts from the issue of how a service is accessed, that is, through network addresses, protocols, and data formats. As we refine service relationships into WSDL Web service definitions, these aspects need to be specified.

Each service operation comprises a set of messages exchanged between a service user and a service provider. In line with the WSDL specification (W3C, 2001), we differentiate between one-way, request-response, solicit-response, and notification operations. Both one-way and notification operations consist of a single message sent by the service user and the service provider, respectively. In the case of request-response and solicit-response operations, two correlated messages are exchanged, the difference being who initiates the dialog (the service user in the former and the service provider in the latter).

In the process of identifying potential service operations we therefore look for causal paths in the UCM model that cut across component boundaries. The path segments consisting of the last responsibility or condition along those paths in the source component and the first responsibility or condition in the destination component can be identified with a message. Their names can be concatenated to serve as a unique handle for the message. This information can be automatically extracted from a UCM by using the UCMNAV tool. The next section provides further details on extracting messages from a UCM model.

However, whether responsibilities or conditions will actually be exposed as service operations also depends on other considerations. In general only some of the interactions at the business process level will result in Web service interactions. In our case, since we are working here within the scope of the WS-I case study, our target will be a service-oriented implementation. It should also be pointed out that one important feature of UCM models is that the mapping from a UCM model to an implementation architecture is not one-to-one and that the same causal dependency between components can be realized using multiple protocols and communication mechanisms, or not mapping into implementation-level concepts at all. In this section, we are suggesting one way in which UCM models can be mapped to Web service interactions. The process and template described below are intended to provide the foundation for an automatic mapping from UCM models into Web services.

Having identified path segments that represent messages between components, we need to decide which service operations they belong to. At present this decision needs to be made manually, although one could expect to use pattern matching to classify messages into operations given the structure of the UCM model. Subsequently, we need to group those operations into services. As a simple illustration of this process, consider the interactions between consumer and retailer.

From the UCM model, we can extract the following path segments that correspond to messages exchanged between the consumer and retailer components:

> c.NavigateToSite-r.PresentCatalog (Navigate)
>
> r.PresentCatalog-c.EnterOrderInfo (Catalog)
>
> c.EnterOrderInfo-r.ReceiveOrder (OrderInfo)
>
> r.OrderSuccessful-c.ShipmentConfirmed (ShipmentConfirmed)
>
> r.NoSuchProduct-c.RejectOrder (RejectOrder)
>
> r.NoItemCanBeShipped-c.RejectOrder (RejectOrder)

To ensure uniqueness, we prefix the name of the responsibility or condition with the corresponding component identifier (c, r, m, or w). In parenthesis we also show the name that is manually assigned to the message during detailed service design (to be discussed in the next section) in order to provide traceability to the MSC model. The message exchange above can be interpreted as two request-response operations, both provided by the retailer component. We can give them more expressive names such as getCatalog() and submitOrder(). Note that submitOrder() has two possible responses: either the order is rejected or shipment is confirmed.

Our approach suggests grouping related operations into services. In some cases, a component may therefore offer multiple services if they bundle different functionalities. In the example, however, getCatalog() and submitOrder() are both operations related to the ordering process, and we decide to group them into a single Retailer service. In this example the name of the service is simply derived from the name of the component that provides it.

We propose the following template for documenting the assignment of operations to services. For a given service user and given service provider, we list the messages exchanged and label them according to their role in an operation (request, response, solicitation, or notification). Finally, we group the messages into operations. The interaction between the consumer and the retailer actors can now be documented as follows:

Consumer-Retailer

Operation: getCatalog()

    Request: c.NavigateToSite-r.PresentCatalog (Navigate)

    Response: r.PresentCatalog-c.EnterOrderInfo (Catalog)

Operation: submitOrder()

    Request: c.EnterOrderInfo-r.ReceiveOrder (OrderInfo)

    Response: r.OrderSuccessful-c.ShipmentConfirmed (ShipmentConfirmed)

    OR Response: r.NoSuchProduct-c.RejectOrder (RejectOrder)

    OR Response: r.NoItemCanBeShipped-c.RejectOrder (RejectOrder)

Similarly, a request-response operation shipGoods() belonging to a Warehouse service can be derived from the interaction between the retailer and its warehouses. However, the interaction between warehouses and manufacturers leads to a different type of operation. The messages exchanged between a warehouse and a manufacturer are as follows:

Warehouse-Manufacturer

Operation: submitPurchaseOrder()

    Request: w.PlaceOrder-m.ValidateWHorder (PlaceOrder)

    Response: m.ValidOrder-w.AckToWH (Ack)

    OR Response: m.InvalidOrder-w.reject (reject)

Manufacturer-Warehouse

Operation: submitShippingNotice()

    Notification: m.UpdateInventory-w.ShippingNotice (ShippedItems)

The first message exchange can be mapped to a request-response operation in the Manufacturer service submitPurchaseOrder(). The reply is in fact a partial acknowledgement of the request, and the actual reply is sent with the next message. The second message exchange corresponds to a notification, resulting in a callback of the Warehouse service. We can, therefore, add a submitShippingNotice() operation to the Warehouse service.

Figure 16. Service provisioning relationships

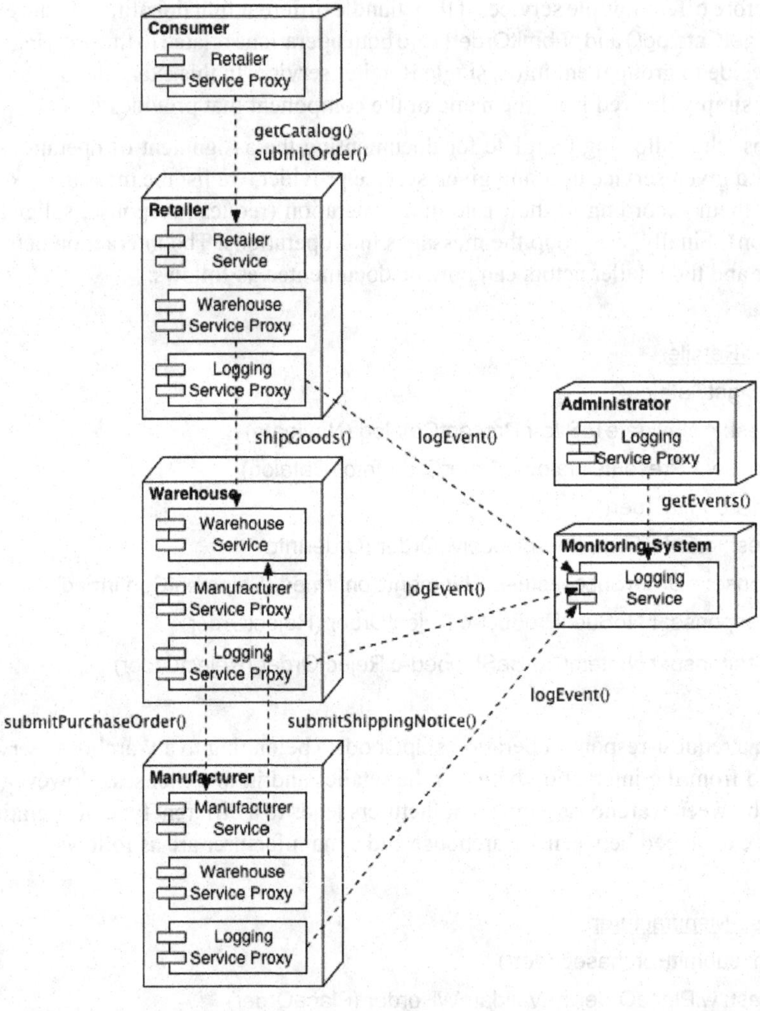

Finally, the interactions with the MonitoringSystem can be exposed as a Logging service. It provides the operations logEvent() and getEvents(). The service provisioning relationships between the components can be visualized as a UML deployment diagram (see Figure 16). In this diagram we use a convention introduced by (Carlson, 2001) to show both service deployment, as well as service invocations in a way similar to a collaboration diagram.

Toward Detailed Service Design and Validation

The previous section already motivated the need for messages between components in the context of operations for Web services. This section presents a tool-supported technique, based on scenario definitions and a UCM path traversal algorithm, for automating part of the process of generating messages. This technique has application in the understanding, visualization, simulation, and analysis of UCM models, as well as the generation of design-level scenarios and test goals for validating designs and implementations.

Scenario Definitions

The UCM notation supports a very simple *path data model* that can be used to traverse paths in a deterministic way. Global Boolean control variables can be used to formalize conditions. Responsibilities can also modify the content of these variables with new values resulting from the evaluation of Boolean expressions.

In our case study several such variables are needed, and Annex B defines them. Using these variables, formal conditions can be attached to branching points in a model, that is, to OR-forks (for selecting alternative branches), dynamic stubs (for selection policies), and timers (to decide whether or not a timeout occurs).

For instance the selection policy of the ManufactureFinishedGoods dynamic stub in Figure 7 is:

$$SufficientInventory \rightarrow \text{Select plug-in Default}$$
$$\neg SufficientInventory \rightarrow \text{Select plug-in ManufactureFinishedGoods}$$

For the OR-fork in the SourceGoods UCM (Fig. 4), the guarding conditions on the two branches are formalized as follows:

$$[\text{NeedToCheckNextWH}] = WarehouseLeft \wedge (\neg ItemListEmpty)$$
$$[\text{AllShippedOrNoMoreWH}] = (\neg WarehouseLeft) \vee ItemListEmpty$$

A UCM model may include several groups of *scenario definitions*. Each such definition consists of initial values for the variables, a set of start points initially triggered, an optional post-condition expected to be satisfied at the end of the execution of the scenario, and a description. Here are two examples (note that T means true and F means false):

Scenario: **PrimaryScenario**

Description: The warehouse has the desired item.

Starting point: PurchaseGoods (in map BusinessProcessRoot)

Variable initializations:

   $ProductExists = T$

   $SufficientStock = T$

> *WarehouseLeft = F*
> *MoreItems = F*
> *ItemListEmpty = T*
> *StockStillSufficient = T*

Scenario: **CheckButStocksSufficient**

Description: The periodic replenishment is checked but stocks are sufficient.

Starting point: StartPeriodicRep (in map PeriodicReplenishment)

Variable initializations:

> *ReplenishTimer_timeout = T*
> *SufficientStock = T*

In our model, we created 20 such scenario definitions categorized in five groups. Together these scenarios cover all the paths from all the root maps and submaps used in our case study. The scenarios resulting from the above two definitions will be illustrated with Message Sequence Charts in the next subsection.

Generation of Message Sequence Charts (MSCs)

The use of scenario definitions for UCM analysis and transformations was pioneered by Miga et al., 2001), who proposed a UCM path traversal analysis that took as input a UCM model and scenario definitions and produced as output a *Message Sequence Chart* (ITU-T, 2004) for each scenario. This functionality was prototyped in UCMNav. The same mechanism was used to highlight the path traversed in the UCM model according to the scenario definitions, hence helping with the understanding of complex or lengthy individual scenarios. The algorithm was generalized in URN Focus Group (2003b) and then re-implemented in UCMNav, this time to generate the output of the traversal in XML (Amyot, Cho, He, & He, 2003). In a nutshell the new algorithm uses a depth-first traversal of the graph that captures the UCMs' structure and generates scenarios where sequences and concurrency are preserved but where alternatives are resolved using the Boolean variables. If conditions cannot be satisfied or evaluated, then the algorithm reports an error. Another tool, UCMEXPORTER (Amyot, Echihabi, & He, 2004), takes these scenarios in XML and converts them to message sequence charts and UML sequence diagrams (OMG, 2003).

MSCs give a linear view of scenarios that traverse multiple UCMs, a situation that occurs frequently when plug-in maps are used. They are composed of component instances, shown as vertical lines, and of messages shown as arrows. Figure 17(c) gives a brief summary of a subset of the notation, which includes actions, conditions, timers, and concurrent behavior.

Fig. 17 provides two examples of MSCs automatically generated from the two scenarios defined in the previous section. UCMEXPORTER generates these MSCs in Z.120 textual form, which can then be rendered graphically by tools such as Tau (Telelogic, 2004). To preserve

Figure 17. Two MSC examples, illustrating typical MSC features

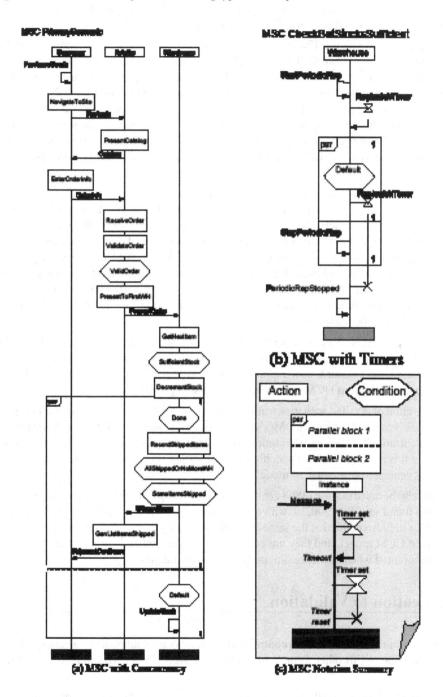

(a) MSC with Concurrency

(b) MSC with Timers

(c) MSC Notation Summary

the semantics of UCMs and traceability to the original model, UCM components are shown as MSC instances, start and end points as messages, condition labels and selected plug-in names as conditions, and responsibilities as actions.

In the first scenario (Figure 17a), we can observe that a Navigate message shows up in the MSC while it is absent from the UCM model. This message is synthesized automatically by UCMExporter in order to preserve the causal flow between a responsibility in the Consumer component and another responsibility in the Retailer component (see Figure 2). Message names between pairs of components are provided in a configuration file and can be refined by concrete message exchanges, for example, in a way consistent with the message names used in the Web service operations defined in the previous section. Consequently MSCs can be re-generated as the UCM model evolves or when different architectures are being evaluated.

Figure 17(a) illustrates the primary scenario for the business process (Figure 1) with triggered replenishment (Figure 11). The linear nature of MSCs makes it easy to follow and inspect this scenario, which otherwise would require the stakeholders to flip back and forth through six different UCMs in order to get the same understanding. This scenario is also interesting because it preserves the concurrency specified at the UCM level (e.g., with AND-forks). The MSC in Figure 17(b) describes a situation where a timer is used (shown in the PeriodicReplenishment submap in Figure 12). The ReplenishTimer is set when first traversed, times out, is set again in a second iteration of the looping UCM path, and is finally reset when StopPeriodicRep occurs.

The MSC notation is more interesting than UML 1.5 sequence diagrams because of its support for concurrency and timers. However, the new UML 2.0 sequence diagrams, being based on the MSC standard, now support the same concepts. Hence, generating UML 2.0 sequence diagrams from UCMs is a valid alternative to generating MSCs.

The generation of detailed scenarios from higher-level UCM descriptions respects the spirit of model-driven development. In OMG's model driven architecture (OMG, 2004), platform-independent models are refined into models containing platform-specific information. Indeed, as seen in this section, platform-specific communication information can be added to the scenarios generated from a UCM model.

It should also be noted that the MSCs generated here are comparable in content to the sequence diagrams found in WS-I (2003b), with the addition of concurrency and timer information. The MSCs are also defined at the same level of granularity and abstraction, they are traceable to the UCM model, and they are consistent with each other. These aspects cannot be taken for granted when sequence diagrams are created manually.

Application to Validation

Scenario definitions based on path control variables, together with path traversal algorithms and transformations to other formalisms, contribute greatly to many validation activities:

- The UCM model itself can be "simulated." For instance, this section presented several scenario definitions (based on variables described in Annex B) used to generate end-to-end scenarios, that is, executions of the model in a given context. Scenario definitions can be seen at test cases that can be used to ensure nothing is broken as the UCM services or architecture evolve, in a way somewhat compatible with the test-development approach proposed by the *agile* development community (Beck, 2003). Errors are reported when the traversal stops (because of non-determinism, unsatisfied conditions, or a start point that is not triggered) or when scenario post-conditions are not met.

- Different stakeholders can review, inspect, and validate individual MSC scenarios extracted from a UCM model in order to create a shared understanding or reach agreement on issues identified in GRL models. MSCs provide a projection of a UCM model for a specific context (a scenario definition) whose existence can be motivated by a GRL model (Amyot, 2003). Additionally, an MSC provides a view to the UCM model that may be more familiar to stakeholders that are closer to the implementation of the system or that have previous knowledge of UML sequence diagrams.

- Test goals can be generated from these scenarios. For instance, Amyot, Weiss, and Logrippo (2004) illustrate the benefits of using UCMNav to automate the generation of test goals from UCM models when compared to approaches based on testing patterns or transformations to formal executable specification languages. These test goals, whether represented as MSCs, in XML, or with some other format, can be refined into concrete test cases for the implementation or for the design, if specified in an executable formalism. The traceable correspondence between the names of the messages used in the MSCs of the previous subsection and those used to implement the operation of the Web services improves the reusability of the scenarios in a testing context, for example, for Web service testing. Amyot, Roy, and Weiss (2005) automated such an approach based on UCMNav and the FitNesse framework for testing Web applications.

- Performance annotations can be added to UCM models in order to generate analyzable performance models in languages such as layered queueing networks. Such a transformation was automated and integrated to UCMNav by Petriu, Amyot, and Woodside (2003). This approach has been successfully applied to several examples from online bookstores to video servers and telephony systems (Petriu & Woodside, 2002). Performance tradeoffs that are difficult to resolve qualitatively at the level of a GRL model can hence benefit from quantitative results (e.g., throughput, bottlenecks, service times and demands, resource utilization) generated by these performance models. In our case study, although we have not done it here, one could derive performance models to determine the best value for the replenishment period or the messaging overhead of central logging, that is, models that allow us to substantiate the existing models (GRL, UCM) with greater level of detail and precision.

Related Work

This section discusses related work, with a particular emphasis on use case-driven design, service-oriented architectures, and conceptual value modeling.

Use-Case Driven Design

Use cases can be supplemented or, to some extent, replaced by URN models. The use case approach has a number of well-known disadvantages that can be averted by using UCMs to model the early requirements of a business process. Using *extends* and *includes* relationships, if often difficult, whereas the same functionality is achievable in a simpler way with UCM stubs and plug-ins. UCM models provide a more systematic way of modeling concurrent behavior and analyzing the interaction of multiple scenarios. Use-case driven approaches rarely provide notions of modeling design goals and linking them to other design artifacts.

The modeling exercise described in this chapter, using URN to describe the WS-I example, uncovered a number of inconsistencies and redundancies in the use case model (WS-I, 2003a). These are due to a number of factors but in particular to the lack of support for showing scenarios belonging to different use cases in the same model and a lack of an abstraction mechanism similar to that provided by stubs and plug-ins. Activity diagrams, which lack the equivalent of dynamic stubs, 2D component layouts, and scenario definitions, tend to be less readable and harder to use than UCMs for documenting individual scenarios.

Service-Oriented Architecture

The service-oriented architecture (SOA) approach proposed by Endrei et al. (2004) aims to align services with business goals. In this approach, services are large-grained activities at the use-case level that a business exposes to be incorporated into other business processes. SOA aims to support many design activities, including domain decomposition, goal-service model creation, and subsystem analysis. During domain decomposition, a value chain model of the business domain showing the main functional areas and their interaction is created. The functional areas are further decomposed into business processes and business use cases.

During goal-service model creation, high-level business goals are decomposed into lower-level subgoals that can be realized by services. This is done to ensure traceability between business needs and implementation using services. During subsystem analysis, business use cases are refined into system use cases, which are then associated with subsystems. Components within each subsystem realize system use cases. For example, a business use case *Purchase Goods* could be refined into the system use cases *Get Catalog* and *Submit Order*. Both would be realized by a RetailerService component.

URN provides support for these three parts, as well as better guidance on what should do be done at each step, and better modeling of scenario interactions.

Conceptual Value Modeling

Conceptual value modeling or e^3-value (Gordijn, 2002; Gordijn & Akkermanns, 2003) is an approach for precisely describing and evaluating innovative e-business ideas. It provides means to evaluate the feasibility of an e-business model focusing on the creation, exchange, and consumption of objects (i.e., the revenue streams) in a multi-actor network. Value models are different from business process models in that the former show how objects of economic value are created and handled by actors, whereas the latter focus on how exchanges of value objects are put into operation from a business process perspective.

E^3-value is similar to our approach in terms of its use of scenarios to model causal flows. It also provides a means for performing value-based trade-offs. However, unlike in URN, value is mainly expressed in monetary terms; other non-functional goals cannot be modeled directly but need to be mapped to how they generate revenues for an actor. On one hand, e^3 value is much more specific in scope than URN. On the other hand, we can think of e^3-value as an intermediary view between general GRL models and operational UCM models. Both approaches could therefore be integrated for modeling e-commerce systems.

Other Related Approaches

The User Requirements Notation and similar languages have been exploited in various contexts, some of which are related to the one presented here:

- UCMs are used by de Bruin and van Vliet (2001) for describing and selecting appropriate architectures. An architecture generator produces a candidate software architecture based on feature-solution graphs (which could be expressed to some extent in GRL) connecting quality requirements and solutions (expressed as potential UCM plug-ins for a reference architecture). The architecture is then evaluated, mainly by inspection, against functional and non-functional requirements.

- Both UCM and GRL are used by Liu and Yu (2003) to model information systems in a social context specified in terms of dependency relationships among agents and roles. Their approach includes an iterative process where the use of GRL and UCM is intertwined: scenarios refine solutions to goals (*tasks*), and the elaboration of scenarios can lead to the discovery of new goals. It is illustrated with a Web-based training system.

- Many GRL concepts are formalized in the TROPOS agent-oriented methodology (Lau & Mylopoulos, 2004) explore the use of TROPOS in the context of Web service design with a greater emphasis on actors and their dependencies (also supported by GRL) than what was presented here. They provide a customer relationship management system example. It is suggested to use the Agent-based Unified Modeling Language to refine the goal and actor models, especially with activity and sequence diagrams, prior to defining Web services in WSDL. However, this step is not well illustrated in their example.

- Bleistein, Aurum, Cox, and Ray (2003) use GRL to link requirements for strategic-level e-business systems to business strategy, as well as to document patterns of best business practices. They explore goal modeling for providing traceability and alignment between strategic levels (business model and business strategy) and tactical and operational ones (business process model and system requirements). This work is still preliminary, but it provides encouraging insights regarding the scalability of GRL for strategic business issues.

- Weiss and Esfandiari (2005) use both GRL and UCMs to model Web services and their interactions. However, their focus is not on modeling business processes per se but on detecting undesirable interactions among services. We see this work as complementary to ours. It could be used to discover architectural alternatives where they are not apparent and to strategize about ways of restructuring a business process to meet business goals.

Conclusion and Future Work

In this section, we summarize our contributions and identify areas of future work.

Contributions

We have made a case for using URN as an approach for business process modeling, and illustrated the approach and its benefits using a supply chain management case study. In the following, our goal is to evaluate the approach by reviewing how URN addresses the requirements for a BPM approach identified in the introduction:

- How does URN address the "W5 questions" (*why, what, who, when,* and *where*)?
- How does it support the analysis of the business model?
- How does it allow multiple stakeholders to participate in the modeling process?

As described, URN comprises two notations: GRL for goal-oriented modeling and UCM for modeling scenarios. Together, these notations help address the W5 questions:

- *Why* do this activity? GRL models allow the analyst to link business or system goals to architectural alternatives, and thus to document the rationale for a particular activity.
- *What* should this activity be precisely? Starting from high-level business goals, GRL supports their iterative refinement into high-level tasks. Further refinement of these tasks into concrete low-level responsibilities, plug-ins, or scenario definitions can be achieved via a UCM model. In particular, its hierarchical abstraction capability allows us to scale our models to large business processes.
- *Who* is involved in this activity? A UCM model does not only provide a refinement of high-level tasks into low-level responsibilities but can also capture the structure of the organization supporting the business process. Components can be defined for each role in the business process. Furthermore, component visibility can be restricted as required by nesting them.

- *Where* and *when* should this activity be performed? A UCM model also allows us to define how responsibilities are allocated to components, as well as their temporal ordering via constructs for expressing sequence, choices, concurrency, and synchronization.

Additionally, a business process model should enable ways of (formally) analyzing the processes and goal satisfaction. Analysis of the business process is supported in two ways. The level propagation mechanism in GRL lets us analyze the impact of architectural alternatives (e.g., centralized logging) on high-level goals (of both functional and non-functional nature), as illustrated in the section on architectural change analysis By capturing architectural reasoning in a GRL model, we can compare alternatives as they apply to a particular context. Unlike use cases, UCM models are not based on an informal textual representation, and can therefore also provide input to various validation activities such as testing and performance analysis. Thus, UCM provides mechanisms for ensuring the validity and traceability of the model, and supports more detailed analysis.

Business process models should be understandable to various stakeholders, including customers. With URN, we can model a business process at different levels of formality supporting all development stages from early requirements to early design. A GRL model can describe "soft" aspects of a business process, for example, high-level business goals such as customer satisfaction and their refinement into operational goals (e.g., the number of orders handled successfully). The hierarchical abstraction mechanism of UCM models (via stubs and plug-ins) allows us to hide lower-level details in defining a business process while preserving a sense of its overall operation. In a UCM model we can simulate scenarios by defining various conditions on the operation of the system and walking through their execution. The interaction of scenarios and the concurrency properties of a UCM model can be analyzed informally or formally by mapping the UCM model into a suitable target language. In this chapter, we have illustrated the usefulness of representing UCM scenarios as message sequence charts to support visualization, shared understanding, and analysis. Mappings to other languages exist, as discussed in Amyot (2003) and Amyot et al. (2004).

Finally, as suggested in the previous section, URN can be integrated partially or entirely into an existing business process modeling approach. It does not have to replace current ways of creating and analyzing models to be useful.

Hence, URN satisfies the requirements of a business modeling language independently of the application area.

Future Work

In the near-term, we expect to work on three research objectives related to the extraction of test goals and test case generation, extraction of service operations, and performance analysis of business processes described in a UCM model:

- Deriving test goals and test cases for the case study. This work will be done in relation to our work on validation described elsewhere (Amyot et al., 2004).

- Add support to the UCMNav tool for recognizing messages that are part of the same service operation (e.g., messages that form request/response pairs or are notification operations in response to an earlier request/response operation).

- Study ways of describing a complex business process as a composition of smaller business processes, to make them more usable as the complexity of the model increases.

- Create a performance model for architectural trade-off scenarios.

- Support relationships between GRL and UCM views of a URN model in a single tool. Recent work has lead to jUCMNav, an Eclipse plug-in for the editing of UCM models (Kealey, Tremblay, Daigle, McManus, Clift-Noël, & Amyot, 2005). This tool is currently being extended to support GRL models (editing and evaluation), scenario generation, and integration with requirements management systems.

A longer-term objective is to map UCM models to a Web services implementation. Here we envision work on two research objectives:

- Generate WSDL descriptions from Web services templates.
- Map UCM scenarios to the Business Process Execution Language (BPEL) for Web services (Andrews et al., 2003) that can be directly executed by a BPEL execution engine.

Another topic for future research is the possibility of using URN for organizational design and the analysis of business models. One important feature of a UCM model is that the *same* scenarios can be mapped to a different set of components. For example, we could explore the architectural impact of different business models, such as replacing the retail business model with a direct-to-customer business model, by defining a set of components that excludes the retailer but reusing the scenarios we have already documented. This topic of research is explored in more detail in Weiss and Amyot (2005).

Acknowledgments

This work has been supported financially by the Natural Science and Engineering Research Council of Canada, through its Strategic Grants and Discovery Grants programs.

References

Amyot, D. (2003). Introduction to the user requirements notation: Learning by example. *Computer Networks, 42*(3), 285-301. Retrieved June 21, 2006, from http://www. usecasemaps.org/pub/ComNet03.pdf

Amyot, D., Cho, D. Y., He, X., & He, Y. (2003, November). Generating scenarios from use case map specifications. In *Proceedings of Third International Conference on Quality Software (QSIC'03)*, Dallas, TX.

Amyot, D., Echihabi, A., & He, Y. (2004, June). UCMEXPORTER: supporting scenario transformations from use case maps. In *Proceedings of NOTERE'04*, Saïdia, Morocco.

Amyot, D., Roy, J. F., & Weiss. M. (2005, June). UCM-driven testing of Web applications. In *Proceedings of 12ᵗʰ SDL Forum (SDL 2005)*, Grimstad, Norway.

Amyot, D., Weiss, M., & Logrippo, L. (2004, November). *UCM-based generation of test goals*. ISSRE'04 Workshop on Integrated-reliability with Telecommunications and UML Languages (WITUL), Rennes, France.

Andrews, T., et al. (2003). *Business process execution language for Web services*, Version (1.1). Retrieved on June 21, 2005, from http://www-106.ibm.com/developerworks/ library/ws-bpel

Beck, K. (2003). *Test-driven development: By example*. Addison-Wesley.

Bleistein, S. J., Aurum, A., Cox, K., & Ray, P. K. (2003). Linking requirements goal modeling techniques to strategic e-business patterns and best practice. In D. Zowghi & B. Al-Ani (Eds.), *Proceedings of 8ᵗʰ Australian Workshop on Requirements Engineering (AWRE'03)*, Sydney. Retrieved August 15, 2004, from http://www.caeser.unsw.edu. au/publications/pdf/Tech03_2.pdf

Buhr, R. J. A. (1998). Use case maps as architectural entities for complex systems. *IEEE Trans. on Software Engineering, 24*(12), 1131-1155. Retrieved on June 21, 2005, from http://www.usecasemaps.org/pub/ucmUpdate.pdf

Buhr, R. J. A., & Casselman, R. S. (1996). *Use case maps for object-oriented systems*. Prentice Hall. Retrieved on June 21, 2005, from http://www.usecasemaps.org/pub/ UCM_book95.pdf

Carlson, D. (2001). *Modeling XML applications with UML*. Addison-Wesley.

Chung, L., Nixon, B. A., Yu, E., & Mylopoulos, J. (2000). *Non-functional requirements in software engineering*. Kluwer Academic Publishers.

de Bruin, H., and van Vliet, H. (2001). *Scenario-based generation and evaluation of software architectures*. Generative and Component-Based Software Engineering (GCSE'01), LNCS 2186. Springer.

Endrei, M., Ang. J., Arsanjani, A., et al. (2004, April). Patterns: service-oriented architecture and Web services, IBM Redbook. Retrieved on June 21, 2005, from http://www. redbooks.ibm.com/redbooks/pdfs/sg246303.pdf

Gordijn, J. (2002). *Value-based requirements engineering: Exploring innovative e-commerce ideas*. (Doctoral dissertation, Vrije Universiteit, The Netherlands, 2002.) SIKS

Dissertation Series No. 2002-08. Retrieved on June 21, 2005, from http://www.cs.vu. nl/~gordijn/thesis.htm

Gordijn, J., & Akkermans, J. (2003). Value-based requirements engineering: Exploring innovative ecommerce ideas. *Requirements Engineering Journal, 8,* 114-135.

ITU-T – *International Telecommunications Union* (2003). Recommendation Z.150 (02/03), user requirements notation (URN) – Language requirements and framework. Geneva, Switzerland.

ITU-T – *International Telecommunications Union* (2004). Recommendation Z.120 (04/04) message sequence chart (MSC). Geneva, Switzerland.

Kealey, J., Tremblay, E., Daigle, J. P., McManus, J., Clift-Noël, O., & Amyot, D. (2005). jUCMNav: une nouvelle plateforme ouverte pour l'édition et l'analyse de modèles UCM. In *Proceedings of NOTERE 2005,* Gatineau, Canada.

Lau, D., & Mylopoulos, J. (2004). Designing Web services with TROPOS. In *Proceedings of IEEE International Conference on Web Services (ICWS'04),* San Diego, CA.

Liu, L., & Yu, E. (2004). Designing information systems in social context: A goal and scenario modelling approach. *Information Systems, 29*(2). Retrieved on August 15, 2006, from http://jucmnav.softwareengineering.ca/twiki/bin/view/UCM/VirLibIs04

OMG – Object Management Group (2003). *Unified Modeling Language Specification* (UML), version (1.5), March 2003. Retrieved on June 21, 2005, from http://www. omg.org/uml/

OMG – Object Management Group (2004). *Model Driven Architecture* (MDA). Retrieved on June 21, 2005 from http://www.omg.org/mda/

Petriu, D. B., & Woodside, C. M. (2002). Software performance models from system scenarios in use case maps. In *Computer Performance Evaluation/TOOLS, Lecture notes in computer science 2324,* 141-158. Springer.

Petriu, D. B., Amyot, D., & Woodside, C. M. (2003, July). Scenario-based performance engineering with UCMNav. In *Proceedings of 11ᵗʰ SDL Forum* (SDL'03), *Lecture notes in computer science* 2708, 18-35. Retrieved on June 21, 2005, from http://www. usecasemaps.org/pub/SDL03-UCM-LQN.pdf

Telelogic, A.B. (2004). *Tau SDL suite.* Retrieved on June 21, 2005, from http://www.telelogic.com/products/tau/sdl/index.cfm

UCM User Group. (2003). *UCMExporter.* Retrieved on June 21, 2005, from http://ucmexporter.sourceforge.net/

UCM User Group. (2004). *UCMNav* 2. Retrieved on June 21, 2005, from http://www. usecasemaps.org/tools/ucmnav/index.shtml

URN Focus Group. (2003a). Draft Rec. Z.151 – *Goal-oriented requirement language* (GRL). Geneva, Switzerland, Sept. 2003. Retrieved on June 21, 2005, from http://www.UseCaseMaps.org/urn/. See also http://www.cs.toronto.edu/km/GRL/

URN Focus Group. (2003b). Draft rec. Z.152 – *use case map notation* (UCM). Geneva, Switzerland, Sept. 2003. http://www.UseCaseMaps.org/urn/. See also http://www. UseCaseMaps.org/

Weiss, M., & Amyot, D. (2005). Design and evolution of e-business models. In *Proceedings of International Conference on Electronic Commerce (CEC)* (pp. 462-466). IEEE.

Weiss, M., & Esfandiari, B. (2005). On feature interactions among Web services. *International Journal of Web Services Research, 2*(4), 21-45

WS-I – Web Services Interoperability Organization. (2003a). *Supply chain management: Use case model*, version (1.0). Retrieved on June 21, 2005, from http://www.ws-i.org

WS-I – Web Services Interoperability Organization. (2003b). *Supply chain management: Sample application architecture*, version (1.0.1). Retrieved on June 21, 2005, from http://www.ws-i.org

W3C (2001). *Web services description language* (WSDL) 1.1. Retrieved on June 21, 2005, from http://www.w3.org/TR/wsdl

Yu, E. (1997). Towards modelling and reasoning support for early-phase requirements engineering. In *Proceedings of 3rd IEEE Int. Symp. on Requirements Engineering (RE'97)* (pp. 226-235).

Yu, E., & Liu, L. (2000). *Organization modelling environment* (OME). Retrieved on June 21, 2005, from http://www.cs.toronto.edu/km/ome/

Yu, E., & Mylopoulos, J. (1998). Why goal-oriented requirements engineering. In *Proceedings of the 4th REFSQ* (pp. 15-22).

Annex A: Summary of the
User Requirements Notation

Figure 18. Summary of the GRL notation

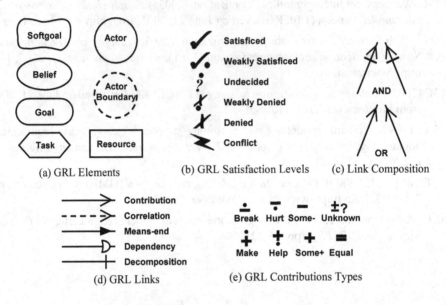

(a) GRL Elements   (b) GRL Satisfaction Levels   (c) Link Composition

(d) GRL Links   (e) GRL Contributions Types

Figure 19. Summary of (a subset of) the UCM notation

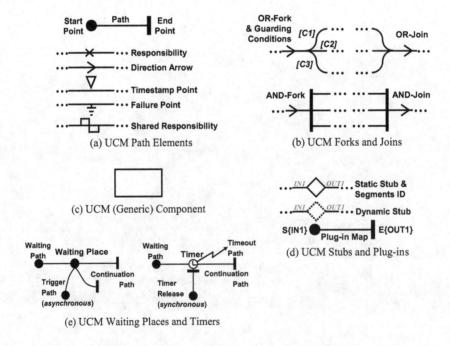

(a) UCM Path Elements   (b) UCM Forks and Joins

(c) UCM (Generic) Component   (d) UCM Stubs and Plug-ins

(e) UCM Waiting Places and Timers

Annex B: Path Control Variables for Scenario Definitions

The following are the global Boolean path control variables used in the supply chain management UCM model:

- CanAccessLog: Is the requester allowed to access the event logs?
- ItemListEmpty: Is the list of remaining items to order empty?
- LogRequestValid: Is the log access request valid?
- MoreItems: Are there more items that can be provided by the current warehouse?
- ProductExists: Does the requested product exist?
- ReplenishTimer_timeout: Will the replenishment timer time out?
- RepositoryAvailable: Is the log repository available?
- SomeItemsShipped: Are there any items being shipped to the consumer?
- StockStillSufficient: Will the stocks be sufficient for the next product (for simulation)?
- SufficientInventory: Is the inventory sufficient? (If not, goods need to be manufactured.)
- SufficientStock: Are the stocks sufficient for the current product?
- ValidOrder: Is the order valid?
- WarehouseLeft: Any warehouse left to which the remaining items could be ordered?

Chapter IX

How E-Services Satisfy Customer Needs:
A Software-Aided Reasoning

Ziv Baida, Free University Amsterdam, The Netherlands

Jaap Gordijn, Free University Amsterdam, The Netherlands

Hans Akkermans, Free University Amsterdam, The Netherlands

Hanne Sæle, SINTEF Energy Research, Norway

Andrei Morch, SINETEF Energy Research, Norway

Abstract

We outline a rigorous approach that models how companies can electronically offer packages of independent services (service bundles). Its objective is to support prospective Web site visitors in defining and buying service bundles that fit their specific needs and demands. The various services in the bundle may be offered by different suppliers. To enable this scenario, it is necessary that software can reason about customer needs and available service offerings. Our approach for tackling this issue is based on recent advances in computer and information science, where information about a domain at hand is conceptualized and formalized using ontologies and subsequently represented in machine-interpretable form. The substantive part from our ontology derives from broadly accepted service management and marketing concepts from business studies literature. In earlier work, we concentrated on the service bundling process itself. In the present chapter, we discuss how to ensure that the created bundles indeed meet customer demands. Experience of Norwegian energy utilities shows that severe financial losses can be caused when companies offer service bundles without a solid foundation for the bundle-creation process and without an in-depth understanding of customer needs and demands. We use a running case example from the Norwegian energy sector to demonstrate how we put theory into practice.

Introduction

More and more businesses nowadays offer their services via the Internet, either parallel to or instead of traditional physical channels. Statistics show an immense growth in the percentage of households with Internet access that actually shop online, from 27 percent in 1998 to nearly 50 percent in 2000 (Xue, Harker, & Heim, 2003). Almost 30 percent of Internet users in the European Union use online banking services, with the Nordic countries as leaders; nearly 65 percent of Internet users in Finland use online banking (Centeno, 2003). Airlines sell more and more tickets online instead of through traditional travel agencies; check-in is performed online rather than at the check-in counter in the airport. Companies such as DHL and FedEx allow customers to follow their shipments through a so-called track-and-trace system. Governments are considering online voting. These are all examples showing the dominant and growing role and importance of e-services in a variety of industries.

Online service offerings introduce a new challenge with which traditional service suppliers do not have to deal. It no longer is sufficient that only service personnel understand customer needs; if a supplier wishes to offer customized services through an automated online process, software must be able to reason out these customer needs and the possible service offerings satisfying such needs, so that the whole process can be provided online. The need for an automated process becomes even greater when a customer wants to buy a service bundle (Grönroos, 2000), a package of more elementary services, which may be offered by multiple suppliers. Each supplier offers its added value, and together suppliers provide a complete answer for a customer need. In such a case, software should be able to decide whether and how to combine services of multiple suppliers into one service bundle.

Our study on creating customer-driven service bundles aims at this new challenge. We present a method for formalizing customer needs and available service offerings, and we relate the two to each other. We do not directly address the problem of how to elicit and understand customer needs (although, as we will show, our method helps gain insights into these needs) but focus on the issues of conceptualizing and formalizing customer needs, such that software can configure service bundles satisfying customer needs.

Our research uses well-known and accepted knowledge, concepts, ideas, and terminology from business research literature (Grönroos, 2000; Kotler, 1988; Zeithaml, Parasuraman, & Berry, 1990) to describe services from a supplier perspective as well as from a customer perspective. The idea is to conceptualize and formalize well-known business research concepts, not to invent new ones. Additionally, we use practices and ideas from computer science as a means to process this knowledge in order to enable automated support for the bundling process of customer-driven service bundles. One of these practices is the use of an ontology, which is a formal, shared conceptualization of something we assume to exist (Borst, 1997; Quine, 1961); in our case, needs and e-services. The unique contribution of this chapter is in the combination of well-known business research terminology on services with the modeling and conceptualization rigor of computer science.

The work presented in this chapter is not limited to e-services but can be applied to traditional services as well. Nevertheless, our work is of much greater importance for e-services, since the realization of e-service offerings requires automating processes that may otherwise be performed in the minds of service personnel. For e-services realization, it is absolutely necessary that business knowledge is conceptualized, formalized, and made machine-readable and machine-processable. This is what we aim to achieve in our work.

Our method consists of three steps to be performed in advance, followed by one runtime step to be performed each time a customer wants to create (design) a bundle for need satisfaction:

1.   Identify and model customer needs and demands;
2.   Identify and model available services;
3.   Identify and model relations between demands and available services; and
4.   Create service bundles out of available services, based on customer needs and demands.

Whereas our earlier work (Akkermans, Baida, Gordijn, Peña, & Laresgoiti, 2004; Baida, Akkermans, & Gordijn, 2003a; Baida, Gordijn, Sæle, Morch, & Akkermans 2004b); focused on steps two and four of the presented method, in the current chapter we present the whole method and focus on steps one and three.

In the remainder of this chapter, we will use a case study in the energy domain to present our work. After introducing the energy domain, we discuss our research approach, followed by a discussion of a service ontology. We then present a four-step method for ensuring that e-services are demand-driven and discuss it using examples from the energy case study. Finally, we review related work and present our conclusions.

Case Study: Bundling Electricity Supply with Other Services

Since the deregulation of the electricity market in Norway in 1991, production and trade of electric energy have been liberalized, while the transmission and distribution are maintained as regulated monopolies. Nowadays, after evolving for almost 15 years of deregulation, the Norwegian power market has become mature. The electricity generation and supply sectors are characterized by fierce competition, due to which the difference in electricity retail prices per kWh between different suppliers is diminishing. Also in other European countries power is shifting from suppliers to customers, and more and more end-user customers in Europe are able to choose a preferred electricity supplier.

Commercially, one of the disadvantages of the electricity product is that for power supply companies it is hard to distinguish themselves, due to the anonymous nature of this product: electricity from different suppliers is delivered according to the same standard, with the same physical characteristics, and is consumed through the same electricity socket in a customer's home. Therefore, companies face difficulties in competing with each other. Consequently, many suppliers are seeking ways to improve marketing via differentiation of their product to increase their market share. One way to differentiate is to offer additional services such as Internet access, (software) application service provisioning, and home comfort management. Another way to improve marketing is to create more complex and elaborate electricity retail contracts, which are more beneficial to customers because they better fit their needs. At the same time, choosing the best electricity contract becomes a demanding task for electricity consumers.

Many of the additional services can be ordered and provisioned via the Internet. Moreover, suppliers can use existing infrastructure and/or available business processes to deploy such extra services, so bundling these services with the traditional electricity product can be done with relatively modest effort. Experience, however, shows that the bundling of services without sound logical fundaments of the bundles design process and disregarding customers' demands may cause severe financial losses, as can be seen by the example of KanKan (Flæte & Ottesen, 2001). KanKan was launched on January 23, 2001, as a new market offer of one of the biggest distribution system operators in Norway. It was marketed as an integrated bundle of services, including electricity supply and transmission, Smart Home features, home insurance, telephone, and an Internet service provider (ISP) service. Despite the expectations and costly market campaigns, very few households showed interest in the new service offering. After several attempts to revise the concept, it was removed from the market (Flæte & Ottesen, 2001; Martinussen, 2002). Several reasons for the failure were identified later; misunderstanding of customer needs and meeting them in product offers was the most visible one. The need for such a solid and formal foundation for a successful online process is the driving force behind our study in the energy sector. Furthermore, the KanKan example highlights the necessity for evaluation methods for the feasibility of offering service bundles, a topic that we have addressed in Baida, Gordijn, Morch, Sæle, and Akkermans (2004a). In this chapter, therefore, we focus on the aspect of customer demands.

Notes on Research Method and Design

Our research approach represents a departure from traditional quantitative as well as qualitative modes of scientific research in information systems (IS) on several scores. First, the nature and role of theory; we employ formal ontology as a device for rigorous theory articulation. Ontologies are formal conceptualizations of a real-world domain such that they have a computational representation that is fit for automated reasoning. This work is much improved now that there are international standards such as resource description framework (RDF) and OWL for knowledge representation on the Web (developed in the context of W3C's Semantic Web effort; OWL stands for Ontology Web Language and was finalized in February 2004). As theories, ontologies are formal (in a logical and/or knowledge-based inferencing sense) yet typically are not expressed in the variable and measure parlance of the common quantitative modes of social and business research (although, of course, this is not strictly excluded). So, usually, ontologies are formalized qualitative theories concerning conceptual structures shared by a community of practice in a domain.

Yet this does not imply (at least not necessarily) that they are congruent with the interpretivist or naturalist perspectives common in qualitative research. Ontologies are intended to be reusable (this is the typical computer science term; i.e., generalizable across other settings, contexts, and applications). Therefore, they formalize the agreed-upon (explicit or more often implicit) common understanding in a domain. For example, the ontology partly discussed in the present chapter only reflects and formalizes consensus aspects of service management and marketing as, for example, typically found in textbooks; it does not attempt to express the latest issues as debated in academic literature on services where there is no consensus, nor does it represent highly domain-specific or even organization-specific elements that one will undoubtedly encounter in any thick-description field empirical study. This implies a clear difference in the resulting theory from a strict interpretivist or naturalist perspective. Ontology is better seen as a model-based approach, whereby the quality and success of the model is assessed in terms of whether it is good enough to help in problem solving, as posed by the research goals. This notion of a model-based stance that is different from the standard fare in both quantitative and qualitative approaches has already been recognized and debated a long time ago in the knowledge systems literature (Ford & Bradshaw, 1993; Schreiber, Akkermans, Anjewierden, de Hoog, Shadbolt, Van der Velde, et al., 2000) and references therein.

Further, qualitative and quantitative approaches have in common that they (often tacitly) assume that scientific aims lie in (different forms of) explanation. In contrast, our ontology approach is more tailored toward problem solving and innovation in business and industry practice. Thus, its aim is closer to what Hevner, March, Park, and Ram (2004) call design science in IS. We mention in passing that, based on previous research, engineering science, and industry experiences, we would take issue with some of these authors' proposed guidelines for academic quality design research, in particular design as a search process and as an (instantiated) artifact, but this is beyond the scope of the present chapter. But certainly in e-business and e-service research, where the field is in a constant state of change and emergence, research goals that go beyond observation, measurement, statistical-variable, or qualitative-interpretive explanation are of prime importance.

All this does have implications for the empirical and test/validation parts of research studies in IS. Ontologies can be tested by computer tooling, modeling, simulation, and analysis. This establishes what is sometimes called their computational adequacy and some aspects of their theoretical adequacy (soundness, consistency, completeness). Their empirical, epistemological adequacy can be tested by (as in our research) case studies in the field. Given the different nature and role of our approach to theory formation, such case studies do not sit well with the conventional typology of exploratory, descriptive, or explanatory case study. They serve a dual goal. On the one hand, they help validate (part of) generalizable ontological theory. To this extent, they might be viewed as tending toward being explanatory (although not necessarily in terms of causal explanation). On the other hand, however, they aim at helping to solve problems and achieve goals, as specifically perceived by our partners or clients in the study, which are, in the present case, not of an explanatory but of a business development and design nature. A consequence of this positioning of our empirical research is that case study design is not along the traditional lines of external-observer style empirical research but has much more in common with action research.

From Customer Needs to E-Services

In this chapter, we present a four-step approach (see Figure 1) to find alternative bundles of e-services that satisfy customer needs. Our approach is based on the following key ideas:

1. A service can be seen as a bundle of benefits (Kasper, van Helsdignen, & de Vries Jr., 1999), which satisfy customer needs.

2. When customers buy products (services or goods), in fact they are not interested in the products themselves, but in the benefits—the value—that these products presents for them (Lancaster, 1966; Teare, 1998). These benefits are satisfiers of customer needs.

3. A customer view on services differs from a supplier view (Vasarhelyi & Greenstein, 2003); thus two service descriptions are required for automated service provisioning. Typically, a supplier description is required for selecting and comparing service instances. A customer description is required in order to decide which available services fit specific customers.

4. Services differ from goods in their intangibility (Grönroos, 2000; Kasper et al., 1999; Kotler, 1988; Lovelock, 2001; Zeithaml & Bitner, 1996). As a result, services cannot be described by their physical properties—as is the case with goods—so that customers and suppliers can refer to them unambiguously. Services therefore need to be

Figure 1. Serviguration: Configuring service bundles based on customer demands

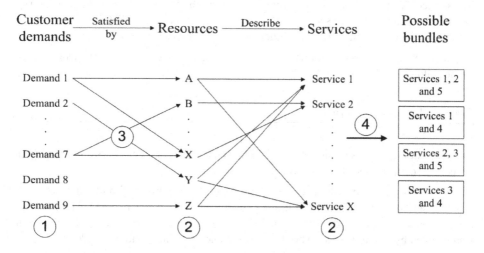

described differently. We describe services by the benefits (value) they provide and by the sacrifices (value) they require.

In short, with the help of business experts, we first model needs and demands of customers in a given sector and then describe available services. Since customer demands are satisfied by providing some customer value, we identify relations between demands and outcomes of services (*resources*, as we call them) that reflect a customer's benefits from a service. When searching for possible services or service bundles that satisfy customer needs, demands (described possibly by subjective quality criteria) are used as selection criteria for resources (benefits, described by objective quality criteria). In other words, instead of saying "demand X can be satisfied by service Y," we say "demand X can be satisfied by resource Y," and we then search for all services that provide resource Y. This is possible because resources are descriptors of services. Hence, selecting specific demands implies not only selecting certain resources but also certain services that must or can be part of a bundle. Then, based on business knowledge on inherent dependencies between services (Baida et al., 2004b), other services may be included in bundles or substituting services may be suggested as solutions. The causal chain, from needs and demands through resources to services, ensures that the offered service bundles will, indeed, meet customer needs.

Formalizing Business Knowledge using a Service Ontology

We formalize business knowledge on services using a service ontology (Baida, 2006; Baida et al., 2003a). On a high level of abstraction, our service ontology embodies two inter-related top-level viewpoints or perspectives: service value and service offering.

The service value perspective (see Figure 2) captures knowledge about adding value. It represents a customer viewpoint on value creation by expressing customer needs, expectations, and experiences, and is driven by a customer's desire to buy a certain service of a certain, often vaguely defined, quality, in return for a certain sacrifice (including price but also intangible costs such as inconvenience costs and access time).

The service offering perspective, in contrast, represents the supply-side viewpoint; it describes service components (a core service and supplementary services) and outcomes, as they are actually delivered by the service provider in order to satisfy customers' needs.

The service value perspective and the service offering perspective will be presented shortly in the following subsections.

Service Value Perspective

The sub-ontology representing the service value (customer) perspective is sketched in Figure 2. Its main concepts are discussed below.

Needs, wants and demands. The starting point for the discipline of marketing, whether it refers to services or not, lies in the human needs and wants (Kotler, 1988). The term *need* refers to what humans need and want (to buy) and is quite straightforward. A formal definition is given by Kotler (1988), who distinguishes needs, wants, and demands:

Figure 2. Service sub-ontology representing the service customer value perspective

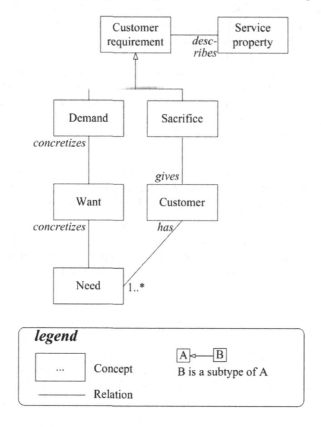

- A human need is a state of felt deprivation of some basic satisfaction.
- Wants are desires for specific satisfiers of these deeper needs.
- Demands are wants for specific products that are backed up by an ability and willingness to buy them.

Needs are often vague; the need for financial security, for example, can be interpreted in many ways. Customers concretize their needs by transforming them into wants and demands, based, for example, on their exposure to existing services and to marketing campaigns. In many cases, when a customer is interested in some service, he or she has already transformed needs into wants and demands. As a matter of fact, the customer already has a solution in mind for his or her need (e.g., indoor comfort [need]; lighting [want]; energy supply [demand]).

Sacrifice. The customer's long-term sacrifice includes the price of the service as well as relationship costs. These can be direct (e.g., investment in office space, additional equipment), indirect (related to the amount of time and resources that the customer has to devote to maintaining the relationship), or psychological costs (lack of trust in a service provider; unpleasant sensory experiences such as noise) (Grönroos, 2000) (e.g., time spent waiting to be served, travel costs, switching costs from one supplier to another).

Service quality. Service quality is the degree and direction of the discrepancy between a customer's expectations and the perception of the service (Bigné, Martinez, & Miquel, 1997). Customer expectations embrace several different elements, including desired service, predicted service, and a zone of tolerance that falls between the desired and adequate service levels (Berry & Parasuraman, 1991). Expectations are based on word-of-mouth communications, personal needs, past experiences, and external communications from service providers (Zeithaml et al., 1990). At least two widely accepted generic methods for defining service quality exist: that of the Nordic school (Grönroos, 2000) and that of the North American school (SERVQUAL) (Zeithaml et al., 1990). Nevertheless, quality definition is domain- and market-specific (e.g., high level of reliability, highly individualized service, and fancy conference location).

Next to quality description, other criteria also may play a role (e.g., quantitative description, or time, when the service should be provided). For this reason, we have introduced the concept **service property** in our ontology; *service quality* is described as *service properties*.

Similarly to demands, also sacrifices may be described by service properties. We refer to demands and sacrifices as **customer requirements**. Service quality, technically speaking, is a property of a customer requirement. In the rest of this chapter, whenever we use the term *desired quality*, we refer also to non-qualitative service properties.

Service Offering Perspective

The service offering (supplier) perspective, lengthily discussed in Baida et al. (2004b), describes how a business intends to add value (see Figure 3). It is centered on the concept of **service element**, which is what the service marketing literature defines as business ac-

Figure 3. Service sub-ontology representing the service supplier perspective

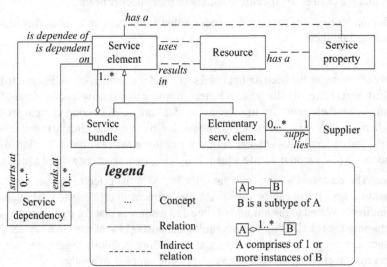

tivities, deeds and performances of a mostly intangible nature (Grönroos, 2000; Kasper et al., 1999; Kotler, 1988; Zeithaml et al., 1990). We showed in Akkermans et al. (2004) that service bundling can in fact be seen as a component configuration task, once the business essence of a service is described with constructs from configuration theory. Configuration is a constructive task where predefined components are assembled (configured) into a larger, complex component, based on the availability of a set of predefined connections, and associated parameters and constraints (Gruber, Olson, & Runkel, 1996; Löckenhoff & Messer, 1994; Mittal & Frayman, 1989).

A service element is a business activity that involves the exchange of values between the actors involved. Hence, it requires a set of *service inputs*, and results in the availability of a set of *service outcomes*. Very often, the outcomes of a service reflect the customer benefits from a service, whereas the customer sacrifice is expressed as service inputs (e.g., payment). Service inputs and service outcomes are referred to as **resources**. Resources are described using objective, measurable parameters. For example, the service element *broadband Internet access* has an outcome resource *broadband Internet capability* with properties *download speed* and *upload speed*, specified in Kbps. Hence, the resource description provides the objective and measurable benefit of a service; this objective benefit may be interpreted differently by customers who have differing expectations and quality perceptions, leading to their subjective value perceptions of the same service.

Service elements can be offered as a bundle and thus form a complex service element. To facilitate automated reasoning about bundling, the **service dependency** is used; it is a relation between service elements. For instance, a substitute dependency between elements A and B represents that service element B is a substitute service for service A (but not necessarily vice versa).

Figure 4 is an example service element from our energy study—the supply of electricity. The service is described by its resources. Two service inputs are required to provide this service (payment and lock-in, a commitment to consume this service for a predefined period), and it results in the availability of one service outcome (energy of type electricity).

Figure 4. Example service element: Electricity supply

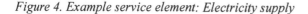
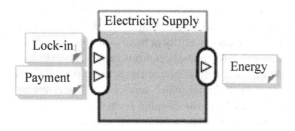

Relating the Service Value and Service Offering Perspectives

The process of service configuration—serviguration (Baida, 2006; Baida et al., 2003a)—spans both perspectives, service value and service offering. Serviguration is the process of defining bundles of service elements (a supply-side description of services, part of the service offering perspective) that satisfy the customer description of his desired service (service value perspective). Serviguration (see Figure 1) can be split into four steps: (1) identify and model customer needs and demands; (2) identify and model available services; (3) identify and model relations between demands and available services; and (4) use knowledge of steps 1, 2 and 3 to create service bundles out of available services, based on a given set of customer needs and demands. Whereas our earlier work concentrated on steps two and four (Baida et al., 2004a), the present chapter concentrates on steps one and three.

Step 1: Identify and Model Customer Needs and Demands

Understanding customer needs has been acknowledged by service marketing and service management researchers as an important early phase in business initiatives (Aschmoneit & Heitmann, 2002; Kotler, 1988; Mentzer, Rutner, & Matsuno, 1997; Teare, 1998). But also in the field of Requirements Engineering (RE), a sub-discipline of computer science, significant effort has been put into understanding stakeholder needs to be satisfied by information systems (Liu & Yu, 2001; Mylopoulos, Chung, Liao, Wang, & Yu, 2001; Mylopoulos, Chung, & Yu, 1999; Sharp & Galal, 1999; Van Lamsweerde, 2000). A specific contribution of RE is goal oriented requirements engineering (GORE). In GORE, needs are called goals, and formal and semi-formal modeling techniques are used to model goals and relations between these. We employ these techniques to represent and to reason about needs. The advantage of doing so is that this enables us to reuse existing mechanisms for reasoning about such needs.

In the first step of our method, we identify and model customer needs. Needs identification has been studied by marketing researchers (Kärkkäinen & Elfvengren, 2002; Kotler, 1988; McCullough, 2002; Murthi & Sarkar, 2003; Reynolds & Gutman, 1988; Teare, 1998) and is beyond the scope of our study. Instead, we consider customer needs to be known in advance by business experts. We then use need hierarchies to model these needs in accordance with our service ontology (needs, wants, and demands). Table 1 presents our hierarchy of needs, wants, and demands for the energy utility at hand. The notations H/I refer to the customer type, household or industrial. As can be seen from Table 1, some demands relate to concrete services (e.g., a demand for a mobile phone line), while others are more abstract when a customer does not necessarily know which service can satisfy his or her need or when a diversity of solutions exists (e.g., the demand *temperature regulation* does not specify a concrete service; it can be satisfied by a variety of services).

Table 1 shows examples of needs, wants, and demands, as we modeled in the energy study.

Table 1. Customer needs, wants, and demands for the energy utility TrønderEnergi

Customer needs	Customer wants	Customer demands
Indoor comfort (H,I)	Lighting (H,I) Home services (cooking, washing, etc.) (H) Comfort temperature (H,I)	Energy supply (H,I) Hot tap water (H,I) Room heating (H,I) Air conditioning (H,I)
	Energy regulation for budget-control (H,I)	Energy regulation for budget control (H,I), with different characteristics (manual / automated, on-site regulation / location-independent)
	Temperature regulation for increased comfort (H,I)	Temperature regulation (H,I) with different characteristics (manual / automated, on-site regulation / location-independent)
Social contacts and recreation (H) Business contacts (I)	Communication (H,I)	Telephone line (H,I) Mobile phone line (H,I) Internet (broadband) (H,I) E-mail facilities (H,I)
Safety (H,I)	Increased security (H,I) Reduced insurance premium (H)	Safety check of electrical installation (H) Internal control of electrical installation (I)
IT support for business (I)	IT services (I)	ASP services (I) Hardware (I) Software (I)

As can be seen from the table, customers specify demands in their own terminology (e.g., "room heating") or in supplier terminology (e.g., "telephone line"). The latter happens when customers are already familiar with available services that can satisfy their needs. In our study, the energy utility TrønderEnergi wanted to explore possible ways to bundle electricity supply with other (not energy-related) services, such that the bundles provide a good solution for customer needs. Therefore, the list of needs, wants and demands presented in Table 1 is not complete; it includes only those needs, wants, and demands that TrønderEnergi considered to satisfy through existing or new service offerings.

Customer requirements for services are captured by (1) needs, wants, and demands, and (2) acceptable sacrifice. Each may further be described by quality criteria or by other service properties. Demands often describe the functionality of a desired solution, whereas the desired quality prescribes the expected performance level of a service. Hence, the desired quality describes a certain level that applies to demands. The acceptable sacrifice captures the price, switching costs, psychological costs, and more to be paid for satisfaction of a need. Two important remarks have to be made:

- While our discussion in this chapter concentrates on deriving a set of desired service outcomes (resources) based on customer demands, we use the same mechanisms also to transform the customers' acceptable sacrifice (in customer terminology) to a set of acceptable service inputs (in supplier terminology).

- Conceptually, resources provide solutions for demands. Hence we discuss relations between demands and resources. However, due to computational considerations, the service ontology relates the concept "demand," through its super-type "customer re-quirement," to the concept "requirement expression." The latter is related to a "design element," the super-type of "resource."

Reasoning about Customer Needs

Often when customers first indicate requiring something, only partial (or no) knowledge of their *concrete* demands exists. We then need (1) to reason about relations between needs, wants, and demands, and derive concrete demands based on more abstract needs, and sub-sequently (2) to match between these demands and available service offerings of service suppliers. In the rest of this section, we show how we perform the first of these reasoning processes.

The relation between needs, wants, and demands can be described by a hierarchy:

> ... a structure by which classes of objects are ranked according to some subor-dinating principle.
>
> (Stephens & Tripp, 1978, p. 102)

Need hierarchies are comprised of three levels of aggregation, using the above definitions of needs, wants, and demands as a subordinating principle.

Similar hierarchies have been used in the field of GORE to transform high-level organizational needs to concrete system requirements (Donzelli, 2004). *Needs* capture the answer for the question why a service (either an elementary one or a service bundle) is offered. Similarly, in system/software design *goals* represent why a system/software is needed.

Similar to customer needs, goals are also defined at different levels of abstraction. They capture the various objectives that the system under consideration should achieve (Van Lamsweerde, 2000, 2001). Unlike GORE literature on goal hierarchies (Fuxman, Liu, Pistore, Roveri, & Mylopoulos, 2003), the marketing literature discusses hierarchies (of needs) (Kotler, 1988) without providing well-defined relations between elements in the need hierarchies, while such well-defined relations are required for software reasoning about needs. We fill this gap by introducing AND/OR/XOR refinements. An AND decomposition means that all siblings of a higher-level object (need, want) must be satisfied to satisfy the higher-level object. An

OR decomposition means that a higher-level object can be satisfied by satisfying an arbitrary number of its siblings. A XOR decomposition means that exactly one of the siblings of a higher-level object must be satisfied to satisfy the higher-level object. These constructs can be combined; for example need N1 may be decomposed into wants W1, W2, W3 and W4 as follows: (W1 AND W2) XOR (W3 AND W4).

We model need hierarchies similar to goal trees. In our case, hierarchies are directed graphs, rather than trees, because a demand or want may be related to more than one want or need respectively, so multiple paths may exist between two nodes, which is not allowed in trees. Needs are the top-level nodes of the graph; then come wants, and finally demands are leafs. AND/OR/XOR refinements describe the relations between a node in the hierarchy (graph) with related nodes in an adjacent level of the hierarchy. Edges that connect nodes have the semantics "concretized by." This relation does not apply to nodes of the same level, because they have the same level of granularity. Therefore, we do not connect nodes of the same hierarchical level. Using this technique and knowledge that business experts possess, we can reason about how an abstract customer need can be specified by more concrete demands, for which a solution (satisfier) can be searched. The left part of Figure 5 presents a visualization of part of Table 1 as a need hierarchy.

Our experience from studies in the energy sector, the health sector (Baida, 2006) and online music provisioning (Baida, de Bruin, & Gordijn, 2003b) shows that the use of above refinement structures requires adding a *context* dimension, since customer needs (or stakeholder needs, as in De Bruin, Van Vliet, and Baida (2002)) differ per customer type, and thus the refinement changes per customer type. Different needs, wants, demands, and their decompositions may apply to different customer types. In fact, per customer group (or per stakeholder) we may define a separate need hierarchy. Customer grouping criteria may differ per case. Examples are the nature of consumption (e.g., households vs. industrial customers), the customer's role (e.g., a patient vs. an informal carer of that patient), or the customer's age group (e.g., teenagers typically have a different interpretation of their needs than adults). For example, the customer want for "communication" can be refined to several demands, including (landline) telephone line, mobile phone line, and Internet access. Whereas one customer may require a landline, another may want Internet access and a mobile phone line, and no landline. Consequently, reasoning on need satisfaction (i.e., which service can satisfy a customer want for communication) should be done on the level of customer demands rather than on the level of (more abstract) customer wants or needs. Note that quality criteria also typically describe demands; wants or needs are often too abstract to be described by some well-defined desired quality criteria.

Step 2: Identify and Model Available Services

In step two of our method, we use the service offering perspective of the presented service ontology to model available services of suppliers. We describe services by their resources—their required inputs and their outcomes. Our study of the energy domain involves a group of financially independent enterprises that provide a variety of services. Together with business experts, we investigated and modeled services, including electricity supply, electricity transmission through a high-voltage network, hot water supply (for room heating), energy control (for controlling the temperature; that is, to lower the temperature during the night and to switch appliances on and off), temperature remote control, broadband Internet access, ASP (application service provider) services, and more. A detailed description of this step can be found in Baida et al. (2004b). For our current discussion, we will provide a shorter summary.

When a customer searches for a service or a service bundle to buy through a Web site, he is, in fact, not interested in the service itself but in the value that the service presents. This principle was acknowledged in the literature (Holbrook, 1999; Kotler, 1988; Lancaster, 1966; Teare, 1998) and can be traced back in the acknowledgment of how important customer value is in e-service offerings. The customer value of a service is reflected very often by the benefits of the service. Benefits often are expressed as the service outcomes (Kasper et al., 1999). The term *benefit* has to be understood in a broad sense; a benefit may also be negative. For example, some services require customers to perform some of the work by themselves (e.g., self-service restaurants). Also, payment—a sacrifice in terms of the service ontology—is seen as a negative benefit. Thus, the benefits of a service reflect not only the positive value of a service (from a customer's perspective) but also the negative value thereof. We describe benefits with resources. A service thus is described by its resources—its required service inputs and its produced service outcomes. Example resources from the current study are energy (of type hot water or electricity), air conditioning, and payments. Since resources represent a supplier perspective on services, they are described in objective terms rather than as a customer perceives them to be—subjective. The objective description is necessary in order to compare services, calculate prices, and provide specifications of the delivered service. Every resource is described by generic attributes (i.e., name and type) and possibly domain-specific properties (to describe a state, productivity, speed, etc.). Accordingly, the quality level of a service is described by the properties of the resources associated with the service.

In other words, resources specify not only the functional benefits of a service (e.g., ability to surf on the Internet) but also an objective description of its quality (e.g., download speed). Consequently, a list of resources—including required positive benefits and acceptable negative benefits—can be used as requirements for service selection when bundling (configuring) elementary services into a value-adding service bundle. To summarize, since resources (inputs and outcomes) describe the customer benefits of a service, they will be used for the selection of services to include in a service bundle.

The use of resources to select services can be manifested by the following example. Both the service electricity supply and the service hot water have an outcome: energy. However, the service *electricity supply* provides an energy resource with the property *type: electricity*, whereas the service *hot water* provides an energy resource with the property *type: hot water*. These are, in fact, two different resources. Suppose now that a customer is interested in energy. A reasoning engine—software that can use business logics and business rules to derive solutions suitable for customers—will then look for services with the outcome resource *energy* (without specifying the resource properties). If a variety of *electricity supply* and *hot water* services are available (possibly provided by different suppliers), each of them will have the outcome *energy*, so each of them will be a suitable solution. If, on the other hand, the property *type: electricity* also is specified, any of the *electricity supply* services (but not the *hot water* services) may be (part of) a solution.

We created a prototype software tool for modeling services in accordance with the presented service ontology. The tool (available at http://www.baida.nl/research/serviguration.html) presents a user-friendly graphical user interface that hides the technical details of the underlying service ontology. Once services are graphically modeled by the user, the tool is capable of creating a service-ontology-based machine-readable version of the model using the RDFS-W3C standard. This is an XML-based standard used for describing information; it adds a layer of semantics to information, and it is suitable for reasoning with ontologies over the Web.

Step 3: Identify and Model Relations between Customer Demands and Available Services

The purpose of building a need hierarchy is twofold. First the hierarchy is used to find context-depending demands, based on more abstract wants and needs. Second, concrete demands are used to search for services that provide satisfiers (service outcomes, resources) for these demands and for more abstract needs.

To this end, we use another requirements engineering technique; namely, feature-solution graphs (De Bruin & Van Vliet, 2001; De Bruin & Van Vliet, 2002; De Bruin et al., 2002). A transformation between customer demands (the satisfaction of which is the goal of the service offering) and resources (descriptors of available services, or solutions) can be viewed as a production system consisting of *production rules*, a knowledge representation formalism used in the AI (artificial intelligence) field. Production rules have the following form: if situation X is encountered, then select solution Y. De Bruin et al. suggested the use of context-aware *feature-solution graphs* (FS-graphs) to model these production rules (De Bruin & Van Vliet, 2002; De Bruin et al., 2002). The suggested graph captures and documents context-sensitive business knowledge so that it becomes possible to reason about feasible solutions and the demands (requirements) they support. A feature-solution graph (adapted to our case) includes three spaces, organized in hierarchies of AND/OR/XOR decompositions:

1. **Feature space.** Describes the desired properties of the system (or service) as expressed by the user. In our case, these are customer demands.

2. **Solution space.** Contains the internal system (services) decomposition into resources that are required for or delivered by available services.

3. **Context space.** Contextual domain knowledge that influences relations between elements of the feature space and elements of the solution space (e.g., customer type, geographic restrictions).

Relations between elements of the feature space (demands) and elements of the solution space (resources) may have the semantics of selection (if demand A is requested, select resource B), rejection (if demand A is requested, then do not select resource B), or weaker relations (positively influenced by or negatively influenced by). These are further referred to as SEL(demand, resource), REJ(demand, resource), POS(demand, resource) and NEG(demand,

Figure 5. Partial FS-graph of the energy study

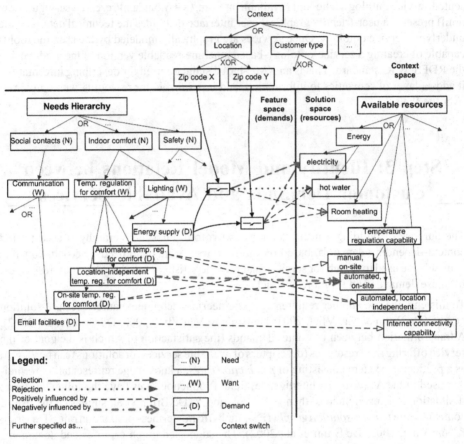

resource). An example FS-graph, adapted for our case, can be found in Figure 5. For visualization reasons, we explicitly mention the type of hierarchy (AND/OR/XOR) only in a few places. Note the context space, where context information as location or the type of customer may influence the behavior of a relation. The hierarchy uses AND/OR/XOR structures. As explained before, an AND structure means that all lower-level elements (demands or resources) must be satisfied in order to satisfy the higher-level element. An OR structure means that any, or a combination of the lower-level elements, can be satisfied in order to satisfy the higher-level element. A XOR structure means that any, but not more than one, of the lower-level elements can be satisfied to satisfy the higher-level element.

Our experience in using FS-graphs with business experts shows that graphs are a good means to visually *communicate ideas*, but when a substantial number of production rules is involved, and in the absence of a dedicated software tool to support this task, the use of *Excel* sheets is preferred by business experts, because the graph becomes too complex to comprehend and to manage. Yet *Excel* also presents a difficulty: it is two dimensional, while the FS-graph is three dimensional. To provide automated support for modeling production

Figure 6. Production rules for transforming customer terminology to supplier terminology

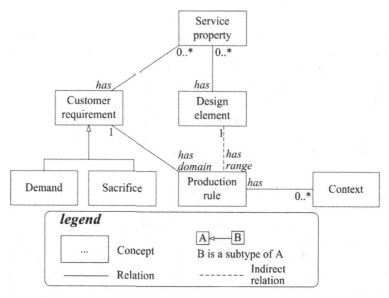

rules, we added constructs of the FS-graph to the earlier-presented service ontology. Figure 6 shows how we incorporate FS-graph structures in the service ontology.

In step one of our method, we identified and modeled customer need hierarchies using the service value perspective of our service ontology. These will now be considered features. In step two, we used the service offering perspective of our service ontology to model available services described by resources. The latter will now be considered solutions. In the third step of our method, we define relations between demands (features) and resources (solutions), as can be seen in Figure 5. These relations have the advantage that they can easily be formalized by logical and programming constructs, making it possible to do a systematic analysis of customer needs and their corresponding solutions (available services) and to automate the reasoning for the selection of resources (and thus, services) to meet certain customer demands.

Complexity in Reasoning with Production Rules

Very often demands and resources include qualitative and/or quantitative descriptors (referred to as service properties in the service ontology). For instance, in Table 1 and in Figure 5, we can find the demand for temperature regulation, specified by the descriptors "manual," "automated," "on-site," and "location-independent." Service properties may influence production rules. For example, imagine a demand for "e-mail facilities" that may be specified by the service property "capacity: small enterprise," and an "Internet connectivity capability" resource that may be specified by the service property "connection type: ISDN." We model two production rules between these demand and resource:

1. **SEL** ("e-mail facilities," "Internet connectivity capability"): if a customer has a demand for 'e-mail facilities", any solution bundle must include a service that provides an "Internet connectivity capability" resource.

2. **NEG** ("e-mail facilities" with property "capacity: small enterprise", "Internet connectivity capability" with property "connection type: ISDN"): the availability of a service that provides the resource "Internet connectivity capability" with property "connection type: ISDN" in a bundle has a negative influence on satisfying the customer demand for "e-mail facilities" for a small enterprise.

Hence, two different production rules apply to these demand and resource, depending on the question whether or not the demand and resource are described by service properties. If a customer asks for "e-mail facilities" for a small enterprise, we search a service that provides an "Internet connectivity capability" resource without service property "connection type: ISDN." This example shows that it does not suffice to model one production rule between any pair (demand, resource). Service properties that describe demands and resources need to be taken into consideration as well. As demands and resources may be described by multiple service properties, theoretically every pair (demand D with service property Qx; resource R with service property Qy) may require a production rule. This discussion can also be extended to demands and resources that are described by more than one service property. For example, a capability resource "Internet connectivity" may be described by a service property "download speed: 8000 Kbit/s," as well as by a service property "upload speed: 1024 Kbit/s." A very large number of production rules may have to be modeled, resulting in an extensive modeling effort.

Also in the domain of telecommunication services, the problem of explosion of combinations has been studied (Keck & Kuehn, 1998), and suggested solutions include tools for context generation and information acquisition. Our experience from large-scale studies in the energy sector and in the health sector (Baida, 2006) is that the majority of the combinations (demand D1 with property Qx, resource R1 with property Qy) require no production rule, so the modeling effort is reasonable. Customer demands and available services that we model are described typically on a higher level of abstraction than in the case of (executable) telecommunication services as in Keck and Kuehn (1998). For example, we model demands as "(landline) telephone line" and resources as "Internet connectivity" with a certain download speed and upload speed, but when these services are made operational, a much richer description of QoS (quality of service) and desired/available features is required, resulting in a much larger number of feature combinations to deal with.

A study we carried out in the health sector (Baida, 2006) yielded a means to decrease complexity. Demands can be divided into clusters, where a cluster includes all demands that are related to a single need. Because resources are solutions for demands, very often also clusters of resources can be observed that are related (by production rules) to clusters of demands. An important observation from our study in the health sector is that the vast majority of production rules exist between single clusters of demands and single clusters of resources. Only a small number of production rules exist between the same cluster of demands and other clusters of resources.

An important conclusion from this observation is that most modeling work can be performed by modeling experts with a reasonable effort and time investment. We can divide the space of demands and resources into clusters, identify related clusters of demands and resources, and first focus the modeling effort on production rules between these clusters. The vast majority of production rules will be modeled between pairs of clusters. Since clusters are sets of related demands and solutions for these demands, in the health study identifying clusters was natural for business experts.

Conflict Identification in Reasoning with Production Rules

Conflicts may arise in three situations when reasoning with production rules. The first situation occurs when various production rules involve the same resource (which may or may not be described by some service properties). This may cause conflicts between production rules. Imagine that we have two demands, D1 and D2, one resource, R1, and the following production rules: SEL(D1, R1) (meaning that resource R1 must be selected if demand D1 is triggered) and REJ(D2, R1) (meaning that resource R1 mustn't be selected if demand D2 is triggered). A conflict occurs when a customer has demands D1 *and* D2. On the one hand, resource R1 must be part of any service bundle, and on the other hand, it may not be part of a solution (bundle). In cases that we modeled in the health sector and in the energy sector, this situation was only theoretical, but it did not appear in practice. Namely, in reality when two conflicting production rules involve two different demands D1 and D2, business experts declared that these demands cannot co-exist, so the conflicting production rules involving (D1, R1) and (D2, R1) will not be triggered at the same time.

The second situation is similar to the first one, but the conflict occurs due to two different service properties Q1 and Q2 that specify the same demand D1. Conflicts occur when two production rules involve the same demand D1 with different service properties (e.g., D1Q1 and D1Q2) and a single resource R1, specified by service property Q3. Demand D1Q1 may require resource R1Q3, while demand D1Q2 has a rejection relation with R1Q3. What must be done when both D1Q1 and D1Q2 apply? This situation is different from the first situation, because here the conflicting production rules involve the same demand (only with different service properties), while the first situation involved two completely different demands.

Some terminology needs to be introduced for the discussion on a third situation of conflict. We distinguish between *global* production rules and *local* production rules.

- Global production rules relate a demand D1 with a resource R1, when neither the demand nor the resource is specified by any service properties (this production rule applies independently of any service property).
- Local production rules relate a demand D1 with a resource R1, when either the demand or the resource, or both are specified by service properties (this production rule applies only when specific service properties are specified).

The third situation occurs when a demand and a resource have a global production rule as well as local production rules. Let us take as an example the earlier presented demand "energy consumption regulation for budget control" (D1) with the service property "mode of operation: manual" (Q1), and resource "temperature regulation capability" (R1) with service property "mode of operation: automated" (Q4). Two production rules are relevant here:

- **POS(D1, R1):** resource R1 has a positive influence on satisfying demand D1. This is a global production rule; it does not take into consideration the properties of D1 and of R1.

- **REJ(D1Q1, R1Q4):** when demand D1 is specified by property Q1, the solution must not include a resource R1 with property Q4. This is a local production rule; it holds for D1 and R1 only when they are specified by service properties Q1 and Q4, respectively.

To automate reasoning with production rules, one must know how the two production rules should be used together. Does the POS production rule apply when a user specifies demand D1 with quality descriptor Q1, because it is global (it holds for any pair (D1, R1), independent of their properties), or does the REJ production rule apply because it is a strong relation (while POS is a weak relation) or because it is more specific? Similar conflicts may occur also between other pairs of production rules, for example, NEG and SEL, or POS and NEG.

Conflict Resolution in Reasoning with Production Rules

As mentioned above, case studies we performed showed that the first situation is theoretical. In order to solve conflicts of the second situation, we classify conflicts based on their *severeness*, as done by Baida et al. (2003b), who used FS-graphs for an assessment of an e-business case study:

- A *major conflict* is a conflict between two strong production rules. It involves a SEL relation and a REJ relation. No solution is possible, so no service bundle can satisfy the given demands.

- A *minor conflict* is a conflict between two weak production rules. It involves a POS relation and a NEG relation. Satisfying the demands is possible, but it requires compromises (typically, the suggested service is not "exactly" what the customer wanted, yet the customer may accept this solution if no better option exists or if its price is significantly lower than the price of other solutions).

- The third type of conflict involves a strong production rule and a weak production rule: either a SEL relation and a NEG relation, or a REJ relation and a POS relation. In these cases, we analyze the impact of the conflict and classify it as a major one or as a minor one. We refer to this as "the third type of conflict."

Table 2. Conflict resolution in case of conflicting production rules

Conflict severeness	Conflict resolution
Major conflict	No solution exists (no service bundle can satisfy the demands)
Minor conflict	Business experts should decide whether the conflict can be solved or not. If the conflict is declared solvable, the resource at hand may (but need not necessarily) be included in a bundle (i.e., consider only the POS relation; disregard the NEG relation). If the conflict is declared unsolvable, the resource at hand may not be part of a bundle. Yet because the resource didn't necessarily have to be part of a bundle (as it did not have the selection relation), a solution is yet possible.
Third type of conflict	Our experience shows that it would be safe to say that no solution exists (no service bundle can satisfy the demands). Yet business experts may still wish to analyze every such case independently to see whether there are some exceptional cases where a solution may exist nevertheless.

In order to resolve conflicts of the second situation mentioned above, we modeled production rules in studies in the health sector (Baida, 2006) and in the energy sector, analyzed the nature of conflicts, and applied the above classification of conflicts. In cases concerning conflicts between two local production rules involving the same demand (but with different service properties; that is the second situation described above):

- No major conflicts were identified

- Minor conflicts turned to be divergent: either the conflict could be ignored (i.e., the POS relation was stronger than the NEG relation), or the conflict was unsolvable (and hence the resource at hand could not be part of a solution).

- In all cases of the third type of conflict, there was no solution for the conflict (and hence no service bundle could satisfy the demands).

Based on these findings and on Baida et al. (2003b), we determine rules for conflict resolution. These are described in Table 2. As can be seen from the table, mainly minor conflicts require human intervention to understand the nature of the conflict and to assess how the conflict should be handled.

The third conflict situation that we described in the previous section occurs when a demand and a resource have a global production rule (that applies independently of any service property) as well as local production rules (that apply only when specific service properties are specified).

The need for local production rules next to global production rules stems from differing levels of reasoning. In reality, most demands and resources are specified by some service properties. Various similar demands and resources may exist that differ only in some property, or in the value of a property. For example, two Internet connectivity capability resources may exist, both with the service property "download speed" and "upload speed," but yet every resource will have different values for these properties (i.e., different download/upload speed). Reasoning with global production rules, we may say that a demand for e-mail facilities may be satisfied by an Internet connectivity capability resource without specifying any properties (i.e., without requiring certain download speed or upload speed). This is a global production rule. However, if the same demand is set with a quality descriptor "capacity: household," we will set requirements also on the download/upload speed, resulting in local production rules. Note that the service ontology allows us to describe whether the values of resources in production rules specify a minimum value, a maximum value, or an exact value. A production rule may then define that when a demand for "e-mail facilities" is set with the service property "capacity: household," a resource "Internet connectivity capability" must be selected with service property "download speed" with a value of *at least* 800 Kbit/s.

Imagine we have a global production rule between demand D1 and resource R1 (without specifying service properties), as well as a local production rule between demand D1 with property Q1 (further referred to as D1Q1) and resource R1 with property Q2 (further referred to as R1Q2; it does not matter whether Q1 and Q2 are the same property or not). We need to define the relations between the global production rule between D1 and R1 ("parents") and the local production rule between D1Q1 and R1Q2 ("siblings"). Different relations may apply for different combinations of parents and siblings (any of them may be one of four types: SEL, REJ, POS, NEG). We analyzed every possible combination of production rules (parent, sibling), resulting in the following guidelines for conflict resolution:

- A global production rule between demand D1 and resource R1 applies whenever demand D1 is set, unless it is overridden by a local production rule. The global production rule holds for resource R1, independent of its quality descriptors.

- A local production rule between D1 and R1Q2 restricts R1 only when R1 is specified by a property Q2, whenever demand D1 is set without being specified by any service properties.

- As a rule of the thumb, a production rule of siblings (local) is more specific than the production rule of the parents (global), and therefore it overrides the parent's production rule. Yet a production rule of siblings may override a production rule of parents only if the siblings' production rule is *strong*. A local *weak* production rule (POS or NEG) may only add selection criteria for selecting resources, but it may not override a global *strong* relation (SEL or REJ).

- Seemingly contradicting production rules may co-exist, if one is global and the other is local. For example, the global production rule SEL(D1, R1) and the local production rule REJ(D1, R1Q2) should be interpreted as follows: when demand D1 is set, any solution must include a resource R1, and this resource must not have service property Q2.

- If the parents have an REJ relation, a service that provides resource R1 *mustn't* be part of a service bundle. In this case, there is no logic behind modeling any other relation (SEL, POS, NEG) on the siblings level, because the strong REJ relation cannot be overridden. Modeling a REJ relation on the siblings level is possible but redundant, so it can be ignored.

Figure 7. Ordering among solutions

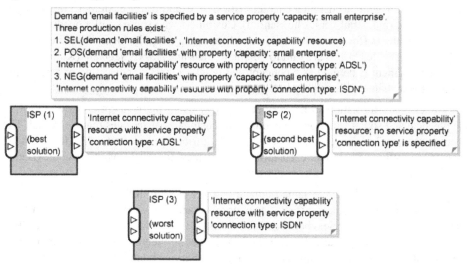

Cases where weak relations are involved (POS or NEG) can be used to define an ordering among solutions, as we show in Figure 7. For example, a solution that involves a POS relation is better than a solution that does not involve such a relation; a solution that involves an NEG relation is worse than a solution that does not involve such a relation. Our experience in modeling real-world situations shows that when a NEG relation is involved, and there exist solution bundles that do not involve this relation (i.e., solutions that do not provide a resource as specified by a NEG relation), in fact there is no need to offer those bundles that provide the resource for which a NEG relation exists, because customers would not choose for it (in Figure 7, small enterprises seeking "e-mail facilities" will not select service ISP (3) when the other options exist). Therefore, if there are solutions that do not provide a resource specified by a NEG relation, we do not generate solutions that *do* include this relation (in Figure 7 this means that service ISP (3) will not be offered as a solution).

Context: How One Customer Differs from Another

The service value perspective of our service ontology—including the concepts *needs, wants, demands, sacrifice,* and *service property*—reflects a customer view on services. As such, it is by definition context-sensitive: every customer or customer type may have a different viewpoint on a service based on his/her situation (time, location, role), on different expectations, and on past experiences (Zeithaml et al., 1990). In this section, we show how the context of a customer can be taken into consideration in the design of customer-tailored service bundles.

A customer's context may either relate to his personal situation or to his belonging to a target group. For example, when we offer medical services to patients, we take into consideration their *personal* medical dossiers with knowledge about their health state. On the other hand, when we offer services to customers without knowledge of them as individuals, we base our offering on more general customer characteristics, for example, the customer's age group or customer type (industrial versus household). Customers who share similar needs/demands in similar contexts (for example, the demand for energy supply for industrial customers within a geographic region) are said to belong to the same *market segment* (Kotler, 1988): "a market segment is defined as a concept that breaks a market, consisting of actors, into segments that share common properties" (p. 69).

We model this information in the service ontology using the concept *context*, reflecting the physical and social situation of (in our case) customers of services that we model. The concept "context" in the service ontology has the attributes name and value; for example, "name: age, value: 65" or "name: customer type, value: industrial." Multiple contexts may be valid simultaneously.

Two customers may have the same demand and yet require different services to satisfy this demand because of their different ages or customer types. Hence, the transformation (captured by production rules) between needs/wants/demands and available resources (that are provided by services), and the choice of services to be included in a bundle, depend on the context of a given customer or a customer group. Service bundles are to be designed for customers who have certain needs and are in a certain context. Throughout this chapter we refer to Figure 1, presenting a simplification of the whole *serviguration* process. Context information is taken into consideration explicitly twice in the process:

1. Some context information describes the conditions under which a whole service element qualifies (or does not qualify) as a solution (we refer to this as "context on the service level"). This is supported by the relation "service element has context" in the service offering perspective. Services that require another context than the one specified by the current customer are not valid candidates to be included in a service bundle by the service configuration task.

    Example:
    A service for hot water (for room heating) is provided only to customers who live in a certain region. We model this geographical restriction as context information, related to the hot water service.

2. Some context information describes the conditions under which a benefit (resource) can satisfy a demand (we refer to this as "context on the resource level"). We model such relations by defining that production rules depend on a customer's context.

    Example (from the health care domain):
    Demand D1: Discussion group concerning how to cope with the changing behavior of a dementia patient
    Resource R1: Coping advice for informal carers of dementia patients
    Production rule: SEL(D1, R1)

Context: Customer type: informal carer

Explanation: The SEL relation will be triggered only in queries where the customer type is "informal carer." Consequently, when an informal carer asks for "discussion group concerning how to cope with the changing behavior of a dementia patient," we will search for a service that offers "coping advice for informal carers of dementia patients." When a different customer (e.g., a patient) has the same demand, the SEL production rule will not be triggered, and therefore we will not offer a service that provides coping advice for informal carers. Different resources exist for different customer types because patients and informal carers require different advice and support (yet a single service may provide resources for both).

Some context information can be considered as global assumptions that narrow the scope of the information we model and of information systems that can use this model. For example, when developing an information system for service offerings within a specific geographic region, the location is assumed to be a global assumption, and it is not necessary to explicitly constrain all service offerings to that region. Global assumptions of a model (of services and customer needs) are considered to be known by all the users of the model and are not made explicit in the *serviguration* process.

Step 4: Create Service Bundles

The process of ensuring customer value of service offerings is termed *serviguration* (Baida, 2006; Baida et al., 2003a) and sketched in Figure 1. Customer demands and acceptable sacrifices are mapped to possible service benefits (referred to as resources). These describe available services. They are then used as a trigger for the service bundling (configuration) process, resulting in zero or more sets of services that provide the required customer benefits, within the limitations of the acceptable sacrifice. Customer benefits, therefore, are criteria (or requirements) for the service configuration process. Each benefit can be related to some higher-level demand, want, or need of a customer. The process of creating service bundles, based on a given set of available services and on a set of requirements expressed in resources, is discussed at length in Akkermans et al. (2004) and Baida et al. (2004b) and is beyond the scope of this chapter. For the current discussion, it suffices to say that we use research on configuration theory from the field of knowledge engineering. By describing services in a way that corresponds with existing configuration ontologies, we simplify the bundling process to a configuration task, for which a wealth of research exists (Borst, 1997; Borst, Akkermans, & Top, 1997; Gruber et al., 1996; Schreiber et al., 2000; Stefik, 1995).

To automate the process of service bundling (or configuration), we combine our service tool with a configuration software tool developed by our partner, Fundacion LABEIN in Bilbao, Spain. The configuration tool uses service models created by the service modeling tool (see step two) to create service bundles based on a given set of requirements. The created service bundles are then imported back to the service tool, where they are visualized to enhance user friendliness.

Lessons Learned from the Electricity Supply Case Study

Needs can be Expressed using Goal Hierarchies

This lesson falls into two parts. First, we can use goal-hierarchies to represent needs. This is important because we then can utilize existing knowledge about goal-reasoning.

Second, need-hierarchies are of use during elicitation of other needs. Business experts provided us with an initial list of identified customer needs. By asking the question *why*, requirements engineers elicit more abstract goals than those first identified in order to find

Figure 8. Three different service bundles for three similar customer demands

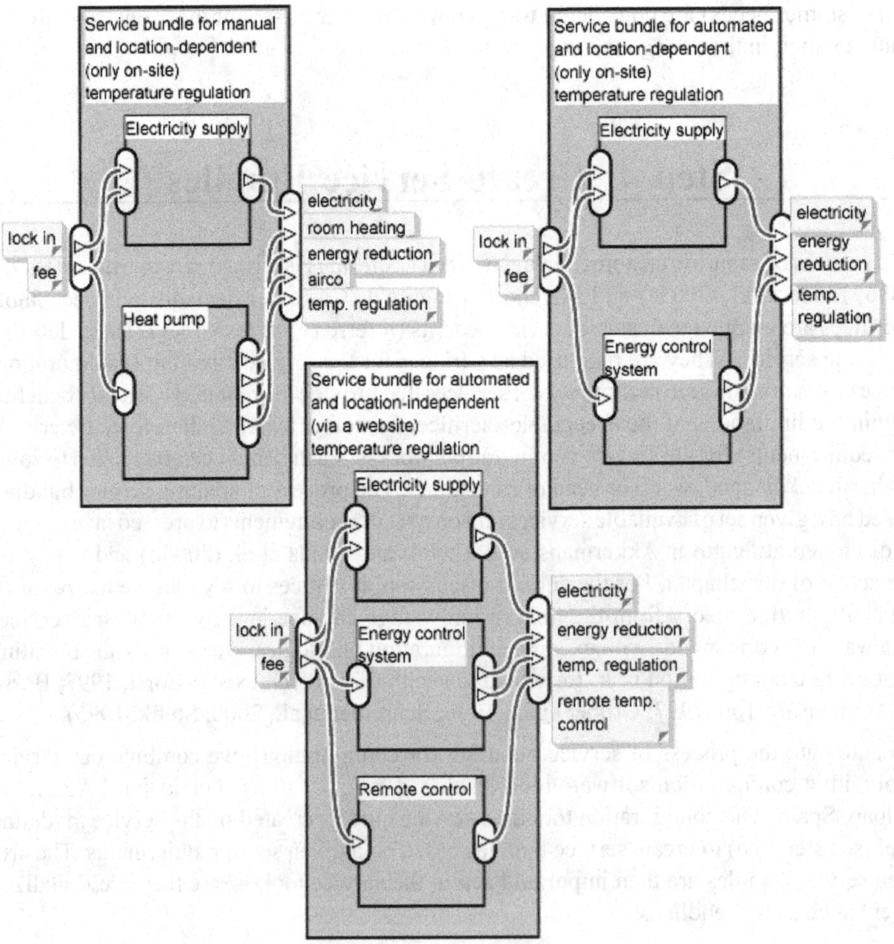

out other important sub-goals of the more abstract goals that were overlooked in the first place (Van Lamsweerde, 2000). Our eventual need hierarchy (see Table 1) evolved from the initial one by applying two methods: asking the question *why* about existing needs and also asking the question *why* about existing solutions (available services and their provided resources or results). We found that both techniques help identify new needs as well as concretize vaguely defined customer needs. Furthermore, asking the question *why* about existing needs helps understand the granularity of needs; it helps define whether a need should indeed be seen as a need or actually is a more concrete want or demand.

Service Ontology Allows for Reasoning on Inconsistencies and Bundles

Relations, as specified by the FS-graph, can cause inconsistencies; for example, in a situation in which a customer specifies conflicting quality criteria for a demand (e.g., a top quality, low-budget service). Handling such inconsistencies (referred to as *conflict management*) must be performed during the reasoning process. We defined guidelines for conflict management based on this and earlier case studies (Baida, 2006; Baida et al., 2003b; De Bruin et al., 2002).

From a business perspective, reasoning on potential service bundles is of most interest. For example, (1) some services require other supporting services; (2) other services may have substitutes that also provide a good solution for a customer; (3) suppliers may prefer to bundle specific services for better utilization of existing infrastructure, and so forth. All these business rules can be expressed in a computer-interpretable way, so that software can implement them. We have built a prototype software tool that does exactly this kind of reasoning. Now that we have a set of required resources, we have to create bundles of services that offer these resources. Any of the required resources may be offered by multiple services, so typically more than one service or service bundle will include these resources and, hence, fulfill the customer's demands. This last process—service configuration—is discussed thoroughly in Baida et al. (2004b) and in Akkermans et al. (2004) and includes the already-mentioned business rules. The service configuration process implements production rules of the type *add service Y to every bundle that includes service X, services X and Y may not be part of the same bundle*, and so forth.

Reflecting Back on the Case Study Domain

We modeled a variety of services in the energy case study, including electricity supply, broadband Internet access, hot water supply, energy control, and more (Baida et al., 2004b), analyzed relations between services and customer demands, and created service bundles to satisfy customer demands. As a result of the modeling of service elements and the automated generation of service bundles, the energy utility at hand succeeded in defining service bundles for specific groups of customers in such a way that these bundles fit the requirements of their respective customers. Furthermore, our analysis helped understand which service bundles should not be offered to specific groups of customers, because they do not satisfy the requirements of these customers well enough or because other bundles can satisfy the same requirements better.

An important advantage of ontologies is that they help reason with domain knowledge. Our ontological approach, summarized in Figure 1, enables automated reasoning. For example, the customer need for "indoor comfort" is reduced to three wants, including "temperature regulation." We found three service bundles that satisfy this want (see Figure 8). All of them include electricity supply plus extra services, supplied by different suppliers. In other words, these service bundles compete with each other. An electricity supplier can then decide whether to offer all of these bundles or just a subset thereof. The choice of a bundle to offer implies also a choice of a business partner to work with, since the extra services are offered by other suppliers. The same want is further specified by several demands. Reasoning on the demand level, we see that the competing bundles provide differing quality levels, so in fact they may address different market segments. It is then up to the supplier(s) to decide which service level(s) to offer.

Related Research

When our method is used by marketing personnel for developing (e-)service offerings, the use of our service ontology can be complemented by the means-end theory, which provides an even more abstract view on service offerings. The means-end theory (Gutman, 1982; Zeithaml, 1988) uses relations between customer values and product/service attributes and benefits in order to explain customer behavior and his or her preference for one product/service or another. A means-end chain is: "a model that seeks to explain how a product or service selection facilitates the achievement of desired states" (Gutman, 1982, p. 60); customers seek means to achieve their ends (goals). The means-end theory uses a hierarchical model to describe this customer goal-oriented behavior. The model consists of three related concepts: values, benefits/consequences, and (product/service) attributes. The hierarchy is created by relating values to underlying benefits and attributes. In their studies, Gutman (1982), Herrmann, Huber, and Braunstein (2000), and Mentzer et al. (1997) present examples of means-end chain models in different sectors: the railway sector, the automobile industry, and the beverages industry. Examples are provided for values, benefits, and attributes (the three elements of a means-end chain model ordered in a decreasing level of abstraction). We have presented in this chapter a need hierarchy with needs, wants, and demands (ordered in a decreasing level of abstraction). Comparing these three studies with ours, we can make the following observations about relations between the means-end theory and the service ontology:

1.   Values in the means-end theory either can be terminal or instrumental. Terminal values are more abstract than any concept in the service ontology; instrumental values correspond to needs in the service ontology.

2.   Benefits/consequences in the means-end theory correspond to wants and needs in the service ontology.

3.   Attributes in the means-end theory either can be abstract or concrete. Abstract attributes correspond to wants in the service ontology; concrete attributes correspond to demands in the service ontology.

The existence of a similar and equivalent structure (hierarchy) and concepts makes it possible to incorporate the use of our method and ontology with means-end chain models by marketing departments. The added value that our method presents in this context is twofold:

1.   Value hierarchies, as in the means-end theory, define relations between values, benefits, and attributes. By adding AND/OR/XOR refinements to hierarchies, we enable a much more detailed and useful analysis of these relations. For example, an OR refinement implies that any low-level element (e.g., demand or attribute) can satisfy a higher-level element (e.g., want or benefit). Consequently, it may not be necessary for a service provider to implement all lower-level attributes. Such knowledge cannot be inferred from means-end hierarchies in their traditional form.

2.   The means-end theory does not consider the possible solutions (actual service offerings of suppliers) for a customer's demands. Customer needs are refined to the degree of desired product attributes, but these are not related further to any elements that provide these attributes. The service ontology, on the other hand, includes both customer needs and available solutions. By using our method and ontology, it becomes possible to relate not only product attributes, but also possible solutions (available or future service offerings) to a customer's needs and values. This can be used for marketing analyses, but it is of greatest importance for e-service offerings because they require that all elements of the process (from customer needs to actual solutions) be linked so that information systems can reason about the process and provide a customer with a suitable solution for his or her needs.

In addition, Herrmann et al. (2000) argued that the means-end theory needs to be complemented with a means to transform customer needs to more concrete, implementation-related measurements. They suggested combining the means-end theory with quality function deployment (QFD). Their approach is similar to ours in that both approaches facilitate a transformation process from vaguely defined customer needs to concrete measurements. While Herrmann et al. (2000) focus on how to understand customer behavior as a key to design new services, our work assumes that knowledge exists about customer behavior, and we focus on how a software can use this knowledge to design service bundles out of available services.

An interesting observation is that we perform conflict resolution in the *relations* (production rules) between features (demands) and solutions (resources). This is opposed to conflict resolution in software engineering (Van Lamsweerde, Darimont, & Leiter, 1998) and software architecture, where conflicts are managed on the feature side: goals and requirements. A possible explanation for this difference is the fact that in software design all requirements and goals refer to the same single artifact: the system to be developed. In the case of service bundling, on the other hand, customer demands need not depend on each other, and the solution may be comprised of totally independent services (artifacts) that can be consumed at different times. For example, a customer may have a demand for home entertainment as well as entertainment outside home. These two demands do not conflict, because a solution service bundle may include a service that delivers home entertainment (e.g., a TV subscription) and a service that delivers entertainment outside home (e.g., a subscription for the national ballet), and the two may be consumed independently, at different times and locations.

Conclusion and Future Work

We proposed an ontology for understanding customer needs for e-services. Using this ontology, it is possible to reason about possible service bundles that satisfy needs. The bottom line of the energy study was that the analysis performed made it possible for the energy utility involved to define service bundles for specific groups of customers in such a way that bundles fit the demands of their respective customers. Furthermore, it helped understand which service bundles should not be offered to specific groups of customers, because they do not satisfy the demands of these customers well enough or because other bundles can satisfy the same demands better. For example, to satisfy a customer demand for energy supply, a bundle theoretically may include combinations of the following services: electricity supply, heat pumping, and hot water. However, customers would prefer bundling electricity supply with hot water to bundling electricity supply with heat pumping due to a lower price. If there had not been a geographical limitation on the supply of hot water, the bundle electricity supply and heat pumping would not have been of interest. Another example is the customer demand of temperature regulation for indoor comfort. The following service elements result in benefits (resources) that satisfy this demand for industrial customers: heat pumping, energy control system, and remote control. However, given the desired quality criteria for this demand (automated vs. manual, location-independent vs. on-site), different combinations of these (and other) services need to be offered.

Knowledge and expertise from business research, information science, and computer science have been intertwined in our research to solve the problem at hand. We spilt the process into a customer perspective (step one of our method), a supplier perspective (step two of our method), and a transformation process between the two (step three of our method). By expressing both perspectives using a formal ontology, also expressible in a machine-interpretable language (RDF), we facilitate checking business knowledge for consistency, using it for reasoning by software, and performing a systematic analysis of the domain.

Business research literature concerning customer needs acknowledges the existence of (need) hierarchies. However, it lacks a few elements necessary for making business knowledge machine-interpretable: (1) a definition of hierarchical decompositions (e.g., AND/OR/XOR structures) of customer needs; (2) a well-defined (in computational terms) description of services; (3) a definition of possible relations (links) between needs and solutions; and (4) an understanding of how demands (functional requirements) differ from desired service quality (non-functional requirements). As we have shown in this chapter, we use existing requirements engineering practices to add the necessary formalism to business concepts: we use goal hierarchies and production rules to relate features (needs, demands) to solutions (services, described by resources). By embedding these constructs and business concepts in a service ontology, expressible in a machine-interpretable language, we create a framework for software-based reasoning: first customer demands trigger the selection of resources (benefits), and then a configuration process creates bundles of services that provide these customer benefits.

The method presented in this chapter uses conceptual modeling and formalizing techniques, widely accepted in computer science and information science, and applies them to concepts from business research. Despite the elusive nature of important business concepts such as quality, benefit, and value, it is possible to derive concrete parameters out of more abstract ones by using several layers between the two. Abstract notions can be transformed to somewhat less-abstract notions; these can then be transformed or mapped to even more concrete notions. The QFD approach uses this technique, and so do means-end hierarchies and requirements engineering goal hierarchies. However, both QFD and means-end models have a limited perspective: supplier's solution or customer needs, respectively. Our method, on the other hand, connects both perspectives using FS-graphs. The two perspectives must be related in order to allow an automated process that finds a solution for a specific high-level need.

By applying our approach for the Norwegian energy sector, we managed to elicit business knowledge and to formalize it in such a way that it can be expressed in computer-interpretable terms. The service offering perspective was implemented in a software tool. Using our service ontology as its fundaments, the tool is capable of creating bundles of services when requirements are specified in terms of resources. In the present chapter, we have shown how we derive such requirements: by (1) adding an earlier step in which we formalize customer demands, and (2) mapping them onto available resources. Our service ontology includes a perspective dedicated to these demands: the service value perspective.

The service ontology includes the notion of quality criteria to describe customer demands. Demands, however, are subjective and context-sensitive. A wealth of knowledge exists within business research about service quality (Grönroos, 2000; Zeithaml et al., 1990). The service ontology includes constructs for modeling the quality related to demands and to services. So far, the available constructs have proven to be suitable and sufficient. Future research can be directed at incorporating existing service quality models (e.g., SERVQUAL) (Zeithaml et al., 1990) into the service ontology.

We considered in this chapter the complexity problem, caused by the large number of pairs (demand, resource) for which business experts have to consider whether a production rule must be modeled. We observed that clusters of demands and resources can be identified, such that the vast majority of production rules will be between pairs of clusters. Only limited effort needs to be put into modeling production rules outside these pairs of clusters, so the modeling effort is reasonable. At the same time we acknowledge that more empirical studies are required to make a sound statement about the complexity problem in modeling production rules.

Also, we investigated production rules involving only one demand and one resource. These were enough to model realistic and complex domains. Yet more empirical studies are required to investigate the necessity for production rules involving multiple resources (e.g., IF demand X THEN resource Y *or* Z). Complexity can also be reduced by prioritizing customer needs. This will also be a topic of future research.

Acknowledgments

This work has been partially supported by the European Commission, as project No. IST-2001-33144 OBELIX, and by the Dutch Ministry of Economic Affairs, as the FrUX project (Freeband User eXperience). This chapter is an updated and extended version of an article entitled "Finding e-service offerings by computer-supported customer need reasoning" published in the *International Journal of E-Business Research (IJEBR) 1*(3), 91-112.

References

Akkermans, H., Baida, Z., Gordijn, J., Peña, N., & Laresgoiti, I. (2004). Value webs: Using ontologies to bundle real-world services. *IEEE Intelligent Systems, 19*(4), 57-66.

Aschmoneit, P., & Heitmann, M. (2002). Customer centred community applica¬tion design: Introduction of the means-end chain framework for product design of community applications. *The International Journal on Media Management, 4*(1), 13-21.

Baida, Z. (2006). *Software-aided service bundling; intelligent methods & tools for graphical service modeling*. Unpublished doctoral dissertation, Vrije Universiteit, Amsterdam.

Baida, Z., Akkermans, H., & Gordijn, J. (2003a). Serviguration: Towards online configurability of real-world services. In *Proceedings of the Fifth International Conference on Electronic Commerce* (ICEC03), Pittsburgh, PA.

Baida, Z., de Bruin, H., & Gordijn, J. (2003b). E-business cases assessment: From business value to system feasibility. *International Journal of Web Engineering and Technology, 1*(1), 127-144.

Baida, Z., Gordijn, J., Morch, A. Z., Sæle, H., & Akkermans, H. (2004a). Ontology-based analysis of e-service bundles for networked enterprises. In *Proceedings of the 17th Bled e-commerce Conference*, Bled, Slovenia.

Baida, Z., Gordijn, J., Sæle, H., Morch, A. Z., & Akkermans, H. (2004b). Energy services: A case study in real-world service configuration. In *Proceedings of the 16th International Conference on Advanced Information Systems Engineering (CAiSE 2004)*, Riga, Latvia.

Berry, L., & Parasuraman, A. (1991). *Marketing services: Competing through quality*. New York: The Free Press.

Bigné, E., Martínez, C., & Miquel, M. J. (1997). The influence of motivation, experience and satisfaction on the quality of service of travel agencies. In P. Kunst & J. Lemmink (Eds.), *Managing service quality (vol. iii)* (pp. 53-70). London: Paul Chapman Publishing.

Borst, P. (1997). *Construction of engineering ontologies for knowledge sharing and reuse*. Unpublished doctoral dissertation, Universiteit Twente, Enschede, The Netherlands.

Borst, P., Akkermans, H., & Top, J. (1997). Engineering ontologies. *International Journal of Human-Computer Studies, 46*, 365-406.

Centeno, C. (2003). *Adoption of internet services in the enlarged European union: Lessons from the internet banking case.* Retrieved August 2004 from http://fiste.Jrc.Es/download/eur20822en.Pdf

De Bruin, H., & Van Vliet, H. (2001). Scenario-based generation and evaluation of software architectures. In *Proceedings of the Third Symposium on Generative and Component-Based Software Engineering (GCSE2001),* Erfurt, Germany.

De Bruin, H., & Van Vliet, H. (2002). Top-down composition of software architectures. In *Proceedings of the 9th International Conference and Workshop on the Engineering of Computer-Based Systems (ECBS2002),* Lund, Sweden.

De Bruin, H., Van Vliet, H., & Baida, Z. (2002). Documenting and analyzing a context-sensitive design space. In *Proceedings of the 3rd Working IFIP/ IEEE Conference on Software Architecture (WICSA-02),* Montreal, Canada.

Donzelli, P. (2004). A goal-driven and agent-based requirements engineering framework. *Requirements Engineering, 9*(1), 16-39.

Flæte, A., & Ottesen, G. (2001, October). Telefiasko for viken. *Dagens Næringsliv (Norwegian newspaper),* pp. 7.

Ford, K., & Bradshaw, J. (Eds.). (1993). *Knowledge acquisition as modeling.* New York: John Wiley & Sons.

Fuxman, A., Liu, L., Pistore, M., Roveri, M., & Mylopoulos, J. (2003). Specifying and analyzing early requirements: Some experimental results. In *Proceedings of the 11th IEEE International Requirements Engineering Conference (RE'03),* Monterey Bay, CA.

Grönroos, C. (2000). *Service management and marketing: A customer relationship management approach.* Chichester, UK: John Wiley & Sons.

Gruber, T., Olsen, G., & Runkel, J. (1996). The configuration design ontologies and the vt elevator domain theory. *International Journal of Human-Computer Studies, 44*(3/4), 569-598.

Gutman, J. (1982). A means-end chain model based on consumer categorization processes. *Journal of Marketing, 46*(2), 60-72.

Herrmann, A., Huber, F., & Braunstein, C. (2000). Market-driven product and service design: Bridging the gap between customer needs, quality management, and customer satisfaction. *International Journal of Production Economics, 66*(1), 77-96.

Hevner, A., March, S., Park, J., & Ram, S. (2004). Design science in information systems research. *MIS Quarterly, 24*(1), 75-105.

Holbrook, M. B. (1999). *Consumer value: A framework for analysis and research.* New York: Routledge.

Kärkkäinen, H., & Elfvengren, K. (2002). Role of careful customer need assessment in product innovation management empirical analysis. *International Journal Production Economics, 80*(1), 85-103.

Kasper, H., van Helsdingen, P., & de Vries Jr., W. (1999). *Service marketing management: An international perspective.* Chichester, UK: John Wiley & Sons.

Keck, D. O., & Kuehn, P. J. (1998). The feature and service interaction problem in telecommunications systems: A survey. *IEEE Transactions on Software Engineering, 24*(10), 779-796.

Kotler, P. (1988). *Marketing management: Analysis, planning, implementation and control.* Englewood Cliffs, NJ: Prentice Hall.

Lancaster, K. J. (1966). A new approach to consumer theory. *Journal of Political Economy, 74*(2), 132-157.

Liu, L., & Yu, R. (2001). Requirements to architectural design: Using goals and scenarios. In *Proceedings of the First International Workshop "From Software Requirements to Architectures" (SREAW-01),* Toronto, Canada.

Löckenhoff, C., & Messer, T. (1994). Configuration. In J. Breuker & W. V. d. Velde (Eds.), *Commonkads library for expertise modelling: Reusable problem solving components* (pp. 197-212). Amsterdam, The Netherlands: IOS Press.

Lovelock, C. (2001). *Services marketing, people, technology, strategy* (4th ed.). Englewood Cliffs, NJ: Prentice Hall.

Martinussen, K. F. (2002). *Kankan som kunne.* (presentation at the itenergi 2002 conference). Retrieved December, 2005, from http://www.itenergi.com/kari_martinussen.ppt

McCullough, D. (2002). A user's guide to conjoint analysis. *Marketing Research, 14*(2), 18-23.

Mentzer, J. T., Rutner, S. M., & Matsuno, K. (1997). Application of the means-end value hierarchy model to understanding logistics service value. *International Journal of Physical Distribution and Logistics, 27*(9/10), 630-643.

Mittal, S., & Frayman, F. (1989). Towards a generic model of configuration tasks. *Proceedings of the Eleventh International Joint Conference on Artificial Intelligence (IJCAI-89),* San Francisco.

Murthi, B., & Sarkar, S. (2003). The role of the management sciences in research on personalization. *Management Science, 49*(10), 1344-1362.

Mylopoulos, J., Chung, L., Liao, S., Wang, H., & Yu, E. (2001). Exploring alternatives during requirements analysis. *IEEE Software, 18*(1), 92-96.

Mylopoulos, J., Chung, L., & Yu, E. (1999). From object-oriented to goal-oriented requirements analysis. *Communications of the ACM, 42*(1), 31-37.

Quine, W. V. O. (1961). *From a logical point of view, nine logico-philosophical essays.* Cambridge, MA: Harvard University Press.

Reynolds, T. J., & Gutman, J. (1988). Laddering theory, method, analysis and interpretation. *Journal of Advertising Research, 28*(1), 11-29.

Schreiber, A. T., Akkermans, J. M., Anjewierden, A. A., de Hoog, R., Shadbolt, N., Van der Velde, W., et al. (2000). *Knowledge engineering and management.* Cambridge, MA: MIT Press.

Sharp, H., & Galal, A. F. G. (1999). Stakeholder identification in the requirements engineering process. In *Proceedings of the 10th International Conference and Workshop on Database and Expert Systems Applications (DEXA 99),* Florence, Italy.

Stefik, M. (1995). *Introduction to knowledge systems*. San Francisco: Morgan Kaufmann.

Stephens, S. A., & Tripp, L. L. (1978). Requirements expression and verification aid. In *Proceedings of the 3rd international conference on Software engineering (ICSE 1978)*, Atlanta, Georgia.

Teare, R. E. (1998). Interpreting and responding to customer needs. *Journal of Workplace Learning, 10*(2), 76-94.

Van Lamsweerde, A. (2000). Requirements engineering in the year 00: A research perspective. In *Proceedings of the 22nd International Conference on Software Engineering*, Limerick, Ireland.

Van Lamsweerde, A. (2001). Goal-oriented requirements engineering: A guided tour, invited minitutorial. In *Proceedings of the International Joint Conference on Requirements Engineering (RE'01)*, Toronto, Canada.

Van Lamsweerde, A., Darimont, R., & Letier, E. (1998). Managing conflicts in goal-driven requirements engineering. *IEEE Transactions on Software Engineering, 24*(11), 908-926.

Vasarhelyi, M., & Greenstein, M. (2003). Underlying principles of the electronization of business: A research agenda. *International Journal of Accounting Information Systems, 4*(1), 1-25.

Xue, M., Harker, P. T., & Heim, G. R. (2003). *Incorporating the dual customer roles in e-service design (Working paper No. 03-04)*. Retrieved August 2004 from http://fic. Wharton.Upenn.Edu/fic/papers/03/0304.Pdf

Zeithaml, V. A. (1988). Consumer perceptions of price, quality, and value: A means-end model and synthesis of evidence. *Journal of Marketing, 52*(3), 2-22.

Zeithaml, V. A., & Bitner, M. J. (1996). *Services marketing*. New York: McGraw-Hill.

Zeithaml, V. A., Parasuraman, A., & Berry, L. (1990). *Delivering quality service: Balancing customer perceptions and expectations*. New York: The Free Press.

Chapter X

Personalization of Web Services:
Concepts, Challenges, and Solutions

Zakaria Maamar, Zayed University, UAE

Soraya Kouadri Mostéfaoui, Oxford Brookes University, UK

Qusay H. Mahmoud, University of Guelph, Canada

Ghita Kouadri Mostéfaoui, Oxford University, UK

Djamal Benslimane, Claude Bernard Lyon 1 University, France

Abstract

This chapter presents a context-based approach for personalizing Web services so that user preferences are accommodated during the performance of Web services. Preferences are of different types varying from when the execution of a Web service should start to where the outcome of this execution should be delivered. Besides user preferences, this chapter argues that the computing resources on which the Web services operate have an impact on their personalization. Indeed, resources schedule the execution requests that originate from multiple Web services. To track this personalization, three types of contexts are devised, namely user context, Web service context, and resource context. A fourth type of context denoted by security enables protecting the content of each of these three contexts. The objective of the security context is to report on the strategies, which permit protecting, overseeing, and assessing the content of the contexts subject to management operations.

Introduction

With the latest development of information and communication technologies, academia and industry are proposing several concepts that can hide the complexity of developing a new generation of user applications. Among these concepts, we cite Web services, which are suitable candidates for achieving the integration of distributed and heterogeneous applications.

A Web service is an accessible application that other applications and humans can discover and trigger to satisfy various needs. It is known that Web services (also called services in the rest of this chapter) have the capacity to be composed into high-level business processes known as composite services. Composing services rather than accessing a single service is essential and offers better benefits to users (Casati, Shan, Dayal, & Shan, 2003; Maamar, Sheng, & Benatallah, 2004b). Composition addresses the situation of a user's request that cannot be satisfied by any available service, whereas a composite service obtained by combining a set of available services might be used (Berardi, Calvanese, De Giacomo, Lenzerini, & Mecella, 2003). For example, applying online for a loan requires identifying the Web site of the appropriate financial institution, filling in an application, submitting the application for assessment, and collecting the analyst's comments back for decision making and applicant notification.

Because users' expectations and requirements constantly change, it is important to include their preferences in the composition and provisioning of Web services. Indeed some users, while on the move, would like receiving answers according to their current locations (Maamar, Yahyaoui, & Mansoor, 2004c). This simple example sheds the light on personalization and its impact on making applications adjustable. Personalization is of types explicit or implicit (Muldoon, O'Hare, Phelan, Strahan, & Collier, 2003). Explicit personalization calls for a direct participation of users in the adjustment of applications. Users clearly indicate the information that needs to be treated or discarded. Implicit personalization does not call for any user involvement and can be built upon learning strategies that automatically track users' behaviors.

Personalization depends on the features of the environment in which it is expected to happen. These features can be about users (e.g., stationary, mobile), computing resources (e.g., fixed, handheld), time of day (e.g., in the afternoon, in the evening), and physical locations (e.g., meeting room, shopping center). Sensing, collecting, assessing, and refining the features of a situation permit the definition of its context. Context is the information that characterizes the interaction between humans, applications, and the surrounding environment (Brézillon, 2003). Prior to integrating context into Web services, various issues need to be addressed (adapted from Satyanarayanan, 2001): how is context structured, how does a Web service bind to context, where is context stored, how frequently does a Web service consult context, how are changes detected and assessed for context update purposes, and what is the overload on a Web service of taking context into account?

Web services composition and provisioning are a very active area of research and development (R&D) (Papazoglou and Georgakopoulos, 2003). However, very little has been accomplished to date regarding their context-based personalization. Several obstacles still hinder personalization, such as: (i) current Web services are not active components that can be embedded with context-awareness mechanisms; (ii) existing Web services composition languages (e.g., Web Services Flow Language [WSFL] and Business Process Execution Language [BPEL]) typically facilitate orchestration only, while neglecting context of users, Web services, and computing resources; and (iii) lack of support techniques for modeling and specifying the integration of personalization into Web services. In this chapter, we present our approach for personalizing Web services using context. The major features of this approach are as follows and will be detailed throughout this chapter: three types of contexts are devised and three types of policies are developed for regulating the personalization of Web services.

The rest of this chapter is organized as follows. The next section overviews some basic concepts such as Web service, context, and personalization. The approach for personalizing Web services is afterwards presented. This will be followed by a discussion on the way context is secured. Prior to concluding the chapter, some related works are presented.

Some Definitions

For the World Wide Web Consortium (W3C), a Web service is *"a software application identified by a URI, whose interfaces and binding are capable of being defined, described, and discovered by XML artifacts and supports direct interactions with other software applications using XML based messages via Internet-based applications"* (Web Services Glossary, 2002). Several standards back the development of Web services, such as universal description discovery and integration (UDDI), Web Service Definition Language (WSDL), and simple object access protocol (SOAP) that define service discovery, description, and messaging protocols, respectively (Milanovic & Malek, 2004). For composition requirements, a composite service is always associated with a specification that describes, among other things, the list of component Web services that participate in the composite service, the execution order of these component Web services, and the corrective strategies in case of exception handling.

Dey defines context as any information that is relevant to the interactions between a user and an environment (Dey, Abowd, & Salber, 2001). This information is about the circumstances, objects, or conditions by which the user is surrounded. Many other researchers have attempted defining context (Brézillon, 2003; Doulkeridis, Valavanis, & Vazirgiannis, 2003), among them Schilit, Adams, and Want (1994), who decompose context into three categories: computing context, such as network connectivity and nearby resources; user context, such as profile and location; and physical context, such as lighting and temperature. In an environment populated with mobile devices, context awareness has been categorized along three components (Spriestersbach, Volger, Lehmann, & Ziegert, 2001): activity, environment, and self. The activity component describes a user's habits while he performs a certain task. The environment component describes the physical and social surroundings of the user in terms of current location and ongoing activities, just to cite a few. Finally, the self component contains the current status of the mobile device itself.

Personalization has attracted the attention of several researchers (Schiaffino & Amandi, 2004). It aims at integrating users' preferences into the process of delivering any information-related content or outcome of service computing. Preferences are of multiple types and vary from content and format to time and location. It is shown, for instance, that the needs of mobile users regarding information access are quite different from the needs of stationary users. Needs of mobile users are not about browsing the Web but about receiving personalized content that is highly sensitive to their immediate environment and respective requirements.

Context and Web Services Personalization

Foundations

Figure 1 illustrates the proposed approach for the personalization of Web services. The core concept in this approach is context, from which three sub-contexts are derived: U-context, W-context, and R-context. Muldoon et al. define the user context of a user as an aggregation of his location, previous activities, and preferences (Muldoon et al., 2003). Sun adopts the same definition of the user context but adds physiological information to this context (Sun, 2003). In this chapter, we comply with Muldoon et al.'s (2003) definition. We define the Web service context of a Web service as an aggregation of its simultaneous participations in composite services, locations, and times of execution that users set, and constraints during execution. Finally, we define the resource context of a resource as an aggregation of its current status, periods of unavailability, and capacities of meeting the execution requirements of Web services.

Figure 1. Representation of the context-based personalization approach

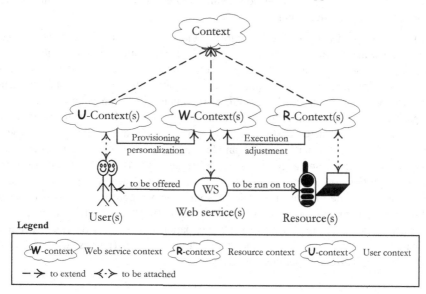

In Figure 1, U-context, W-context, and R-context are inter-connected. From R-context to W-context, "execution adjustment" relationship identifies the execution constraints on a Web service (e.g., execution time, execution location) vs. the execution capabilities of a resource (e.g., next period of availability, scheduling policy) on which the Web service will operate. A resource checks its status before it agrees on supporting the execution of an additional Web service. From U-context to W-context, "provisioning personalization" relationship identifies the preferences of a user (e.g., when and where a Web service needs to be executed, and when and where the execution's outcome needs to be returned) vs. the capabilities of a Web service to accommodate these preferences (e.g., can a service be executed at a certain time or in a certain location). A Web service checks its status before it agrees on satisfying an extra user's need.

A Web service is personalized because of user preferences and adjusted because of resource availabilities. Users and resources are the triggers that make Web services change so they can accommodate preferences and consider availabilities. Besides both triggers, a third one exists, which is a personalized Web service. The personalization of a Web service can trigger the personalization of some peers, which are in relationship with this personalized Web service. We call this type of relationship causal. For example, if a service is personalized in order to accommodate a certain time preference, it is important to ensure that the preceding services are all successfully executed before the time that features the execution of this service. This means that the respective execution times of these services have to be checked and adjusted if needed.

Types and Roles of Context

The role of U-context is to track the current status of a user and reflects his personal preferences in terms of "execution location" or "execution time" of services. The following parameters populate U-context: label, previous locations/services, current location/services, next locations/services, previous periods of time/services, current period of time/services, next periods of time/services, and date.

The role of W-context is to oversee the current status of a Web service and its respective execution constraints. These constraints are tightly-dependent on the preferences of users of type "execution-time requested" and "execution-location requested". A Web service is triggered each time it receives an invitation of participation in a composite service (details are given in Maamar, Kouadri Mostéfaoui, & Bataineh, 2004a, on what an invitation of participation means). Before a service accepts an invitation, it carries out some verifications, including the number of current participations vs. number of allowed participations, expected completion time of current participations, and features of the newly received invitation with regard to execution time and execution location. It happens that a Web service refuses an invitation of participation in a composite service because of multiple reasons: period of unavailability for some maintenance work, resource unavailability, or overloaded status. The following parameters populate W-context: label, status per participation, previous services per participation, next services per participation, regular actions, starting time per participation (requested and effective), location per participation (requested and effective), reasons of failure, corrective actions, and date.

The role of R-context is to monitor the current status of a resource. Before a resource accepts supporting the execution of a service, it performs some verifications, including number of Web services currently executed vs. maximum number of Web services under execution, approximate completion time of ongoing executions, and execution time of the newly received request. It happens that a resource turns down a request of executing a Web service because of multiple reasons: period of unavailability due to some maintenance work or potential overloaded status. The following parameters define R-context: label, previous periods of time/services, current period of time/services, next periods of time/services, previous locations/services, current location/services, next locations/services, and date.

Operation

Figure 2 represents the interaction diagram of the context-based personalization of Web services. When a user selects a Web service, he proceeds next with its personalization according to time and location preferences. On the one hand, time preference is organized along two parts: (i) when the execution of the service should start, and (ii) when the outcome of this execution should be returned to the user. On the other hand, location preference is organized along two parts: (i) where the execution of the service should occur, and (ii) where the outcome of this execution should be returned to the user.

Once the user's preferences are submitted to the Web service, this one ensures that the dates and locations are valid and no conflicts could emerge during deployment. For instance, the delivery time cannot occur before the execution time of a service. Moreover, the user has to be continuously reminded that he has to explicitly identify his current location so that execution location and delivery location are both properly handled. Prior to identifying the resources on which it will be executed, the Web service checks its W-context with regard to the number of Web services currently under execution vs. the maximum number of Web services under execution, and the next period of unavailability. After a positive check of the W-context, the identification of a resource can be launched now. A resource needs mainly to accommodate two things: the starting time of the execution of a service, and the time that the execution of a service lasts, since the outcome of this execution needs to consider the delivery time as per user indication. To this purpose, a resource checks its associated R-context regarding the next periods of time that will feature the execution of Web services and the next period of maintenance. After a positive check, the resource notifies the service, which itself notifies the user.

Before the personalized Web service notifies the user as shown in Figure 2, an additional personalization process is triggered. This process consists of adjusting the Web services that are linked, through the causal relationship, to the recently personalized Web service. The description given in the previous paragraphs also applies to the extra Web services, which assess their current status through their respective W-contexts and search for the resources on which they will operate. To keep Figure 2 clean, the interactions that the extra personalized Web services undertake to search for the resources are not represented. Once all the Web services are personalized, a final notification is sent out to the user about the deployment of the Web service that he has initially requested.

Figure 2. Interactions between participants of personalized Web services

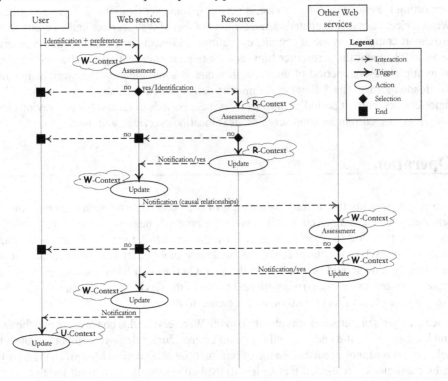

Role of Policies in Personalization

Because of user preferences and resource availabilities, a Web service has to be adjusted so that it accommodates these preferences and takes into account these availabilities. To ensure that the adjustment of a Web service is efficient, we developed three types of policies (providers of Web services are normally responsible for developing the policies). The first type, called consistency, checks the status of a Web service after being personalized. The second type, called feasibility, ensures that a personalized Web service can find a resource on which it executes according to the constraints of time and location. Finally, the third type, called inspection, ensures that the deployment of a personalized Web service complies with the adjusted specification.

A consistency policy guarantees that a Web service still exactly does what it is supposed to do after personalization. Personalization could alter the initial specification of a Web service when it comes, for instance, to the list of regular events that trigger the Web service. Indeed, time- and location-related parameters are now new events to add to the list of regular events. Moreover, because of QoS-related parameters (e.g., response time and throughput) of a Web service, it is important to verify that these QoS parameters did not change and are still satisfied despite the personalization.

A feasibility policy guarantees that a personalized Web service always succeeds in the identification of a resource on which it will operate. Because services have different requirements (e.g., periods of request, periods of delivery) and resources have different constraints (e.g., period of availabilities, maximum capacity), an agreement has to be reached between what services need in terms of resources and what resources offer in terms of capabilities.

An inspection policy is a means by which various aspects are considered, such as what to track (time, location, etc.), who asked to track (user, service itself, or both), when to track (continuously, intermittently), when and how to update the arguments of the different contexts, and how to react if a discrepancy is noticed between what was requested and what has effectively happened. The inspection policy is mainly tightened to the parameters of types requested and effective of the W-context of a Web service. If there is a discrepancy between these parameters, the reasons have to be determined, assessed, and reported. One of the reasons could be the lack of appropriate resources on which the personalized service needs to be executed. It should be noted that this reason is in contradiction with the aim of the feasibility policy.

Security and Web Services Personalization

This section continues our investigation of Web services personalization with emphasis, this time, on securing the contexts of users, Web services, and resources.

Motivations

To track the progress of the interactions that happen, first, between users and Web services and, second, between Web services and resources, context was specialized into user context, Web service context, and resource context. It is agreed that any tracking operation relies on the quality of information that is collected, refined, and used for feeding this operation. A poor quality of information results in making wrong decisions, which affect, for example, the chronology of operations for execution or the planning of resources for scheduling. The support information for tracking purposes represents the content of a context. We discuss below the rationale of securing the content of contexts and the mechanisms we set up for authorizing or restricting the management of this content by using specific policies.

Our security approach is built upon a fourth type of context, which we extend from context and refer to as security context (S-context) in Figure 3. While the three aforementioned types of context are responsible for providing information on the status of user, Web service, and resource components, respectively, the security context is responsible for overseeing the contents of U/S/R-contexts of these components (Figure 3). Therefore, the security context is specialized into three types referred to as S-context$_U$ (security context of user context), S-context$_W$ (security context of Web service context), and S-context$_R$ (security context of resource context). Figure 3 illustrates two types of links between contexts: to extend for specialization purposes and to oversee for tracking purposes. It should be noted that Figure 3 is a refinement of Figure 1. By promoting security context, our objective is to track all the

Figure 3. Types of context for securing Web services personalization

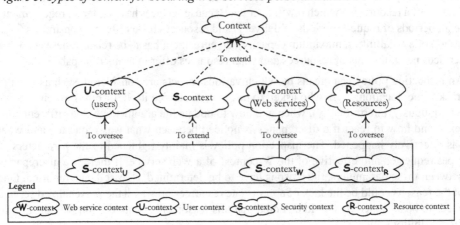

concerns and threats that affect the content of a context, deploy appropriate measures based on previous security contexts, and adjust the measures subject to the feedbacks obtained out of this tracking. Some of the elements that could be identified through a security context are multiple, including the regular actions that are used for identification and encryption/decryption, the types of violation that targeted the protective measures, and the corrective actions that are run for fixing misuse or alteration situations.

The separation between S-context (dedicated to security) and U/W/R-context (dedicated to components) permits a better management of the matters that each type of context is concerned with. On the one hand, U/W/R-context focuses on the changes in a component whether user, Web service, or resource. These changes are about availability, commitment, location, etc. On the other hand, S-context focuses on the protection strategy of the content of these three contexts from any misuse or alteration attempts.

Protection of Context Content

The aim of the security context is twofold. The first aim is to announce the security mechanisms, which guarantee the necessary protection of U/W/R-contexts in terms of authentication, message safety, and data integrity. This aim has already been looked into as part of our previous research on context ontologies (Maamar et al., 2005). A non-authorized access to a context could result in an inaccurate assessment of multiple elements like location of user, execution status of a Web service, or capacity of a resource. The second aim, which is the focus of this chapter, is to keep track at the level of the security context (S-context$_{U/W/R}$) of all the operations that users/Web services/resources initiate over the content of their respective U/W/R-contexts. By tracking these operations, it would be possible to know what happened, what is happening, and what would happen to the content of a context. Operations on the content of a context are multiple, ranging from consultation and modification to content exchange between contexts. The sensitive nature of the content of contexts, as

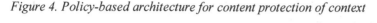

Figure 4. Policy-based architecture for content protection of context

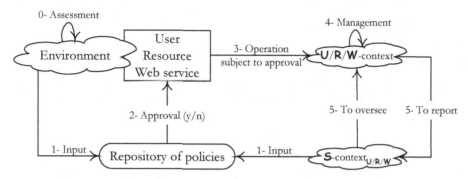

emphasized by the first aim of the security context, has motivated the development of a set of policies for framing the performance of these operations based, first, on the status of the environment surrounding users/Web services/resources and, second, on previous experiences of running similar operations. For instance, a Web service could refrain from consulting its W-context's parameters if this Web service finds out that the resource on which it operates, can intercept and modify content. In this chapter, we use Ponder (Damianou, 2002) to specify the various policies per type of context and per type of operation to be run over the content of this type of context.

Figure 4 illustrates our proposed policy-based architecture for protecting the content of a context. The architecture highlights three components namely user, resource, and Web service, and a repository of policies (to be associated with an authorization engine). To keep Figure 4 clear, the way these components are "plunged" in the surrounding environment is just represented with the shape overlapping between "user/resource/Web service" rectangle and "environment" cloud. Each component binds to a context that is overseen by a security context. A component carries out operations over the content of its context upon receiving approval from the repository of policies (i.e., the authorization engine). This approval is the result of triggering policies based on the inputs that the repository receives after assessing the environment (environment assessment is outside this chapter's scope, but readers are referred to Maamar et al., 2005, for additional details) and consulting the security context. At this time, two types of policies are put forward in compliance with the types of policies in Ponder (an object-oriented policy language for the management of distributed systems and networks): authorization and restriction. Input from the environment is about user (location, day time, status$_{\{busy, resting, etc.\}}$, etc.), Web service (current status$_{\{active, suspended, etc.\}}$, provider identifier, QoS, etc.), and resource (current load$_{\{high, low, etc.\}}$, provider identifier, QoS, etc.). And the input from the security context is about previous experiences, which have dealt with the content of context. Previous experience refers here to a similar operation over a context content that occurred in the past and was reported at the level of the security context. Any change in the content of a context is immediately communicated to the security context. A change could be illustrated with setting new values to parameters of contexts, modifying the update flag of a parameter from "permitted" to "un-permitted," modifying the consultation flag of a parameter from "authorized" to "un-authorized," etc. In Figure 4, number duplication means concurrent operations.

Security Strategy

Our development strategy for a security context of types user (S-context$_U$), Web service (S-context$_W$), and resource (S-context$_R$) revolves around three steps: threat identification, security-context organization, and policy specification.

1. Threat identification step. This step consists of listing the threats that could abstain a component (user/resource/Web service) from managing the content of its context. We classify the threats according to their origin. The various origins of threats reinforce the relationships that exist between users and Web services and between Web services and resources.

    •   Threats on the content of U-context of user primarily originate from Web services. Once a Web service is selected for participation in a composition, the Web service could turn out to be untrustworthy during run-time. Indeed, subject to personalization at the levels of execution time or execution location, a Web service might aim at modifying some preferences of a user without consulting him or her. A motivator for the modification could be the large number of user requests that the Web service has accepted to satisfy, thus exceeding its capabilities. Since contexts' parameters overlap, the user is requested to modify the values of some of his U-context's parameters (e.g., next locations per Web services) in accordance with the latest changes in the W-context's parameters. If the Web service is classified as untrustworthy and a similar modification request has repetitively been issued by the same Web service, restriction policies should prevent the user from modifying U-context. Details on the trust level of a Web service and type of request are contained in the security context (see Step 2 for details). Contrary to restriction policies, authorization policies permit the modification of the U-context's parameters if, for example, the recent changes in the preferences of the user at the Web service level still meet the requirements of the user.

    •   Threats on the content of W-context of a Web service have two origins: user and resource. Regarding the user origin, the aforementioned scenario that describes the threats on U-context of user is still valid once the threat direction is reversed. This time the user, instead of the Web service, aims at modifying his preferences without consulting the Web service. The Web service either accepts or rejects modifying the W-context. Modification rejection could be motivated by the lack of resources on which the Web service would run. And modification acceptance could be motivated by the confidence level that the Web service aims at increasing toward this user.

    Regarding the resource origin, a Web service needs computing resources on which it operates. In addition to the overlapping situation between W-context's and R-context's parameters (where a change at the W-context level has to be reflected at the R-context level, too), the resource can request some private data from the

W-context of a Web service for different purposes related to tracing current executions or scheduling forthcoming executions. A resource could accept additional Web services for execution if it could establish the various participations of this Web service in other compositions. While this threat (private-data access) could be addressed using authentication, the resource needs to be informed about the authentication mechanism that it needs to comply with prior to any attempt of consulting W-context. This mechanism type is known per the first aim of the security context (Maamar et al., 2005).

- Threats on the content of R-context of a resource originate from Web services. The aforementioned scenario that describes the threats on W-context of a Web service is still valid once the threat direction is reversed. This time the Web service, instead of the resource, aims at modifying some execution parameters without consulting the resource. The resource either accepts or rejects modifying the R-context. Modification acceptance could be motivated by the availability of the resource on which the Web service was planned to run. And modification rejection could be rejected by the repetitive requests that originate from this Web service.

2.   Security-context organization step. This step consists of identifying the parameters of the security context (S-context$_{U/W/R}$) per component type, so that, first, overseeing the changes in the content of contexts properly happens and, second, building a bank of previous experiences occurs too (Figure 4). At this stage of our research, we have identified the following parameters independently of the security-context type:

- **Label context:** identifies the context of the component that the security context is associated with.

- **Operation source:** identifies the component that intends to run an operation over a context content.

- **Operation type:** indicates if it is a consultation or modification operation.

- **Source trustworthiness:** indicates how much the component that binds to a context trusts the component that intends to run an operation over this context content (null if both components are the same).

- **Parameter list:** indicates the parameters of a context that are included in the operation of the component.

- **Last operation(s) outcome:** identifies the performance outcome in terms of success or failure of a similar operation(s) that the component binding to a context has received in the past from another component.

- **Operation validation and outcome:** indicates if the current operation over a context content is approved or denied (if *trustworthiness of source* is set to null, then *operation validation* is by default set to approved) and what the outcome of this performance is in terms of success or failure.

- **Date:** identifies the time of updating the parameters above.

Example of S-context$_{U/W/R}$'s parameters instantiation

- **Label context:** U-context$_1$ (context of user$_1$).
- **Operation source:** Web service$_2$.
- **Operation type:** modification
- **Source trustworthiness:** high (user$_1$ highly trusts Web service$_2$).
- **Parameter list:** parameter$_1$, parameter$_2$.
- **Last operation(s) outcome:** null (first time).
- **Operation validation and outcome:** approved/failure (the operation of Web service$_2$ was approved but its execution failed).
- **Date:** 5/5/2005

3.   **Policy specification step.** This step consists of working on the policies that will be responsible for managing the content of U/W/R-contexts. Policies permit a dynamic management of the content of a context. Each management request is verified using policies. Furthermore, policies can be changed on the fly in response to changing conditions.

Development of the Security Strategy

Our motive for adopting policies is to frame the operations that are carried out over the content of contexts according to the state of the surrounding environment and previous experiences. The selection of a policy definition language is guided by some requirements that need to be satisfied as reported in Tonti, Bradshaw, Jeffers, Montanari, Suri, and Uszok (2003): expressiveness to support the wide range of policy requirements arising in the system being managed, simplicity to ease the policy definition tasks for people with various levels of expertise, enforceability to ensure a mapping of policy specification into concrete policies for various platforms, scalability to guarantee adequate performance, and analyzability to allow reasoning about and over policies. In this chapter, we employ Ponder (Damianou, 2002). Ponder is an object-oriented policy language for the management of distributed systems and networks.

Ponder permits developing different types of policy: authorization (positive or negative), obligation, etc. In this chapter, we only use the first type. The following illustrates an authorization policy to modify the content of a context. The modification request originates from Web service$_i$ to U-context of user$_j$. The conditions that this request are subject to are associated with "when" label and summarized as follows: trustworthiness level of Web service$_i$ is high, type of operation is modification, and outcome of a similar operation in the past is success. Once these conditions are satisfied, various actions are performed, namely setting the values of the parameters of U-context, updating the operation validation with approval, and, finally, updating the operation outcome with either success or failure.

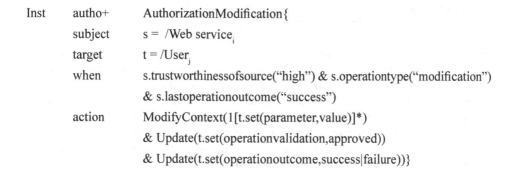

Inst   autho+   AuthorizationModification{
           subject $s = $ /Web service$_i$
           target $t = $ /User$_j$
           when   s.trustworthinessofsource("high") & s.operationtype("modification")
                       & s.lastoperationoutcome("success")
           action   ModifyContext(1[t.set(parameter,value)]*)
                       & Update(t.set(operationvalidation,approved))
                       & Update(t.set(operationoutcome,success|failure))}

Figure 5. Interactions during Web services personalization (after considering security)

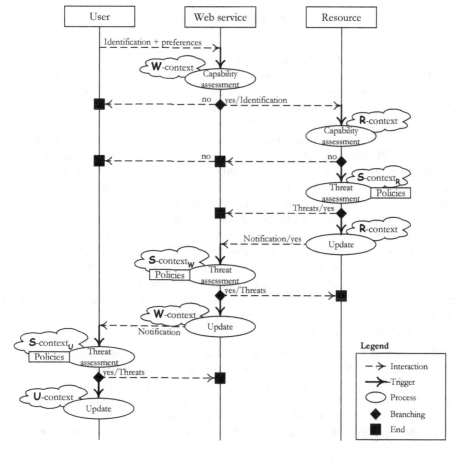

Impact of Security Context on Personalization

Figure 2 illustrated the interactions that occur during Web services personalization prior to including the security of the content of context. These interactions have mainly shown how context contributes to assessing the capabilities and tracking the commitments of Web services and resources. Upon personalization acceptance, contexts of user, Web service, or resource were updated. Now we discuss the way these interactions are adjusted because of the security context. Figure 5 presents the way security contexts and policies are combined for threat assessment on the content of contexts. In the same figure, this assessment always occurs before any update process of the content of context.

Compared to Figure 2, Figure 5 shows the additional processing that occurs during assessing threats. While this processing might constitute an extra load on users, Web services, and resources, it permits, however, a better decision-making process of the actions to take due to the consistency now featuring the context content. We strengthened that a poor quality of information affects, for example, the chronology of operations to execute or the planning of resources to schedule.

Related Work

Hegering, Kupper, Linnhoff-Popien, and Reiser present a strategy that homogenizes the notion of context through the use of three categories (Hegering, Kupper, Linnhoff-Popien, & Reiser, 2003): device, environment, and user. The three categories greatly overlap with the types of context of Figure 1. Independently of the user context, the device context category corresponds to the resource context, and the environment context corresponds to the Web service context. Zuidweg, Pereira Filho, and van Sinderen use the W3C's platform for privacy preferences (P3P) standard (W3C, 2003) in a Web service-based context-aware application (Zuidweg Pereira Filho, & van Sinderen, 2003). The intention of P3P is to automatically negotiate on a Web site's privacy practice. A user defines his privacy preferences and stores them in a machine-readable format such as APPEL(A P3P Preferences Exchange Language) (W3C, 2003). When a user wants to browse a Web site, a user agent that resides in the user's browser retrieves first the Web site's P3P policy. Next, the user agent compares the policy with the user's preferences. If the policy complies with these preferences, then the Web site will be made available. Otherwise, the user may be prompted to further evaluate the Web site, otherwise his request or her will be cancelled. While we have discussed in this chapter that preferences are related to execution time and execution location of Web services, preferences can also be associated with privacy when it comes, for instance, to disclosing some sensitive information on users.

Barkhuus and Dey have identified three levels of interactivity for context-aware applications (Barkhuus & Dey, 2003): personalization, active context awareness, and passive context awareness. According to the authors, personalization, also referred to as customization and tailoring, is motivated by the diversity and dynamics featuring nowadays applications. In an active context-awareness mode, it concerns applications that, on the basis of sensor data, change their content autonomously. In a passive context-awareness mode, applications merely present the updated context to the user and let the user specify how the application should change. In this chapter, we adopted a passive context-awareness style with the manual feeding of the user's current location. While we mentioned that this type of feeding presents some limitations vs. an automatic feeding, this has, however, enabled an efficient handling of the privacy concern of users.

In this chapter, context is used for overseeing Web services personalization. Other projects such as Breener and Schiffers (2003) use Web services for managing context provisioning. Breener and Schiffers envision that context information will typically be provided by autonomous organizations (or context providers), which means heterogeneity and distribution challenges to deal with. Additional challenges are cited in Breener and Schiffers (2003) including (i) what is the optimal sequence for gathering and combining the required context information, (ii) how to secure the whole context provisioning process, and (iii) how is the cooperation between the providers of context achieved, and even enforced?

The separation of concerns between user, Web service, and resource is backed by Poladian, Pedra Sousa, Garlan, and Shaw (2004). In their dynamic configuration of resource-aware services project, they have considered three spaces—user utility, application capability, and computing resources—and two mappings. A mapping from capability space to utility space expresses the user's needs and preferences (similar to "provisioning personalization" in Figure 1). A mapping from capability space to resource space expresses the fidelity profiles of available application (similar to "execution adjustment" in Figure 1). In Poladian et al. (2004), by configuring the system it is meant to find a point in the capability space that, first, maximizes user utility, and, second, satisfies the resource constraints. In our Web services personalization approach, a Web service could represent this point, since it aims at conciliating between what a user needs and what a resource offers.

Other languages for policy specification exist, such as the Web service policy framework (WS-Policy) (Nolan, 2004). A WS-Policy specification defines a syntax and semantics for service providers and service requestors to describe their requirements, preferences, and capabilities. The syntax provides a flexible and concise way of expressing the needs of each domain in the form of policies. A domain in this context is a generic field of interest that applies to the service and can illustrate one of the following aspects: security, privacy, application priorities, user account priorities, and traffic control. A WS-Policy specification also describes processing models for the policies that operate independently of the domains.

Other service-specific policies have been proposed. Privacy policies discussed in Yee and Korba (2004) are an example. Yee and Korba propose a privacy policy negotiation approach to protect privacy of Web services users. Along the same direction, Indrakanti Varadharajan, and Hitchens make use of the XML Access Control Language (XACL) to specify authorization policies for patient records in healthcare systems implemented as Web services (Indrakanti Varadharajan, & Hitchens, 2004). The use of another policy specification language, namely Rei, is also reported in Masuoka et al. (2005). Policies were used for implementing access control over resources like networked devices, offered in an ubiquitous configuration.

Conclusion

In this chapter, we presented a context-based approach for Web services personalization. Three types of contexts, namely U-context, W-context, and R-context, are the cornerstone of the approach by storing details related to personalization, such as preferred execution time and preferred execution location of Web services. The effect of changes of a Web service because of user preferences and resource availabilities has required the development of three types of policies, referred to as consistency, feasibility, and inspection. The use of policies aims at guaranteeing that Web services still do what they are supposed to do despite personalization.

Research on security for Web services has particularly investigated low-level aspects like message privacy, data integrity, and authentication. In a dynamic environment like the Internet, this is by far not enough. A continuous assessment of the threats and regular change in the security strategy are critical. Context permits feeding this strategy with information about various elements related to location of user, execution status of a Web service, load of a resource, etc. Therefore, it was deemed appropriate to protect the content of a context from alteration or misuse risks by framing the management operations over this content. These operations were built upon a context of type security and specified with policies defined in Ponder.

References

Barkhuus, L., & Dey, A. (2003). Is context-aware computing taking control away from the user? Three levels of interactivity examined. In *Proceedings of The 5th International Conference on Ubiquitous Computing (UbiComp 2003)*, Seattle, Washington.

Berardi, D., Calvanese, D., De Giacomo, G., Lenzerini, M., & Mecella, M. (2003). A foundational vision for e-services. In *Proceedings of The Workshop on Web Services, e-Business, and the Semantic Web (WES 2003) held in conjunction with The 15th Conference On Advanced Information Systems Engineering (CaiSE 2003)*, Klagenfurt/Velden, Austria.

Breener, M., & Schiffers, M. (2003). Applying Web services technologies to the management of context provisioning. In *Proceedings of The 10th Workshop of the OpenView University Association (OVUA 2003)*, Geneva, Switzerland.

Brézillon, P. (2003). Focusing on context in human-centered computing. *IEEE Intelligent Systems, 18*(3), 62-66.

Casati, F., Shan, E., Dayal, U., & Shan, M. C. (2003). Business-oriented management of Web services. *Communications of the ACM, 46*(10), 55-60.

Damianou, N. C. (2002). *A policy framework for management of distributed systems*. Doctoral dissertation, University of London, Imperial College of Science, Technology and Medicine.

Dey, A. K., Abowd, G. D., & Salber, D. (2001). A conceptual framework and a toolkit for supporting the rapid prototyping of context-aware applications. *Human-Computer Interaction Journal, Special Issue on Context-Aware Computing, 16*(1), 97-166.

Doulkeridis, C., Valavanis, E., & Vazirgiannis, M. (2003). Towards a context-aware service directory. In *Proceedings of The 4th Workshop on Technologies for E-Services (TES'03) held in conjunction with The 29th International Conference on Very Large Data Bases (VLDB 2003)*, Berlin, Germany.

Hegering, H. G., Kupper, A., Linnhoff-Popien, C., & Reiser, H. (2003). Management challenges of context-aware services in ubiquitous environments. In *Proceedings of The 14th IFIP/IEEE International Workshop on Distributed Systems: Operations and Management (DSOM 2003)*, Heidelberg, Germany.

Indrakanti, S., Varadharajan, V., & Hitchens, M. (2004). Authorization service for Web services and its implementation. In *Proceedings of The IEEE International Conference on Web Services (ICWS 2004)*, San Diego, California.

Maamar, Z., Kouadri Mostéfaoui, S., & Bataineh, E. (2004a). A conceptual analysis of the role of conversations in Web services composition. In *Proceedings of The 2004 IEEE International Conference on e-Technology, e-Commerce and e-Service (EEE-04)*, Taipei, Taiwan.

Maamar, Z., Sheng, Q. Z., & Benatallah, B. (2004b). On composite Web Services provisioning in an environment of fixed and mobile computing resources [Special issue]. *Information Technology and Management Journal, 5*(3), 251-270.

Maamar, Z., Yahyaoui, H., & Mansoor, W. (2004c). Design and development of an M-commerce environment: The E-CWE project. *Journal of Organizational Computing and Electronic Commerce, 14*(4), 285-303.

Maamar, Z., Kouadri Mostéfaoui, S., & Yahyaoui, H. (2005). Towards an agent-based and context-oriented approach for Web services composition. *IEEE Transactions on Knowledge and Data Engineering, 17*(3), 686-697.

Maamar, Z. Narendra, N. C., & Sattanathan, S. (in press). Towards an ontology-based approach for specifying and securing Web services. *Journal of Information & Software Technology*.

Masuoka, R., Chopra, M., Labrou, Y., Song, Z., Chen, W., Kagal, L., & Finin, T. (2005). Policy-based access control for task computing using Rei. In *Proceedings of The 14th International World Wide Web Conference (WWW2005)*, Chiba, Japan.

Milanovic, N., & Malek, M. (2004). Current solutions for Web service composition. *IEEE Internet Computing, 8*(6), 51-59.

Muldoon, C., O'Hare, G., Phelan, D., Strahan, R., & Collier, R. (2003). ACCESS: An agent architecture for ubiquitous service delivery. In *Proceedings of The 7th International Workshop on Cooperative Information Agents (CIA2003)*, Helsinki, Finland.

Nolan, P. (2004). *Understand WS-policy processing*. Technical report, IBM Corporation.

Papazoglou, M., & Georgakopoulos, D. (2003). Introduction to the special issue on service-oriented computing. *Communications of the ACM, 46*(10).

Poladian, V., Pedro Sousa, J., Garlan, D., & Shaw, M. (2004). Dynamic configuration of resource-aware services. In *Proceedings of The 26th International Conference on Software Engineering (ICSE 2004)*, Edinburgh, Scotland (pp. 604-613).

Satyanarayanan, M. (2001). Pervasive computing: Vision and challenges. *IEEE Personal Communications*, 8(4).

Schiaffino, S., & Amandi, A. (2004). User-interface agent interaction: Personalization issues. *International Journal of Human Computer Studies, 60*(1), 129-148.

Schilit, B., Adams, N., & Want, R. (1994). Context-aware computing applications. In *Proceedings of The IEEE Workshop on Mobile Computing Systems and Applications*, Santa Cruz, CA (pp. 85-90).

Spriestersbach, A., Volger, H., Lehmann, F., & Ziegert, T. (2001). Integrating context information into enterprise applications for the mobile workforce: A case study. In *Proceedings of The 1st ACM International Workshop on Mobile Commerce (WMC 2001) held in conjunction with The Seventh Annual International Conference on Mobile Computing and Networking (MobiCom 2001)*, Rome, Italy.

Sun, J. (2003). Information requirement elicitation in mobile commerce. *Communications of the ACM, 46*(12).

Tonti, G., Bradshaw, J., Jeffers, R., Montanari, R., Suri, N., & Uszok, A. (2003). Semantic Web languages for policy representation and reasoning: A comparison of KAoS, Rei, and Ponder. In *Proceedings of The 2nd International Semantic Web Conference (ISWC 2003)*, Sanibel Island, FL.

Uszok, A., Bradshaw, J., Jeffers, R., Johnson, M., Tate, A., Dalton, J., & Aitken, S. (2004). Policy and contract management for semantic Web services. In *Proceedings of The 2004 AAAI Spring Symposium on Semantic Web Services Series*, Stanford, CA.

Web services glossary (2002). Retrieved September 27, 2006, from http://www.w3.org/2002/ws/arch/2/06/wd-wsa-gloss-20020605.html

W3C (2003). *Platform for privacy preferences (P3P) project*. Retrieved June 2004 from http://www.w3.org/P3P/

Yee, G., & Korba, L. (2004). Privacy policy compliance for Web services. In *Proceedings of The IEEE International Conference on Web Services (ICWS 2004)*, San Diego, CA.

Zuidweg, M., Pereira Filho, J. G., & van Sinderen, M. (2003). Using P3P in a Web services-based context-aware application platform. In *Proceedings of The 9th Open European Summer School and IFIP Workshop on Next Generation Networks (EUNICE 2003)*, Balatonfured, Hungary.

Section I V

Electronic Communication Adoption and Service Provider Strategy

Chapter XI

Managing Corporate E-Mail Systems:
A Contemporary Study

Aidan Duane, Waterford Institute of Technology, Ireland

Patrick Finnegan, University College Cork, Ireland

Abstract

As the criticality of e-mail for electronic business activity increases, ad-hoc e-mail imple-
mentation, prolonged management neglect and user abuse of e-mail systems have generated
negative effects. However, management's ability to rectify problems with e-mail systems
is hindered by our understanding of its organisational use. Research on e-mail systems is
often dated and based on quantitative methodologies that cannot explain the interaction
between various controls in organisational settings. Updating our understanding of the
organisational aspects of e-mail systems utilizing qualitative methods is necessary. This
chapter presents a multiple case study investigation of e-mail system monitoring and con-
trol. The study examines the interaction between key elements of e-mail control identified
by previous researchers and considers the role of such controls at various implementation
phases. The findings reveal eight major elements to be particularly important in monitor-
ing and controlling e-mail systems within the organisations studied. These are: (1) form a
cross-functional e-mail system management team; (2) implement and regularly update e-mail
management software; (3) formulate a detailed and legally sound e-mail policy; (4) engage

in structured e-mail system training; (5) create and maintain ongoing awareness of e-mail policy; (6) engage in a process of hybrid feedback and control-based e-mail monitoring; (7) firmly enforce discipline in accordance with the e-mail policy; and (8) conduct regular reviews and updates of the e-mail management programme.

Introduction

Internet-based electronic commerce applications constitute a significant departure from traditional information technologies, posing more risks to the organisation because of their extensive direct electronic interaction with other entities (De & Mathew, 1999). In particular, an e-mail system introduces a new set of threats and legal issues to an organization, and the dramatic increase in e-mail usage is commensurate with the rising number of workplace incidents and disputes (American Management Association (AMA), 2003; Attaran, 2000; Hancock, 1999; PriceWaterhouseCoopers (PWC), 2002; Simmers, 2002; Weber 2004). As organisations struggle to derive value from information technologies (Agarwal, 2001) and scrutinise spending on all applications, including e-mail (Graff, 2002c), particularly in periods of reduced information technology (IT) budgets (PWC, 2002), organisations waste money buying technology if they don't create the human infrastructure, policies and procedures to curb information systems abuses (Hancock, 1999).

E-mail systems have traditionally been initiated by IT departments without being part of a business-led strategy. Nevertheless, e-mail has evolved over time to become more of a corporate-wide service (Jackson, Dawson, & Wilson, 2000). The e-mail infrastructure is now a mission critical component of the enterprise information infrastructure and an essential component in all implementations of e-commerce platforms, especially for enterprises striving to become more virtual, resilient, and efficient (Graff, 2002b). E-mail systems have also become heavily integrated with mobile technologies, particularly portable telephones, and thus there is an increasing importance on Web or wireless access to central e-mail servers (Graff & Grey, 2002). This mobile e-mail access provides users with more flexibility and mobility but increases the pressure on the organisation to maintain and improve the reliability of the core e-mail system infrastructure (Graff & Grey, 2002). Mobile e-mail access also brings new pathways for the entry of viruses or the exit of confidential information (Graff & Grey, 2002). The more that organisations rely on e-mail, the more reliable if must be, because the risk of business interruption increases dramatically (Graff & Grey, 2002). Organisations must secure, expand and manage this communication medium effectively to meet new challenges (Graff & Grey, 2002; Weber, 2004).

Simmers (2002) contends that vague, unmonitored, unenforced, or absent e-mail policy exposes the organisation to a number of legal, financial, and operational risks such as losses of confidential information, network congestion, threats to network integrity, diversion of employee attention, and increased liability. Simmers (2002) and Weber (2004) contend that the nature and incidence of problematic e-mail use requires particular attention because of the costs it imposes on organisations. Consequently, organisations are increasingly challenged to get e-mail under control (Graff, 2002e) and must become more focused on stabilising and protecting their e-mail systems, gaining more control over the use of their systems and managing risk associated with these systems (Graff & Grey, 2002). Only when an e-mail system is used and managed properly will an organisation be able to reap its benefits (Graff, 2002e; Ruggeri, Stevens, & McElhill, 2000). Thus, it is imperative that underlying all uses of e-mail, current and expanded, is careful planning, monitoring, and management of the e-mail infrastructure (Graff & Grey, 2002; Simmers, 2002; Sipior & Ward, 2002; Weber, 2004). In particular, organisations should anticipate the potentially harmful effects of e-mail systems and seek to prevent them from occurring (Van den Hooff, 1997). However, organisations lack analytical tools and understanding to examine their existing practices and to assist in reasserting e-mail systems for corporate rather than individual purposes (Ruggeri et al., 2000; Weber, 2004).

The appropriate design, management, and application of any communication system depend to a great extent upon appropriate ongoing research of those systems from technical, organizational, and social perspectives (Rice, 1990). However, Weber (2004) contends that we still lack a deep understanding of the impacts of e-mail on organizations, and our understanding of these impacts remains fragmented and superficial. Although the unsatisfactory understanding of the impacts of communication media provided by quantitative research has long been recognised (Rogers, 1986), it is evident that the majority of the research produced over the past two decades on e-mail systems research utilizes quantitative methods to examine the social and technical concerns of e-mail systems. The need for organizationally based research has been highlighted in the past by researchers such as Fulk and Desanctis (1995) and Rudy (1996) in calling for situational studies that recount organisational environments in which electronic communications systems are used. Nevertheless, laboratory-like experiments (Cappel, 1995; Culnan & Markus, 1987; Fulk, Schmitz, & Steinfield, 1990; Mantovani, 1994) and mass surveys (AMA, 2000; AMA 2003; Hoffman, Hartman, & Rowe, 2003; Lim, Thompson, & Geok, 2002; Schulman, 2001) dominate the literature on e-mail studies. As a result, there has been relatively little published advice on how to take an organisational view of e-mail systems (Ruggeri et al., 2000; Weber 2004). Weber (2004) comments that:

> ... many of us claim that as members of the information systems discipline we are well placed to study phenomena associated with human-computer interactions. It is somewhat ironic, therefore, that with few exceptions we find little research on e-mail published in our major journals. (p. xi)

Weber (2004) argues that we still have "human, technological, and organisational problems to solve" (p.iv) in relation to e-mail systems and calls for "better ways of managing e-mail and assisting users of e-mail to deal with the problems it poses" (p. iv).

This chapter presents the results of multiple case studies that investigate how organisations monitor and control their e-mail systems. The next section examines the theoretical grounding for the study. This is followed by a discussion of the research method and a presentation of the research findings. The chapter concludes by identifying key factors in a programme for e-mail system electronic monitoring and control.

Theoretical Grounding

In the push to increase business use of e-mail, many organisations failed to fully consider the implications of its implementation (Ruggeri et al., 2000) and many have not attended to developing or communicating e-mail policies (Urbaczewski & Jessup, 2002). Other organisations left staff to establish the purpose and use of e-mail systems (Ruggeri et al., 2000) while some organisations even encouraged playful use of the e-mail system without controlling activities, to facilitate learning (Belanger & Van Slyke, 2002). However, as IT evolves, its social construction changes (Benbunan-Fich, 2002). Users do not passively receive the technology in a pre-existing form; rather, they actively adapt the technology to their own ends. IT users choose what features of the technology they will use and how they will use those features (Benbunan-Fich, 2002). Therefore, a technology in use should be conceived as a set of social practices that emerge and evolve over time (Giddens, 1979; Poole & DeSanctis, 1990).

Consequently, the initial technical success of e-mail system implementation does not guarantee long-term usefulness or political harmony and can culminate in devastating side-effects during latter stages of implementation (Graff, 2002e; PWC, 2002; Romm, Pliskin, & Rifkin, 1996). In fact, numerous organisations worldwide are repeatedly reporting increasing negative effects of e-mail systems (Attaran, 2000; PWC, 2002; Weber 2004). Some major companies have settled multi-million dollar sexual harassment lawsuits as a result of internally circulated e-mail (Siau, Fui-Hoon Nah, & Teng 2002; Sipior & Ward, 2002). In many instances, it is reported that adequate systems control structures are absent (PWC, 2002; Sipior & Ward, 2002; Weber, 2004). Rice and Aydin (1991) suggest that organisations fail to anticipate and control the negative effects of information systems because they are less visible and expected, and, thus, less assessed or managed. Noticeably, PWC (2002) reports that it tends to be organisations that have experienced information systems abuse that implement controls. However, such results are not confined to e-mail systems. Rogers' (1986) work on communications technology concluded that those who introduce communication technologies must see beyond the desirable, direct, and anticipated impacts, and realise that more of the indirect, undesirable, and unanticipated impacts of communication technologies occur as time elapses. Weber (2004) suggests that technological developments associated with e-mail use may prove to be ineffective if they are not informed by social science research.

It has been proposed that the effects of computer-mediated communication can be categorised from a two-level perspective, as technology can have both first-level and second-level effects (Sproull & Kiesler, 1991). Researchers have identified the first-level negative effects of e-mail systems as productivity drain (Anderson, 1999; Graff & Grey, 2002; Lim et al., 2002; PWC, 2002); security breaches; urgent communications overlooked; excessive non-business communication (Lim et al., 2002; PWC, 2002; Sipior & Ward, 2002); an increasing cost of usage; information overload and redundancy (Graff & Grey, 2002; Lim et al., 2002; Sproull & Kiesler, 1991; Weber, 2004). Researchers have identified the second-level negative effects of e-mail systems as depersonalisation; disinhibition (Markus, 1994; Siau et al., 2002; Weber, 2004); profanities, bad news, negative sentiment and illicit use (Hodson, Englander, & Englander, 1999; Siau et al., 2002); deindividuation (Kwong & Lee, 2002; Sproull & Kiesler, 1991;); gender imbalance; electronic protestation and revolt (Sipior and Ward, 2002; Sproull & Kiesler, 1991); and gaining leverage (Rudy, 1996).

When electronic communication can potentially undermine management control, management predictably asserts the control more vigorously (Sproull & Kiesler, 1991). The negative effects of information systems challenge managers to formulate policies and procedures that control but do not discourage use (Anadarajan, Simmers, & Ibgaria, 2000). An effective programme of monitoring and control is a commonly identified success factor in assimilating new technologies (Hoffman & Klepper, 2000). Control in organisations is achieved in many ways, ranging from direct surveillance to feedback systems, to social and cultural controls (Simons, 1995). Control can be interpreted as both monitoring activities and then taking action to ensure a preferred behaviour of a system being controlled (Aken, 1978; Otley & Berry, 1980). Electronic monitoring extends the scope of control, transforming personal control to systemic control, and as technical controls emerge, personal, social, structural, and cultural controls extend through electronic mediation (Orlikowski, 1991). Thus, monitoring and control are intertwined (Otley & Berry, 1980).

There is increasing sentiment among managers that a more hands-on approach to e-mail systems management is needed (Simmers, 2002). However, too much or too little e-mail systems management can be dysfunctional for an organisation (Simmers, 2002). Many organisations do little more than ask their employees to comply with a formal e-mail policy (Simmers, 2002). However, Oravec (2002) suggests that some hard-line e-mail policies that exert zero tolerance of personal e-mail use are so nebulous that every employee could be deemed in violation. Thus, Weber (2004) argues that "in our efforts to improve e-mail technology, we need to take care that we do not exacerbate problems with e-mail use" (p. xi). Thus, some organisations adopt electronic monitoring of e-mail and restrict e-mail use (Belanger & Van Slyke, 2002; Ruggeri et al., 2000; Weber, 2004). In fact, the number of organisations engaging in some form of electronic monitoring of e-mail is steadily increasing year on year, as is reflected in studies by AMA (2000), AMA (2003), Hodson et al. (1999), Lim et al. (2002), PWC (2002), and Sipior and Ward (2002). The main arguments in justification of e-mail monitoring practices include prevention of systems abuse; to detect non-business use; to capture communication metrics; prevention of the loss of confidential information; prevention of competition; quality control; avoidance of liability for defamation; prevention of harassment and pornography; protection from computer viruses; and security (Oliver, 2002; PWC, 2002; Sipior & Ward, 2002). Simmers (2002) contends that managing the usage of the policy and enforcing the policy by monitoring/filtering software enhances alignment of individual usage with organisational priorities.

However, e-mail monitoring is contentious as it may conflict with staff privacy expectations (Sipior & Ward, 2002) and erodes the trust between employer and staff (Urbaczewski & Jessup, 2002). Furthermore, zero-tolerance of personal use of e-mail is debatable as organisations lose an effective means to increase their staff's work-related knowledge (Belanger & Van Slyke, 2002). Weber (2004) argues that organisations must permit some level of non-business e-mail as they also expect employees to engage in work activities outside of work hours. Thus, well-intended but non-analytical efforts by organisations to manage e-mail will result in problems at later stages of its diffusion (Ruggeri et al., 2000). Thus, it is imperative that underlying all uses of e-mail, current and expanded, is careful planning, monitoring, and management of the e-mail infrastructure (Graff & Grey, 2002; Simmers, 2002; Sipior & Ward, 2002; Weber, 2004). Sipior and Ward (2002) suggest that a strategic response to information systems abuse can consist of a combination of factors, including assessing current operations, implementing proactive measures to reduce potential misuse, formulating a usage policy, providing ongoing training, maintaining awareness of issues, monitoring internal sources, regulating external sources, securing liability insurance, keeping up-to-date with technological advances, legislative and regulatory initiatives, and identifying new areas of vulnerability. However, individual controls can have dysfunctional effects if isolated solutions are provided for specific problems (Dhillon, 1999). Thus, the key to an effective control environment is to implement a strong "set" of controls (Dhillon, 1999).

Some classifications of control exist, as shown in Table 1, and are used here even though the distinction between categories is open to debate. Formal controls (Dhillon, 1999), or control through social structure (Pennings & Woiceshyn, 1987), involve developing rules that reflect the emergent structure with control embedded in explicit policies, procedures, and rules. Informal controls (Dhillon, 1999) or control through culture (Pennings & Woiceshyn, 1987), consist of increased awareness supplemented with ongoing education and training so that the shared norms and values of workers shape behaviour, order perception, and influence attitudes. With technical control (Dhillon, 1999), or control through technology (Pennings and Woiceshyn, 1987), the role of management changes from direct supervision to enforcing the operation of the technical system. Thus, electronic monitoring and control enables a matrix of control, fusing together a range of capabilities to facilitate a more embedded means of control (Orlikowski, 1991).

Table 1. Components of a strategy of e-mail system electronic monitoring and control

Category of e-mail system control	Components of a strategy of e-mail system electronic monitoring and control	
Technical e-mail system controls	1.	Reconfigure the e-mail system software
	2.	Implement e-mail system anti-virus software
	3.	Implement e-mail system scanning, filtering and blocking software
	4.	Implement e-mail system monitoring software
Formal e-mail system controls	5.	Formulate an e-mail system policy
	6.	Form an e-mail system management team
	7.	Audit e-mail system accounts
	8.	Create and maintain awareness and provide feedback on e-mail system controls
	9.	Discipline e-mail system policy abuse
	10.	Adopt e-mail system pricing structures
	11.	Establish methods of e-mail system buffering
	12.	Formulate an automatic e-mail system disclaimer
Informal e-mail system controls	13.	Engage in e-mail system training
	14.	Create incentives to contribute to e-mail management
	15.	Enable e-mail system social forums
Professional / legislative e-mail system controls	16.	Incorporate professional and legislative e-mail system controls

Table 2. Possible dysfunctional effects of the components of a strategy of e-mail system electronic monitoring and control

Components of a strategy of e-mail system electronic monitoring and control		Possible dysfunctional effects
Technical	1. Reconfigure the e-mail system software.	Organisations fail to adequately consider the configuration of the e-mail application (Rudy, 1996).
	2. Implement e-mail system anti-virus software.	Organisations fail to update anti-virus software (Lindquist, 2000).
	3. Implement e-mail system scanning, filtering, and blocking software	Organisations fail to use filtering software effectively (Jackson et al., 2000).
	4. Implement e-mail system monitoring software.	E-mail monitoring can be contentious for economic, ethical, legal (Hodson et al., 1999) and health reasons (Clement & McDermott, 1991).
Formal	5. Formulate an e-mail system policy.	E-mail policies can be poorly designed (Sproull & Kiesler, 1991).
	6. Form an e-mail system management team.	Organisations fail to appoint an individual/committee to oversee e-mail management (Sipior et al., 1996).
	7. Audit e-mail system accounts.	Organisations fail to assess policy effectiveness and resolve problems (Flood, 2003).
	8. Create and maintain awareness and provide feedback on e-mail system controls	Management fails to raise awareness against risks associated with inappropriate e-mail activities (Sipior & Ward, 2002); fail to communicate the policy effectively (Whitman et al., 1999); and fail to continually raise awareness of the policy, particularly to new employees (Sipior & Ward, 2002).
	9. Discipline e-mail system policy abuse.	Organisations fail to consistently and fairly enforce e-mail policies (Flood, 2003).
	10. Adopt e-mail system pricing structures.	Pricing structures penalise those with fewer resources to pay for communications or have more useful information to communicate (Sproull & Kiesler, 1991).
	11. Establish methods of e-mail system buffering.	Buffering, by limiting interaction and information exchange to work-compatible colleagues/group members, can re-establish hierarchical channels of communication by pre-defining who staff can communicate with but separates staff from critical information or personnel (Sproull & Kiesler, 1991).
	12. Formulate an automatic e-mail system disclaimer	May be insufficient protection for an organisation against a lawsuit if badly written (Graff, 2002d).
Informal	13. Engage in e-mail system training.	Training is inadequate, voluntary, or one-shot (Banerjee et al., 1998).
	14. Create incentives to contribute to e-mail management	Employees should not be encouraged to seek rewards to comply with organisational policy as it effectively holds the organisation to ransom (Ruggeri et al. 2000).
	15. Enable e-mail system social forums.	May lead to conflict where in self-policing behaviour, forum members point out inappropriate e-mails (Steinfield, 1990)

Table 2. continued

Professional / legislative	16.	Incorporate professional and legislative e-mail system controls.	Government or legislative authorities may fail to develop clear and concise directives for organisations to follow when formulating and implementing e-mail policy or may be reactive rather than proactive in developing directives for controlling problems encountered with electronic communication technologies (Chociey, 1997; Sipior & Ward, 1995).

Applying the classification of technical, formal and informal controls identified by Dhillon (1999) to e-mail systems monitoring and control, Table 2 summarises the conclusions from a number of studies to identify some dysfunctional effects associated with certain controls.

Weber (2004) suggests that somehow technological developments need to reinforce and reward appropriate behaviours and curb inappropriate behaviours among e-mail users. Organisations must strive to identify a strategy of e-mail system monitoring and control that simultaneously enables managers to influence employees and is acceptable to employees (Urbaczewski & Jessup, 2002).

However, Ruggeri et al. (2000) and Weber (2004) report that there is little support or insight to assist organisations in reasserting e-mail systems for business use. Despite the importance of an e-mail system, and even though for many of us it represents perhaps the most significant computer application we use, it is an under-researched topic within the information systems discipline, and there is little published research about e-mail in the major information systems journals (Weber, 2004). Weber (2004) calls for a deeper understanding of the impacts of e-mail on organisations and contends that by focusing research on developing improved protocols to guide behaviours when we use e-mail, we can be more confident in the appropriateness of any measures we use to enforce use of these protocols. Rudy (1996) reported that the continued experience of the negative effect of e-mail systems may imply that not enough research has been done in this area. Little appears to have changed. Thus, e-mail phenomena provide a rich lode to mine for research purposes (Weber, 2004).

Method

This study aims to provide an organisational analysis of the monitoring and control of e-mail systems. The case studies method is considered suitable as it is a rich source of data, and analytic generalisation can be applied where prior theory is used as a template for comparing the empirical results (Yin, 1994). Multiple case designs are desirable when the intent of the research is description, as it allows for cross analysis and extension of theory (Benbasat, Goldstein, & Mead 1987). The appropriateness of the multiple case approach for this study is clarified in Table 3.

Four organisations (see Table 4) were deemed suitable for participation in this study based on the following criteria:

Table 3. The suitability of a case study for the requirements of the research

Research requirements	Case study method
To address the lack of research into how to take an organisational view of e-mail.	Enables exploration of an area in which few previous studies have been carried out (Benbasat et al., 1987), focusing on organisational rather than technical issues (Yin, 1994).
To establish how organisations control and monitor their e-mail systems.	Enables the capture of reality in more significant detail, permitting analysis of more variables than possible with other research method (Galliers, 1992) .
To gain an understanding of the contextual environment in which the e-mail system functions.	Provides a natural context within which a contemporary phenomenon is to be studied where the focus is on understanding the dynamics present (Benbasat et al., 1987).

- the organisation agrees to participate fully in the study;
- the organisation has a large community of e-mail users;
- the e-mail system is installed for a long period of time;
- the organisation considers the e-mail system to be a vital component of its electronic business infrastructure; and
- the organisation is taking measures to exert control over its e-mail system.

According to Rogers (1986), high-quality communications research should:

- obtain multiple measures from several independent sources;
- use objective data sources such as computer monitored data, corporate records, archival materials, etc., rather than just individuals' self-reports as gathered in personal interviews and by questionnaires; and
- utilise unobtrusive measures so that obtaining the data does not affect the data being gathered.

Following the approach outlined by Rogers (1986), data collection in each organisation took place over a 15-month period using semi-structured interviews, focus group interviews, document analysis, and electronic data collection. A semi-structured interview method was used to facilitate a more contextual understanding of the phenomena and to develop a rich, descriptive impression of the events while exploring their occurrence in each organisation. Such interviews took place with the human resources (HR) and IT managers in each organization, as existing studies indicate that such managers play an integral role in managing organisational e-mail systems. Semi-structured focus group interviews with other staff were conducted in order to triangulate findings. Documents analysed included e-mail policies, manuals, documentation, and e-mail notifications about e-mail use from each organisation. Finally, 15 months of e-mail monitoring data gathered from each organisation was gathered and analysed. These data flows provide opportunities to understand the application, manage-

Table 4. Organisational input into the study

	HealthCo	InsureCo	InvestCo	TeleCo
Industry	Manufacturing	Financial services	Financial services	Telecommunications
No. employees	1200	500	600	650
Year that e-mail was installed	1995	1998	1998	1998
Managers and no. of interviews	HR (x5), IT(x5).	HR (x5), IT(x5).	HR (x5), IT(x5), Rep.	HR (x5), IT(x5).
No. of group interviews	5 (staff) x 3 (interviews)	5 (staff) x 3 (interviews)	5 (staff) x 3 (interviews)	5 (staff) x 3 (interviews)
Documentation	E-mail policy, logs, notices, handbook	E-mail policy, logs, notices, handbook	E-mail policy, logs, notices, handbook	E-mail policy, logs, notices, handbook
Research period	Jul02-Sept03	Feb02-Apr03	May02-Jul03	Apr02-Jun03

Table 5. E-mail controls prior, during, and post e-mail monitoring implementation

Controls	HealthCo	InsureCo	InvestCo	TeleCo
Pre-implementation of e-mail monitoring				
Technical	Installed e-mail in 1995. Irregularly updated anti-virus software since 1996.	Installed e-mail in 1998. Irregularly updated anti-virus software since 1998. Basic filtering/ blocking software since 1998.	Installed e-mail in 1998. Irregularly updated anti-virus software since 1998. Basic filtering/blocking software since 1998.	Installed e-mail in 1998. Irregularly updated anti-virus software since 1998. Basic filtering/ blocking software since 1998.
Formal	IT formally responsible for e-mail. E-mail accounts only examined to eliminate viruses or technical errors. Staff e-mail contacts buffered internally.	IT formally responsible for e-mail. Basic informal local policy but poorly communicated and poor availability. E-mail accounts audited if incidents reported by staff.	IT and HR formally responsible for e-mail. Basic informal local policy but poorly communicated and poor availability. Mailboxes only examined to eliminate viruses/ technical errors.	IT and HR informally responsible for e-mail. Basic informal local policy but poorly communicated and poor availability. Mailboxes only examined for viruses/ technical errors.
Informal	Basic e-mail training on technical issues for all staff.	Technical e-mail manual provided.		
Initial implementation of e-mail monitoring (first month)				
Technical	Initial covert monitoring begins in July 2002 to generate metrics. New e-mail application installed. Basic e-mail filtering.	Initial covert monitoring begins in March 2002 to generate metrics.	Overt monitoring begins in May 2002.	Initial covert monitoring begins in April 2002 to generate metrics.
Formal	E-mail management group (EMMG) assumes formal e-mail management. Basic e-mail policy created. Gradual implementation of monitoring and control chosen in order to set and visibly attain targets.	IT reluctantly continue e-mail management.	E-mail management committee assumes formal e-mail management. E-mail policy updated. Policy published on Intranet and in staff handbook. Presentation and copy of policy on e-mail for all staff.	HR and IT continue informal e-mail management. New e-mail policy drafted from U.S. policy.
Informal			Staff trained on e-mail, filtering, anti-virus software, and monitoring.	
Early implementation of e-mail monitoring (two to seven months)				
Technical	New anti-virus software.	Receipt facility disabled except for urgent e-mail.	IT support filtering, virus, and mailbox management.	

Table 5. continued

Formal	Staff e-mailed about policy and monitoring. E-mail presentation for managers and supervisors. Policy only available by e-mailing HR. Staff e-mailed to compel relevant e-mail subject headings. Staff formally reprimanded for e-mail abuse. All staff reminded by e-mail to read and adhere to policy.	Staff and managers e-mailed about policy and monitoring. Policy on Intranet and in staff handbook. Some staff warned by e-mail about abuse. Staff e-mailed over e-mail abuse and policy. Staff e-mailed to compel relevant subject headings. Some staff given verbal warning. Some staff receive second warning.	Dedicated e-mail address created for the e-mail management committee so that staff can provide feedback or queries about e-mail use and management. Staff sent monthly feedback on monitoring. E-mail policy sent to staff for suggestions.	Policy only available by e-mailing HR. Overview of policy on login screen.
Informal			Supervisors urged to coach staff after minor policy infractions.	
Latter implementation of e-mail monitoring (8-15 months)				
Technical	Automatic online anti-virus software updates. Extensively reconfigured filtering/ blocking software. Many file attachments blacklisted. Web-based e-mail accounts blocked except for contact with five nominated family/ friends.	Filtering/blocking software upgraded for internal e-mail. Failed attempt to technically configure time limits on unopened e-mail. Automatic online anti-virus updates. E-mail reconfigured for receipt only and reduced storage for some staff. All Web-based e-mail blocked.	E-mail system reconfigured to automatically purge deleted e-mail. Filtering/ blocking software upgraded to filter internal e-mail and attachments. Automatic online anti-virus updates enabled. Attachments to/from Web-based e-mail accounts subject to permission.	Automatic online anti-virus software updates.
Formal	E-mail privileges revoked for gross violations of policy and backup failure. Staff e-mailed monthly with feedback to encourage policy compliance. Business contacts warned that non-business e-mail would be reported. Staff must sign liability form to accept private attachments	Disciplinary report placed in some staff files but later rescinded.	Staff informed that attachments to/from Web based e-mail accounts would be subject to permission. Staff informed that attachments transmitted internally would be limited to a list of approved file types. Staff e-mailed monthly feedback and tips on improving mailbox management.	Staff member suspended for disclosing sensitive data by e-mail. Extensive review of the audit trail generated by e-mail monitoring undertaken. Automatic e-mail policy reminder sent.

Table 5. continued

Informal	Staff contribute addresses to anti-spam catalogue. One-day e-mail course for managers and supervisors	E-mail security awareness course covering technical, content and legal issues for all staff . Supervisors instructed to coach staff individually.	Training programme devised for new members of staff. Supervisors asked to coach staff.	

ment, and consequences of e-mail systems. The data gathered was analysed through "time frame analysis" denoted by pre, initial, early and latter implementation of e-mail monitoring similar to those utilised by Rice (1990).

Results

All four companies exercised little control over e-mail system use in the early stages of diffusion, allowing staff unrestricted e-mail communication. This approach to e-mail management changed dramatically after the introduction of e-mail monitoring software in each company in 2002. Table 5 presents the time frame analysis of the technical, formal, and informal controls adopted by each organisation during the pre-implementation stage and during the initial, early, and latter stages of e-mail monitoring implementation. Table 5 also illustrates that there are a number of differences in how each of these organisations monitor and control their e-mail systems. All four IT managers were concerned that there was a problem with e-mail use. Prior to implementing e-mail monitoring, they had no way of achieving an organisational perspective of e-mail use. HealthCo decided to implement monitoring in order to establish greater transparency and visibility of e-mail use, to ensure it wasn't negatively effecting business transactions, and to smooth movement to future communication tools. InsureCo's and TeleCo's primary objectives were to improve the management and efficiency of e-mail and to control personal use. InvestCo was directed by corporate headquarters to monitor e-mail after productivity concerns related to personal use arose in another division.

Technical controls formed the thrust of all four organisations' efforts to monitor and control e-mail use prior to the implementation of e-mail monitoring software in 2002. Yet these technical controls were poorly implemented with redundant anti-virus software and ineffective filtering/blocking rules. Furthermore, the IT department dominated systems implementation and management, relying on technically focused training and/or technically written user manuals. E-mail policies, where they did exist, were poorly written and inadequately communicated. E-mail accounts were not audited, as it was considered too time consuming. Accounts were only accessed to eliminate viruses or to rectify malfunctions. Initial monitoring reveals quite a number of problems with e-mail use in each of these organisations as outlined in Table 6. Interestingly, it took the implementation of another technical control (i.e., e-mail monitoring software) to inject some effort by each of the companies into developing

Table 6. Initial problems exposed by e-mail monitoring in each organisation

Organisation	% Non-business e-mail	Initial problems exposed by monitoring in each of the organisations
HealthCo	40%	Substantial non-business use; group-specific information e-mailed company-wide; excessive e-mail storage; volumes of undeleted e-mail.
InsureCo	32%	Relatively high level of non-business e-mail use; widespread forwarding internally; e-mail unopened for excessive periods.
InvestCo	15%	Knee-jerk reaction to overt monitoring may have contributed to low levels of non-business e-mail abuse.
TeleCo	28%	Reasonably high level of non-business e-mail use; relative efficiency when managing e-mail; satisfactory e-mail-turnaround; attachments infrequent.

formal e-mail system controls. It is also worth noting that after the implementation of e-mail monitoring software feedback from this technical control was also the primary motivator for every update and fine-tuning of formal and informal controls, while also identifying areas where further controls were necessary.

Analysis and Discussion

The case studies reveal eight major elements to be particularly important in monitoring and controlling e-mail systems within the organisations studied. These are: (1) form a cross-functional e-mail system management team; (2) implement and regularly update e-mail management software; (3) formulate a detailed and legally sound e-mail policy; (4) engage in structured e-mail system training; (5) create and maintain ongoing awareness of e-mail policy; (6) engage in a process of hybrid feedback and control based e-mail monitoring; (7) firmly enforce discipline in accordance with the e-mail policy. Finally, it is imperative to recognise that this is an ongoing process that the management team should (8) conduct regular reviews and updates of the e-mail management programme, to adapt for changes in technology, changes in work-practices, changes in legislative, and industry requirements, etc.

Form a Cross-Functional E-Mail System Management Team

Stanton and Stam (2003) suggest that e-mail management should occur within the context of a negotiatory process that brings management, employees, and IT professionals to the same

Table 7. Delegation of responsibility for e-mail management in each company

	HealthCo	InsureCo	InvestCo	TeleCo
Legal input	No	No	Yes	No
User input	No	No	Yes	No
HR input	Yes	Yes	Yes	Yes
IT input	Yes	Yes	Yes	No
Other managers	Yes	No	No	No
E-mail management style	Formal	Formal	Formal	Informal

table. Previous research (Wolinsky and Sylvester, 1992) has suggested that organisations should establish a formal committee, consisting of the IS manager, a company lawyer, a HR official, an executive management representative, a union representative, and a general power user to oversee e-mail management. Siau et al. (2002) consider it imperative for staff to be involved in the e-mail management process. Table 7 outlines the organisational members responsible for e-mail management in each of the four companies.

HealthCo established the E-Mail Management Group (EMMG), consisting of the IT and HR managers, a business process improvement manager and an operations manager. Interestingly, InvestCo was the only company to seek legal input and to allow an elected staff representative to join the e-mail management committee. Responsibility in InsureCo was reluctantly accepted by the IT manager. Wolinsky and Sylvester (1992) concluded that failing to formally appoint an individual or to form a committee to manage the e-mail system, may mean that nobody will assume this responsibility, leading to an uncoordinated and disjointed approach to managing the system and a lack of direction for users, which could result in systems failure. TeleCo failed to formalise responsibility for pursuing improvements in e-mail use, and neither the HR or IT managers voluntarily accepted the task. Although processing and analysis of monitored data occurred monthly, neither manager reviewed the data effectively.

Implement and Regularly Update E-Mail Management Software

There are an estimated 30,000 viruses in existence with approximately 300 new viruses created monthly (Sipior & Ward, 2002). Thus, protecting the e-mail environment from viruses, malicious code, and spam is now keenly appreciated as the cost of doing business as failure to protect the e-mail environment will result in a real loss of system availability and productivity and a real loss of income (Graff & Grey, 2002). Although each of the companies had some version of e-mail installed for four to seven years, anti-virus software updates were extremely irregular. Only three of the companies had installed e-mail filtering/blocking software, but again, this was very basic and was largely ineffective.

HealthCo installed an upgraded e-mail system during the initial implementation of e-mail monitoring software in 2002, but each of the other organisations persisted with their existing e-mail system. However, the more communication metrics that were generated by the e-mail monitoring software, the more apparent it became to all of the organisations that their e-mail systems' technical controls were seriously flawed. Only HealthCo took the initiative and installed more powerful anti-virus software following the feedback from the e-mail monitoring software in the early stages. InsureCo and InvestCo took more of a big-bang approach in the latter stages, implementing anti-virus software automatically updated online and installing updated filtering/blocking software. Metrics in the latter stages of e-mail monitoring also prompted HealthCo, InsureCo, and InvestCo to extensively reconfigure their filtering/blocking software to limit personal e-mail use and to block incoming/outgoing web-based e-mail (e.g., to/from Yahoo! e-mail addresses) and attachments unless necessary for business use. InsureCo also reduced e-mail transmission/receipt capacity for some staff while InvestCo also reconfigured the e-mail system to automatically purge deleted e-mail every 48 hours. TeleCo took the least robust approach, choosing to only update the anti-virus software for automatic online updates in the latter stages of e-mail monitoring while paying little attention to filtering/blocking incoming/outgoing e-mail. According to PWC (2002), virus infection is the single-largest cause of serious security breaches in organisations because organisations often fail to regularly update the e-mail system anti-virus software, rendering it ineffective.

Formulate a Detailed and Legally Sound E-Mail Policy

Graff (2002d) suggests that organisations should formulate an e-mail system policy to maximise user efficiency, protect sensitive data, and reduce the risk of inappropriate message content. However, Attaran (2000) suggests that organisations often lack clear policies to prevent the negative effects of e-mail. Siau et al. (2002) also suggest that most e-mail policies are not formally worded or legally sound and strongly recommend that legal assistance should be obtained in developing e-mail policies. This view is confirmed by this study as the policies analysed were generally found to be poorly written, often confusing and contradictory, and predominantly lacking any legal basis. Furthermore, Siau et al. (2002) and Graff (2002d) recommend that organisations should make it clear in the e-mail policy that the primary purpose of an e-mail system is for business purposes.

In this research it was found that although the e-mail policy of each company stated that e-mail should only be allocated if the user had an explicit business use for it, each organisation provided universal access to the corporate e-mail system. Some researchers would argue that this may not be detrimental as e-mail is an essential business tool (Anderson, 1999), and if there is no access or if access is severely limited, organisational outcomes may suffer (Simmers, 2002). However, only InvestCo and TeleCo clearly describe and explain the value of e-mail as a critical business tool in their e-mail policies and manuals. Furthermore, despite several managers being involved in drafting HealthCo's e-mail policy during the implementation of monitoring, their combined contributions amounted to copy/pasting paragraphs from the policies of other organisations. TeleCo's revised e-mail policy, drafted six weeks after implementing monitoring, is 15 pages long, legalistic, and jargon-laden. The informal management of the e-mail system effectively led the HR manager to modify the e-mail policy of a corporate division based in the U.S. to fit the Irish division, rather than engage in a discussion with other stakeholders. InvestCo's HR manager believes the implementation of monitoring forced a rethinking about e-mail policy and its communication, as the HR and IT managers, corporate legal department, and a staff representative were engaged to draft the new policy. InsureCo never updated its e-mail policy after implementing monitoring. Some authors (Wolinsky & Sylvester, 1992) suggest that staff should sign the e-mail policy to acknowledge an understanding of its contents and compliance, but none of the managers interviewed believed this prudent, as failure to sign updates could be problematic.

Hodson et al. (1999), Oliver (2002), Hoffman, Hartman, and Rowe (2003), and Weber (2004) believe that the need for employees to rely on e-mail to manage personal matters is particularly true in an era of longer workdays, multiple career households, and the increased sharing of earning and household management responsibilities. However, this personal use of e-mail is only appropriate as long as it does not affect work patterns, productivity, and performance, or compromise the organisation in any way (Hoffman et al., 2003). Zero-tolerance of personal use of e-mail is unacceptable to staff in each organisation investigated for this study, as many staff depend on e-mail to maintain personal communications with family and friends. Limited personal use appears to be acceptable to management and staff in all companies. Confusingly, this is not reflected in HealthCo's e-mail policy, which explicitly prohibits personal use of e-mail while the e-mail policies of InsureCo and TeleCo only permit personal use of e-mail outside of working hours. InvestCo's policy permits limited personal use during working hours only.

Interviewees at all companies believe that policies should outline prohibited keywords and attachments to increase compliance and reduce misunderstandings, yet only HealthCo attempted to do so. However, HealthCo's HR manager warns that "specific definitions leave you open to oversights and the possibility of definition expiry." This seems consistent with Hoffman et al. (2003), who found that although 92% of organisations surveyed allowed employees reasonable personal use of e-mail, fewer than half of these organisations clearly defined what they considered reasonable use.

According to Simmers (2002), organisations must be honest about monitoring, announcing when the monitoring will happen, and why and how it will be done. However, only HealthCo and TeleCo have clear references to e-mail monitoring in their e-mail policy. InsureCo's policy expresses *"the right to monitor all e-mail"* but specifically refers to *"MAILsweeper filtering software."* InsureCo's *"E-mail Procedures"* document states that *"internal e-mail shall not be subject to interception or inspection."* InvestCo's policy does not mention monitoring but states that staff *"should have no reasonable expectation of privacy of communication."* Many researchers recommend that organisations should also define how breaches of e-mail policy will be dealt with (Banerjee, Cronan, & Jones, 1998). Only HealthCo's and TeleCo's policies assert the right to take disciplinary action up to, and including, dismissal. However, TeleCo's policy cites heavily from several acts of U.S. law that have no legal basis in Ireland. In addition, interviewees found such laws difficult to assimilate. InsureCo's e-mail policy does not mention disciplinary action anywhere. Although InvestCo's policy cautions that *"improper e-mail use is subject to disciplinary action,"* staff members are referred to a *"Corporate Code of Discipline,"* which contains no reference to e-mail abuse. Table 8 reveals the attitude of the study participants to elements of an e-mail policy identified as important by previous researchers. Furthermore, Table 8 evaluates the inclusion of such elements in each company's policy.

Table 8. The consideration of important elements of e-mail policy by each company

	HealthCo	InsureCo	InvestCo	TeleCo
1. Ensure that policy is easy to read	Adequate	Adequate	Extensive	Not
2. Personally present the e-mail policy to staff	Not	Not	Extensive	Not
3. State critical nature of e-mail	Not	Not	Extensive	Extensive
4. Explain technical implications of e-mail use	Poor	Poor	Adequate	Adequate
5. Explain legal implications of e-mail use	Poor	Poor	Poor	Extensive
6. Explain ethical implications of e-mail use	Poor	Poor	Poor	Extensive
7. Establish rules for sending/receiving e-mail	Adequate	Poor	Poor	Poor
8. Establish rules for receiving/sending attachments	Extensive	Poor	Poor	Poor
9. Establish rules for virus and security checks	Poor	Poor	Poor	Poor
10. Explain why e-mail folders need to be managed	Not	Adequate	Adequate	Not
11. Explain why monitoring is necessary	Adequate	Poor	Not	Adequate
12. Explain how e-mail is monitored	Adequate	Not	Not	Adequate
13. Explain why filtering is necessary	Adequate	Not	Poor	Adequate
14. Explain how e-mail is filtered	Poor	Extensive	Poor	Poor
15. Define prohibited content and attachments	Adequate	Not	Not	Not
16. Define limitations on internal and external contacts	Extensive	Not	Not	Not
17. Define limitations on personal use of e-mail	Poor	Adequate	Adequate	Poor
18. Establish privacy of personal use	Poor	Poor	Adequate	Poor
19. Describe disciplinary action for violating policy	Adequate	Not	Poor	Poor
20. Identify what training/support is available for staff	Not	Not	Extensive	Not
21. Obtain written/electronic confirmation of policy acceptance	Not	Not	Not	Poor
22. Schedule regular reviews of policy content	Not	Not	Not	Not

Legend: Not = Not Performed; Poor = Performed Poorly; Adequate = Performed Adequately; Extensive = Performed Extensively

Engage in Structured E-Mail System Training

According to Jackson and Burgess (2005), e-mail training is significantly successful at improving an employee's ability to write e-mails, to use a subject line to convey information about the content more effectively, and to write clearer e-mails that are more concise, thus reducing the cost associated with e-mail. However, research (Attaran, 2000) has shown that organisations rarely train employees not to misuse e-mail systems. The majority of managers interviewed in this study cite the allocation of staff, time, and financial resources as major detractions from the training and education process. This contributes to a greater reliance on technical controls. Consequently, none of the managers initially had a positive attitude to training. Only one company made any significant effort to rectify its approach to training staff to use and manage e-mail more effectively. However, the majority of managers interviewed believed focusing primarily on technical issues when training staff to use e-mail is an oversight and that an equal, if not greater, portion of training should focus on e-mail behaviour and policy.

InvestCo trained all staff when introducing the monitoring software as the HR manager was confident that "once staff knew the negative impacts of e-mail and how it could affect the company, better e-mail management would prevail." The IT manager believes that allowing the "staff representative to deliver a large portion of the non-technical training greatly contributed to staff acceptance of e-mail policy" as training was "delivered at their level of understanding by one of their colleagues, so staff were supportive of the process". InsureCo waited 14 months after implementing monitoring to conduct a security awareness course highlighting technical, content, and legal issues for all staff. While permanent staff at HealthCo had availed of initial technical training on e-mail, the withdrawal of e-mail privileges from summer interns, who had received no training whatsoever, revealed a glaring need for ongoing training. After 11 months of monitoring, HealthCo tried to redress training by holding a one-day course for managers and supervisors, but yet again other staff members were overlooked. However, this approach is questionable as some researchers (Banerjee et al., 1998) argue that one-off training sessions may not be sufficient to combat e-mail system abuse.

Weber (2004) considers it essential that employees be familiar with and capable of using technologies that will assist them to deal effectively with the negative effects of e-mail. However, with the general exception of staff from InvestCo, focus group participants were rather critical of the support and training provided by the IT department with filtering and mailbox maintenance. Interestingly, informal controls in the guise of staff coaching became very appropriate after a failed attempt in InsureCo to create a technical control to force time limits on unopened customer e-mail enquiries for more efficient response times. Unable to reconfigure the e-mail software, staff supervisors were charged with providing staff with further instruction on reducing volumes of unopened e-mail and responding to e-mail more efficiently. At no point has TeleCo engaged in e-mail training, despite taking serious disciplinary actions against one employee. Table 9 reveals the attitude of the study participants to elements of e-mail training identified as important by previous researchers. In particular, Table 9 highlights the time line for the delivery of these elements in each of the companies.

Table 9. The delivery of important elements of e-mail training/coaching in each company

	HealthCo	InsureCo	InvestCo	TeleCo
1. Explain how to send an e-mail	Pre*	Latter	Initial	Never
2. Explain how to send and receive and attachment	Pre*	Latter	Initial	Never
3. Explain how to archive, backup, delete, and empty folders	Never	Never	Initial	Never
4. Explain e-mail's impact on the corporate network	Never	Latter	Initial	Never
5. Describe how to deal with spam/unsolicited/unwanted e-mail	Pre*	Latter	Initial	Never
6. Explain how to check for and remove viruses or suspicious files	Pre*	Latter	Initial	Never
7. Explain how to set up and use internal distribution lists	Never	Never	Never	Never
8. Explain how to deal with inappropriate e-mail	Never	Never	Never	Never
9. Explain how to establish personal filtering rules	Pre*	Never	Initial	Never
10. Discuss the critical nature of e-mail as a business tool	Never	Never	Initial	Never
11. Discuss the current e-mail practices of staff in the organisation	Latter**	Latter	Never	Never
12. Discuss the legal and ethical implications of e-mail abuse	Latter**	Latter	Initial	Never
13. Describe what communications are unsuitable for e-mail	Never	Never	Never	Never
14. Discuss the organisation's efforts to filter and monitor e-mail	Latter**	Latter	Never	Never
15. Discuss prohibited e-mail addresses and content	Latter**	Latter	Initial	Never
16. Discuss how staff report violations of e-mail policy	Latter**	Never	Never	Never
17. Request staff to encourage more appropriate e-mail use by colleagues	Latter**	Never	Never	Never
18. Discuss disciplinary action for violations of e-mail policy	Latter**	Latter	Initial	Never
19. Obtain feedback on further training requirements	Never	Never	Latter	Never

*Legend: Never = Never Implemented; Pre = Pre-implementation of e-mail monitoring; Initial = initial implementation-1st month; Early = early implementation-1-6 months; Latter = latter implementation-7-15 months; *All Staff; **Supervisors & Managers Only*

Create and Maintain Ongoing Awareness of E-Mail Policy

According to Sipior and Ward (2002) the primary defense against inappropriate information systems activities is to increase the awareness and understanding of what the risks are and how they arise. Simmers (2002) suggests that once the policy is written and reviewed by the management and legal staff, it should be widely publicised through seminars, performance reviews, and informal discussion sessions, and it should be given to all new employees. Lim et al. (2002) and Sipior and Ward (2002) also propose that organisations can create awareness of e-mail policy by formally presenting it to all employees, including it in the employee handbook, in memos, at meetings and by publishing it on the company Intranet. Nevertheless, creating and maintaining awareness of e-mail policy is weak in three of the companies. Table 10 shows that only InvestCo formally presented the e-mail policy to all staff, while HealthCo only presented the policy to managers and supervisors.

The primary method for conveying e-mail policy appears to be by e-mail. However, this may not be sufficient or appropriate to achieve a change in users' attitudes toward e-mail systems use. Overt communication approaches, such as broadcasting the e-mail policy on the computer screen every time the e-mail system is accessed (Hoffman et al., 2003) and frequent reminders to staff that their computer activities are subject to monitoring (Panko & Beh, 2002) should be adopted by organisations. Although TeleCo is the only company to place the e-mail policy on the e-mail system login screen, it is the only way in which the company creates and maintains awareness of the e-mail policy and only consists of a rather brief synopsis of the policy. Rather than choose any form of personal communication, it is clearly evident from Table 10 that each organisation depends on the e-mail system to convey reminders, updates, feedback, warnings, and user tips. However, interviewees in two companies revealed that notifications were often deleted or filed without being read.

Engage in a Process of Hybrid Feedback and Control-Based E-Mail Monitoring

Urbaczewski and Jessup (2002) argue that a hybrid of feedback and control monitoring is most appropriate for most organisations. Simmers (2002) suggests that the monitoring

Table 10. Creating awareness of e-mail policy in each company

	HealthCo	InsureCo	InvestCo	TeleCo
Policy on the Intranet	No	Yes	Yes	No
Policy e-mailed to staff	Yes	Yes	Yes	No
Copies of policy distributed	No	No	Yes	No
Policy in the handbook	No	Yes	Yes	No
Policy on log-in screen	No	No	No	Yes
Presentations on e-mail use	Managers and Supervisors only	No	Yes	No

function should be more than the technology and that it should include periodic (weekly, monthly, bimonthly) generation of usage reports to allow feedback on policy compliance and discussion of these reports at appropriate levels of the organisation to enable action taken against those who violate the policy. It is reasonable to suggest that the four companies participating in this study focused more on the control aspects of the monitoring software than the extensive possibilities for providing positive feedback to staff on their e-mail activities. This appeared to be because management was desperate to bring e-mail under control and predominantly believed that this could only be achieved by formal warnings and coercions to bring e-mail use back in line with business needs.

Management in HealthCo, InsureCo, and InvestCo provided monthly communications to staff on overall e-mail use, but HealthCo's and InsureCo's communications were primarily hostile and provided little in the way of positive feedback to staff. InvestCo's approach was much more positive from the early stages, providing staff with positive and encouraging feedback while requesting staff add their own suggestions as to how e-mail could be managed more effectively. InvestCo also e-mailed staff with tips on improving mailbox management. The resultant effect of this was a much more positive e-mail management environment, according to staff in InvestCo. TeleCo's sole effort at providing any feedback was to implement a monthly automated e-mail policy reminder sent to all staff.

Firmly Enforce Discipline in Accordance with the E-Mail Policy

Siau et al. (2002) argue that organisations should always back up policies with decisive actions if a violation of policy occurs. In the U.S., this seems to be in practice as the AMA (2003) reports that more than 25 percent of U.S. organisations have terminated an employee contract for e-mail infractions. Three of the four companies in this study took decisive disciplinary action. InvestCo were the only company to not punish staff for infringements. Both HealthCo and InsureCo initiated disciplinary action from the early stages of e-mail monitoring. HealthCo formally reprimanded staff and revoked e-mail privileges for some staff after gross violations of the e-mail policy were detected. InsureCo issued verbal and written warnings to some staff for e-mail policy breaches before finally disabling some staff's send e-mail option and placing a disciplinary report on their staff file. However, this was later rescinded. TeleCo initiated the strongest response to a breach of e-mail policy, suspending a staff member for disclosing sensitive business data by e-mail. This prompted an extensive review of the e-mail audit trail for all staff.

Furthermore, Siau et al. (2002) encourage establishing a chain of command between the IT department and other departments as this enables the supervisors of those who violate the policy to be responsible for discipline instead of overloading the IT department. This chain of command is reflected in the formation of a cross-functional e-mail systems management team in HealthCo and InvestCo and appeared to work quite effectively. However, the IT managers still suggested that too much responsibility for detecting e-mail policy violations and enforcing discipline was placed on their shoulders.

Conduct Regular Reviews and Update of the E-Mail Management Programme

Continuous evaluation for technology misuse is needed (Romm et al., 1996), and as e-mail monitoring evolves, organisations need to review their policies and practices and revise them (Flood, 2003; Hoffman et al., 2003). As the evidence from these cases suggest, organisations do conduct regular reviews of their e-mail management programmes. These reviews predominantly revolve around the feedback from the e-mail monitoring data and are usually accompanied by one or more changes to how e-mail is managed. These changes vary from minor adjustments to how e-mail is filtered or blocked to more significant changes such as disabling the send e-mail function on some staff e-mail accounts. Siau et al. (2002) recommend that when there is a new policy or changes to an existing policy, employees should be notified. However, none of the organisations updated their policies since implementing e-mail monitoring despite making changes to e-mail management procedures on a number of occasions.

Conclusion

Careful planning, monitoring and management of the e-mail infrastructure must underlie all uses of e-mail, current and expanded. Failing to protect the e-mail environment will result in possible losses to system availability, productivity, and income. It is evident that a clear vision of controls should be developed as implementing patches in an illogical and incoherent manner, particularly when something goes wrong, may further compromise an organisation. This study aims to improve our understanding of the operation of e-mail monitoring and control methods in organisational contexts. The findings highlight the need to formulate a coordinated response consisting of technical, formal, and informal controls as part of an organisational approach to e-mail management. Based on the analysis of the study findings, Table 11 identifies the key technical, formal, and informal controls for monitoring and control of e-mail systems.

Table 11. Key factors of an effective strategy of e-mail system electronic monitoring and control

Technical	• implement and regularly update e-mail management software
Formal	• form a cross-functional e-mail system management team • formulate a detailed and legally sound e-mail policy • create and maintain ongoing awareness of e-mail policy • engage in a process of hybrid feedback and control based e-mail monitoring • firmly enforce discipline in accordance with the e-mail policy • conduct regular reviews and updates of the e-mail management programme
Informal	• engage in structured e-mail system training

These controls are a subset of those identified by previous researchers (outlined earlier in Table 1) and reflect the findings of the study on the interaction between controls. This conclusion is not an attempt to downplay the importance of other controls but rather to highlight the importance of certain controls in an organisational context. Overall, the study has advanced our understanding of the application of e-mail monitoring and control methods in an organisational context by applying a qualitative methodology to complement the results of previous quantitative studies. Nevertheless, the findings from the study are tentative, and further research is required.

Acknowledgments

The researchers would like to acknowledge the assistance of the Irish Research Council for the Humanities and Social Sciences (IRCHSS), without whose kind support this project would not have been possible. The researchers would also like to thank the organisations and individuals who participated in this study for their generous cooperation and contribution.

References

Agarwal, R. (2001). Research in information systems: What we haven't learned. *MIS Quarterly, 25*(4), v-xv.

Aken, J. E. (1978). On the control of complex industrial organisations. American Bank Association (1972) *Results of the National Automation Survey*, Washington, DC.

American Management Association (AMA) (2000). *Workplace testing: Monitoring and surveillance.* New York. Retrieved on October 9, 2006, from http://www.amanet.org/press/archives/elecmont.htm

American Management Association (AMA) (2003). *E-mail rules, policies and practices survey.* New York. Retrieved on October 9, 2006, from http://www.amanet.org/press/amanews/Email_Survey2003.htm

Anandarajan, M., Simmers, C., & Ibgaria, M. (2000). An exploratory investigation of the antecedents and impact of Internet usage: An individual perspective. *Behaviour and Information Technology, 19*(1), 69-85.

Anderson, S. (1999). Managing agency e-mail systems. *Rough Notes, 142,* 12, Indianapolis, Dec, 16-18.

Attaran, M. (2000). Managing legal liability of the Net: A ten step guide for IT managers. *Information Management and Computer Security, 8*(2), 98-100.

Banerjee, D., Cronan, T. P., & Jones, T. W. (1998). Modeling IT ethics: A study in situational ethics. *MIS Quarterly, 22*(1) 31-60.

Belanger, F., & Van Slyke, C. (2002). Abuse or learning? *Communications of the ACM, 45*(1), 64-65.

Benbasat, I., Goldstein, D. K., & Mead, M. (1987). The case research strategy in studies of information systems. *MIS Quarterly 11*(3), 368-385.

Benbunan-Fich, R. (2002). *Information technology in organisations: Paradigms and metaphors.* CIS Working Paper Series, Zicklin School of Business, Baruch College, City University of New York. Retrieved from Http://Cisnet/Baruch.Cuny.Edu/Fich

Cappel, J.J. (1995). A study of individuals' ethical beliefs and perceptions of e-mail privacy. *Journal of Business Ethics, 14,* 819-827.

Clement, A., & McDermott, P. (1991) Electronic monitoring: Worker reactions and design alternatives. In Van den Besselaar, A. Clement, & P. Jarvinen (Eds.), *Information systems, work and organization design* (pp. 187-199). Amsterdam: Elsevier Science Publishers.

Culnan, M.L., & Markus, L.M. (1987). Information technologies. In F. M. Jablin, K. H. Roberts, L. L. Putnam, & W. P. Lyman (Eds.), *Handbook of organisational communication: An interdisciplinary perspective* (pp. 420-443). Newbury Park, CA: Sage.

De, R., & Mathew, B. (1999). Issues in the management of Web technologies: Conceptual framework. *International Journal of Information Management, 19,* 427-447.

Dhillon, G. (1999). Managing and controlling computer misuse. *Information Management and Computer Security, 7*(4), 171-175.

Flood, L. (2003, February 9). Close monitoring provides protection. *The Sunday Business Post.* Retrieved on October 9, 2006, from http://archives.tcm.ie/businesspost/2003/02/16story187978038.asp

Fulk, J., & Desanctis, G. (1995). Electronic communication and changing organisational forms. *Organisation Science, 6*(6), 337-349.

Fulk, J., Schmitz, J., & Steinfield, C.W. (1990). A social influence model of technology use. In J. Fulk & C. Steinfield (Eds.), *Organisations and communication technology* (pp. 117-140). London: Sage.

Galliers, R.D. (1992). Choosing information systems research approaches. In R. D. Galliers (Ed.), *Information systems research: Issues, methods and practical guidelines* (pp. 144-162). Henley-on-Thames: Alfred Waller Ltd.

Giddens, A. (1979). *Central problems in social theory.* Berkeley: University of California Press.

Graff and Grey (2002). *E-mail and IM as essential platform components in 2002.* Gartner Group, 13th December, Note Number SPA-15-0931. Retrieved on July 7, 2005, from Http://www.gl.iit.edu/gartner2/research/103200/103210/103210.html

Graff, J. (2002a). *Management update: How to set up an e-mail retention policy.* Gartner Group, 10th April, Note Number IGG-04102002-02. Retrieved on July 7, 2005, from Http://www.Gl.Iit.Edu/Gartner2/Research/105800/105861/105861.Html

Graff, J. (2002b). *Building e-mail: Economy, resilience and business value.* Gartner Group, 22nd March, Note Number LE-15-6155. Retrieved on July 7, 2005, from Http://www.Gl.Iit.Edu/Gartner2/Research/105300/105369/105369.html

Graff, J. (2002c). *Maximising business value through e-mail*. Gartner Group, 22nd March, Note Number AV-15-6154. Retrieved on July 7, 2005, from Http://www.Gl.Iit.Edu/Gartner2/Research/105300/105366/105366.html

Graff, J. (2002d). *Establishing and reinforcing an e-mail usage policy*. Gartner Group, 13th March, Note Number TU-15-8120. Retrieved on July 7, 2005, from Http://www.gl.iit.edu/gartner2/research/105000/105085/105085.html

Graff, J. (2002e). *Building a high performance e-mail environment*. Gartner Group, 21st March, Note Number M-15-8182. Retrieved on July 7, 2005, from Http://www.gl.iit.edu/gartner2/research/105300/105322/105322.html

Hancock, B. (1999). Security views. *Computers and Security*, *18*, 184-198.

Hodson, T. J., Englander, F., & Englander, V. (1999). Ethical, legal and economic aspects of monitoring of employee e-mail. *Journal of Business Ethics*, *19*, 99-108.

Hoffman, M. W., Hartman, L. P., & Rowe, R. (2003). You've got mail and the boss knows: A survey by the center for business ethic, e-mail and Internet monitoring. *Business and Society Review*, *108*(3), 285-307.

Hoffman, N., & Klepper, R. (2000). Assimilating new technologies: The role of organisation culture. *Information Systems Management 17*(3), 36-42.

Jackson. T. W., & Burgess, E. (2005, May 14-18). Optimising the e-mail communication environment. In *Proceedings of the International Resources and Management Association Conference, Managing Modern Organisations with Information Technology*, San Diego, CA.

Jackson, T. W., Dawson, R., & Wilson, D. (2000, May). The cost of e-mail within organisations. In *Proceedings of the Information Resources Management Association Conference (IRMA00)*, Anchorage, AK.

Kwong, T. C. H., & Lee, M. K. O. (2002). Behavioral intention model for the exchange mode Internet music piracy. In *Proceedings of the 35th Hawaii International Conference on Systems Sciences*. IEEE Computer Society.

Lim, V. K. G., Thompson, S. H. T., & Geok L. L. (2002). How do I loaf here? Let me count the ways. *Communications of the ACM*, *45*(1), 66-70.

Lindquist, C. (2000) You've got dirty mail. *ComputerWorld, 34*(11), 72-73.

Mantovani, G. (1994). Is computer-mediated communication intrinsically apt to enhance democracy in organisations? *Human Relations*, *47*(1), 45-62.

Markus, L. M. (1994). Finding a happy medium: Explaining the negative effects of electronic communication on social life at work. *ACM Transactions on Information Systems*, *12*(2), 119-149.

McFarlan, F. W., & McKenney, J. L. (1982). The information archipelago: Gaps and bridges. *Harvard Business Review*, *60*(5), 109-119.

Oliver, H. (2002). E-mail and Internet monitoring in the workplace: Information privacy and contracting out. *The Industrial Law Journal, 31*(4), 321-352.

Oravec, J. A (2002). Constructive approaches to Internet recreation in the workplace. *Communications of the ACM*, *45*(1), 60-63.

Orlikowski, W. J. (1991). Integrated information environment or matrix of control? The contradictory implications of information technology. *Accounting, Management and Information Technology, 1*(1), 9-42.

Otley, D. T., & Berry, A. J. (1980). Control, organisation and accounting. *Accounting, Organisation and Sociology, 5*(2), 231-244.

Panko, R. R., & Beh, H. G. (2002). Monitoring for pornography and sexual harassment. *Communications of the ACM, 45*(1), 84-87.

Pennings, J. M., & Woiceshyn, J. (1987). A typology of organisational control and its metaphors. In S.B. Bacharach & S.M. Mitchell (Eds.) *Research in sociology of organisations* (pp. 73-104). Greenwich, CT: JAI Press.

Poole, M.S., & Desanctis, G. (1990). Understanding the use of group decision support systems: The theory of adaptive structuration. In J. Fulk & C. Steinfeld (Eds.), *Organizations and communication technology* (pp. 173-193). Newbury Park, CA: Sage.

PriceWaterhouseCoopers (PWC) (2002). *Information security breaches survey 2002.* Retrieved on July 7, 2005, from http://www.Pwc.Com

Rice, R. E. (1990). Computer-mediated communication system network data. *International Journal of Man-Machine Studies, 32,* 627-647.

Rice, R. E., & Aydin, C. (1991). Attitudes towards new organisational technology: Network proximity as a mechanism for social information processing. *Administrative Science Quarterly, 36,* 219-244.

Rogers, E. M. (1986). *Communication technology: The new media in society.* New York: Free Press.

Romm, C. T., Pliskin, N., & Rifkin, W. D. (1996). Diffusion of e-mail: An organisational learning perspective. *Information and Management, 31,* 37-46.

Rudy, I. A. (1996). A critical review of research on e-mail. *European Journal of Information Systems, 4*(4), 198-213.

Ruggeri, G., Stevens, & McElhill, J. (2000). A qualitative study and model of the use of e-mail in organisations. *Internet Research: Electronic Networking Applications and Policy, 10*(4), 271-283.

Schulman, A. (2001). The extent of systematic monitoring of employee e-mail and Internet use. Retrieved on July 7, 2005, from http://www.privcyfoundation.org/workplace/technology

Siau, K., Fui-Hoon Nah, F., & Teng, L. (2002). Acceptable Internet use policy. *Communications of the ACM, 45*(1), 75-79.

Simmers, C. A. (2002). Aligning Internet usage with business priorities. *Communications of the ACM, 45*(1), 71-74.

Simons, R. (1995). *Levers of control.* Boston: Harvard Business School Press.

Sipior, J.C., Ward, B.T., & Rainone, S.M. (1996.) The Ethical dilemma of employee email privacy in the united states. *Proceedings of European Conference on Information Systems (ECIS)* (pp. 989-992).

Sipior, J. C., & Ward, B. T. (2002). A strategic response to the broad spectrum of Internet abuse. *Information Systems Management, 19*(4), 71-79.

Sproull, L., & Kiesler, S. (1991). *Connections: new ways of working in the networked organisation.* Cambridge, MA: MIT Press.

Stanton, J. M., & Stam, K. R. (2003). Information technology, privacy and power within organisations: A view from boundary theory and social exchange perspectives. *Surveillance & Society, 1*(2), 152-190.

Urbaczewski, A., & Jessup, L. M. (2002). Does electronic monitoring of employee Internet usage work? *Communications of the ACM, 45*(1), 80-83.

Van Den Hooff, B. (1997). *Incorporating e-mail: Adoption, use and effects of e-mail in organisations.* Universite IT van Amsterdam. ISBN 90-75727-72-0.

Weber, R. (2004). The grim reaper: The curse of e-mail. Editor's Comments, *MIS Quarterly, 28*(3), Iii-Xiii.

Whitman, M. E., Townsend, A. M., & Aalberts, R. J. (1999). The communications decency act: An update for IS management. *Information Systems Management, 16*(1), 91-94.

Wolinsky, C., & Sylvester, J. (1992). Privacy in the telecommunications age. *Communications of the ACM, 35*(2), 23-25.

Yin, R. K. (1994). Case study research, design and methods. London: Sage.

Chapter XII

Predicting Electronic Communication System Adoption:
The Influence of Adopter Perceptions of Continuous or Discontinuous Innovation

Gary Hunter, Illinois State University, USA

Steven Taylor, Illinois State University, USA

Abstract

This study examines whether perceptions of the type of innovation (discontinuous relative to continuous) influences predictions of electronic communication system adoption. The factors that influence adoption and their relative importance are hypothesized to differ depending on whether the electronic communication system is perceived as continuous or discontinuous by the adopter. A survey of firms' intentions to adopt customer relationship management software is used to test the hypotheses. The theoretical bases of the study are the Gatignon and Robertson (1989) model of diffusion and the behavioral delineation of continuous and discontinuous innovations (Rogers, 1983).

Introduction

Customer relationship management (hereafter referred to as CRM) is a form of electronic communication system that is growing in importance in today's business environments. For example, at a recent National Retail Federation convention, all of the executives indicated that they intended to invest in customer relationship management (CRM) activities in the coming year (Levy & Weitz, 2004). The Aberdeen Group (2003) predicts that CRM total spending (software, services, and related hardware) will grow at a compounded annual growth rate of 6.7% from 2003 to 2006, by which time it will attract $17.7 billion in spending.

CRM is defined as

> ... a business strategy to select and manage the most valuable customer relationships. CRM requires a customer-centric business philosophy and culture to support effective marketing, sales, and service processes. CRM applications can enable effective customer relationship management, provided that an enterprise has the right leadership, strategy, and culture.
>
> (Thompson, 2002, p. 1)

Thus, while CRM is a business strategy that does not require an electronic communication program to implement, in practice it often involves the use of such a program.

However, research is limited regarding the different factors that influence a firm's likelihood of adopting such a communications program. Research examining the differential impact of factors when a firm is upgrading an existing program rather than initially adopting a program is even more limited. This assertion provides the foundation for our study concerning the diffusion of communication-related technology. Rogers (2004) reports that to date more than 5,000 academic publications have been reported related to the concept of diffusion of innovation across a multitude of social science domains. The goal of this study is to contribute to this line of inquiry by determining whether the factors influencing the initial adoption of electronic communication technologies differ from the factors influencing upgrades of electronic communication technologies. The theoretical bases of the study are the diffusion of high technology products framework tested by Gatignon and Robertson (1989) and that of continuous/discontinuous innovations (Rogers, 1983).

Results of the study are important because they should provide strategic guidance to electronic communication service providers. The results should also offer information regarding whether service providers should use a differentiated or non-differentiated strategy. Using the correct strategy should offer cost savings to communication service providers. Finally, the study is important because it offers guidance on the relative importance of the factors influencing adoption. Electronic communication service providers could use this information to focus on those factors seen as relatively more important by their customers.

Conceptual Background

We suggest that electronic communication programs can be perceived by customers as either continuous or discontinuous innovations. An innovation is defined as "an idea, practice, or object that is perceived as new by an individual or other unit of adoption" (Rogers, 1983, p. 11). Rogers suggests that the innovation does not have to be new to the world as long as it is new to the adopter. Innovations have been described along a continuum anchored on one end by innovations that are really new to the organization (i.e., discontinuous) and anchored on the other end by those innovations that involve incremental changes to an existing product (i.e., continuous) (Arnould, Price, & Zinkhan, 2004). The position of an innovation along such a continuum is based on the amount of behavioral change it causes the organization (cf. Robertson, 1971).

While recognizing the existence of continuous as well as discontinuous innovations, many marketing studies to date have focused specifically on the diffusion of discontinuous innovations (Gatignon and Robertson, 1989). Some recent studies in marketing do examine the adoption of continuous innovations or upgrades but with the intent of developing a mathematical model to predict diffusion rates, not examination of the behavioral constructs and characteristics influencing adoption (e.g., Danaher, Hardie, & Putsis, 2001; Padmanabhan, Rajiv, & Srinivasan, 1997).

Robertson and Gatignon (1986) summarize the literature on diffusion of innovations to offer a propositional framework that suggests diffusion is influenced by factors from several

Figure 1.

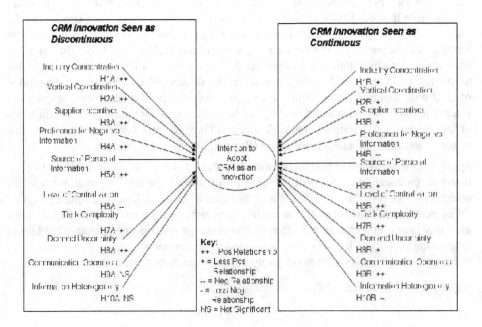

sources, including supply-side factors, organizational factors, characteristics of the decision maker, and adopter industry factors. Gatignon and Robertson (1989) empirically test the propositions developed in their framework and find that supply-side, adopter industry, and personal characteristics of the decision maker influence the adoption of discontinuous technological innovations. Specifically, they find that industry concentration in the adopter industry, vertical coordination and incentives between the supplier and the adopter, and a preference for negative information as well as exposure to personal and impersonal information are significantly related to adoption of a discontinuous innovation by an organization. Importantly, they test their propositions in the context of a sales force's adoption of laptop computers, an innovation that was presumably more discontinuous than continuous at that time.

Gatignon and Robertson (1989) suggest that a topic worthy of future research is to examine the relationship between the factors they identify as influencing adoption and the type of innovation (i.e., continuous or discontinuous). We therefore apply the model developed and tested by Gatignon and Robertson to determine whether different factors or the relative influence of factors change based on the innovation type.

Conceptual Model

The research model empirically validated herein derives from Gatignon and Robertson (1989). However, Brown (2003) points out that some believe that technology diffusion represents a unique form of innovation because, unlike most innovations, information technology (IT) cannot be adopted as a black box solution for a variety of reasons. First, there is a substantial knowledge burden placed on adopters of technology. We would add the condition that this might be particularly problematic for discontinuous technology communication innovations. Second, the use of technology is often intertwined within organizational routines. This suggests that individuals' interaction with the communication technology must fit within some larger organizational process in order to be effective (Leonard-Barton & Deschamps, 1988). Third, while classical diffusion theory focuses on individuals' willingness to adopt, with technology diffusion the more telling question may concern the ability to adopt (see Cohen & Levinthal's, 1990, discussion of an organization's "absorptive capacity"). Finally, Attewell (1992) asserts that the diffusion of complex organizational technologies may be better understood as a process largely driven by decreasing knowledge barriers than as a process driven by communication and social influences. In other words, he asserts that complex technologies create a "knowledge barrier" that inhibits diffusion. We therefore develop a research model that investigates the potential for variance from Gatignon and Robertson's (1989) original results in technology diffusion models based on perceived (dis)continuous innovation.

Gatignon and Robertson's (1989) model first offers evidence that the industry concentration of the adopter industry influences the rate of adoption of a discontinuous innovation. They report that increased competition leads to more rapid adoption of an innovation as industry participants pay closer attention to each other's competitive maneuvers. A continuous innovation would suggest that experience with the innovation would be more important in driving future adoption decisions relative to concentration within the industry. Frambach and Schillewaert (2002) suggest that heavy users of a preceding technology might be more receptive to innovations based on or replacing that technology. Those using preceding versions of the innovation would most likely consider future versions of the innovation as continuous. Therefore:

H1a: In situations in which the innovation is seen as discontinuous, industry concentration will have a positive relationship with intention to adopt an innovation.

H1b: In situations in which an innovation is seen as continuous, industry concentration will have less influence, relative to a discontinuous innovation, on intention to adopt.

In terms of the competitive environment of the supplier, Gatignon and Robertson (1989) offer evidence that vertical coordination and the use of incentives have a positive relationship with the adoption of innovations. Vertical coordination refers to the coordination between a supplier and its customers. Vertical coordination has a positive influence on the rate of diffusion of an innovation because of increased information flow (Gatignon & Robertson, 1985). Increased information flow reduces the risk of a discontinuous innovation. Because continuous innovations are assumed to involve less risk than discontinuous innovations due to increased experience with the product, the flow of information is not as necessary relative to a discontinuous innovation. Easingwood and Beard (1989) suggest that reducing risks increases the likelihood of adoption of an innovation. Therefore:

H2a: In situations in which an innovation is seen as discontinuous, vertical coordination will have a positive relationship with intention to adopt.

H2b: In situations in which an innovation is perceived as continuous, vertical coordination will have less of an influence, relative to a discontinuous innovation, with intention to adopt.

Related to vertical coordination, supplier incentives (e.g., price) are found by Gatignon and Robertson (1989) to be positively related to the rate of diffusion for discontinuous innovations. Under a continuous innovation, supplier price incentives should be less relevant to the adopter's decision because other transaction costs (e.g., decreased uncertainty) have locked the firm into the installed communications program (cf. Williamson, 1981). It should be noted that these hypotheses are developed from the viewpoint of a firm trying to sell their product to new customers or upgrading current customers. When trying to switch customers currently using another brand of communication program, there should be an increased focus on price to overcome transaction costs. Therefore:

H3a: In situations in which an innovation is seen as discontinuous, supplier incentives will have a positive relationship with intention to adopt.

H3b: In situations in which an innovation is perceived as continuous, supplier incentives will have less of an influence, relative to situations of discontinuous innovation, on intention to adopt.

A preference for negative information is a personal characteristic of the decision maker that Gatignon and Robertson (1989) found to have a positive relationship with the adoption of discontinuous innovations. In the context of continuous innovations, a preference for negative information would have a negative relationship with adoption of incremental improvements because negative information would suggest failures on the part of the electronic communications program are being made more salient. Therefore:

H4a: In situations in which an innovation is seen as discontinuous, a preference for negative information will have a positive relationship with intention to adopt.

H4b: In situations in which an innovation is perceived to be continuous, a preference for negative information will have a negative relationship with intention to adopt.

Finally, Gatignon and Robertson (1989) find a positive relationship between the number of sources of impersonal information and the number of sources of personal information with the adoption of discontinuous innovations. Continuous innovations, requiring less information due to decreased risk, should require fewer contacts relative to discontinuous innovations; hence the importance of these types of information should decrease. Therefore:

H5a: In situations in which an innovation is seen as discontinuous, a positive relationship should exist between exposure to sources of impersonal information and intention to adopt.

H5b: In situations in which an innovation is perceived to be continuous, exposure to impersonal information will be of less importance, relative to discontinuous innovations, in predicting intention to adopt.

While Gatignon and Robertson (1989) found support for a limited number of characteristics influencing organizational adoption of a technological innovation, numerous other variables were hypothesized that were not supported. However, research suggests that these variables might be related to intention to adopt an innovation seen as continuous. The following paragraphs present these variables.

Company centralization was found to not have a significant relationship with adoption of a discontinuous innovation. However, Rogers (1983) reports the results of several studies that suggest otherwise. Perhaps these studies used innovations that were more continuous than that used as a context by Gatignon and Robertson (1989). Centralization's importance may increase when a more continuous innovation is examined. Initial decisions to adopt may be more rapid when a single decision maker is responsible for the decision (Damanpour, 1991).

Decisions to upgrade an electronic communications program would entail incorporating the experiences of the individuals using the program in a more centralized firm. The individuals using the communications program would be more likely to push to expend resources to gain benefits that are more salient to them because of their familiarity and working knowledge of the software. Therefore:

H6a: In situations in which an innovation is seen as discontinuous, a negative relationship should exist between the level of centralization of a firm and intention to adopt.

H6b: In situations in which an innovation is seen as continuous, a positive relationship between centralization and intention to adopt should exist.

Gatignon and Robertson (1989) also found that task complexity was not related to adoption of laptop computers by the sales force. Intuitively, one would reason that a laptop would decrease the complexity of the sales task over the long run. However, perhaps the short-term complexity involved in learning to use a discontinuous innovation overwhelmed the long-term benefits of simplifying the sales task (cf. Frambach & Schillewaert, 2002), whereas a continuous innovation requiring a lesser degree of short-term behavioral change may not exceed the long-term benefits of the technology. Therefore:

H7a: In situations in which an innovation is perceived as discontinuous, task complexity will have less of an influence, relative to situations in which the innovation is continuous, on intention to adopt.

H7b: In situations in which an innovation is perceived as continuous, task complexity will have a positive relationship with intention to adopt.

Gatignon and Robertson (1989) also find that demand uncertainty is not related to whether a firm chooses to adopt or reject a new technology. Gatignon and Robertson (1989) hypothesize that demand uncertainty will increase adoption of innovations because of increased competition and heterogeneity in the marketplace. In such markets, innovations are used to decrease demand uncertainty. Demand uncertainty is defined as the degree of certainty an adopting firm has of the demand for their good or service. Overall uncertainty grows when increased uncertainty associated with discontinuous relative to continuous innovations is combined with demand uncertainty. In a situation of demand uncertainty, adoption of a continuous innovation would decrease the level of uncertainty regarding the marketplace while only slightly increasing the level of uncertainty associated with adoption of the innovation. In the case of discontinuous innovations, the innovation must offer a much larger decrease in demand uncertainty to offset the increase in uncertainty due to adoption of the innovation (cf. Frambach and Schillewaert, 2002). Therefore:

H8a: Demand uncertainty will be positively related to intention to adopt when the innovation is perceived as continuous.

H8b: Demand uncertainty will have less of an influence, relative to continuous innovation, on intention to adopt when the innovation is perceived as discontinuous.

Gatignon and Robertson (1989) also hypothesized that communication openness (operationalized as the number of conventions and trade shows that are held in the industry) would be positively related to adoption of an innovation. However, no significant relationship was found. We suggest two possible explanations. One explanation for this finding may be that network competence mediates the relationship between communication openness and adoption of technology in the case of CRM software. Ritter and Gemunden (2003) define network competence as the company-specific ability of a firm to handle, use, and exploit interorganizational relationships. Second, and the focus of the current research, we postulate that as communication openness increases, news of failures and successes with continuous innovations spreads, hence a relationship between communication openness and adoption of innovations would be significant. Therefore, the lack of significant results in Gatignon and Robertson's study could be due to the discontinuous nature of the innovation. Such a discontinuous innovation could suggest that the industry had not had the opportunity to communicate regarding the benefits and costs associated with the new innovation. While it is arguable that laptops were a discontinuous innovation in the context of sales in 1989, Gatignon and Robertson (1989) assumed that laptops were seen as discontinuous innovations and did not query respondents regarding the degree of behavioral change necessitated by adoption of the innovation. Therefore, we propose:

H9a: Communication openness will not be related to intention to adopt for discontinuous innovations.

H9b: Communication openness will be positively related to intention to adopt for continuous innovations.

Information heterogeneity represents the degree to which a decision maker is willing to consider information sources outside the industry (Gatignon & Robertson, 1989). Gatignon and Robertson (1989) do not find support for their assertion that adoption is more likely for those with information networks that extend beyond the industry. However, we propose that information heterogeneity is not related to intention to adopt discontinuous innovations, but is negatively related to intention to adopt continuous innovations. We defend this proposition based upon Burt's (1992) suggestion that possessing information sources outside the industry can be a competitive advantage. In order to maintain this advantage, the firm may be motivated to limit the spread of information about innovations within the industry. As such, the firm may be the first to know of the innovation but avoid adoption in an attempt to maintain control of information. If the innovation is seen as continuous, then the firm will have greater sources of information regarding upgrade benefits, thus they will not upgrade unless it is seen as offering significant improvements. Therefore:

H10a: Information heterogeneity will not be related to intention to adopt for discontinuous innovations.

H10b: Information heterogeneity will be negatively related to intention to adopt for continuous innovations.

Method

Sample

The sample was composed of 10,000 randomly selected e-mail addresses from a purchased list of individuals subscribing to a magazine popular with chief information officers (CIOs). We chose this sample for two reasons. First, interviews with salespeople for a firm in this industry indicated the key decision maker was the CIO. Second, Brown (2003) similarly relied on CIOs in her study on technology diffusion.

Results offer evidence that the respondent was the decision maker (44.79 percent report sole authority for the decision and 46.88 percent report influencing and making recommendations). E-mail was sent to the sample asking the recipient to participate in the survey. Three hundred and ten responses were received; nine of the respondents reported that they could not complete the survey because of technical difficulties. Thus, an estimated 3 percent of the sample could not respond due to technical difficulties. Hence, the sample size used in calculating response rate was reduced to 9700. While this response rate is low (3.1 percent) relative to a traditional mail survey, because the e-mail list was rented from the vendor we cannot ensure all of the e-mails were delivered. Hence, this is arguably a conservative estimate of the actual response rate.

The respondents were predominately male (87.4 percent), primarily holding an undergraduate (44.2 percent) or a masters degree (42.2 percent). The respondents were primarily from firms with annual revenues of 25 million dollars or less (60.4 percent) and from firms with fewer than 100 employees (47.6 percent). The respondents were employed in a variety of industries, with the majority being from manufacturing (12.41 percent) or consulting industries (11.72 percent), followed closely by software (11.03 percent) and telecommunications (10.34 percent). Seventy-eight percent of the respondents reported they held the position of CIO or a CIO equivalent within the firm, and half of the respondents reported using CRM software for less than 6 months (50 percent). Of the 301 respondents, 56.8 percent reported not using CRM software. Some respondents did not complete all of the survey questions, thus an imputation procedure was used to replace missing values with means.

The imputation method used was mean substitution. Not unusual in survey research, many of the questionnaires were missing at least one response to an item. In such situations, researchers must choose between: (1) using an imputation method that will allow consideration of all respondents or (2) ignoring respondents whose responses are incomplete. Ignoring respondents with incomplete responses is optimal when "the extent of missing data is small, the sample is sufficiently large to allow for deletion of cases with missing data, and the relationships in the data are so strong as to not be affected by any missing data process" (Hair, Anderson, Tatham, & Black, 1998, p. 51). In this case, we chose to use mean substitution to replace missing values because we believe that in cases in which the response rate is already low, to ignore respondents would limit our findings to a greater degree than using imputation. We acknowledge that mean substitution has disadvantages, including understatement of the true variance of the data, distorted distribution, and depression of correlations (Hair et al., 1998).

Electronic communication programs were operationalized as customer relationship management software. CRM software was used because it represents a discontinuous or continuous innovation to many firms. It also represents a significant investment to many firms and is perceived as important because it communicates information about customers throughout the firm.

Survey Instrument

Respondents completed a survey instrument that measured the variables identified by Gatignon and Robertson (1989), a scale designed to measure whether the innovation was continuous or discontinuous, and the degree to which they intended to adopt CRM software. Each of the constructs and the items measuring that particular construct are provided in Appendix A. The scales were built around and included the examples from the study by Gatignon and Robertson (1989). While it is true that Gatignon and Robertson (1989) used a variety of scale formats ranging from dichotomous items to 100-point continuous scales, we chose to largely employ seven-point Likert scale items. The use of such scales affords us the opportunity to use standard regression techniques to assess our research hypotheses. Due to the disparity of industries represented in the sample, a combination of revenues and number of employees was used to represent firm size. Continuous or discontinuous innovation was operationalized by a scale measuring the amount of behavioral change necessary to adopt an innovation. We use a median split of scores on this scale to group respondents into those that consider adoption of the software to be a continuous or discontinuous innovation. Those scoring below the median on this scale perceive CRM to be a continuous innovation, and those scoring above perceive CRM to be a discontinuous innovation.

Intention to adopt is also operationalized as a scale, modeled after the rejection scale used by Gatignon and Robertson (1989). Because rejection is seen as a continuum instead of a dichotomy, a scale allows us to measure whether a firm has decided not to adopt or they are considering adoption but have not yet come to a conclusion (cf. Gatignon & Robertson, 1989).

We also investigated evidence of reliability and validity based on the recommendations of Churchill (1979). Churchill's paradigm for measurement, widely accepted in the marketing literature, is based on the domain sampling model. Churchill (1979) ultimately calls for demonstration of construct validity, which includes both reliability and a variety of measures of validity. Evidence of reliability and validity of the scales was obtained in the current research by analysis of internal consistency and correlation analysis. While the scales showed evidence of discriminant and convergent validity through a correlational analysis, reliability as judged by internal consistency (Cronbach, 1951) was low for some of the scales. While scores on most scales were above suggested levels, two scales (measuring demand uncertainty and information heterogeneity) were suspect (Nunnally, 1978). However, we note that Gatignon and Robertson (1989) similarly experienced attenuated reliability scores as measured by coefficient alpha when measuring constructs within this area of inquiry. We adopt the position of the authors of that seminal article on diffusion of innovations, that is, that the scales used herein possess sufficient construct validity to support empirical analyses (see Appendix A).

Results

Regression is used to test the hypotheses. Prior to testing the hypotheses, variable means were compared based on firm size. Using an ANOVA, only one variable, supplier incentives, showed a significant difference in means based on the size of the firm. A Scheffe procedure revealed no significant difference between any size pairings for this variable, so all firms were included in the analysis of the hypotheses.

Hypotheses

In order to test the hypotheses, regression results for continuous and discontinuous innovations are compared. For a number of hypotheses, comparisons were relative to another predicted relationship. If the predicted relationship was not statistically significant, hypothesized comparisons were moot and the hypotheses are not supported. This occurs for H1, H5, and H8, and subsequently these results are not discussed. See Table 1 for the regression results for each of the hypotheses.

Supporting H2a, a significant positive relationship is found between vertical coordination and intention to adopt for discontinuous innovations ($t = 3.480$, $p < .05$). Results also suggest a positive relationship between vertical coordination and intention to adopt for continuous innovations ($t = 2.286$, $p < .05$). A lower r^2 provides evidence that vertical coordination has less influence when the innovation is continuous. Thus H2b is supported.

Regression results provide support for H3a. Supplier incentives do have a positive relationship with intention to adopt a discontinuous innovation ($t = 2.503$, $p < .05$). Results do not support a statistically significant relationship between supplier incentives and intention to adopt a continuous innovation. Thus, H3b, hypothesizing less influence for continuous innovations, is supported.

Evidence does not support H4a, hypothesizing a positive relationship between a preference for negative information and intention to adopt a discontinuous innovation. However, evidence does support H4b, predicting a negative relationship between a preference for negative information and intention to adopt a continuous innovation ($t = - 4.386$, $p < .05$). Results do not support H6a. Results do suggest a relationship between firm centralization and intention to adopt a continuous innovation, as hypothesized in H6b. However, the relationship is opposite to that hypothesized. As firm centralization increases, intention to adopt a continuous innovation decreases. Thus, no support is offered for either H6a or H6b.

Hypothesis 7a predicts that task complexity will have less of an influence on the adoption of discontinuous innovations relative to continuous innovations. While a significant positive relationship exists between task complexity and the intention to adopt a discontinuous

Table 1. Relation of variables to intention to adopt

Innovation	Discontinuous	Continuous	Discontinuous	Continuous	Discontinuous	Continuous
Hypothesis	H2a	H2b	H3a	H3b	H4a	H4b
Independent variables	Vertical coordination	Vertical coordination	Supplier incentive	Supplier incentive	Negative information	Negative information
Dependent var.	Intention to adopt	Intention to adopt	Intention to adopt	Intention to adopt	Intention to adopt	Intention to adopt
R^2	.137	.061	.079	.032	.002	.105
F-statistic	12.113	5.226	6.266	2.673	.157	23.392
p-value	< .05	< .05	< .05	.106	.693	< .05
Beta coefficients[a]	.371	.248	.281	.178	.040	-.324
t-statistics	3.480*	2.286*	2.503*	1.635	.396	-4.836*

[a] *Standardized coefficients are used throughout. * p < .0001*

Table 1. continued

	Discontinuous	Continuous	Discontinuous	Continuous	Discontinuous	Continuous	Discontinuous	Continuous
Hypothesis	H6a	H6b	H7a	H7b	H9a	H9b	H10a	H10b
Independent Variables	Firm centralization	Firm centralization	Task complexity	Task complexity	Comm. openness	Comm. openness	Information heterogeneity	Information heterogeneity
Dependent var.	Intention to adopt	Intention to adopt	Intention to adopt	Intention to adopt	Intention to adopt	Intention to adopt	Intention to adopt	Intention to adopt
Adjusted R^2	.001	.129	.094	.031	.002	.144	.001	.121
F-statistic	.101	11.813	10.063	6.424	.181	33.770	.098	27.448
p-value	.752	<.05	<.05	<.05	.671	<.05	.755	<.05
Beta coefficients[a]	-.036	-.359	.307	-.176	-.043	.380	-.032	-.347
t-statistics	-.317	-3.437	3.172*	-2.535*	-.425	5.811*	-.312	-5.239*

[a] *Standardized coefficients are used throughout.* * $p < .0001$

innovation (t = 3.172, p < .05), a significant negative relationship was found between task complexity and adoption of a continuous innovation (t = -2.535, p < .05). The negative relationship is opposite to the relationship hypothesized in H7b. Moreover, examination of the r^2 for each equation suggests that task complexity has a greater influence on intention to adopt a discontinuous innovation. Hence, hypothesis 7a and 7b are not supported, but evidence supports a relationship opposite to that hypothesized.

Offering support for H9a and H9b, communication openness is not related to intention to adopt a discontinuous innovation (t = -.425, p > .05) but is related to intention to adopt a continuous innovation (t = 5.811, p < .05).

Results offer evidence supporting H10a and H10b. Evidence suggests that information heterogeneity is not related to intention to adopt a discontinuous innovation (t = -.312, p < .05) but is positively related to intention to adopt a continuous innovation (t = -5.239, p < .05).

Discussion

The results of our empirical analyses support our basic proposition that different diffusion factors predict adoption for continuous relative to discontinuous innovations. Therefore, the following paragraphs focus on the similarities and differences based on continuous/discontinuous innovations and intention to adopt. See Table 2 for a summary of the factors influencing intention to adopt for discontinuous and continuous innovations.

The results first suggest that the intention to adopt discontinuous and continuous innovations is sometimes influenced by similar factors; however, the degree or direction of influence may often vary. For example, vertical coordination and task complexity were associated with intention to adopt for both continuous and discontinuous innovations. However, vertical coordination was more influential in persuading firms to adopt a discontinuous relative to a continuous innovation. Task complexity demonstrated a positive relationship with intention to adopt a discontinuous innovation but a negative relationship with a continuous innovation. Moreover, the influence was weaker for continuous innovations relative to discontinuous.

Table 2. Factors influencing intention to adopt by type of innovation

Type of adoption	Type of innovation	
	Discontinuous	Continuous
Intention to adopt	Vertical coordination (+). Supplier incentives (+). Task complexity (+).	Vertical coordination (+). Preference for negative information (-). Firm centralization (-). Task complexity (-). Communication openness (+). Information heterogeneity (-).

Second, there seems to exist some issues related to valence of the influences in diffusion of innovation relative to whether or not the innovation is perceived as continuous or discontinuous. For example, intention to adopt a discontinuous innovation is positively related to vertical coordination, supplier incentives, and task complexity. Interestingly, no negative relationships exist between intention to adopt a discontinuous innovation and the predictor variables, whereas most of the relationships for continuous innovations are negative. Similarly, the intention to adopt a continuous innovation is positively related to vertical coordination and communication openness. Intention to adopt a continuous innovation has a negative relationship with a preference for negative information, firm centralization, task complexity, and information heterogeneity. Together, these findings offer evidence that intention to adopt an electronic communication program is predicted by a different set of factors, depending on whether the program is perceived to be a continuous or discontinuous innovation.

Managerial Implications

Numerous managerial implications are apparent based on the results of the study reported herein. First, many industries depend on consumers to regularly upgrade current brands (e.g., consumer electronics, software, automobiles), yet much of marketing research has focused on the factors that influence the adoption of discontinuous innovations (cf. Gatignon & Robertson, 1989). Results from this study could inform managers as to the types of firms most likely to upgrade from a current version to a more powerful or comprehensive version of electronic communication and allow them to more efficiently use marketing resources.

Second, differences in the importance of vertical coordination suggest that electronic communication service providers gear their marketing strategies toward establishing closer relationships with customers when initially encouraging them to adopt. Findings regarding incentives suggest that one method of doing so would include offering incentives to those new to such programs. This recommendation appears consonant with industry calls for enhancing relationship marketing practices (e.g., see CRMGuru.com for relevant examples).

Third, the finding that task complexity has differential effects implies that electronic communication service providers may be overselling their products. High task complexity should have a positive relationship with intention to adopt, regardless of continuous or discontinuous. Perhaps the initial adoption created more complexity in the short term and they are attempting to avoid a recurrence. Assuming this explanation is true, electronic communication service providers should present accurate representations of the time required for a program to be effective.

Fourth, results suggest that electronic communication service providers should vary their marketing strategy depending on whether the product is perceived as a discontinuous or continuous innovation. If the service provider is attempting to persuade a firm to initially adopt a program, the focus should be on establishing a relationship with a potential customer. The relationship can be furthered through the use of supplier incentives, and the provider should emphasize the complexity of the customer's market.

This, of course, also implies that both businesses considering CRM communication technologies and those offering such technology for exchange should develop a research agenda to fully understand issues related to both complexity of CRM communication technologies and whether or not such technology is being perceived as continuous or discontinuous in nature. If the program is perceived to be a continuous innovation (e.g., upgrading an existing program) then electronic communication service providers should emphasize different factors. In this case, service providers should de-emphasize and accurately describe the adoption process. Again, relationships with the customer are important but not as important as when the program was initially adopted (i.e., discontinuous innovation). In this case, supplier incentives do not add to the relationship and would be a waste of resources. Perhaps the best resource would be past performance and accuracy of provided information (e.g., the time frame for effectively adopting the program).

Fifth, and similarly, findings regarding a preference for negative information suggest that accuracy should increase intention to upgrade an electronics communication program. Findings offer evidence of a negative association between company centralization and intention to upgrade an electronic communications program; thus emphasis should be on firms with decentralized decision making. However, this result could also indicate that service providers must be sure they are talking to the correct decision maker(s) within the organization. Perhaps upgrades to existing communication programs require greater input across the customer firm because an existing system permeates the customer firm. Initial adoption decisions are made by fewer individuals because less is known about such systems by the rest of the customer firm. Having greater input could cause delays or postponement in upgrading an electronic communications program. Information heterogeneity has a negative relationship with intention to upgrade an electronic communications program. Electronic communication service providers should stress the benefits of the upgrade over existing technology, being careful not to oversell the upgrade. The benefits must be stressed because customers with varied sources of information can easily ascertain the value of these benefits from their connections within and outside the industry.

Finally, we suggest that our results may be managerially consistent with the recommendations of Riemenschneider, Hardgrave, and Davis (2002) relative to software development as a technological innovation. These authors found that individuals are more likely to adopt new technological software methodologies when: (1) the technology is regarded as useful by users, (2) an organizational mandate exists to use the technology, (3) the technological innovation is compatible with existing technologies, and (4) the opinions of users in regard to the adoption of such technology is proactively solicited. We suspect that those individuals associated with communication-related technologies may mimic such behaviors and encourage managers to be aware of these findings. The basis for this assertion lies in the congruency between these recommendations and service marketing theory and practice. In fact, Mathiassen, Andersson, and Hanson (2003) specifically argue that management in technology services can improve their diffusion practices by adopting the role of a service provider rather than simply a technology provider. The next section identifies a pair of limitations associated with the reported study.

Limitations

While the response rate is comparable to other Web-based studies (e.g., Meuter, Ostrom, Roundtree, & Bitner, 2000), it is low by traditional standards for mail surveys. This is not surprising given that a general declining trend in response rates is widely recognized across social science disciplines in terms of all forms of survey research (Griffis, Goldsby, & Cooper, 2003; Sheehan, 2001). Smith, Olah, Hansen, and Cumbo (2003) present evidence how the length of a survey instrument exacerbates this phenomenon. This suggests that the representativeness of the sample may be questionable (i.e., nonresponse error). In order to provide support for the representativeness of the sample, we compared the brand names of software that respondents reported using to published data regarding the market positions of these companies. The positions represented in the sample were similar to the positions reported in the published source (www.crmguru.com). For further evidence of representativeness, comparisons were made between the demographic profiles of customers and the demographic profile of customers for one CRM firm. Again, the comparisons were similar, offering some evidence of the representativeness of the sample.

There also remain measurement issues connected to this area of inquiry. The low reliability of the scales measuring demand uncertainty and information heterogeneity in our study is similar to those found in the study by Gatignon and Robertson (1989). Thus, the lack of a significant relationship between demand uncertainty and intention to adopt, although the finding is consistent with the results of Gatignon and Robertson (1989), should be viewed with a jaundiced eye. Future inquiries into this exciting and potentially enlightening area of inquiry will benefit from increased emphasis on the development of more reliable scales of the relevant constructs.

Future Research

First, as stated above, much work remains in terms of developing better measures of the relevant constructs in this area of inquiry. In addition, replication studies will likely inform managers in terms of identifying the types of customers that are most likely to upgrade an electronic communication program.

A second broad direction for future research could involve a closer examination of *the process* by which each of the variables in the research model influences intention to adopt an electronics communication program. While reasoning was offered for the relationships between the variables and the likelihood of adoption, the actual basis for these influences was not tested due to the broad nature of the study. More precise studies focused on the individual elements (i.e., adopter competitive environment, supplier competitive environment, organizational characteristics, and individual decision maker characteristics) would further both theoretical and practical knowledge concerning strategies to speed up the adoption process.

Yet a third direction for future research might be to further explore the role of the individual characteristics of the decision maker in choosing whether to adopt. Evidence from this study suggests that individual differences such as a preference for negative information plays a role in the adoption decision. Such findings suggest that some of the influences on consumer decisions to adopt could also influence organizational decision makers. Therefore, future research should examine the role of the individual decision maker in the adoption decision for an organization.

There are also a plethora of lines of inquiry from the emerging social science literatures that could be associated with future investigations of diffusion of communication technologies.

For example, we previously discussed the potential relationship between network competence and diffusion of technology innovations such as CRM (Ritter and Gemunden, 2003). These authors identify a link between integration of intraorganizational communication and technology adoption. We encourage future research to sift out the potential mediating or moderating role of network competence in the success of diffusion of communication-related technology innovations.

Fourth, there are also a number of recent marketing-based studies related to the diffusion of technology-related innovations that could be addressed specific to communication-related technologies. For example, Maholtra, Citrin, and Shainesh (2004) discuss the distinction between "technology marketing" and the "marketing of technology oriented products and services." These authors assert that technology marketing is focused on acquisition and turnover market of technology. Thus, technology marketing involves the use of new production and delivery systems to market new products and services. The marketing of technology-oriented products and services, on the other hand, involves a range of marketing activities necessary to successfully market such products. Uslay, Maholtra, and Citrin (2004) extend this discussion by reviewing the literature to identify (1) the most recent marketing "toolkit" available to marketers associated with technology-related products and services, and (2) outstanding research questions that could form the basis for research agendas related to this area of inquiry. Future research should consider investigating such distinctions and the efficacy of the identified marketing "tools" related to the diffusion of communication-related technological innovations.

Fifth, we identified a number of recent studies that might be extended by incorporating the results of the study reported herein. Jensen (2004) provides a new theoretical explanation for why larger firms tend to adopt sooner. Green, Collins, Webb, and Alan (2004) link perceived control (a psychological construct related to attitude models) to the diffusion of software process innovations. Ranganathan, Dhaliwal, Teo Jasbir, and Thompson (2004) report results suggesting that internal assimilation and external diffusion of Web technologies both significantly affect the benefits realized by supply chain management. Marinova (2004) similarly links market knowledge diffusion on innovation efforts and subsequent firm performance. Finally, Redmond (2004) articulates an explanation for how market competition has an unintended effect of accelerating the diffusion of innovations, particularly those associated with new communication technologies. We assert that all of these areas of inquiry might benefit from incorporation of diffusion of innovation theory into these emerging models.

Sixth, there are a number of more comprehensive modeling efforts related to technology innovation diffusion that could specifically benefit inquiries into communication-related technological innovations. For example, Greenhalgh, Robert, MacFarlane, Bate, and Kyriakidou (2004) provide an extensive literature review concerning the spread and sustaining of innovations in the health services sector. Venkatesh, Morris, Davis, and Davis (2003) present a comprehensive model of user acceptance of information technology. Lee, Lee, and Eastwood (2003) provide a two-step methodology for estimating consumer adoption of technology-based service innovations. Finally, both Baskerville and Pries-Heje (2003) and Bruun and Hukkinen (2003) assert that competing models of diffusion of information technology can provide distinctly different, yet complementary, knowledge about marketing practices related to the diffusion of such innovations. Model comparisons appear a particularly fruitful avenue of future inquiries in this domain.

Finally, we encourage future research to consider the long-term societal impacts of diffusion of communications-related technologies. For example, Gani and Sharma (2003) go so far as to link the effects of information technology achievement and diffusion on foreign direct investment. Kirkman (2001) calls for the promotion of truly global Internet diffusion as a mechanism for helping to equalize life satisfaction and wealth distribution worldwide. We support such noble inquiries.

Conclusion

The results of this study suggest that firms' decisions to adopt electronic communication programs are influenced by their perceptions of whether the program is perceived to be a continuous or discontinuous innovation. Adoption of discontinuous electronic communication programs is predicted by different factors relative to those that predict the adoption of upgraded (e.g., continuous) electronic communication programs. Results offer guidance to electronic communication service providers seeking to find new customers and those seeking to have customers upgrade their existing communication programs.

References

Aberdeen Group (2003), *Worldwide CRM spending: Forecast and analysis 2002-2006*. Author unknown. Retrieved January 2005 from http://www.aberdeen.com

Arnould, E. J., Price, L. L., & Zinkhan, G. M. (2004). *Consumers* (2nd ed.). New York: McGraw Hill.

Attewell, P. (1992). Technology diffusion and organizational learning: The case of business computing. *Organization Science, 3*(1), 1-19.

Baskerville, R., & Pries-Heje, J. (2003). Diversity in model diffusion of information technology. *Journal of Technology Transfer, 28*(3-4), 251-64.

Brown, M. M. (2003). Technology diffusion and the 'knowledge barrier': The dilemma of stakeholder participation. *Public Performance & Management Review, 26*(4), 345-59.

Bruun, H., & Hukkinen, H. (2003). Crossing boundaries: An integrative framework for studying technological change. *Social Studies of Science, 33*(1), 95-117.

Burt, R. S. (1992). *Structural holes: The social structure of competition*. Cambridge, MA: Harvard University Press.

Churchill, G. A., Jr. (1979). A paradigm for developing better measures of marketing constructs. *Journal of Marketing Research, 16*, 64-73.

Cohen, W. M., & Levinthal, D. A. (1990). Absorptive capacity: A new perspective on learning and innovation. *Administrative Science Quarterly, 35*, 128-52.

CrmGuru (2002). *Multi-function CRM suites for medium to large enterprises*. Author unknown. Retrieved May 14, 2002, from http://www.crmguru.com/members/papers/solutions_guide.pdf

Cronbach, L. J. (1951). Coefficient alpha and the internal structure of tests. *Psychometrika, 16*, 297-334.

Damanpour, F. (1991). Organizational innovation: a meta-analysis of effects of determinants and moderators. *Journal of the Academy of Management, 34*, 555-590.

Danaher, P. J., Hardie, B. G. S., & Putsis, W. P., Jr. (2001). Marketing-mix variables and the diffusion of successive generations of a technological innovation. *Journal of Marketing Research, 38*, 501-514.

Easingwood, C., & Beard, C. (1989). High technology launch strategies in the UK. *Industrial Marketing Management, 18*, 125-138.

Frambach, R. T., & Schillewaert, N. (2002). Organizational innovation adoption: A multi-level framework of determinants and opportunities for future research. *Journal of Business Research, 55*, 163-176.

Gani, A., & Sharma, B. (2003). The effects of information technology achievement and diffusion on foreign direct investment. *Perspectives on Global Development and Technology, 2*(2), 161-78.

Gatignon, H., & Robertson, T. S. (1985). A propositional inventory for new diffusion research. *Journal of Consumer Research, 11*(May), 849-867.

Gatignon, H., & Robertson, T. S. (1989). Technology diffusion: An empirical test of competitive effects. *Journal of Marketing, 53*(January), 35-49.

Green, G. C., Collins, R., Webb, H., & Alan, R. (2004). Perceived control and the diffusion of software process innovations. *Journal of High Technology Management Research, 15*(1), 123-44.

Greenhalgh, T., Robert, G., MacFarlane, F., Bate, P., & Kyriakidou, O. (2004). Diffusion of innovations in service organizations: Systematic review and recommendations. *The Milbank Quarterly, 82*(4), 581-629.

Griffis, S. E., Goldsby, T. J., & Cooper, M. (2003). Web-based and mail surveys: A comparison of response, data, and cost. *Journal of Business Logistics, 24*(2), 237-58.

Hair, J. F., Jr., Anderson, R. E., Tatham, R. L., & Black, W. C. (1998). *Multivariate data analysis* (5th ed.). Upper Saddle River, NJ: Prentice Hall.

Jensen, R. A. (2004). Multiplant firms and innovation adoption and diffusion. *Southern Economic Journal, 70*(3), 661-71.

Kirkman, G. S. (2001). Out of the labs and into the developing world: Using appropriate technologies to promote truly global Internet diffusion. *Journal of Human Development, 2*(2), 191-237.

Lee, E., Lee, J., & Eastwood, D. (2003). A two-step estimation of consumer adoption of technology-based service innovations. *The Journal of Consumer Affairs, 37*(2), 256-82.

Leonard-Barton, D., & Deschamps, I. (1988). Managerial influence in the implementation of new technology. *Management Science, 34*, 1252-65.

Levy, M., & Weitz, B. A. (2004). *Retailing management* (5th ed.). New York: McGraw-Hill.

Maholtra, N. K., Citrin, A. V., & Shainesh, G. (2004). Editorial: The marketing of technology oriented products and services – An integration of marketing and technology. *International Journal of Technology Management, 28*(1), 1-7.

Marinova, D. (2004). Actualizing innovation effort: the impact of market knowledge diffusion in a dynamic system of competition. *Journal of Marketing, 68*(July), 1-20.

Mathiassen, L., Andersson, I., & Hanson, K. (2003). Service provision in a software technology unit. *Journal of Information Technology, 18*, 195-209.

Meuter, M., Ostrom, A. L., Roundtree, R. I., & Bitner, M. J. (2000). Self-service technologies: Understanding customer satisfaction with technology-based service encounters. *Journal of Marketing, 64*(July), 50-64.

Nunnally, J. C. (1978). *Psychometric theory* (2nd ed.). New York: McGraw-Hill.

Padmanabhan, V., Rajiv, S., & Srinivasan, K. (1997). New products, upgrades, and new releases: A rationale for sequential product introduction. *Journal of Marketing Research, 34*(November), 456-472.

Ranganathan, C., Dhaliwal, J., Teo Jasbir, S., & Thompson, S. H. (2004). Assimilation and diffusion of Web technologies in supply-chain management: An examination of key drivers and performance impacts. *International Journal of Electronic Commerce, 9*(1), 127-61.

Redmond, W. H. (2004). Interconnectivity in diffusion of innovations and market competition. *Journal of Business Research, 57*(11), 1295-1302.

Riemenschneider, C. K., Hardgrave, B. C., & Davis, F. D. (2002). Explaining software developer acceptance of methodologies: A comparison of five theoretical models. *IEEE Transactions on Software Engineering, 28*(12), 1135-46.

Ritter, T., & Gemunden, H. G. (2003). Network competence: Its impact on innovation success and its antecedents. *Journal of Business Research, 56*(9), 745-55.

Robertson, T. S. (1971). *Innovative behavior and communication.* New York: Holt, Rinehart and Winston, Inc.

Robertson, T. S., & Gatignon, H. (1986). Competitive effects on technology diffusion. *Journal of Marketing, 50*(July), 1-12.

Rogers, E. M. (1983). *Diffusion of innovations.* New York: The Free Press.

Rogers, E. M. (2004). A prospective and retrospective look at the diffusion model. *Journal of Health Communications, 9*, 13-19.

Sheehan, K. (2001). E-mail survey response rates: A review. *Journal of Computer Mediated Communication, 6*(2). Retrieved January 18, 2005, from http://www.ascusc.org/jcmc/vol6/issue2/

Smith, R., Olah, D., Hansen, B., & Cumbo, D. (2003). The effect of questionnaire length on participant response rate: A case study in the US cabinet industry. *Forest Products, 53*(11/12), 33-6.

Thompson, B. (2003). *What is CRM?* Retrieved Septmember 20, 2006, from http://www.crmguru.com/members/primer/01.html

Williamson, O. E. (1981). The economics of organization: The transaction cost approach. *American Journal of Sociology, 87*(3), 548-577.

Uslay, C., Maholtra, N. K., & Citrin, A. V. (2004). Unique marketing challenges at the frontiers of technology: An integrated perspective. *International Journal of Technology Management, 28*(1), 8-31.

Venkatesh, V., Morris, M. G., Davis, G. B., & Davis, F. D. (2003). User acceptance of information technology: toward a unified view. *MIS Quarterly, 27*(3), 425-78.

Appendix A

Adopter Industry Competitive Characteristics

Competitive price intensity (reliability = .89)

How frequently does price-cutting take place in your industry?

Our industry is very price competitive.

How often does your firm cut its price in response to competitors' price cuts?

In our industry, we have to be very competitive in terms of price.

Demand uncertainty (reliability = .40)

- How would you describe the market for your company's products?
- With what degree of certainty are you able to predict demand for your company's products?
- Demand in our market fluctuates greatly from one year to the next (R).
- How would you describe the demand for your company's products?

Communication openness (reliability = .64)

- How many regional or national conventions and trade shows are held in your industry each year?
- How many opportunities do you have to interact with others holding the same position as you in your industry?
- Very few opportunities exist to exchange information within my industry (R).
- Communication within my industry is open.

Supply Side Competitive Environment

Vertical coordination (reliability = .86)

- How many supplier seminars for customer relationship management software have you been invited to attend in the past year?
- Suppliers of customer relationship management software often contact me to invite me to information sessions.
- Suppliers of customer relationship management software have often offered their support to my firm.
- I would describe the relationship between my firm and suppliers of customer relationship management software as good.

Supplier incentives (reliability = .83)

- My company has received "key customer" discounts on new customer relationship management software.
- Suppliers of customer relationship management software have offered my firm incentives to adopt their software.
- My firm relies on supplier incentives to help defray the costs of adopting new software packages.
- Suppliers of customer relationship management software often offer service incentives to offset the cost of their software.

Organization/Task Characteristics

Company Centralization (reliability = .60)

- I can take very little action on my own without senior management approval.
- I would describe the organizational structure of my firm as centralized.
- I have a lot of autonomy in making decisions within my company (R).
- I make many important decisions without the input of more senior management (R).

Task complexity (reliability = .76)

- It has become very complicated to stay connected with our customers.
- Contacting customers has become very complex.
- It is a difficult task to track and use the information that we collect from our customers.
- I would describe our customer contact center as overloaded.

Change required to adopt software (reliability = .90)

- For my firm to shift to the use of customer relationship management software would require a great deal of change in our current business practices.

- My firm's adoption of customer relationship management software would require a great deal of change in the manner in which we currently interact with consumers.

- Customer relationship management software would be a completely new innovation for my firm.

- It would be extremely difficult to implement customer relationship management software within my firm.

- The implementation of customer relationship management software in my firm would require the redesign of a significant number of our business processes.

Intention to adopt CRM software (reliability = .83)

- We have completely rejected the idea of installing customer relationship management software (R).

- We are considering the adoption of customer relationship management software.

- We have accepted the idea of using customer relationship management software.

- We do not want to automate customer relationship management (R).

Decision Maker Information Processing Characteristics

Preference for negative information (reliability = .60)

- When I am faced with both positive and negative information and advice about a new technology, I favor the positive information (R).

- I tend to rely on the positive information that I have available in choosing to adopt a new technology (R).

- Negative information is more credible than positive information.

- I believe negative information about new software offers insights that positive information does not provide.

Preference for information heterogeneity (reliability = .56)

- Firms outside my industry are usually a better source of information about customer relationship management software than firms in my industry.

- I rely on information from within my industry more than I do on information from outside my industry (R).

- Information about customer relationship management software from inside my industry is not reliable.
- To be dependable, information must come from sources within and outside my industry.

Exposure to personal information (NA)

- I have a great deal of personal contacts with individuals within the industry, not in the industry, customers, and within my company that are able to provide me with information about customer relationship management software.

Exposure to impersonal information (NA)

- I have access to a large number of impersonal sources (e.g., articles, advertisements, and brochures) that provide me with information about customer relationship management software.

Endnote

R indicates an item is reverse scored.

Chapter XIII

Computer Self-Efficacy and the Acceptance of Instant Messenger Technology

Thomas Stafford, University of Memphis, USA

Abstract

AOL instant messenger (IM) is a widely used Internet chat technology. There are indications that users do not find it easy to use initially, and this concerns AOL management; they think that if popular applications are not easy to use, the ability of AOL to attract and hold loyal customers will be impeded. In this chapter, the acceptance of IM technology is investigated within the familiar framework of the technology acceptance model (TAM), in which ease of use plays a pivotal role in promoting acceptance and subsequent use of a given technology. Computer self efficacy (CSE) is examined for possible antecedent roles in structural models of acceptance processes. It is determined that CSE does operate in a mediating relationship between some of the critical subcomponents of the TAM model but that it does not operate within the strictly defined theoretical boundaries established for general antecedents to the overall TAM process.

Introduction

A leading Internet service provider (ISP), America Online (AOL), considers ease of use to be the defining feature of its consumer Internet access service; this company has secured its market position in the Internet culture by promoting ease of use and convenience (Stafford, 2003; Wired.com, 1998). AOL instant messenger is now one of the key differentiators that the company promotes as it expands its market coverage to business and industrial markets, and IM remains a critical feature with which it intends to maintain its competitive advantage in the consumer ISP market (Joyce, 2002). Managers at AOL view the instant messenger product as a potentially useful business communication tool for use in collaborative communications among work teams, in addition to its well-established reputation as a trendy consumer communication application (Stafford, 2003). They believe that business IM use increases business user involvement with AOL services.

AOL believes this high degree of visibility and user involvement in its IM product will ultimately lead to more profit for the company, as its use promotes increased online activity and subsequently increased opportunities to up-sell users with various e-commerce offers, in addition to the increased audience power for the benefit of online advertising that such online longevity engenders (Gonier, personal communication, May 2001). For these reasons, AOL has been very interested in determining how users are motivated to use IM, as well as in assessing the convenience of the IM utility to new users who may be experimenting with it (Stafford, 2001). This interest on the part of the IM developer in understanding IM user motivations is the basis for the observations and results reported here.

In this chapter, the results of an analysis of data from a large sample of AOL customers is reported in order to demonstrate the motivational factors that influence user acceptance of the instant messenger application. The effects of computer self-efficacy are examined as antecedents to technology acceptance processes related to motivated use of IM. The influence of well-understood usefulness and ease of use motivational constructs are considered in light of user self-efficacy with the IM application, and implications for developing user expectations in order to maximize acceptance and use of IM technologies are examined.

Theoretical Perspectives on IM User Motivations

CSE: User Self-Efficacy for Computer Technology

Bandura's work in psychology (Bandura 1977, 1978, 1982) is the basis for the modern computer self-efficacy construct. Bandura determined that the degree to which an individual feels capable of performing a task is related to subsequent task performance. Compeau and Higgins (1995a) adapted Bandura's work to the use of computer technology, and subsequently developed and validated a scale for assessing user perceptions of technological capabilities, which most scholars refer to as the "CSE" scale, for computer self-efficacy. A number of researchers have utilized this CSE scale in the investigation of the evolving TAM, or technology acceptance model (cf. Chau, 2001; Fenech, 1998; Igbaria & Iivari, 1995; Venkatesh, 2000), on the consideration that important variables leading to acceptance of computer technology—notably the usefulness of a given technology and its ease in use—would naturally be interrelated with user perceptions of their capability to make use of technology. There have been, however, conflicting indications as to ability of CSE to explain fully the variation of constructs in the technology acceptance model, chief of which is the influence CSE might have on ease of use perceptions among users (cf. Chau, 2001; Fenech, 1998). TAM in its basic form is quite well understood, but efforts to expand its application and context through the use of hypothetically related constructs (such as CSE and other potential antecedents to key TAM constructs) require the investigation of empirical effects that might demonstrate the antecedence of such constructs (e.g., Venkatesh, Morris, Davis, & Davis, 2003).

While the influence of CSE on TAM constructs is still much of an open question (Fenech, 1998), CSE has been empirically useful in the study of other sorts of information systems use (Compeau & Higgins, 1995a). Computer self-efficacy can be used to predict user performance with technology training (Nahl, 1996), the Internet in general (Fenech, 1998; Nahl & Meer, 1997), and CSE may well be the critical link in explaining how usefulness and ease of use generate usage intentions for the World Wide Web (Fenech, 1998).

CSE as a TAM Antecedent

CSE and TAM seem to go together in studies of technology use (Stafford, 2003), though results have been mixed depending on the user context and the target technology. Venkatesh's (2000) evolving conceptualization of the TAM has used CSE to explain ease of use perceptions as a function of user internal source of control (the locus of control perspective). Igbaria and Iivari (1995) tested CSE as a TAM antecedent in a sample of Finnish personal computer users. Chau's (2001) results, however, suggested little influence between CSE and ease of use and usefulness perception.

CSE research involving the TAM has typically taken an antecedent approach, with CSE influencing one of the key TAM constructs, and the rising generalization is that increases in self-efficacy lead to improved perceptions of perceived ease of use among technology users (Wexler, 2001). In accordance with Bandura's (1982) original views, it is typically found that improvements in user technology acceptance can be found through increasing user confidence regarding the process of using the technology. Thus, on the consideration that experience and self-efficacy are inter-related, technology training should be able to increase technology usage (Jawahar & Elango, 2001; Piccoli, Ahmad & Ives, 2001). Even so, much of the work done on CSE and TAM has not followed the established specific empirical criteria for testing TAM antecedents (e.g., Venkatesh & Davis, 2000), which takes the form of mediation testing between a putative antecedent and a given TAM construct.

In light of the general focus in the literature on CSE linkages with ease of use measures in the TAM (e.g., Wexler, 2001), little work on the nature of TAM antecedents appears to have investigated antecedents to the more important perceived usefulness (PU) construct (Venkatesh & Davis, 2000). The research reported in this chapter involves an investigation of the antecedent role of CSE to its influence on PU, though the more orthodox perceived ease of use (PEOU) antecedent tests are also considered.

Instant Messenger as a Target Technology

The diffusion of the Internet has made its many applications, in particular computer-mediated communication, highly popular (Riva, 2002). Of the many features of the Internet that have proven attractive to users, the potential for facilitating social interaction, appears to be one of the most important emerging uses (Cummings, Butler, & Kraut, 2002). Of the several communicative functionalities of the Internet, instant messenger is a transport layer procedure for sending text messages and data between people and applications; unlike other Internet-mediated communications channels, it provides "presence," the ability to determine if a recipient of a message is logged on to receive in real time (Oliva, 2003).

Though it was developed as a consumer market application, IM has seen increasing use as a collaborative communication technology in business work groups (Zhou, 2005; Zhou & Zhang, 2005) and as a venue for customer service in marketing organizations (Froehle & Roth, 2004). As a mode of social interaction, IM is expected to become as ubiquitous as e-mail (Huang & Yen, 2003), and regardless of usage function, IM has become a primary human communication channel (Lee & Perry, 2004).

Fast-paced message exchanges and support for multimedia are aspects of IM technology that have led to increased usage (Zhou & Zhang, 2005). IM closely resembles speech as a communications modality (Zhou, 2005), though its pared-down nature in usage lacks some of the rules of spoken interchange, as well as lacking some of the cues to flow that normal speech has (Riva, 2003). Since presence detection is a key function of IM (Oliva, 2003), it is considered to be a "permission-based" channel, where users must be on each others' buddy lists for effective communication (Chen, Yen, & Huang, 2004).

Research on IM has typically investigated factors leading to adoption and increased usage (e.g., Stafford, 2005). Some studies have considered the role of CSE in furthering adoption processes, typically as characterized in the TAM model (e.g., Chau, 2001; Igbaria & Iivari, 1995; Venkatesh, 2000), although adoption and acceptance research has looked specifically at the role of self-efficacy on the effectiveness of computer use. Deng, Doll, and Truong (2004), for example, demonstrated that self-efficacy has influences beyond initial adoption and can play an ongoing role in computer use and effectiveness of use. Hasan (2006) identified both general and application-specific CSE, noting that efficacy in general influenced uses of general technology, and efficacy related to computer applications was more effective in explaining training outcomes for user-specific computer technology and "near-transfer" learning. Both general and application-specific CSE decreased anxiety in training and improved ease of use perceptions for target technologies.

Ilie, Van Slyke and Green (2005) find gender differences for IM use, noting that women tend to value ease of use and innovation visibility as a basis for innovation behavior, while men value pure diffusion variables more—variables such as relative advantage, results demonstrability, and perceived critical mass. Even so, they found that critical mass, the perception by users that an innovation had reached self-sustaining levels (that it had "succeeded") was the best predictor of usage intentions. Hence, we can see that the few studies that have been done on IM adoption have approached the application from a technology acceptance framework, and while the technology acceptance research tradition has considered the role that CSE plays in furthering acceptance processes, very little has been done to examine the impact of self-efficacy in the adoption and acceptance of emerging consumer sector Internet applications such as IM.

The Special Case of IM, CSE, and America Online

Uses and gratifications for Internet use is an emergent Internet usage motivation paradigm that has been adapted from communications theory research. According to Stafford, Stafford, and Schkade (2004), Internet uses and gratifications appear to be in some ways quite similar to the motivations for the use of other media, in terms of distinct process gratifications (enjoyment of using the medium) and content gratifications (enjoyment of the content the medium brings the user). However, consumer Internet usage has also been shown to be substantially motivated by social gratifications, in addition to the more usual gratifications of usage processes and sought media content (Stafford, 2001). Applications like IM have clear and important social attractions for Internet users, and the likelihood of increased acceptance and increased use of ISP services is related to user experiences with and motivations related to IM use (Gonier, 2001). For this reason, it could be expected that IM uses and gratifications would be substantially social in their makeup.

Major ISPs are interested in applications that engage users, causing them to spend more time online and subsequently become more profitable subscribers for the service provider (Gonier, 2001), but this presents a particular motivational problem to ISP managers seeking to influence users in their adoption of technologies such as IM. For example, the typical new user at America Online is a late adopter (Stafford, 2003) and will be less comfortable with AOL technologies such as instant messenger (Stafford, 2001). The managerial issue at hand is that new users don't appear to have an easy time learning how to use the IM utility (Gonier, 2001), which is an issue that bears consequences beyond the consumer user segment, since AOL expects its user-friendly interface and ease of operation to continue to influence market share gains in new business segments for important applications like IM (Joyce, 2002).

There are indications that high self-efficacy individuals who use instant messenger find the utility significantly more useful and easier to use than individuals with low self-efficacy and end up spending more time with it as a result (Stafford, 2003), which would fit with the objectives of ISP managers. Hence, the influence of self-efficacy on technology acceptance is an important point to understand in a market where most of the new users are inexperienced and unsure of their technical skills, given the self-fulfilling nature of CSE as regards time spent with a technology (Piccoli et al., 2001).

Empirical findings suggest that self-efficacy is linked to ease of use measures (e.g., Wexler, 2001), and could well serve as a critical antecedent in technology acceptance models. This, taken together with more general findings related to the improvement of users' behavioral intentions to use new technology (BI) arising from increases in computer self-efficacy, suggests that IM-specific computer self-efficacy will serve an empirically consistent role in technology acceptance models in the form of an antecedent:

H1: Perceived ease of instant messenger use mediates the influence of self-efficacy for instant messenger use on consumers' behavioral intentions to use the technology.

Little effort has been made to empirically establish antecedents to the powerful perceived usefulness construct (PU) in the TAM (Venkatesh & Davis, 2000), but there are clear indications that CSE can serve in this role with regard to IM use in the TAM framework. Hence, the potential antecedent status of CSE in its influence on the important usefulness-usage intention relationship in the TAM can be specified:

H2: Perceived usefulness of instant messenger will mediate the influence of self-efficacy for instant messenger use on consumers' behavioral intentions to use the technology.

These hypotheses are examined in a structural equation modeling framework using linear structural relations (LISREL) (Jöreskog & Sörbom, 1993), with Internet-specific TAM measures adapted by Stafford (2001) from the work of Venkatesh and Davis (1996; see also Karahanna, Straub, & Chervany, 1999), in addition to a revised version of the 10-item computer self efficacy scale of Compeau and Higgins (1995b) worded to reflect a focus on instant messenger technology.

Method

AOL recruited 1,006 qualified users to respond to a survey about IM use at their Opinion Place research Web site. Participants were compensated in the form of American Airlines frequent flyer points. Ongoing demographics research conducted by AOL indicates a typical demographic mixture at Opinion Place that is comparable to the general profile of Internet users (Stafford & Gonier, 2004). An overview of the AOL demographic comparison is presented in Table 1.

Table 1. AOL demographics

	Internet	AOL
Gender		
- Male	49%	45%
- Female	51%	55%
Age		
- 18 – 24	14%	16%
- 25 – 34	21%	18%
- 35 – 44	26%	27%
- 45 – 54	23%	24%
- 55 +	15%	16%
Married	66%	62%

Results

H1 predicted that CSE would be mediated in its influence on BI through PEOU for instant messenger technology. This mediation scheme fits the empirical scenario identified by Venkatesh and Davis (2000, p. 187) for assessing antecedents to the TAM framework, and permits a test of CSE as a potential antecedent to the model in this context of IM use by consumers. H2 predicted that CSE would be mediated in its influence on BI through PU for instant messenger technology, which is also a specific examination of the potential anteced-ent role of CSE—in this case, to PU in the standard TAM formulation.

The initial step in the testing of these hypotheses within the theoretical framework of the TAM is to fit the basic form of the TAM in a structural model to ensure adequate performance of the basic model, in advance of mediation testing with CSE. This is in keeping with the recom-mended "two-step" structural equation modeling approach to theory testing (e.g., Anderson & Gerbing, 1988). Here, standard TAM measures are modified to assess instant messenger acceptance (TAM/IM) and are verified in a confirmatory analysis that fits the familiar TAM grouping of one exogenous construct (PEOU) and two endogenous constructs (PU and BI). After fitting the TAM/IM, a second model is fitted, specifying structural linkages between CSE, serving as an exogenous construct, and all three of the main TAM constructs are fitted in the endogenous position for mediational assessment. This is done in order to assess the potential antecedent role of CSE in acceptance of IM technology.

Figure 1. TAM structural model for instant messenger (Adapted from Stafford, 2005)

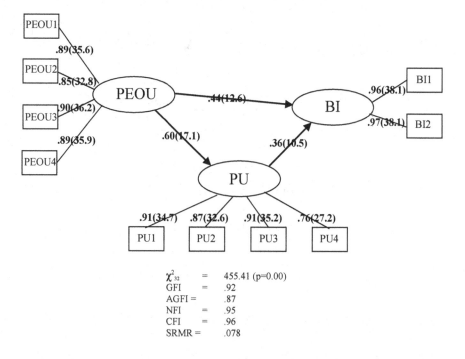

$$\chi^2_{32} = 455.41 \ (p=0.00)$$
$$GFI = .92$$
$$AGFI = .87$$
$$NFI = .95$$
$$CFI = .96$$
$$SRMR = .078$$

Figure 2. TAM/IM structural model with CSE antecedent (Adapted from Stafford, 2005)

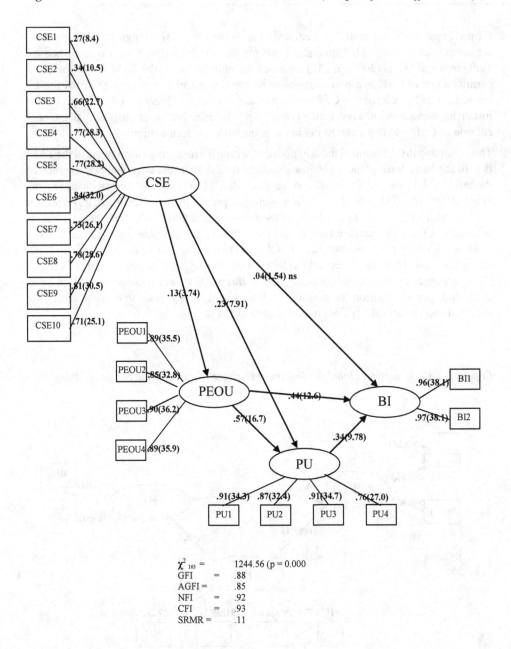

χ^2_{163} =   1244.56 (p = 0.000)
GFI   =   .88
AGFI =   .85
NFI   =   .92
CFI   =   .93
SRMR =   .11

The basic confirmatory analysis of TAM/IM is represented in Figure 1 and the structural model that demonstrating the antecedent testing through mediational paths as specified by Hypotheses 1 and 2 is represented in Figure 2.

The confirmatory analysis of the TAM/IM fits well, with goodness of fit (.92), adjusted goodness of fit (.87), normed fit (.95), and comparative fit indices (.96) all in the expected range for a well-fitting model. Linkages in the model are all strong and significant (loadings are shown with associated t-values in parentheses), and demonstrate the mediational scheme typically expected between PEOU-PU-BI. Hence, the TAM/IM form appears to operate in a theoretically consistent manner.

Fit for the structural model that tests the mediational relationships between CSE and the TAM constructs is not as strong as the fit of the basic TAM/IM form, but the fit indices are distinctly comparable to the range of acceptable fit criteria demonstrated and documented in Bassellier, Benbasat, and Reich (2003, p. 330). In examining the mediational schemes between CSE-PEOU-BI and CSE-PU-BI, it should be noted that structural linkages between CSE and the TAM constructs are not as strong as might be expected. Nor are they significant in every case—specifically, in the case of the CSE-BI linkage, which is a critical link in the empirical test of antecedence as specified by Venkatesh and Davis (2000).

In order to empirically establish that a construct is antecedent to the TAM as an overall model, it is necessary to show that its relationship with BI is mediated by PEOU (Venkatesh & Davis, 2000, p. 187). For that set of relationships to be conclusive evidence of media-tion, which is necessary to establish antecedent status, significant links must be established between all three constructs in the TAM, if the mediational method specified by Baron and Kenny (1986) is followed. In the mediational model, the path between CSE and BI is clearly not significant, and so hypothesis 1 fails in testing. CSE does not serve as a general ante-cedent to the TAM as a whole. Recall that the requirements for antecedents to the TAM are that mediation operate via PEOU, and the three paths specified above would all have to be significant to provide the necessary evidence for mediation, in line with standard mediation testing procedures (e.g., Baron & Kenny, 1986).

It does appear that hypothesis 2 is confirmed, however. The linkages between CSE-PEOU-PU are all significant, and this raises the empirical case for CSE's influence on PU being mediated by PEOU. In short, one could make the case that self-efficacy for IM use influ-ences perceptions of usefulness for IM to the extent that users perceive that the utility is easy to use—if it is easy to use, and if users feel confident in using it, it will be perceived as a useful tool. This does not necessarily mean that CSE serves as an antecedent to the TAM as a complete holistic model, but it does suggest that CSE plays important and theoreti-cally interesting roles with regard to key constructs in the TAM/IM. This can be a useful outcome for managers seeking to improve IM acceptance, as well as theoreticians seeking to understand TAM antecedents more completely.

These results are equivocal in terms of showing CSE to be a basic TAM antecedent, since the specified requirement for antecedent status to the holistic model are clear with regard to the need to show a mediated link to BI through PEOU (Venkatesh & Davis, 2000, p. 187). However, the indication that PEOU mediates between CSE and PU in evaluations of instant messenger (and not BI, as would be required to consider CSE an overall TAM antecedent) is a finding that is both intuitively appealing and theoretically consistent. Moreover, it is in keeping with the specifications for future testing as outlined by Venkatesh and Davis (2000), who noted that specific antecedents to PU had been under-researched.

Discussion

CSE does not serve as an antecedent to the overall TAM model in the context of instant messenger use, at least not in the ways that have been specified for TAM antecedents in prior research. However, since CSE's effect on perceptions of usefulness for IM does appear to be mediated by ease of use perceptions, there are useful considerations for researchers and managers interested in factors that increase adoption of IM technology.

ISP management considers IM to be an important service and an important factor in maintaining their market share in a competitive market. It is a popular utility among Internet users, and the likelihood of increased use seems firmly anchored to perceptions of IM usefulness among users. This is theoretically consistent with prescriptions for ongoing work with technology acceptance constructs (e.g., Venkatesh & Davis, 1996, 2000). To the extent that increasing time spent online is considered to be a function of more involvement with online applications (Gonier, 2001), efforts that improve user self-efficacy with critical applications such as IM will help ISP management attain their goals. It is clearly demonstrated here that ease of use perceptions mediate usefulness perceptions for IM use among a large sample of AOL customers, so it seems clear that managers need to structure training or support resources that boost perceptions of ease of use for IM if they wish the utility to be considered useful; naturally, usefulness has been shown in the past to be a key consideration in boosting perceptions of intentions to use computer technologies. Hence, making IM easy to use can have beneficial outcomes in technology acceptance. Indeed, recent innovations such as AOL Online Coach seem designed with this efficacy training dynamic in mind (Stafford, 2003).

The reason why CSE does not perform as a general antecedent to the TAM is unclear and requires more research to understand. One possibility may be that the investigation of Internet utilities in the TAM framework crosses theoretical boundaries that delimit the study of diffusion-like activities such as technology acceptance from sustained technology usage activities that are better conceptualized in the infusion perspective (Cooper & Zmud, 1990; Kwon & Zmud, 1987; Saga & Zmud, 1994), which presupposes prior adoption of an innovation and concerns itself with the individual user's motivations to make best, fullest, and continued use of technologies already adopted for use (e.g., Agarwal & Prasad, 1997). Or it may be the case that a study of IM use in consumer markets impacts performance of TAM in ways that are inconsistent with the workplace studies of technology diffusion that the model is so often utilized for.

Clearly, there are a host of additional studies that could examine the various implications of the results found here, but the most important unanswered question remains the reason for the lack of a clear mediational effect in the antecedent test of CSE to the general TAM for IM. The self-efficacy literature seems clear on the issue: increased self efficacy should lead to increased technology usage. We see, based on this study, that CSE impacts usefulness perceptions with regard to IM user motivations; we just lack a clear picture of the usefulness-usage intentions relationships in the context of IM/CSE. Hence, this is an issue that should be resolved in future research in this area.

Conclusion

Computer self efficacy for AOL Instant Messenger was posited to serve as an antecedent to the general form of the technology acceptance model for instant messenger use. Based on clearly delineated tests for assessing the antecedent status of variables related to the TAM, a structural model was fitted to test a series of mediation relationships. It was found that CSE is not mediated by PEOU in its influence on BI in the TAM, which is the specific requirement for demonstrating status as a general antecedent to the acceptance model.

Mediation was demonstrated in the form of the intervening influence of PEOU in the relationships between CSE and PU, which is evidence for an antecedent role for CSE with regard to PU. This relationship is important, both because of the need to investigate specific antecedents to PU in the TAM (e.g., Venkatesh & Davis, 2000), and for reasons related to managerial efficacy in increasing use of online utilities related to profitable ISP business performance. The determination of a mediational relationship between CSE-PEOU-PU, in the absence of an expected mediational relationship between CSE-PEOU-BI, is a point that bears much theoretical consideration in light of the current self-efficacy literature and will be the focus of important future research.

References

Agarwal, R., & Prasad, J. (1997). The role of innovation characteristics and perceived voluntariness in the acceptance of information technology. *Decision Sciences, 28*, 557-582.

Anderson, J. C., & Gerbing, D. W. (1988). Structural equation modeling in practice: A review and recommended two-step approach. *Psychological Bulletin, 103*, 411-42.

Bandura, A. (1977). Self-efficacy: Toward a unifying theory of behavioral change. *Psychological Review, 84*(2), 191-215.

Bandura, A. (1978). Reflections on self-efficacy. *Advances in Behavioral Research and Therapy, 1*, 237-269.

Bandura, A. (1982). Self-efficacy mechanism in human agency. *American Psychologist, 372*, 122-147.

Baron, R. M., & Kenny, D. A. (1986). The mediator-moderator variable distinction in social psychological research: Conceptual, strategic and statistical considerations. *Journal of Personality and Social Psychology, 51*, 1173-1182.

Bassellier, G., Benbasat, I., & Reich, B. H. (2003). The influence of business managers' IT competence on championing IT. *Information Systems Research, 14*(4), 317-336.

Chau, P. Y. K. (2001). Influence of computer attitude and self-efficacy on IT usage behavior. *Journal of End User Computing, 13*(1), 26-33.

Chen, K., Yen, D. C., & Huang, A. H. (2004). Media selection to meet communication contexts: Comparing email and instant messaging in an undergraduate population. *Communications of the AIS,* (14) [Article 20], 387-405.

Compeau, D. R., & Higgins, C. A. (1995a). Application of social cognitive theory to training for computer skills. *Information Systems Research, 6*(2), 118-143.

Compeau, D. R., & Higgins, C. A. (1995b). Computer self-efficacy: Development of a measure and initial test. *MIS Quarterly, 19*(9), 189-211.

Cooper, R., & Zmud, R. (1990). Information technology implementation research: A technological diffusion approach. *Management Science, 36*(2), 123-139.

Cummings, J. N., Butler, B., & Kraut, R. (2002). The quality of online social relationships. *Communications of the ACM, 45*(7), 103-108.

Deng, X., Doll, W., & Truong, D. (2004). Computer self-efficacy in an ongoing use context. *Behavior & Information Technology, 23*(6), 395-412.

Fenech, T. (1998). Using perceived ease of use and perceived usefulness to predict acceptance of the World Wide Web. *Computer Networks & ISDN Systems, 30*(1-7), 629-630.

Froehle, C.M., & Roth, A.V. (2004). New measurement scales for evaluating perceptions of the technology-mediated customer service experience. *Journal of Operations Management, 22*(1), 1-21.

Hasan, B. (2006). Effectiveness of computer training: The role of multilevel computer self-efficacy. *Journal of Organizational and End User Computing, 18*(1), 50-68.

Huang, A. H., & Yen, D. C. (2003). Usefulness of instant messaging among young users: Social vs. work perspective. *Human Systems Management, 22*(2), 63-72.

Igbaria, M, & Iivari, J. (1995). The effects of self-efficacy on computer usage. *Omega, 23*(6), 597-605.

Ilie, V., Van Slyke, C., & Green, G. (2005). Gender differences in perception and use of communication technologies: A diffusion of innovation approach. *Information Resources Management Journal, 18*(3), 13-31.

Jawahar, I. M., & Elango, B. (2001). The effect of attitudes, goal setting and self-efficacy on end user performance. *Journal of End User Computing, 13*(2), 40-45.

Jöreskog, K. G., & Sörbom, D. (1993). *LISREL 8.* Chicago: Scientific Software International, Inc.

Joyce, E. (2002). *AOL angles for business market share. ASPnews.com.* Retrieved from http://www.aspnews.com/news/article/0,,4191_1364131,00.html, created 6/11/02, accessed 4/6/03.

Karahanna, E., Straub, D., & Chervany, N. L. (1999). Information technology adoption across time: A cross-sectional comparison of pre-adoption and post-adoption beliefs. *MIS Quarterly, 23*, 183-213.

Kwon, T., & Zmud, R. (1987). Unifying the fragmented models of information systems implementation. In R. Boland & R. Hirschheim (Eds.), *Critical issues in information systems research* (pp. 227-251). West Sussex, UK: John Wiley & Sons.

Lee, K. C., & Perry, S. D. (2004). Student instant messaging use in a ubiquitous computing environment: Effects of deficient self-regulation. *Journal of Broadcasting & Electronic Media, 48*(3), 399-420.

Leung, L. (2002). Loneliness, self-disclosure, and ICQ use. *CyberPsychology & Behavior, 5*(3), 241-251.

Li, D., Chau, P. Y. K., & Lu, H. (2005). Understanding individual adoption of instant messaging: An empirical investigation. *Journal of the AIS, 4*(6), 102-129.

Nahl, D. (1996). Affective monitoring of internet learners: Perceived self-efficacy an success. *Journal of the American Society for Information Science, 33*, 100-109.

Nahl, D., & Meer, M.P. (1997). User-centered assessment of two Web browsers: Errors, perceived self-efficacy, and success. *Journal of the American Society of Information Science, 34*, 89-97.

Oliva, R. A. (2003). Instant messaging comes of age. *Marketing Management, 12*(3), 49-52.

Piccoli, G., Ahmad, R., & Ives, B. (2001). Web-based virtual learning environments: A research framework and a preliminary assessment of effectiveness in basic it skills training. *MIS Quarterly, 25*(4), 410-426.

Riva, G. (2002). The sociocognitive psychology of computer-mediated communication: The present and future of technology-based interactions. *CyberPsychology & Behavior, 5*(6), 581-598.

Saga, V., & Zmud, R. (1994). The nature and determinants of it acceptance, routinization and infusion. In *Proceedings of the 1994 International Federation for Information Processing.*

Stafford, T. F. (2005). Computer self-efficacy as an antecedent to the acceptance of instant messenger technology. *International Journal of Electronic Business Research, 1*(4), 41-50.

Stafford, T. F. (2001). *Motivations related to consumer use of online services.* Unpublished doctoral dissertation, University of Texas – Arlington.

Stafford, T. F. (2003). Computer self-efficacy and internet use: The case of AOL Instant Messenger. In *Proceedings of the 2003 Decision Sciences Institute Conference.*

Stafford, T. F., & Gonier, D. (2004). Gratifications for internet use: What Americans like about being online. *Communications of the ACM, 47*(1), 107-112.

Stafford, T. F., & Stafford, M.R. (2001). Identifying motivations for the use of commercial Web sites. *Information Resources Management Journal, 14*, 22-30.

Stafford, T. F., Stafford, M. R., & Schkade, L. L. (2004). Determining uses and gratifications for the Internet. *Decision Sciences, 35*(2), 259-288.

Venkatesh, V. (2000). Determinants of perceived ease of use: Integrating control, intrinsic motivation, and emotion into the technology acceptance model. *Information Systems Research, 11*(4), 342-365.

Venkatesh, V., & Davis, F. D. (1996). A model of the antecedents of perceived ease-of-use: Development and test. *Decision Sciences, 27*, 451-481.

Venkatesh, V., & Davis, F. D. (2000). A theoretical extension of the technology acceptance model: Four longitudinal field studies. *Management Science, 46*(2), 186-204.

Venkatesh, V., Morris, M. G., Davis, G. B., & Davis, F. D. (2003). User acceptance of information technology: Toward a unified view. *MIS Quarterly, 27*, 425-478.

Wellman, B., Salaff, J., Dimitrova, D., Garton, L., Gulia, M., & Haythornthwaite, C. (1996). Computer networks as social networks: Collaborative work, telework, and virtual community. *American Review of Sociology*, (22), 213-238.

Wexler, J. (2001). Why computer users accept new systems. *Sloan Management Review, 42*(3), 17.

Wired.com (1998). *AOL expects 26 million newbies*. Retrieved from http://www.wired.com/business/0,1367,15035,00.html, created 9/15/98, accessed 4/21/03.

Zhou, L. (2005). An empirical investigation of deception behavior in instant messaging. *IEEE Transactions on Professional Communication, 48*(2), 147-160.

Zhou, L., & Zhang, D. (2005). A heuristic approach to establishing punctuation convention in instant messaging. *IEEE Transactions on Professional Communication, 48*(4), 391-400.

Chapter XIV

User Perceptions of the Usefulness of E-Mail and Instant Messaging

Philip Houle, Drake University, USA

Troy Strader, Drake University, USA

Sridhar Ramaswami, Iowa State University, USA

Abstract

This chapter describes research that explores the impact of unsolicited traffic on the perceived usefulness of electronic message technologies. Two technologies were explored: e-mail and instant messaging. The hypothesis is that unsolicited message traffic would have negative effects on the perceived usefulness of the technologies. However, the findings did not support this expected result. Users of the technologies appear to cope with the unsolicited traffic in a variety of ways. The implications of results are discussed from the perspective of managers, researchers, marketers, service providers, and public policy makers.

Introduction

Using electronic message technologies has become a way of life for many. In the modern workplace, people routinely communicate with each other using a computer in addition to, or instead of, a telephone. Many workers spend a significant fraction of their day producing and processing electronic messages. Outside of the workplace, many use their personal computer to communicate with their family and their friends. In both contexts, such communication facilitated by the Internet spans the globe.

The oldest electronic message technology is e-mail. E-mail began more than 40 years ago when users of time-shared mainframe computer systems wanted to communicate with each other. With the widespread use of the Internet, e-mail has become a standard for communication between its users. As a result, e-mail is typically used as a replacement for a variety of documents such as memorandum, letters, or reports.

Today, e-mail can be sent literally to anyone or everyone. All that is required is that the sender has the needed electronic address or addresses. The marginal cost increase to send an e-mail message to a large number of recipients is hardly more than sending to one recipient. This exceedingly minimal incremental cost of sending e-mail messages to many recipients has lead to a phenomenon called spam.

Spam is typically defined as the sending of unsolicited, identical, or nearly identical, messages to a large number of recipients (Wikipedia, 2006). Historically, the idea of spam has been described with a variety of message technologies, one of which includes e-mail. However, for purposes of our discussion here, spam is a descriptor of a class of messages that are unsolicited and are sent to a large number of recipients via the e-mail system.

Over the years there have been, and continue to be, a variety of electronic communication technologies that are employed in addition to e-mail. One of the more recent electronic communications technologies is instant messaging (IM). Instant messaging is a form of electronic communication that involves immediate exchange of messages between two or more users who are simultaneously connected with each other. Typically, messages are brief, which means they can be composed quickly and, when completed, can be delivered very quickly across the network to connected users, perhaps in a fraction of a second. The overall flow of messages between the simultaneously connected parties functions much like, and often is called, a chat session or chat room.

The popularity of instant messaging was probably best demonstrated by the success of America Online (AOL) and its instant messaging product. Other companies, including Yahoo and Microsoft, have comparable and competing products. The basic idea behind all of these products is an easy-to-use interface that connects the user to a server that provides access to the network via a username and simultaneously connects the user to other users via their usernames. Once connected, all users can "message" each other, that is, send short message of text directly to other connected users.

Instant messaging differs from e-mail as follows: E-mail messages may be lengthy, are sent across the network, and are queued for the recipient. The recipient need not be connected at the time the message is sent and/or arrives. The recipient reads the message, potentially at a much later time, and the transmission latency may be minutes, hours, or days. In contrast, instant messages are short and are immediately sent across the network to a simultaneously connected recipient. A recipient typically will reply immediately. In effect, a conversation, or chat, occurs. For instant messaging to work effectively, the transmission latency must not exceed a few seconds.

Similar to e-mail, it is possible for a sender to target a large number of potential recipients for an unsolicited message. The term spim has been used to describe such activity. For purposes of our discussion, spim is a class of messages that are unsolicited and are sent to a large number of users via an instant messaging system.

The assumption made in this study is that spam and spim are negative factors with the users of electronic messaging technologies. As the proportion of message traffic that is spam or spim increases, users must process increasing numbers of essentially useless messages, wasting time and resources. In addition, the service providers are supporting traffic levels that are artificially high, perhaps by as much as a factor of two or three, due to spam and spim messages. This adds to their costs, which must ultimately be passed on to their customers. However, there are other negatives inherent to spam and spim.

Perhaps one of the most alarming things about spim and spam relates to the potential security threat created by many such messages. One threat is the possibility that a message contains a payload that installs malicious code on the user's computer. Such code might be a virus that corrupts the user's computer or it might be spyware. Spyware is code that installs itself unnoticed on the user's computer, records the user's subsequent actions, and then sends the information to others. Spyware has the potential to capture information about the user that would allow a third party to steal the user's identity and carry out fraudulent transactions against the user.

A second type of security threat posed by spim and spam relates to something called phishing. Phishing is the sending of unsolicited messages designed to appear as a legitimate message from some established entity, such as a bank, that dupes the recipient into doing something that compromises his or her security. A phishing-related compromise can range from something as innocent as opening a malicious Web page to the more serious action of inappropriately revealing login information, such as a username and password, to a third party (Roberts, 2005). Phishing has already evolved from its earliest forms because users have learned to cope with it. A newer version, spear-phishing, relies more heavily on methods of gaining user trust to provide richer, more believable bait and targets a much smaller, more clearly defined group of potential victims (Bauknight, 2005).

In 2003, approximately 2 billion spam messages were sent every day (Swartz, 2004). It is such a pervasive problem that an industry has evolved to fight the problem through development of anti-spam software. In addition, it is commonplace today for users to run anti-virus packages that scan all incoming e-mail looking for threats. However, the same level of threat exists for spim.

Vendors of the more popular instant messaging services report significant increases in the volume of spim. There are estimates that the quantity of spim solicitations doubled from 2002 to 2003, reaching 500 million in 2003 (Claburn, 2004). Other estimates suggest that more than 1 billion spim messages were sent in 2003, and the number could quadruple annually through the mid-2000s (Swartz, 2004). The volume of spim messages is expected to continue growing at a rate at or above that of spam messages because laws and anti-spam technology are primarily focused on spam. In addition, the use of instant messaging continues to grow and has much more room for growth. In 2003, about 70 percent of corporations in North America used instant messaging (Schultz, 2004). About 85 percent used it in 2004 (Garretson, 2005).

Another reported characteristic regarding the content of spim messages relates to the distribution of pornography. According to a report from early 2004 by the Radicati Group, a technology market research firm in Palo Alto, California, in 2004, 70 percent of spim contained material considered pornographic (Biever, 2004). While not a security threat per se, content that is pornographic does create a new dimension to whether spam and spim are factors affecting perceptions of the usefulness of electronic message technologies. Whether the factor is negative or positive may well depend on the recipient.

The purpose of our study is to understand how increasing volumes of spam and spim impact the perceptions of users regarding the usefulness of e-mail and instant messaging. The specific questions explored were:

1.   How do user perceptions of spam affect their perceptions of the usefulness of e-mail?

2.   How do user perceptions of spim affect their perceptions of the usefulness of instant messaging?

Theoretical Background

One of the primary models for predicting whether information technology will be used is the technology acceptance model (TAM) (Davis, 1989). This model identifies the relationships between several factors that predict information technology use. Actual use of information technology is affected by the behavioral intention (BI) to use it. Two primary factors affecting behavioral intention are perceived ease of use (PEOU) and perceived usefulness (PU). Numerous studies have validated and/or extended the model. In this study, we focus on one component of the TAM—user perceptions regarding system usefulness.

Since we were considering e-mail and instant messaging, we decided to extend the technology acceptance model by including two new factors: the perception regarding spam and the perception regarding spim. The items used in the survey instrument for perceived usefulness of e-mail and instant messaging were adapted from an earlier TAM study (Davis & Venkatesh, 1996). The items used for the two new factors, the perception regarding spam and the perception regarding spim, were developed based on dimensions identified in popular press articles. Individual survey items asked for individual perceptions of to what extent spam (or spim) had wasted their time, made it difficult to sort through useful messages, violated their privacy, and potentially could cause harm to their computer. Constructs, survey items, item scale, and reliability measures are included in the Appendix. Factor analysis and reliability tests confirmed that the items identified are credible measures for perceptions of spim and spam as well as system usefulness.

Methodology and Findings

We identified the target population for the study as individuals who are likely to use, or consider using, both electronic mail and instant messaging. One group that is a significant component of this population is young adults. We identified a population of approximately 400 undergraduate and graduate students at a large public university and a medium-sized private university in Iowa. We prepared a survey instrument, including scale items for measuring the study's constructs, and gathered the responses in 2004 using a Web-based survey form. Of the survey respondents contacted to participate, 188 completed the survey, a response rate of 47 percent. The respondents were 57 percent men and 43 percent women.

Impact of Spam on E-Mail Usefulness

Our first finding focuses on perceptions of electronic mail usefulness and spam. The hypothesis was that higher levels of perceived problems associated with spam (wasted time, distractions from important messages, potential privacy loss, and potential harm to computers) would affect perceptions of the usefulness of electronic mail. That is, more spam makes e-mail less useful. To test the hypothesis, we ran a regression model to test the statistical relationship between spam perceptions and e-mail usefulness. Interestingly, we found that there is no statistically significant relationship.

One explanation is that, despite increases in the number of spam messages being sent, users have learned to cope with spam through a combination of technical solutions (anti-spam software) and non-technical solutions (identifying probable spam messages and quickly deleting them without opening the message). At this time, it appears that the benefits of e-mail far outweigh any inconvenience attributed to spam.

Impact of Spim on Instant Messaging Usefulness

Our second finding focuses on perceptions of instant messaging usefulness and spim. The hypothesis was that higher levels of perceived problems associated with spim such as wasted time, distractions from important messages, potential privacy loss, and potential harm to computing devices would affect perceptions of the usefulness of instant messaging. That is, more spim makes IM less useful. To test the hypothesis, we ran a regression model to test the statistical relationship between spim perceptions and IM usefulness. In this instance we found a statistically significant relationship. The relationship was positive. This is counter-intuitive given that we expected to find a significant negative relationship. Our findings suggest that receiving more spim led to higher perceptions of the usefulness of instant messaging.

One explanation is that the use of IM and the amount of spim is still relatively small, so, like the early days of e-mail, this is not yet a significant problem. It may also be true that the IM user base is much smaller and more homogeneous than the large number of e-mail users, enabling marketers that use spim to better target the message to the audience, resulting in less unwanted message content. Another explanation is that the content of spim, primarily unsolicited pitches for porn sites and concerts (Swartz, 2004), is not necessarily unwanted.

Implications and Conclusion

Based on the findings of our study, the counter-intuitive perceptions individuals have regarding the relationship between spam, spim, and electronic communication technology usefulness point to a number of implications for companies utilizing electronic mail or instant messaging for marketing products, providers of e-mail, and IM services as well as companies that directly provide anti-spam/spim services and public policy makers that monitor global electronic communication technology usage.

First, firms that utilize e-mail or IM-based marketing campaigns should realize that, even though it is relatively easy and inexpensive to send large numbers of advertising messages, it will be difficult to get much response to messages if the messages are considered by individuals to be spam or spim. Organizations and individuals can use software to block many of the messages, and even if messages get through, individuals have learned to cope with the obtrusive nature of the messages. The best alternative for firms is to communicate electronically only with those customers who have agreed ahead of time to receive the messages. This reduces the amount of messages considered to be spam and spim, greatly reduces the annoyance related to unsolicited messages, and increases the likelihood that advertising-related messages will result in sales.

These findings also have implications for electronic communication service providers. Although the number of spam and spim messages will likely continue to grow well into the future, individuals are unlikely to pay much for anti-spam/spim software because the annoyance level is not that great. They expect these services to be provided for a nominal charge or as a free service that is part of their regular account subscription. And even if some messages get through, they are able to cope with the problem by ignoring and deleting unsolicited and unwanted messages.

Finally, for public policy makers, there is a need for laws to control spam and spim, not because of the huge cost of time and effort to users but in instances where privacy is being violated or porn-related content is being sent to minors. As with most information technology issues, laws related to electronic communications and electronic commerce will have to be constantly re-evaluated as organizational practices change over time. Spam-related legislation has been implemented in the European Union and United States in 2003 and 2004, but the new laws are unlikely to rein in the dedicated spammers who generate the majority of unwanted e-mail traffic (Nettleton, 2005). At this time, though, individuals perceive the technologies to still be useful despite spam and spim.

The overall finding of this study is that spam and spim are not necessarily perceived by e-mail and IM users to be a major problem. The benefits (for example, usefulness for a wide range of purposes including communication and information sharing) realized by using the communication technologies outweigh the time and effort needed to deal with unsolicited messages.

References

Bauknight, T. (2005). The newest Internet scams. *Business & Economic Review, 52*(1), 19-21.

Biever, C. (2004). *Spam being rapidly outpaced by 'spim'*. Retrieved March 1, 2005, from http://www.newscientist.com/article.ns?id=dn4822

Claburn, T. (2004, January 19). The Rise of 'Spim,' *InformationWeek*, (972), p. 50.

Davis, F. (1989). Perceived usefulness, perceived ease of use, and user acceptance of information technology. *MIS Quarterly, 13*(3), 319-340.

Davis, F., & Venkatesh, V. (1996). A model of the antecedents of perceived ease of use: development and test. *Decision Sciences, 27*(3), 451-481.

Garretson, C. (2005). Bringing security to instant messaging. *Network World*. Retrieved January 3, 2006, from http://www.networkworld.com/news/2005/040405-im-security.html

Nettleton, E. (2005). Getting tough on spam? *Database Marketing & Customer Strategy Management, 12*(4), 357-361.

Roberts, P. (2005). Symantec: spam, phishing grow, botnets shrink in '04. *Network World*. Retrieved January 3, 2006, from http://www.networkworld.com/news/2005/032105symanspam.html

Schultz, M. (2004). *How to stop IM and SPIM abuse*. Retrieved March 1, 2005, from http://news.zdnet.com/2100-9595_22-5201055.html

Swartz, J. (2004). *Spam's irritating cousin, spim, on the loose*. Retrieved March 1, 2005, from http://www.usatoday.com/tech/news/2004-03-01-spim_x.html

Wikipedia. (2006). http://en.wikipedia.org/wiki/e-mail_spam

Appendix: Constructs, Items, and Reliability Statistics

1 = strongly disagree, 7 = strongly agree

Perceived Usefulness: E-Mail (reliability = 0.92)

- Using an electronic mail system would improve my performance in my degree program.
- Using an electronic mail system in my degree program would increase my productivity.
- Using an electronic mail system would enhance my effectiveness in my degree program.
- I find an electronic mail system would be useful in my degree program.

Perceived Usefulness: Instant Messaging (reliability = 0.95)

- Using an instant messaging system would improve my performance in my degree program.
- Using an instant messaging system in my degree program would increase my productivity.
- Using an instant messaging system would enhance my effectiveness in my degree program.
- I find an instant messaging system would be useful in my degree program.

Spam Perception (reliability = 0.71)

- I waste a lot of time processing unwanted e-mail.
- Unwanted e-mail makes it difficult to sort though useful e-mail.
- I believe my privacy is violated by unwanted e-mail senders.
- Because it could harm my computer, I am usually hesitant to open any unwanted e-mail.

Spim Perception (reliability = 0.80)

- I waste a lot of time processing unwanted instant messages.
- Unwanted instant messages make it difficult to sort though useful instant messages.

- I believe my privacy is violated by unwanted instant message senders.
- Because it could harm my computer, I am usually hesitant to open any unwanted instant messages.

Section V

Privacy Policies and Implementation Issues

Chapter XV

Is P3P an Answer to Protecting Information Privacy?

Noushin Ashrafi, University of Massachusetts Boston, USA

Jean-Pierre Kuilboer, University of Massachusetts Boston, USA

Abstract

Increasingly the Internet is used as a common tool for communication, information gathering, and online transactions. Information privacy is threatened as users are expected to reveal personal information without knowing the consequences of sharing their information. To that end, research groups, both from academia and industry, have embarked on the development of privacy enhancement technologies. One such technology is platform for privacy preferences (P3P). Developed by the World Wide Web Consortium (W3C), P3P has a number of prominent stakeholders such as IBM, Microsoft, and AT&T. Yet there is little general knowledge on what P3P is and the extent of its deployment by e-business organizations. This study is exploratory in nature and aims at addressing these questions; in particular, we look at P3P both as a new technology and as a standard. We use our empirical data on top-500 interactive companies to assess its adoption.

Introduction

The computing field today is far from what the environment was 20 years ago. As the distributed networked computing architecture is becoming prevalent and with e-commerce on the rise, the issues of privacy protection and system security have come into focus (Reagle & Cranor, 1999). Some personal information has been available in city hall records and libraries for some time, yet its level of accessibility in electronic form has changed drastically in recent years (Moor, 1997). Easy access to personal information has caused concerns about privacy and security among end-user consumers and information technology (IT) professionals. A number of surveys indicate an increasing concern for privacy. A survey by Teltzrow and Kobsa in 2004 showed that 64 percent of consumers hesitate to use the Internet for online transactions due to the fact that they don't know how their personal information would be used. A more recent study by Acquisti and Grossklags (2005) showed a large portion (89.2 percent) expressing concern about privacy. Furthermore, there are indications that a majority of users (90 percent) are in favor of being asked for permission before companies use their personal information for marketing purposes, 76 percent consider privacy policies quite important, and 55 percent would be willing to provide personal information to the Web sites that have posted privacy policies (Teltzrow & Kobsa, 2004).

Security and privacy issues are considered the two most important issues in modern use of computers. The security issue is often regarded as a technical issue to be solved by off-the-shelf solutions such as virus checkers or firewalls. The privacy problem, however, has received little attention and is likely to get worse without proactive measures. According to a report by Zona Research, a low percentage (16 percent) of managers and IT staffers surveyed said that their company addressed privacy issues (Surmacz, 2001). Until recently, concerns were also expressed that:

> ... the literature on trust in the context of B2C fails to control for privacy, fails to meaningfully consider it, or even completely overlook it.
> (Davidson, Clarke, Smith, Langford, & Kuo, 2003, p. 344)

Why security and privacy issues remain unresolved after so many years is not really a mystery. Dealing with both problems is an ongoing process rather than a "one-time" solution and is accentuated by a changing environment and little resource allocation. Although the new distributed architecture is far from the vault-setting environment that characterized computing systems of 20 years ago, management mentality and budget allotment are evolving slowly. On the other hand, the e-business economy is growing rapidly (Rohde, 2002) creating a sense of urgency for building trust and gaining respect for privacy. Research groups, both from academia and industry, are looking into enhancement technologies and standards.

To that end, P3P is an emerging standard and technology developed by the World Wide Web Consortium. Simplicity and transparency are two characteristics that make P3P so appealing (Karjoth, Schunter, Van Herreweghen, & Waidner, 2003), in that it provides a simple, automated way for users to gain more control over the use of personal information by the Web sites they visit and, for the Web site developers, it offers a simple means to express their Web site information collection, distribution, and retention policies.

Among the proponents of P3P, IBM is distinguishing itself and experimenting with the development of a P3P policy editor (IBM, 2000). AT&T has a research project dedicated to developing a P3P add-on to Microsoft Internet Explorer (AT&T, 2003), which matches personal preferences of the visitors on privacy issues with the extensible markup language (XML) published privacy policies of the companies.

Despite these efforts, there is little knowledge on what actually P3P is, what its capabilities are, and to what extent it is being adopted by e-commerce organizations. This study is exploratory in nature and aims to provide a brief explanation of P3P both as a new technology and as a standard. We use our empirical data to assess its adoption in the e-commerce environment. The next section presents the background on use of technology for privacy protection. We then examine the role of P3P in privacy protection and a brief history of how it started. The three following sections explore P3P capabilities as privacy protection technology and standard, and the extent it is adopted by interactive companies. We then look at P3P as a competitive advantage and how it is used to gain the end user's trust. We conclude with discussion on the limitations of P3P and its future directions.

Background

Alan Westin (1967, p.7) defines privacy as "the claim of individuals, groups, or institutions to determine for themselves when, how and to what extent information about them is communicated to others." In the e-business realm, the transactions have to balance convenience and personalization with measures of privacy protection (Ashrafi & Kuilboer, 2005). With second-generation e-commerce and ubiquitous e-business, opportunities and threats are intertwined. The use of the Internet for online purchasing, home banking, and information search on a daily basis has increased the amount of information exchange and threatens information privacy, as users are expected to share personal information without knowing the consequences. Internationally, national security laws increasing data retention augment the threats of data exposure.

Concerns about ethical issue have been raised in numerous instances when personal information is propagated intentionally, accidentally, or as the result of a security breach with dear consequences. Aspects of privacy laws addressing the right of individuals on the Internet are covered in many disciplines under ethical discussions, technical notes, or as a societal phenomenon (Stewart-Schwaig, Kane, & Storey, 2005; Tavani & Moor, 2001). Often privacy issues are raised by privacy advocacy groups in the context of invasion of privacy, identity theft, or abuse by private industry or government agencies (Rotenberg, 2003; Solove, Rotenberg, & Schwartz, 2006). Efforts are made trying to assert the rights of individuals or organizations to deny or restrict the access, collection, and use of personal information.

According to Spiekermann, Grossklags, and Berendt (2001, p. 8), "three fundamental approaches have evolved over the past decade addressing the privacy issue: ensuring privacy through law, through self-regulation, or through technical standards." Privacy laws and self-regulation practices have been the subject of an ongoing debate since 1996, when the Internet became widely used as a commercial tool. Many organizations have drafted privacy policies, albeit the effective deployment of these policies is not evident (Benassi, 1999; Clarke, 1999; Reagle & Cranor, 1999; Stewart-Schwaig et al., 2005).

 Privacy laws are futile in a global economy because the protection of privacy within and across national borders has been subject to very disparate laws. The power of regulatory agencies is often undermined or limited with respect to global data. For example, trans-border dataflow between countries is difficult to control. In the U.S., most regulations are targeted at particular groups (such as children) or categories of information (such as medical or financial) and are mostly subject to self-regulation. A number of studies have questioned the virtue of the self-regulation practices (Buchholz & Rosenthal, 2002; Greisiger, 2001). There seems to be a need for technical solutions to balance these political deficiencies.

Privacy enhancing technologies (PET) were developed to integrate privacy measures with technology. However, PET introduced a new level of complexity to online communications. Encryption, anonymizer, spam filter, and cookie cutter, as used by PET, are not necessarily easy to use and defeat the main purpose of using the Internet for convenience. Service providers needed an easy-to-use mechanism to assure users the control of their personal information. In 1996, the Platform for Internet Content Selection (PICS), a precursor of P3P, was established primarily to filter the potentially offensive material, particularly to children (Reidenberg, 1997). In 1997, many of the stakeholders started to realize that ad-hoc treatment of privacy would lead to chaos and that both the industry and the consumer would benefit from standardization. Hence, a need for a standardized and automated technique emerged and led to the development of P3P. In April 2002, the World Wide Web Consortium published the platform for privacy preferences, and later it considered wider constraint and incorporated some of the legal and political privacy protection principles into P3P (Cranor, 2003).

P3P, APPEL, EPAL

P3P is a simple Internet standard aimed at facilitating the exchange of information about Web site privacy policies. It includes a set of XML documents illustrating an organization's priorities regarding customer information (Agrawal, Kiernan, Srikant, & Xu, 2003). It strives to keep the information secure and restrains from sharing it with outside parties. It also provides a way to control the use of personal data collected through Web site visits. In its most primitive form, it consists of a set of rules published on the Web server of the organization providing the user with a machine-readable snapshot of the organization privacy position. On the client side, the latest browsers (e.g., Microsoft IE 6, Firefox) contain new privacy features based on the P3P project. P3P was designed from the start for a machine-to-machine dialogue allowing negotiation and matching of stated policies to consumer preferences. An example of such negotiation would involve the visit of a transaction Web site where the potential buyer will be asked to provide personal information such as address, telephone, and credit-card number, and through his/her purchase will disclose his or her various interests. A P3P Preferences Exchange Language (APPEL 1.0) allows the user to express his preferences in a set of preference rules. This scheme can then be used by the user agent to make automated or semi-automated decisions regarding the acceptability of machine-readable privacy policies from P3P enabled Web sites.

The IBM research teams are trying to capture the essence of P3P and potential extension. Given the global reach of the corporation and the fact that its global customers are subject to disparate privacy regulation, these teams are attempting to leverage research from their Zurich, Tokyo, and Australian laboratories. One of their outputs was the development of the Platform for Enterprise Privacy Practices (E-P3P) defining a fine-grained privacy policy model (Ashley, Hada, Karjoth, & Schunter, 2002). "An enterprise privacy policy often reflects different legal regulations, promises made to customers as well as more restrictive internal practices of the enterprise" (Backes, Pfizmann, & Schunter, 2003, p. 375). As enterprises begin to actively manage and promote privacy, some tools can help formalize the resulting policies. The Enterprise Privacy Authorization Language (EPAL) was designed to this effect. The actual flow of the user information inside or outside the enterprise in congruence with the implicit contract resulting from the displayed privacy policies depends on the efficiency of its enforcement. EPAL defines XML syntax to formulate fine-grained practice subject to enforcement.

P3P is based on the "labeling" or "tagging" schemes for filtering unwanted Web content (Grimm & Rossnagel, 2000). The initial P3P draft indicated that users and providers of an Internet service should negotiate privacy practices on a free and equal basis (Grimm & Rossnagel, 2000). Three communications phases were to supply the foundation for this process.

- **Notice:** Web sites provide the user with conspicuous notice of their privacy practices.

- **Choice:** Web sites offer users choices as to how their personal information is used.

- **Negotiation:** Explicit consent by the user allows the transfer of personal data and the supply of service, or the user would break off the relationship.

P3P was to supply the mechanism to formalize the privacy protection policies and deliver the protocol to transfer personal data. The holding point soon appeared with the complexity inherent in the full implementation. As a result, the first version of P3P was modularized, and only elements pertaining to "notice" and "choice" were retained, postponing negotiations for future implementation and hence leaving the user with a simple take-it-or-leave alternative.

Once the principles were established, the challenge was shifted to choosing an easy-to-use deployment technology. The hypertext markup language was showing its shortcomings, noticeably a lack of flexibility and the ability to express semantics as well as format. As a result, XML was developed with its capability to extend the set of tags and include semantics of specialized use. The working group that started under the aegis of the W3C with the mandate of developing solution to the increasing call for privacy solutions promptly adopted XML to express the policies.

P3P: The Technology

P3P is currently implemented using the extensible markup language. While the bulk of the implementation resides on a visited Web site and is managed by the Web server, P3P will not be effective without a client counterpart. In the initial connection protocol, the negotiation will involve the exchange of a TCP/IP address and will validate connection parameters. Once connected, P3P can enter into action by providing the P3P from the company's point of view (e.g., privacy policies elicited in XML addressing the questions of what information will be collected, what will be done with it, how long it will be kept, how it will be shared, the measures taken to protect it, etc.). The client, through a web browser or a customized application, will automatically match these policies with his/her own preferences and accept or deny the connection and ensuing transactions. This will be possible only if the client is sophisticated enough to be able to express the preferences and configure adequately a P3P-enabled browser to match them. This obviously depends on a chain of events and resources on both sides:

1. The organization expresses its policies through valid P3P (i.e., XML) documents.
2. The organization makes the policies available to Web visitors in a standardized way (i.e., location, format, access).
3. The browser on the client side supports the P3P negotiation.
4. The browser knows where to find the policies.
5. The client is able to express the privacy policies preferences.
6. The negotiation of attributes is successful.
7. The client is able to interpret the results of the interaction offered by the browser.
8. The client has preferences applicable to generic Web sites, otherwise the process will be a resource burden.

Support for P3P in modern Web browsers is present but often limited to processing of regular cookies. For example, Microsoft supports features of P3P client in its Internet Explorer version 6.0, which offers six levels of privacy settings from accepting all cookies to rejecting all cookies, hence leaving other customized policies unattended. For example, sites can track their customers with a Web beacon, e-mails, forms, or other, more pernicious methods, such as supercookies tracking through an un-patched Windows Media Player. Other browsers, such as Mozilla, have privacy settings for cookies, images, and forms as well as related security issues such as pop-up management. All browsers will obtain a snapshot of the visited sites' privacy policies if they exist, are valid, and saved in the known location in P3P conformant format. The principle of a snapshot departs from a resilient assurance of privacy protection. While personally identifiable information has been collected, there is neither a mechanism to bind the data to the privacy policy in force at the time of collection nor an enforcement mechanism for compliance.

P3P: The Standard

In 1997, realizing that ad-hoc treatment of privacy would lead to chaos and that both the industry and the consumer would benefit from standardization, the W3C considered the incorporation of other legal or political privacy protection principles. For example, the Organization for Economic Co-Operation and Development (OECD) guidelines on the protection of privacy since 1981 were used as an underlying substrate for the P3P design. Since the beginning of Internet commercialization, stakeholders have been aware that the rules of information transfer had changed from a consumption of information to a full exchange. Following pressures regarding a lack of privacy protection in Internet data exchange, organizations hosting Web sites started to include privacy policies on the sites without standard context, location, or defined format. This made these humanly readable documents virtually unusable. Visitors had difficulty understanding, matching, and comparing differing policies, leading to equally difficult avenues for data collection for the purpose of customer relationship management or mass customization, as there were increasing risks of litigation or negative publicity about abuse of personal data in an equivocal non-regulated environment. This led to the design of an agent-based system based on XML aimed at standardizing and automating the privacy preferences negotiation process.

The P3P standard is endorsed by the W3C and has a number of prominent stakeholders, such as IBM, Microsoft, and AT&T. They work concurrently on the next release of P3P (1.1) and an associated standard effort on a P3P preference exchange language (APPEL) aimed at providing the users with a mechanism to encode their preferences about privacy. The P3P standard is currently in its first inception. With version 1.0 in effect since April 2002, currently the W3C has the next version (1.1) published as a working draft. It includes features left out of the first release, such as a mechanism to allow sites to offer a choice of P3P policies to visitors; a mechanism to allow visitors (through their user agents) to explicitly agree to a P3P policy; mechanisms to allow for non-repudiation of agreements between visitors and Web sites; and a mechanism to allow user agents to transfer user data to services.

P3P: The Adoption

The platform for privacy preferences is emerging as a standard way for Web sites to encode their privacy policies (Cranor, 2002). By mid-March 2002, just before the publication of P3P first recommendation by the W3C, Jupiter's Media Metrix reported that from the top 10 Web sites with the highest traffic, six Web sites had adopted P3P. This led to the erroneous assumption that widespread adoption would follow after the passage of the recommendation by W3C. A study published by Ernst and Young in September 2003, six months after the recommendation by W3C, found only 24 percent of the top 100 sites posting a P3P policy. A follow-up study of 500 sites by Ernst and Young in January 2003 revealed that 18 percent had adopted P3P.

Our study conducted in June of 2003 involved 500 interactive companies and analyzed the rate of the diffusion of P3P practices one year after the initial standard was published. We checked the Web sites of 500 companies that were listed as the top 500 interactive compa-

Table 1. Percentage of companies with a published privacy policy on their Web sites

Have published privacy policy on their Web site		Do not have published privacy policy on their Web site		Out of online business	
67%		25%		8%	
Internet-only	37%	Internet-only	%10	Internet-only/assume out of business	5%
Both	30%	Both	%15	Both	3%

nies by *Interactive Week Magazine,* published in its November 2000 issue. The listing was based on online sales over four quarters ending on June 30th, 2000, included public and private companies in business at the end of June 2000, and was compiled in July with a survey conducted by Advantage Business Research. The pollster sent out questionnaires to more than 40,000 e-commerce executives, interactive managers, chief executive officers, and chief information officers. A team at PricewaterhouseCoopers helped to retrieve online sales figures. The companies were asked questions about their total revenue, online revenue, and their type of business. Information on nearly 1,500 companies was compiled and ranked based upon their online revenue, and the top 500 companies were published in the November issue. We were fortunate that this listing also included the Web sites for the 500 top companies, which we used as the starting point for our study. In the spring of 2002, we visited these 500 Web sites and conducted our research to find out what percentage of the top 500 companies had privacy policies published on their Web sites. In the fall of 2002, we visited the Web sites again to check how many of the top 500 companies still had an online presence. Table 1 summarizes this information.

Two-thirds of the companies examined had privacy policies published on their Web sites; 37 percent had P3P and were engaged only in online trade, while 30 percent had P3P and were conducting business both online and off-line (brick-and-mortar). Table 1 also shows that less than one-third did not have privacy policies published with 10 percent consisting

Table 2. Comparison of P3P adoption studies

Study by	Date	Sample Size	% that adopted P3P
Jupiter Media Metrix	March 2002	10	60
Ernst & Young	September 2002	100	24
Ernst &Young	January 2003	500	18
Our Study	June 2003	500	13

Table 3. Adoption of P3P by company size

Size of company measured by their revenue	Top 100	101-200	201-300	301-400	401-500
Percentage of companies adopting P3P	26%	16%	13%	9%	1%

of companies who were only online and 15 percent consisting of companies who had online and off-line business. Our findings are compatible with of those by the Freedom Foundation that found 77 percent of highly visited Web sites posted a privacy policy (Jensen & Potts, 2004).

In the spring of 2003, we revisited these 500 Web sites and conducted our follow-up research to find out what percentage of the top 500 companies had implemented P3P. We were also interested to find out if company size (based on total revenue) was a factor influencing the implementation P3P. We found that only 13 percent of top 500 interactive companies had adopted P3P as of June 2003. Table 2 compares the results of our study to the results of four previous studies.

These numbers show a decline in the rate of adoption by time and as the sample size increases. A cursory analysis of the study conducted by Jupiter Media Metrix points out that one possible reason for the high rate of P3P adoptions could have been be due to the fact that their small sample included large companies such as Yahoo, MSN, Lycos, and some industry P3P sponsors such as IBM, ATT, and Microsoft. These may have biased the results to a high adoption rate of 60 percent.

Given the tendencies for these large conglomerates to adopt P3P, we decided to stratify our results along company size (overall revenues) and see if the results would be different. Table 3 summarizes these results:

Our results suggest that the rate of adoption for the 100 largest companies was the highest (26 percent) and the rate declined as the company size decreased. For companies in the 101-200 cluster, the adoption rate was 16 percent; for those in the 201-300 range, the adoption rate was 13 percent; and for companies in the 301-400 cluster, the adoption rate was 9 percent. Only 1 percent of the final 100 adopted P3P. This decline can be attributed to the organizational structure and resource levels that allow the larger organizations to experiment with new technology and be more responsive to consumer concerns whereas smaller companies lag behind in adopting P3P and perhaps have privacy as a low item on their priority list.

P3P: As a Competitive Advantage

Organizations are generally adopting technology to gain a competitive advantage. As Narayanan (2001, p. 119) points out, "technology can often be a critically important element in the competitive battles between firms." Among the firms adopting P3P, a perceived advantage would be to enhance the consumers' trust. As Culnan and Armstrong (1999) suggested, one goal of offering high-quality service is to keep customers coming back and to attract new ones through positive word of mouth. Privacy issues are becoming a major concern of the customers (Reagle & Cranor, 1999) and an important aspect of quality service. Hence, an easy-to-use device intended to assure the customer that the organization has a system to protect their privacy may characterize the quality service to which Culnan alludes. AT&T privacy bird, a utility tool that evaluates the degree of equivalence between consumers' concerns and companies' privacy policies, seems to be a move in the right direction. AT& T privacy bird provides the end-user with a tool warning of discrepancy between privacy issues important to them versus those addressed by the company.

The AT&T privacy bird user agent comes with three standard privacy settings: high, medium, and low. We ran our P3P policy evaluator over APPEL rule sets representing each of these three settings. A policy that matches the preferences expressed in a rule set receives a "green bird" from the policy evaluator, while a policy that does not match the preferences expressed in a rule receives a "red bird." The three rule sets encode the following preferences:

- **Low:** Trigger a red bird at sites that collect health or medical information and share it with other companies or use it for analysis, marketing, or to make decisions that may affect what content or ads the user sees. Also trigger a red bird at sites that engage in marketing but do not provide a way to opt-out.

- **Medium:** Same as low, plus trigger a red bird at sites that share personally identifiable information, financial information, or purchase information with other companies. Also trigger a red bird at sites that collect personally identified data but provide no access provisions.

- **High:** Same as medium, plus trigger a red bird at sites that share any personal information (including non-identified information) with other companies or use it to determine the user's habits, interests, or other characteristics. Also trigger a red bird at sites that may contact users for marketing or use financial or purchase information for analysis, marketing, or to make decisions that may affect what content or ads the user sees.

Privacy preferences are divided into four categories: health or medical, financial or purchase, personally identified information, and non-personally identified information, each of which has a set of warning rules. A customer, using the privacy bird, has the option to choose low, medium, high, or customized levels of privacy protection. Table 4 (AT&T, 2003) depicts the privacy preferences categories, rules within each category, and the four levels of protection. The table demonstrates that, for example, a consumer choosing the low level will be protected against three rules as marked under the column "low." If the Web site does not accommodate three privacy issues check-marked in the table under column heading "low," a warning signal will be given. It is then up to the customer to decide whether to continue with his/her transaction on this Web site or simply leave and navigate to another Web site that will provide the same service or product with a higher privacy protection. A consumer with medium-level desire to protect her/his privacy would select medium level protection where six privacy issues are check marked in table under column heading "medium." Consumers with high-level desire for protection could choose high-level protection, where 12 privacy issues are marked under the "high" column. The tool also offers the choice of customizing

Table 4. AT&T privacy categories and rules

Privacy preferences categories and rules	Low	Medium	High	Customized
Health or medical information				
Warn me at Web sites that use my health or medical information for analysis, marketing, or to make decisions that may affect what content or ads I see, and so forth	X	X	X	
Warn me at Web sites that use my health or medical information to share with other companies (other than those helping the Web site provide services to me)	X	X	X	
Financial or purchase information				
Warn me at Web sites that use my financial information or information about my purchases for analysis, marketing, or to make decisions that may affect what content or ads I see, and so forth			X	
Warn me at Web sites that use my financial information or information about my purchases to share with other companies (other than those helping the Web site provide services to me)		X	X	
Personally identified information				
Warn me at Web sites that may contact me to interest me in other services or products via telephone			X	
Warn me at Web sites that may contact me to interest me in other services or products via other means (e-mail, postal mail, etc.)			X	
Warn me at Web sites that may contact me to interest me in other services or products and do not allow me to remove myself from marketing/mailing lists	X	X	X	
Warn me at Web sites that use information that personally identifies me to determine my habits, interests, or other characteristics			X	
Warn me at Web sites that use information that personally identifies me to share with other companies (other than those helping the Web site provide services to me)		X	X	
Warn me at Web sites that do not allow me to find out what data they have about me		X	X	
Non-personally identified information				
Warn me at Web sites that use my non-personally identifiable information to determine my habits, interests, or other characteristics			X	
Warn me at Web sites that use my non-personally identifiable information to share with other companies (other than those helping the Web site provide services to me)			X	

which issues are important to the consumer and check marks them under "custom" column. The biggest advantage of this tool is its ability to accommodate consumers' level of desire to protect their personal information.

There is a trade off between the availability of the services or products that provide the convenience of online transactions and protecting consumer information. Consumers who want to protect all health, financial, personal, and non-personal information may not find many companies with a Web site that promises such protection. Other consumers may ask for some protection against sensitive information such as those check-marked under the "medium" column. We chose the average consumer as the middle-of-the-road person who wants some privacy protection but is not overly sensitive.

To test what percentage of companies will accommodate such users, we visited those companies from the top 500 that have P3P policies. Four results were observed: sites with "positive image results" are those that accommodated six or more criteria for medium privacy protection; sites with "warning results" are those that accommodated some but not all six criteria; sites with negative P3P policies were those that had P3P policies but issue a negative report; and finally sites with "non-functioning" policies were those that have P3P policies, but did not respond to the request of matching privacy bird most likely due to syntax error or non-standard location. The results of the visits are outlined in Table 5 stratified by size.

Table 5 indicates that on average, very small percentages (9 sites among 500) of companies have P3P satisfactory to a pragmatic user, and higher numbers have negative P3P policies potentially detrimental to their customers. Our findings support the earlier data analysis (Liu & Arnett, 2001) that compared the privacy policies of large versus small companies using the Fortune 500 and the Inc. 500 listings. Their conclusions that less than 15% of the Inc. 500 Web sites even contained a privacy policy statement were very disappointing and remain so. Larger companies do better in term of adoption but do not project a trust-enhancing image. The companies in the lowest tier are absolutely non-compliant. Generally the organization could reap the benefits from positive positioning, but surprisingly implementations are less than optimal. To the well-intentioned organization that embarked on the adoption of P3P without full understanding of the business and legal implications, a word of advice would be to get a book on the subject and experiment on a non-production server. Validating the

Table 5. Privacy preference match to P3P adopting sites (using AT&T privacy bird)

	First 100	101-200	201-300	301-400	401-500
Sites with positive image results	11.54%	12.50%	15.38%	22.22%	0.00%
Sites with warning results	15.38%	12.50%	15.38%	11.11%	100.00%
Sites with negative P3P policies	69.23%	68.75%	53.85%	22.22%	0.00%
Proportion of sites with non-functioning policies	3.85%	6.25%	15.38%	44.44%	0.00%

Note that absolute numbers are higher for the largest companies, as indicated before.

privacy policies through the W3C validator and AT&T privacy bird make a smooth transition to the technology.

Implementation of Privacy Policy

P3P is designed to allow Web sites to express their privacy policies in machine-readable format to allow users to automatically make decisions about their privacy preferences. Although on a technological level P3P has been successful, protecting users' privacy involves much more; privacy policies are either absent, incomplete, or lack clarity. Anton, Earp, He, Stuffebeam, Bolchini, and Jensen (2004) have criticized privacy policies written in a language well above the understanding of the ordinary Web surfer. Of the 40 policies they examined, 8 required the equivalent of high school education, 13 required the equivalent of some college education, 12 required 14 to 16 years of schooling, and the remaining 7 required the equivalent of a postgraduate education. They concluded that the ambiguity of the policies leads visitors to distrust or to be misled by the policies.

The implementation of privacy policies is also hindered by the lack of the requirement of active users. Today, making full use of P3P involves downloading a tool like the AT&T privacy bird and setting privacy preferences within the program. This is an unrealistic expectation from the users, as they are required to learn about and set their P3P preferences. A group at IBM T.J. Watson Research Center (Karat, Brodie, & Karat, 2006) advocates the need for a policy workbench, where the user is able to create and transform natural language policies into machine-readable code. Such an initiative will in the future extend the privacy choice dimension to the point that the user can set his/her preferences and be able to understand and verify who has access to their personal information and for what purposes it will be used.

Emerging Legislation

In the U.S., a number of states have started to take actions to remedy the lack of enforcing security and privacy policies and convey to organizations the need to preserve their customers' personally identifiable data. For example, the California SB 1386, operative July 2003, requires all public and private organizations that own or licenses personal computerized data to disclose any breach of security of the data to the owner of the data. For example, in 2005 alone, an estimated 52 millions occurrences of leaks have been reported with data elements useful to identity thieves, such as Social Security numbers, account numbers, and driver's license numbers (PRC, 2006). Under the new laws passed in many states, these occurrences have to be reported. The law also requires a business to take all reasonable steps to destroy customers' records containing personal information when the business will no longer retain those records.

As of January 2006, three more states, Illinois, Louisiana, and New Jersey, are adding laws on the breach of personal information (Vijayan, 2006). As a result, companies are struggling to keep up with a patchwork of states' laws related to data privacy and information security.

As with existing statutes in more than 20 states, these new laws ascertain the consequences that organizations will face in the event of a security breach involving the compromise of personal data about their customers. Overall the breach of personal information under the new laws is becoming costly; direct costs such as free credit report monitoring as compensation and indirect costs such as potential loss of the customers may parallel or even exceed the possible fine imposed for state laws. Although emerging legislations should encourage maintaining personal privacy, they may also add complexity by enforcing different laws for doing business online in different states. As a result of the numerous privacy breaches that occurred during 2005 and complaints for an increasing financial burden from compliance with numerous state laws, a number of bills have been introduced in the Senate to provide:

- Greater protection of and control over the use of key personal data such as Social Security numbers and financial account information.
- Increased penalties for breaches and facilitating identity theft.
- A nationwide standard for notifying consumers when their personal information has been breached.

Conclusion

Like many other innovations in e-commerce, P3P is in its infancy. Successful adoption of P3P and its likely descendants is highly dependent on the degree, stability, and wisdom of administrative sponsorship and on the integration of technical, legal, and market-driven strategies. In the case of P3P, the usefulness of the technology has thus far eluded both technical and top management. The latest survey by Ernst & Young, conducted in May 2004 (after our study) shows an increase in adoption of P3P: the overall adoption in the top 100 has increased to 33% and in the 500 to 24%. Yet these increases compared to the level of concern expressed by the users are minimal. The privacy protection advocate groups such as the Electronic Privacy Information Center (EPIC) have not endorsed P3P, calling it Pretty Poor Privacy. The Center for Democracy and Privacy claims that P3P is not a panacea for privacy, but it does represent an important opportunity to make progress in building greater privacy protections in the Web experience of the average user.

Early adopters and industry proponents have jumped onboard the P3P bandwagon, but as our study reveals, the majority and the mainstream online stakeholders have yet to endorse the W3C recommendation, either waiting for the next iteration, distrusting the proponents of the technology, or merely doubting the business value of the solution.

References

Acquisti, A., & Grossklags, J. (2005). Privacy and rationality in individual decision making. *IEEE Security & Privacy, 3*(1), 26-33.

Agrawal, R., Kiernan, J., Srikant, R., & Xu, Y. (2003, March 2003). Implementing P3P using database technology. In *Proceedings of the 19ᵗʰ International Conference on Data Engineering,* Bangalore, India.

Anton, A.I., Earp, J. B., He, Q., Stuffebeam, W., Bolchini, D., & Jensen, C. (2004) Financial privacy policies and the need for standardization. *IEEE Security & Privacy, 2*(2), 36-45.

Ashley, P., Hada, S., Karjoth, G., & Schunter, M. (2002, November 21). E-P3P privacy policies and privacy authorization. In *Proceedings of the ACM Workshop on Privacy in the Electronic Society,* Washington, DC.

Ashrafi, N., & Kuilboer, J. P. (2005). Online privacy policies: an empirical perspective on self-regulatory practices. *Journal of Electronic Commerce in Organizations, 3*(4), 61-74.

AT&T. (2003). *AT&T privacy bird.* Retrieved October 2003 from http://privacybird.com

Azmi, I. M. (2002). E-commerce and privacy issues: An analysis of the personal data protection bill. *International Review of Law, Computers and Technology, 16*(3), 317-330.

Backes, M., Pfizmann, B., & Schunter, M. (2003). A toolkit for managing enterprise privacy policies. In *Proceedings 8ᵗʰ European Symposium on Research in Computer Security,* Gjovik, Norway.

Benassi, P. (1999). TRUSTe: an online privacy seal program. *Communications of the ACM, 42*(2), 56-59.

Berendt, B., Günther, O., & Spiekerman, S. (2005). Privacy in e-commerce: Stated preferences vs. actual behavior. *Communications of the ACM, 48*(4), 101-106.

Buchholz, R. A., & Rosenthal, S. B. (2002). Internet privacy: Individual rights and the common good. *S.A.M Advanced Management Journal, 67*(1), 34-40.

Clarke, R. (1999). Internet privacy concerns confirm the case for intervention. *Communications of the ACM, 42*(2), 60-67.

Cranor, L. F. (2002). *Web privacy with P3P.* Sebastopol, CA: O'Reilly & Associates.

Cranor, L. F. (2003). P3P: making privacy policies more useful. *IEEE Security & Privacy. 1*(6), 50-55.

Culnan, M. J., & Amstrong, P. K. (1999). Information privacy concerns, procedural fairness, and impersonal trust. An empirical investigation. *Organization Science, 10*(1), 104-114.

Davidson, R. M., Clarke, R., Smith, H. J., Langford, D., & Kuo, B. (2003). Information privacy in a globally networked society: implication for IS research. *Communications of the Association for Information Systems. 12*(2003), 341-365.

Delaney, E. M., Goldstein, C. E., Gutterman, J., & Wagner, S. N. (2003). Automated computer privacy preferences slowly gain popularity. *Intellectual Property & Technology Law Journal, 15*(8), 17.

Ernst & Young P3P dashboard project. (2003). Retrieved October 2003 from http://www. ey.com/GLOBAL/content.nsf/US/AABS_-_TSRS_-_Library

Ernst & Young P3P dashboard project. (2004). Retrieved September, 2004, http:// www.ey.com/global/download.nsf/US/P3P_Dashboard_-_May_2004/$file/ E&YP3PDashboardMay2004.pdf

Greisiger, M. (2001). Securing privacy. *Risk Management, 48*(10), 14-19.

Grimm, R., & Rossnagel, A. (2000, October 30-November 4). *Can P3P help to protect privacy worldwide.* Proceedings of ACM Multimedia Workshop, Los Angeles, CA.

Haller, S. C. (2002). Privacy: What every manager should know. *The Information Management Journal, 36*(3), 33-44.

Hormozi, A. M. (2005). Cookies and privacy. *Information Systems Security, 13*(6), 51-59.

IBM. (2000). *P3P policy editor.* Retrieved October 2003 from http://www.alphaworks.ibm. com/tech/p3peditor

Jensen, C., & Potts, C. (2004). Privacy policies as decision-making tools: An evaluation of online privacy notices. In *Proceedings of CHI 2004,* Vienna, Austria.

Karat, C. M., Brodie, C., & Karat, J. (2006). Usable privacy and security for personal information management. *Communications of the ACM, 49*(1), 56-57.

Karjoth, G., Schunter, M., Van Herreweghen, E., & Waidner, M. (2003). Amending P3P for clearer privacy promises. In *Proceedings of the 14th International Workshop on Database and Expert Systems Applications: 2nd Int'l Workshop on Trust and privacy in Digital Business (TrustBus),* Prague, Czech Republic.

Liu, C., & Arnett, K. P. (2001). WWW privacy policies in large and small business enterprises: Do they ease privacy concerns? In *Proceedings of Seventh Americas Conference on Information Systems.* Boston.

Moor, J. H. (1997). Towards a theory of privacy in the information age. *Computers and Society, 27*(3), 27-32.

Narayanan, V. K. (2001). *Managing technology and innovation for competitive advantage.* NJ: Prentice-Hall.

Palen, L., & Dourish, P. (2003, April 5-10). Unpacking "privacy" for a networked world. In *Proceedings of CHI 2003: New Horizons,* Ft. Lauderdale, FL.

PRC (2006). *A chronology of data breaches reported since the ChoicePoint incident.* Retrieved January 3, 2006, from www.privacyrights.org

Ranganathan, C., & Ganapathy, S. (2002). Key dimensions of business-to-consumer Web sites. *Information & Management, 39,* 457-465.

Reagle, J., & Cranor, L.F. (1999). The platform for privacy preferences. *Communications of the ACM, 42*(2), 48-55.

Regan, P. (2003). Privacy and commercial use of personal data: Policy developments in the United States. *Journal of Contingencies and Crisis Management, 11*(1), 12-18.

Reidenberg, J. R. (1997). The use of technology to assure Internet privacy: adapting labels and filters for data protection. *Lex Electronica 3*(2). Retrieved January 25, 2006, from http://lex-electronica.org/articles/v3-2/reidenbe.html

Roberts, P. F. (2005). Data privacy issues to persist next year. *Eweek, 18*. Retrieved December 19, 2005, from http://www.eweek.com/article2/0,1895,1902909,00.asp

Rohde, L. (2002, November 21). UN: worldwide use of Internet, e-commerce still growing. *IDG News Service*. Retrieved on October 2, 2006, from http://www.computerworld.com/action/article.do?command=viewArticleBasic&articleId=76107

Rotenberg, M. (2003). *The privacy law Sourcebook 2003: United States law, international law, and recent developments*. Washington DC: Electronic Privacy Information Center.

Sanzaro K., & Keating, D. (2000). *Online privacy policies and practices under fire*. Retrieved January 25, 2006, from http://www.gigalaw.com/articles/2000-all/sanzaro-2000-03-all.html

The California Security Breach Information Act *(SB 1386)*.(2002). Senate Bill 1386 Peace. Personal information: Privacy.

Singer, L., Keck, R., Buffington, J., & Poulos, B. (2001). *Roundtable discussion: Internet privacy and the law*. Retrieved from http://www.gigalaw.com/articles/2001-all/rountable-privacy-2001-04-all.%html

Smith, H. J. (2001). Information privacy and marketing: what the U.S. should (and shouldn't) learn from Europe. *California Management Review, 43*(2), 8-33.

Soloman, H. (2002). Privacy policies under fire: Businesses that don't adopt P3P standard will suffer: Commissioner. *Computing Canada, 28*(14):1

Solove, D. Rotenberg, M., & Schwartz, P. M. (2006). *Information privacy law* (2nd ed.). NY: Aspen.

Spiekermann, S. Grossklags, J., & Berendt, B. (2001, October 14-17). E-privacy in 2nd generation e-commerce: privacy preferences versus actual behavior. In *Proceedings of ACM Conference on Electronic Commerce (EC'01)*, Tampa, FL.

Stewart-Schwaig K., Kane, G. C., & Storey, V. C. (2005). Privacy, fair information practices and the Fortune 500: The virtual reality of compliance. *The DATA BASE for Advances in Information Systems, 36*(1), 49-63.

Surmacz, J. (2001, June 20). Privacy a low priority. *CSO Magazine*. Retrieved on October 2, 2006 from http://csoonline.com/metrics/viewmetric.cfm?id=227

Tavani, H. T., & Moor, J. H. (2001). Privacy protection, control of information, and privacy-enhancing technologies. *Computers and Society, 29*(4), 6-11.

Teltzrow, M., & Kobsa, A. (2004, January 30-31). Communication of privacy and personalization in e-business. In *Proceedings of the Workshop "WHOLES: A Multiple View of Individual Privacy in a Network World*. Stockholm, Sweden.

Vijayan, J. (2006, January 6). Three more states add laws on data breach. *Computerworld, 40*(2), 8.

W3C (2003). *P3P*. Retrieved June 2003 from http://www.w3.org/P3P/

Westin, A. R. (1967). *Privacy and freedom*. New York: Atheneum.

World Wide Web Consortium. *Testsuite for the platform for privacy preferences (P3P) project*. Retrieved on September 22, 2006 from: http://p3ptest-1.w3.org/

Chapter XVI

Semi-Automatic Derivation and Application of Personal Privacy Policies[1]

George Yee, National Research Council, Canada

Larry Korba, National Research Council, Canada

Abstract

The recent fast growth of the Internet has been accompanied by a similarly fast growth in the availability of Internet e-business services (e.g., electronic book seller service, electronic stock transaction service). This proliferation of e-business services has in turn fueled the need to protect the personal privacy of e-business users or consumers. We propose a privacy policy approach to protecting personal privacy. However, it is evident that the derivation of a personal privacy policy must be as easy as possible for the consumer. In this chapter, we define the content of personal privacy policies using privacy principles that have been enacted into legislation. We then present two semi-automated approaches for the derivation of personal privacy policies. The first approach makes use of accepted privacy rules obtained through community consensus (from research and/or surveys). The second approach makes use of privacy policies already existing in a peer-to-peer community. We conclude the chapter by explaining how personal privacy policies can be applied in e-business to protect consumer privacy.

Introduction

The rapid growth of the Internet has been accompanied by a similarly rapid growth in e-business services targeting consumers. E-business services (or "e-services;" we use these terms interchangeably) are available for banking, shopping, stock investing, and healthcare, to name a few. However, each of these services requires a consumer's personal information in one form or another. This leads to concerns over privacy.

In order for e-business services to be successful, privacy must be protected. In a recent U.S. study by MasterCard International, 60% of respondents were concerned with the privacy of transmitted data (Greer & Murtaza, 2004). An effective and flexible way of protecting privacy is to manage it using privacy policies. In this approach, each provider of an e-service has a privacy policy specifying the private information required for that e-service. Similarly, each consumer of an e-service has a privacy policy specifying the private information he or she is willing to share for the e-service. Prior to the activation of an e-service, the consumer and provider of the e-service exchange privacy policies. The service is only activated if the policies are compatible (we will define what "compatible" means below). Where the privacy policy of an e-service consumer conflicts with the privacy policy of an e-service provider, we have advocated a negotiations approach to resolve the conflict (Yee & Korba, 2003a, 2003b). However, where do these privacy policies come from? Providers in general have sufficient resources to come up with their privacy policies. Consumers, on the other hand, need help in formulating privacy policies. In addition, the creation of such policies needs to be as easy as possible or consumers would simply avoid using them. Existing privacy specification languages such as platform for privacy preferences (P3P) and A P3P Preferences Exchange Language (APPEL) (W3C APPEL, 2002; W3C Platform, 2002) that are extensible markup language (XML)-based are far too complicated for the average Internet user to understand. Understanding or changing a privacy policy expressed in these languages effectively requires knowing how to program. What is needed is an easy, semi-automated way of deriving a personal privacy policy. In this chapter, we present two semi-automated approaches for obtaining personal privacy policies for consumers and explain how the policies are used to protect consumer privacy. This chapter is an updated and extended version of Yee and Korba (2005).

The specification of privacy policy content section examines the specification of privacy policies by identifying some attributes of private information collection. The semi-automated derivation of personal privacy policies section shows how personal privacy policies can be semi-automatically generated. The privacy management model section presents our privacy management model, which explains how personal privacy policies can be used to protect consumer privacy. The discussion and related work section discusses our approaches and presents related work. The chapter ends with conclusions and future research.

The Specification of Privacy Policy Content

Privacy Legislation and Directives

In Canada, privacy legislation is enacted in the Personal Information Protection and Electronic Documents Act (PIPEDA) (Department of Justice, 2003) and is based on the Canadian
Standards Association's Model Code for the Protection of Personal Information (Canadian
Standards Association, 2003) recognized as a national standard in 1996. This code consists
of 10 Privacy Principles (Canadian Standards Association, 2003) that, for convenience, we
label as CSAPP. Data privacy in the European Union is governed by a very comprehensive
set of regulations called the Data Protection Directive (European Union, 1995). In the United
States, privacy protection is achieved through a patchwork of legislation at the federal and
state levels. Privacy legislation is largely sector-based (Banisar, 1999).

Table 1. CSAPP: The 10 privacy principles from the Canadian Standards Association

Principle	Description
1. Accountability	An organization is responsible for personal information under its control and shall designate an individual or individuals accountable for the organization's compliance with the privacy principles.
2. Identifying purposes	The purposes for which personal information is collected shall be identified by the organization at or before the time the information is collected.
3. Consent	The knowledge and consent of the individual are required for the collection, use, or disclosure of personal information, except when inappropriate.
4. Limiting collection	The collection of personal information shall be limited to that which is necessary for the purposes identified by the organization. Information shall be collected by fair and lawful means.
5. Limiting use, disclosure, and retention	Personal information shall not be used or disclosed for purposes other than those for which it was collected, except with the consent of the individual or as required by the law. In addition, personal information shall be retained only as long as necessary for fulfillment of those purposes.
6. Accuracy	Personal information shall be as accurate, complete, and up-to-date as is necessary for the purposes for which it is to be used.
7. Safeguards	Security safeguards appropriate to the sensitivity of the information shall be used to protect personal information.
8. Openness	An organization shall make readily available to individuals specific information about its policies and practices relating to the management of personal information.
9. Individual access	Upon request, an individual shall be informed of the existence, use and disclosure of his or her personal information and shall be given access to that information. An individual shall be able to challenge the accuracy and completeness of the information and have it amended as appropriate.
10. Challenging compliance	An individual shall be able to address a challenge concerning compliance with the above principles to the designated individual or individuals accountable for the organization's compliance.

Requirements from Privacy Principles

In this section, we identify some attributes of private information collection or personally identifiable information (PII) collection using CSAPP as a guide. We will then apply the attributes to the specification of privacy policy contents. Note that we use "private information" and "PII" interchangeably. We use CSAPP because it is representative of privacy legislation in other countries (e.g., European Union, Australia) and has withstood the test of time, originating in 1996. In addition, CSAPP is representative of the Fair Information Practices, a set of standards balancing the information needs of the business with the privacy needs of the individual (Schwaig, Kane, & Storey, 2005). Table 1 shows CSAPP.

In Table 1, we interpret "organization" as "provider" and "individual" as "consumer." In the following, we use CSAPP.n to denote Principle n of CSAPP. Principle CSAPP.2 implies that there could be different providers requesting the information, thus implying a *collector* attribute. Principle CSAPP.4 implies that there is a *what* attribute, for example, what private information is being collected. Principles CSAPP.2, CSAPP.4, and CSAPP.5 state that there are *purposes* for which the private information is being collected. Principles CSAPP.3, CSAPP.5, and CSAPP.9 imply that the private information can be disclosed to other parties, giving a *disclose-to* attribute. Principle CSAPP.5 implies a *retention time* attribute for the retention of private information. Thus, from the CSAPP we derive five attributes of private information collection: *collector*, *what*, *purposes*, *retention time*, and *disclose-to*.

The privacy principles also prescribe certain operational requirements that must be satisfied between provider and consumer, such as identifying purpose and consent. Our service model and the exchange of privacy policies automatically satisfy some of these requirements, namely principles CSAPP.2, CSAPP.3, and CSAPP.8. The satisfaction of the remaining operational requirements depends on compliance mechanisms (principles CSAPP.1, CSAPP.4, CSAPP.5, CSAPP.6, CSAPP.9, and CSAPP.10) and security mechanisms (Principle CSAPP.7).

Figure 1. Example consumer personal privacy policies

Policy use: E-learning *Owner*: Alice Consumer *Proxy*: No *Valid*: unlimited	*Policy use*: Bookseller *Owner*: Alice Consumer *Proxy*: No *Valid*: June 2005	*Policy use*: Medical Help *Owner*: Alice Consumer *Proxy*: No *Valid*: July 2005
Collector: Any *What:* name, address, tel *Purposes:* identification *Retention time:* unlimited *Disclose-to*: none	*Collector:* Any *What:* name, address, tel *Purposes:* identification *Retention time:* unlimited *Disclose-To*: none	*Collector:* Any *What:* name, address, tel *Purposes:* contact *Retention time:* unlimited *Disclose-to*: pharmacy
Collector: Any *What:* Course marks *Purposes:* Records *Retention time:* 2 years *Disclose-to*: none		*Collector:* Dr. A. Smith *What:* medical condition *Purposes:* treatment *Retention time:* unlimited *Disclose-to*: pharmacy

Privacy Policy Specification

Based on the above exploration, the contents of a privacy policy should, for each item of PII, identify (a) *collector* – who wishes to collect the information, (b) *what* – the nature of the information; (c) *purposes* – the purposes for which the information is being collected; (d) *retention time* – the amount of time for the provider to keep the information; and (e) *disclose-to* – the parties to whom the information will be disclosed. Figure 1 gives three examples of consumer personal privacy policies for use with an e-learning provider: an online bookseller, and an online medical help clinic. The *policy use* field indicates the type of online service for which the policy will be used. For a consumer policy, the *proxy* field holds the name of the proxy if a proxy is employed to provide the information; otherwise, this field has the default value of "no." For a provider policy, the *proxy* field has a default value of "yes," indicating that the consumer can use a proxy to provide the information; otherwise, this field has the value "no." Since a privacy policy may change over time, we have a *valid* field to hold the time period during which the policy is valid. Figure 2 gives examples of provider privacy policies corresponding to the personal privacy policies of Figure 1.

A privacy policy thus consists of "header" information (policy use, owner, proxy, valid) together with one or more 5-tuples or privacy rules:

<collector, what, purposes, retention time, disclose-to>

where each 5-tuple or rule represents an item of private information and the conditions under which the information may be shared. For example, in Figure 1, the personal policy for e-learning has a header (top portion) plus two rules (bottom portion); the personal policy for bookseller only has one rule.

Semi-Automated Derivation of Personal Privacy Policies

A semi-automated derivation of a personal privacy policy is the use of mechanisms (described below) that may be semi-automated to obtain a set of privacy rules for a particular policy use. We present two approaches for such derivations. The first approach relies on third-party surveys of user perceptions of data privacy (Figure 3). The second approach is based on retrieval from a community of peers.

Derivation through Third-Party Surveys

a.   A policy provider makes use of third-party surveys performed on a regular basis, as well as those published in research literature to obtain user privacy sensitivity levels (PSLs) or perceptions of the level of privacy for various combinations of <what,

purposes, retention time> in provider policy rules. We call <what, purposes, retention time> a WPR for short. This gives a range of PSLs for different WPRs in different provider policies. This step may be expressed mathematically as follows:

Let p_i represent a WPR from a provider policy, I represent the set of p_i over all provider policies, $f_{k,i}$ represent the privacy sensitivity function of person k to sharing p_t with a service provider. We restrict $f_{k,i}$ to an integer value in a standard interval [M,N], that is, $M \leq f_{k,i} \leq N$ for integers M, N (e.g., M=1, N=5). Then the PSLs $s_{k,i}$ are obtained as:

$$s_{k,i} = f_{k,i}(p_i) \ \forall k \in K, \ i \in I$$

where K is the set of consumers interested in the provider's services. This equation models a person making a choice of what PSL to assign a particular p_i.

b. Corresponding to a service provider's privacy policy (which specifies the privacy rules required), a *policy provider* (or a software application used by the policy provider) consolidates the PSLs from (a) such that the WPRs are selectable by a single-value privacy level from a "privacy slider" for each service provider policy. There are different ways to do this consolidation. One way is to assign a WPR the median of its PSL range as its privacy level (illustrated below). The outcome of this process is a set of consumer privacy rules (expressed using a policy language such as APPEL), ranked by privacy level, for different providers and with the *collector* and *disclosed-to* fields as "any" and "none," respectively (the consumer can change these fields later if desired). This step may be expressed mathematically using the notation introduced in (a) as follows:

Let P represent a provider's privacy policy. Then for each WPR $p_i \in P$, we have from (a) a set of PSLs: $S_j(P) = \{s_{k,i} \mid p_i \in P, \ \forall k \in K\}$. Our goal is to map $S_j(P)$ to a single privacy level from a privacy slider. Let g be such a mapping. Then this step performs the mapping $g(S_j(P)) = n$, where n is the privacy slider value. The mapping g can be "take the median of" (illustrated below) or "take the average of," for example. We have assumed that the range of slider values is the same as [M,N] in (a). If this is not the case, g would need to incorporate normalization to the range of slider values.

c. Consumers obtain online from the policy provider the privacy rules that make up whole policies. They do this by first specifying the provider for which a consumer privacy policy is required. The consumer would then be prompted to enter the privacy level using the privacy slider for each WPR from the service provider's policy. The selected rules would then automatically populate the consumer's policy. The consumer then completes his/her privacy policy by adding the header information (i.e., *policy use, owner, proxy, valid*) and, if desired, add specific names to *collector* and *disclosed-to* for all rules. This can be done through a human-computer interface that shelters the user from the complexity of the policy language. In this way, large populations of

354 Yee & Korba

consumers may quickly obtain privacy policies for many service providers that reflect the privacy sensitivities of the communities surveyed.

Consumers may interactively adapt their existing privacy policies for new service provider policies based on the PSLs of the WPRs and the new provider policies, as illustrated in Figure 4. In Figure 4, the policy interpreter interactively allows the user to establish (e.g., using a privacy slider) the privacy levels of required rules based on the new provider policy and the PSLs from a policy provider. Policy search then retrieves the user policy that most

Figure 3. Derivation of personal privacy policies from surveys

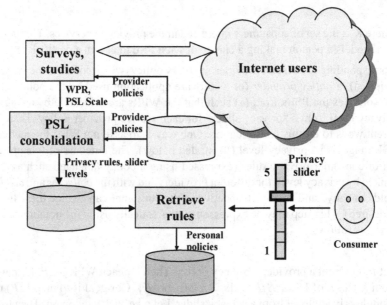

Figure 4. Adapting an existing personal privacy to a new provider

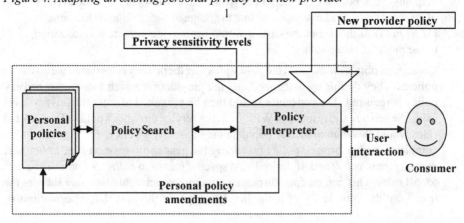

closely matches the user's privacy-established rules. This policy may then be further amended interactively via the policy interpreter to obtain the required personal privacy policy. This assumes the availability of an easy-to-understand interface for the user interaction as well as software to automatically take care of any needed conversions of rules back into the policy language (e.g., APPEL).

Example:

Suppose a consumer wishes to generate a personal privacy policy for E-learning Unlimited. For simplicity, suppose the privacy policy of E-learning Unlimited has only one WPR, namely <course marks, records, 12 months>.

Then the above steps are implemented as follows:

a. The third-party survey generates the following results for the WPR (the lowest privacy sensitivity level is $M = 1$, the highest is $N = 5$).

WPR (p_i)	PSL $(s_{k,i})$
<course marks, records, 6 months>	3
<course marks, records, 6 months>	4
<course marks, records, 6 months>	4
<course marks, records, 6 months>	5
<course marks, records, 12 months>	1
<course marks, records, 12 months>	1
<course marks, records, 12 months>	2
<course marks, records, 12 months>	3

   Note that the higher the number of months that the marks are retained, the lower the PSL (the lower the privacy perceived by the consumer). The different PSLs obtained constitute one part of the privacy sensitivity scale.

b. In this step, the policy provider consolidates the PSL in (a) using the median value from the corresponding PSL range. Thus for the 4 course mark retention times of 6 months, the lowest value is 3, the highest value is 5, and the median is 4. Therefore the rule <any, course marks, records, 6 months, none> is ranked with privacy level 4. Similarly, the rule <any, course marks, records, 12 months, none> is ranked with privacy level 2.

c. To obtain his/her privacy rules, the consumer specifies the service provider as E-learning Unlimited, and a privacy slider value of 4 (for example) when prompted. He/she then obtains the rule

<any, course marks, records, 6 months, none>

and proceeds to complete the policy by adding the header values and, if desired, specific names for *collector* and *disclosed-to*.

Retrieval from a Community of Peers

This approach assumes an existing community of peers already possessing specific use privacy policies with rules according to desired levels of privacy. A new consumer joining the community searches for personal privacy rules. The existing personal privacy policies may have been derived using the third-party surveys as above. Each privacy policy rule is stored along with its privacy level so that it may be selected according to this level and purpose. Where a rule has been adapted or modified by the owner, it is the owner's responsibility to ensure that the slider privacy value of the modified rule is consistent with the privacy sensitivity scale from surveys.

Figure 5. Retrieval of private policy rules from a community of peers

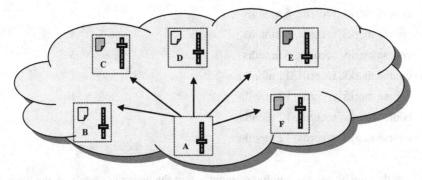

a) New consumer "A" broadcasts request for privacy rules to the community

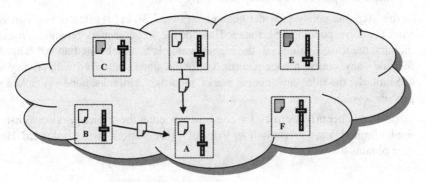

b) Consumers B and D answer A's request

a. All online users are peers, and everyone has a privacy slider. The new consumer broadcasts a request for privacy rules to the community (see Figure 5(a)), specifying *purpose* and slider value. This is essentially a peer-to-peer search over all peers.

b. The community responds by forwarding matching (in terms of *purpose* and slider value) rules to the consumer (see Figure 5(b)). This matching may also be fuzzy.

c. The consumer compares the rules and selects them according to *what*, possibly popularity (those that are from the greater number of peers), and best fit in terms of privacy. After obtaining the rules, the consumer completes the privacy policies by completing the headers and possibly changing the *collector* and *disclosed-to* as in the above derivation from surveys approach.

d. The consumer adapts a privacy policy to the service provider's policy, as in the derivation by surveys approach (Figure 4) to try to fulfill provider requirements.

Privacy Management Model

In this section, we explain how our privacy management model works to protect a consumer's privacy. Our model defines how privacy policies are used and explains how the provider's compliance to a consumer's policy can be assured.

How Privacy Policies are Used

An e-business provider has a privacy policy stating what PII it requires from a consumer and how the information will be used. A consumer has a privacy policy stating what PII the consumer is willing to share, with whom it may be shared, and under what circumstances it may be shared. An entity that is both a provider and a consumer has separate privacy policies for these two roles. A privacy policy is attached to a software agent, one that acts for the consumer and another that acts for the provider. Prior to the activation of a particular service, the agent for the consumer and the agent for the provider undergo a privacy policy exchange, in which the policies are examined for compatibility (see Figure 6). The service is only activated if the policies are compatible, in which case we say that there is a "match" between the two policies.

Figure 6. Exchange of proivacy policies (PP) between consumer agent (CA) and provider agent (PA)

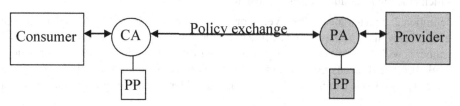

The Matching of Privacy Policies

We define here the meaning of a match between a consumer privacy policy and a service provider privacy policy. Such matching is the comparison of corresponding rules that have the same *purposes* and similar *what*. Let I represent the set of rules in a consumer privacy policy and let J represent the set of rules in a service provider privacy policy. Let $p_{i,c}$, $i \in I$ and $p_{j,p}$, $j \in J$ represent corresponding WPRs of the consumer policy and the provider policy, respectively, that have the same purposes and similar what. We wish to ascribe a function pr that returns a numerical level of privacy from the consumer's point of view when applied to $p_{i,c}$ and $p_{j,p}$. A high pr means a high degree of privacy; a low pr means a low degree of privacy, from the consumer's point of view. It is difficult to define pr universally because privacy is a subjective notion, and one consumer's view of degree of privacy may be different from another consumer's view. However, the privacy rules from the policy provider have corresponding privacy slider values, and they are just what we need. We simply look up $p_{i,c}$ and $p_{j,p}$ in the policy provider database and assign the corresponding privacy slider values to them. This look-up and assignment can be done automatically.

Definition 1 (Matching Collector and Disclosed-To)

The *collector* parameter from a consumer policy matches the *collector* parameter from a provider policy if and only if they are textually the same or the *collector* parameter from the consumer policy has the value "any." The matching of *disclosed-to* parameters is defined in the same way.

Definition 2 (Matching Rules)

There is a match between a rule in a consumer privacy policy and the corresponding (same purposes and similar what) rule in the provider policy if and only if:

$$pr(p_{i,c}) \leq pr(p_{j,p}), \quad i \in I,\ j \in J$$

and the corresponding collector and disclosed-to parameters match. If there is no corresponding rule in the provider policy, we say that the consumer rule corresponds to the null rule in the provider policy (called *consumer n-correspondence*), in which case the rules automatically match. If there is no corresponding rule in the consumer policy, we say that the provider rule corresponds to the null rule in the consumer policy (called *provider n-correspondence*), in which case the rules automatically mismatch.

In definition 2, a match means the level of privacy in the provider's rule is greater than the level of privacy in the consumer's rule (the provider is demanding less information than the consumer is willing to offer). Similarly, a consumer rule automatically matches a provider null rule because it means the provider is not even asking for the information represented by the consumer's rule (ultimate rule privacy). A provider rule automatically mismatches a consumer null rule because it means the provider is asking for information the consumer is not willing to share whatever the conditions (ultimate rule lack of privacy).

Definition 3 (Matching Privacy Policies)

A consumer privacy policy matches a service provider privacy policy if and only if all corresponding (same purposes and similar what) rules match and there are no cases of provider n-correspondence, although there may be cases of consumer n-correspondence.

Definition 4 (Upgrade and Downgrade of Rules and Policies)

A privacy rule or policy is considered upgraded if the new version represents more privacy than the prior version. A privacy rule or policy is considered downgraded if the new version represents less privacy than the prior version.

In comparing policies, it is not always necessary to carry out the comparison of each and every privacy rule as required by definitions 2 and 3. We mention three shortcuts here.

Shortcut 1

Both policies are the same except one policy has fewer rules than the other policy. According to definitions 2 and 3, there is a match if the policy with fewer rules belongs to the provider. There is a mismatch if this policy belongs to the consumer.

Shortcut 2

Both policies are the same except one policy has one or more rules with less retention time than the other policy. According to definitions 2 and 3, there is a match if the policy with one or more rules with less retention time belongs to the provider. There is a mismatch if this policy belongs to the consumer.

Shortcut 3

Both policies are the same except one policy has one or more rules that clearly represent higher levels of privacy than the corresponding rules in the other policy. According to definitions 2 and 3, there is a match if the policy with rules representing higher levels of privacy belongs to the provider. There is a mismatch if this policy belongs to the consumer.

Thus, in the example policies above, there is a match for e-learning according to shortcut 2, since the policy with lower retention time belongs to the provider. There is a mismatch for bookseller according to shortcut 1, since the policy with fewer rules belongs to the consumer. There is a mismatch for medical help according to shortcut 3, since the policy with the rule representing a higher level of privacy is the one specifying a particular collector (Dr. Smith), and this policy belongs to the consumer.

Privacy Policy Compliance

As we have seen, the above privacy principles require a provider to be accountable for complying with the privacy principles (CSAPP.1) and the privacy wishes of the consumer. In practice, a provider is required to appoint someone in its organization to be accountable for its compliance to privacy principles (CSAPP.1). This person is usually called the chief privacy officer (CPO). An important responsibility of the CPO is to put in place a procedure for receiving and responding to complaints or inquiries about the privacy policy and the practice of handling personal information. This procedure should be easily accessible and simple to use. The procedure should also refer to the dispute resolution process that the organization has adopted. Other responsibilities of the CPO include auditing the current privacy practices of the organization, formulating the organization's privacy policy, and implementing and maintaining this policy. We propose that the CPO's duties be extended to include auditing the provider's compliance to the consumer's privacy policy.

Further discussion of privacy policy compliance is beyond the scope of this chapter. We mention in passing that an alternative method of ensuring compliance is the use of a privacy policy compliance system (PPCS) as presented in Yee and Korba (2004).

Discussion and Related Work

We have presented methods for the semi-automatic derivation of personal privacy policies. Given our privacy management model, there has to be a way for consumers to derive their personal privacy policies easily or consumers will simply not use the approach. The only "alternative" that we can see to semi-automated derivation is for the consumer to create his/her personal privacy policy manually. This can be done by a knowledgeable and technically inclined consumer but would require a substantially larger effort (and correspondingly less likely to be used) than the semi-automated approaches we have presented. In addition to ease of use, our approaches ensure consistency of privacy rules by community consensus. This has the added benefit of facilitating provider compliance, since it is undoubtedly easier for a provider to comply with privacy rules that reflect the community consensus than rules that only reflect the feelings of a few.

We believe our approaches for the semi-automatic derivation of personal privacy policies are quite feasible, even taking into account the possible weaknesses described below. In the surveys approach, the consumer has merely to select the privacy level when prompted for the rules from the provider's policy. In fact, the user is already familiar with the use of a privacy slider to set the privacy level for Internet browsers (e.g., Microsoft Internet Explorer under "Internet Options"). We have implemented the surveys approach in a prototype that we created for negotiating privacy policies. We plan to conduct experiments with this implementation, using volunteers to confirm the usability of the surveys approach. In the retrieval approach, the consumer is asked to do a little bit more—compare and select the rules received—but this should be no more complex than today's e-commerce transactions or the use of a word processing program. Likewise, adapting a personal policy to a provider policy should also be the same level of complexity. Like anything else, the widespread use of these methods will take a little time to achieve, but people will come around to using them, just as they are becoming used to e-commerce—it is merely a matter of education and experience. Further, consumers are becoming more and more aware of their privacy rights as diverse jurisdictions enact privacy legislation to protect consumer privacy. In Canada, the Personal Information Protection and Electronic Documents Act has been in effect across all retail outlets since January 1, 2004, and consumers are reminded of their privacy rights every time they visit their optician, dentist, or other business requiring their private information.

An interesting aspect of our approaches is the prospect of continuously updating PII-related information and privacy policies, based upon policy updates fed back to the policy provider from consumers. Users will be changing their policies to suite their desired or perceived needs over time, when interacting with different service providers, and for different services. The policy provider could gather updates made to policies dynamically and analyze them to adjust the typical policies it distributes to better reflect the experiences of the population with different service providers.

We now discuss some possible weaknesses in our approaches.

The surveys approach requires trust in the policy provider. Effectively, the policy provider becomes a trusted third party. Clearly, the notion of a trusted third party as a personal policy provider may be controversial to some. Any error made by the policy provider could affect PII for many hundreds or thousands of people. A certification process for the policy provider is probably required. For instance, in Canada, the offices for the provincial and federal privacy commissioners could be this certification body. They could also be policy providers themselves. Having privacy commissioners' offices take on the role of policy providers seems to be a natural fit, given their mandate as privacy watchdogs for the consumer. However, the process would have a cost. Costs could be recovered via micro-charges to the consumer or the service provider for the policies provided. Aggregated information from the PII surveys could be sold to service providers who could use them to formulate privacy policies that are more acceptable to consumers.

There is a challenge in the retrieval approach regarding how to carry it out in a timely fashion. Efficient peer-to-peer search techniques will collect the rules in a timely manner, but the amount of information collected by the requester may be quite large. As well, since the various rules collected will probably differ from one another, the requestor will have to compare them to determine which ones to select. Quick comparisons to reduce the amount of data collected could be done through a peer-to-peer rules search that employs a rules hash array, containing hashed values for different portions of the rule.

In the section on policy compliance, a weakness of having the CPO be responsible for protecting consumer privacy is that the CPO belongs to the provider's organization. Will he/she be truly diligent about his/her task to protect the consumer's privacy? To get around this question, the CPO can make use of secure logs to answer any challenges doubting his/her organization's compliance. Secure logs automatically record all the organization's use of the consumer's private information, both during and after the data collection. Cryptographic techniques (Schneier & Kelsey, 1999) provide assurance that any modification of the secure log is detectable. In addition, database technology such as Oracle9i can tag the data with its privacy policy to evaluate the policy every time data is accessed (Yee & Korba, 2004). The system can be set up so that any policy violation can trigger a warning to the CPO.

An objection could be raised that our approaches are not general, having been based on privacy policy content that was derived from Canadian privacy legislation. We have several answers for this objection. First, as was pointed out above, Canadian privacy legislation is representative of privacy legislation in many countries. Therefore the content of privacy policies derived from Canadian privacy legislation is applicable in many countries. Second, as was also pointed out above, Canadian privacy legislation is also representative of the Fair Information Practices standards, which have universal applicability. Third, all privacy policies regardless of their content will have to converge on the content that we presented, since such content is required by legislation. Finally, our approaches can be customized to any form of privacy policy, regardless of the content.

We next discuss related work.

The use of privacy policies as a means of safeguarding privacy for e-business is relatively new. There is relatively little research on the use of personal privacy policies. For these reasons, we have not been able to find many authors who have written on the derivation of personal privacy policies. Dreyer and Olivier (1998) worked on generating and analyzing privacy policies for computer systems, to regulate private information flows within the system rather than generating personal privacy policies. Brodie, Karat, Karat, and Feng (2005) describe a privacy management workbench for use by organizations. Within this workbench are tools to allow organizational users tasked with the responsibility to author organizational privacy policies. The tools allow these users to use natural language for policy creation and to visualize the results to ensure that they accomplished their intended goals. These authors do not address the creation of personal privacy policies. Irwin and Yu (2005) present an approach for dynamically asking the user suitable questions to elicit the user's privacy preferences. They present a framework for determining which questions are suitable. However, there is no use of community consensus, which means the resulting policies could be highly subjective. This means that providers would find it more difficult to use such policies to help them formulate provider privacy policies that would be acceptable to the majority of consumers.

Other work that uses privacy policies is primarily represented by the W3C Platform for Privacy Preferences (W3C Platform). This provides a Web site operator with a way of expressing the Web site's privacy policy using a P3P standard format and to have that policy automatically retrieved and interpreted by user agents (e.g., browser plug-in). The user can express rudimentary privacy preferences and have those preferences automatically checked against the Web site's policy before proceeding. However, P3P cannot be used to fulfill the requirements of privacy legislation, has no compliance mechanism, and represents a "take it or leave it" view of privacy—if you don't like the privacy policy of the Web site, you leave it. There is no provision for negotiation as in Yee and Korba (2003b) and Korba (2002). In addition, Jensen and Potts (2004) evaluated the usability of 64 online privacy policies and the practice of posting them, and determined that significant changes needed to be made to the practice in order to meet usability and regulatory requirements. Finally, Stufflebeam, Anton, He, and Jain (2004) presented a case study in which they used P3P and Enterprise

Privacy Authorization Language (EPAL) to formulate two healthcare Web site privacy policies and described the shortcomings they found using these languages.

Conclusion and Future Research

The protection of personal privacy is paramount if e-services are to be successful. A privacy policy approach to privacy protection seems best. However, for this approach to work, consumers must be able to derive their personal privacy policies easily. In order to describe semi-automated approaches to derive personal privacy policies, we first defined the content of a personal privacy policy using the Canadian Privacy Principles. We then presented two semi-automated approaches for obtaining the policies: one based on third-party surveys of consumer perceptions of privacy, the other based on retrieval from a peer community. Both approaches reflect the privacy sensitivities of the community, giving the consumer confidence that his/her privacy preferences are interpreted with the best information available. We then explained our privacy management model, which details how privacy policies are used and the meaning of privacy policy matching. We further described how consumers could be assured that providers will comply with consumer policies.

For future research, we plan to investigate other ways of deriving privacy policies easily. As well, we plan to conduct experiments with volunteers, using the implementation of the surveys approach in our privacy policy negotiation prototype to confirm usability and resolve any scalability/performance issues.

References

Banisar, D. (1999, September 13). Privacy and data protection around the world. In *Proceedings of 21ˢᵗ International Conference on Privacy and Personal Data Protection*, Hong Kong.

Brodie, C., Karat, C. M., Karat, J., & Feng, J. (2005, July 6-8). Usable security and privacy: a case study of developing privacy management tools. In *Proceedings of Symposium On Usable Privacy and Security* (SOUPS), Pittsburgh, PA.

Canadian Standards Association. (2003). *Model code for the protection of personal information*. Retrieved September 5, 2003, from http://www.csa.ca/standards/privacy/code/Default.asp?articleID=5286&language=English

Department of Justice. (2003). *Privacy provisions highlights*. Retrieved August 4, 2003, from http://canada.justice.gc.ca/en/news/nr/1998/attback2.html

Dreyer, L. C. J., & Olivier, M. S. (1998). A workbench for privacy policies. In *Proceedings of The Twenty-Second Annual International Computer Software and Applications Conference* (COMPSAC '98), 350-355.

European Union. (1995). *Directive 95/46/EC of the European parliament and of the Council of 24 October 1995 on the protection of individuals with regard to the processing of personal data and on the free movement of such data.* Retrieved September 5, 2003, from http://aspe.hhs.gov/datacncl/eudirect.htm

Greer, T., & Murtaza, M. (2004, May). E-commerce security and privacy: managerial vs. technical perspectives. In *Proceedings of 15th IRMA International Conference (IRMA 2004)*, New Orleans, LA.

Irwin, K., & Yu, T. (2005, November 7). Determining user privacy preferences by asking the right questions: an automated approach. In *Proceedings of The 2005 ACM Workshop on Privacy in the Electronic Society (WPES 2005)*, Alexandria, VA.

Jensen, C., & Potts, C. (2004, April 24-29). Privacy policies as decision-making tools: an evaluation of online privacy notices. In *Proceedings of the 2004 Conference on Human Factors in Computing Systems (CHI 2004)*, Vienna, Austria.

Korba, L. (2002, January 7-11). Privacy in distributed electronic commerce. In *Proceedings of The 35th Hawaii International Conference on System Science (HICSS)*.

Schneier, B., & Kelsey, J. (May 1999). Secure audit logs to support computer forensics. *ACM Transactions on Information and System Security, 2*(2), 159-176.

Schwaig, K. S., Kane, G. C., & Storey, V. C. (2005). Privacy, fair information practices and the Fortune 500: the virtual reality of compliance. *The DATA BASE for Advances in Information Systems, 36*(1), 49-63.

Stufflebeam, W., Anton, A., He, Q., & Jain, N. (2004, October 28). Specifying privacy policies with P3P and EPAL: Lessons learned. In *Proceedings of The 2004 ACM Workshop on Privacy in the Electronic Society* (WPES 2004), Washington, D.C.

W3C APPEL. (2002). *A P3P preference exchange language 1.0 (APPEL1.0).* W3C working draft 15, April 2002. Retrieved September 2, 2002, from http://www.w3.org/TR/P3P-preferences/

W3C Platform. (2002). *The platform for privacy preferences.* Retrieved September 2, 2002, from http://www.w3.org/P3P/

Yee, G., El-Khatib, K., Korba, L., Patrick, A., Song, R., & Xu, Y. (2004). *Privacy and trust in e-government.* In W. Huang, K. Siau, & K. Kee Wei (Eds.), Electronic government strategies and implementation (pp. 145-189). Hershey, PA: Idea Group Inc.

Yee, G., & Korba, L. (2003a, January). Bilateral e-services negotiation under uncertainty. In *Proceedings of The 2003 International Symposium on Applications and the Internet* (SAINT2003), Orlando, FL.

Yee, G., & Korba, L. (2003b, May). The negotiation of privacy policies in distance education. In *Proceedings of 14th IRMA International Conference*, Philadelphia.

Yee, G., & Korba, L. (2004, July). Privacy policy compliance for Web services. In *Proceedings of 2004 IEEE International Conference on Web Services (ICWS 2004)*, San Diego, CA.

Yee, G., & Korba, L. (2005). Semi-automatic derivation and use of personal privacy policies in e-business. *International Journal of E-Business Research, 1*(1), 54-69.

Endnote

[1]   NRC Paper Number: NRC48479

About the Authors

In Lee is an associate professor in the Department of Information Management and Decision Sciences, College of Business and Technology, Western Illinois University. He received an MBA from the University of Texas at Austin and a PhD from the University of Illinois at Urbana-Champaign. He is a founding editor-in-chief of the *International Journal of E-Business Research*, the primary objective of which is to provide an international forum for researchers and practitioners to advance the knowledge and practice of all facets of electronic business. He has been serving on the excutive council of the Information Resources Management Association since 2003. He has published his research in *Communications of the ACM, IEEE Transactions on Engineering Management, IEEE Transactions on Systems, Man, and Cybernetics, International Journal of Production Research, Computers and Operations Research, Computers and Industrial Engineering, Knowledge and Process Management, Business Process Management Journal, Journal of E-Commerce in Organization*s, and others. His current research interests include e-commerce technology development and mangement, agent-oriented enterprise modeling, and intelligent simulation systems.

* * *

Hans Akkermans is a professor and head of the business informatics section at the Free University Amsterdam, as well as an international consultant. His research interests are interdisciplinary information science, distributed intelligence, and innovation with advanced information and communication technologies (ICT). He is the chair of the board of The Netherlands Graduate Research School of Information and Knowledge Systems, the scientific director of EnerSearch AB, an international industrial consortium on ICT in energy, and the coordinator of this area for the European Commission. He also leads Vubis, the Amsterdam multidisciplinary research center for business information sciences. He holds a *cum laude* PhD in theoretical physics from the University of Groningen.

Daniel Amyot is an assistant professor at the University of Ottawa, which he joined in 2002 after working for Mitel Networks as a senior researcher in software engineering. His research interests include scenario-based software engineering, requirements engineering, formal methods, and feature interactions in emerging applications. Amyot is rapporteur for requirements languages (MSC and URN) at the International Telecommunication Union. He has a PhD and a Master of Science from the University of Ottawa (2001 and 1994), as well as a Bachelor of Science from Laval University (1992). He is also the father of three energetic children.

Rebecca Angeles is an associate professor of MIS with the Faculty of Business Administration, University of New Brunswick Fredericton, Canada. Her research has appeared in such publications as *Information & Management, Decision Support Systems, Supply Chain Management: An International Journal, International Journal of Physical Distribution & Logistics Management, Logistics Information Management, Journal of Business Logistics, Pricing Strategy and Practice: An International Journal, EDI Forum: The Journal of Electronic Commerce,* and *Journal of International Consumer Marketing.* Her research interests are in the areas of radio frequency identification, electronic business, business-to-business exchanges, electronic trading partnerships, electronic data interchange (EDI), Internet-EDI, and interorganizational systems, as well as innovative education approaches in management information systems.

Noushin Ashrafi is a professor of information systems and chair of the executive committee of the faculty council at the University of Massachusetts Boston. Dr. Ashrafi received a PhD from the University of Texas at Arlington. Her area of research includes software process improvement, application of mathematical models to assess fault tolerance in software, and privacy issues in electronic commerce. Her publications have appeared in journals such as *IEEE Transactions, Information and Management, Journal of Electronic Commerce in Organizations,* and *Journal of Database Management.* Dr. Ashrafi has made presentations on various topics of information systems at national and international conferences.

Ziv Baida is a researcher with the Faculty of Economics and Business Administration (Information Systems Group) at the Free University Amsterdam. In his research, he applies conceptual modeling and knowledge management methods and techniques to traditional business topics such as business analysis, inter-organizational control, and service marketing. He developed the serviguration ontology and software tool, which were the topic of his PhD thesis at the computer science group at the Free University Amsterdam. He also runs e-Rational, a consulting firm specializing in business analyses, information management, and requirements engineering.

Djamal Benslimane is a full professor of computer sciences at Claude Bernard Lyon 1 University and a member of LIRIS-CNRS Laboratory, both in Lyon, France. His research interests include database interoperability, Web services, and ontologies. Benslimane received a PhD in computer science from Blaise Pascal University (France).

Tsung-Bin Chang obtained a master's degree in information management from Da-Yeh University. He is a specialist in signal exchange and quality improvement of mobile tele-communication in the mobile business branch at Chunghwa Telecom Co., Ltd., the largest telecom company in Taiwan.

Guoqing Chen received a PhD from the Catholic University of Leuven, Belgium. Currently he is a professor of information systems management at the School of Economics and Management, Tsinghua University. Dr. Chen has been published more than 100 times international in journals, books, and conference proceedings, including two books published by Kluwer Academic Publishers, Boston (1998 and 1999, respectively). He is a co-author of the books *Information Systems: Organization, Management and Modeling* (with K. Reimers, 2002) and *Seizing Strategic IT Advantage in China* (with W. McFarlan and R. Nolan, 2003). Professor Chen serves on several editorial boards of international journals including *Information Processing & Management, Information Sciences,* and others. His teaching and research interests include management information systems, business intelligence, fuzzy logic and data modeling, and IT management and e-business.

Ye-Sho Chen received a PhD from Purdue University in 1985. He is currently a professor of MIS in the Department of Information Systems and Decision Sciences at Ourso College of Business Administration, Louisiana State University. Dr. Chen has published more than 80 papers in journals (such as *Decision Support Systems, Journal of Information Technology,* and *IEEE Transactions on Engineering Management*) and conference proceedings (such as *Proceedings of the International Conference on Information Systems* and *Proceedings of the Hawaii International Conference on System Sciences*). Dr. Chen is the associate director of the International Franchise Forum at LSU. His major function is to conduct the Netchising—combining the power of the Inter*net* for global integration of business processes and international fran*chising* for local responsiveness of demands—research to help organizations grow in the global market.

Aidan Duane holds a Master of Science from University College Cork (UCC). At present he is following the PhD program at UCC with the Department of Accounting, Finance and Information Systems. He also currently lectures in information systems and electronic business at Waterford Institute of Technology (WIT) in Ireland. His research interests include electronic business, electronic communication systems, electronic monitoring, and information systems (IS) ethical issues. His research has been published in leading information systems journals and conferences, including *The Information Systems Journal, The International Journal of E-Business Research*, ICIS, ICEC, and IRMA.

Patrick Finnegan holds a PhD in information systems from the University of Warwick, and is currently a senior lecturer in management information systems at the University College Cork. His research interests include electronic business and IS strategy. He has published his research in a number of international journals and conferences, including *The International Journal of Electronic Commerce, IT& People, Database, Electronic Markets, The Information Systems Journal*, ECIS, ICIS, and AMCIS.

Jørn Flohr Nielsen is a professor of organization and management at the School of Economics and Management, University of Aarhus, Denmark. His research interests include organizational change, organizational aspects of e-commerce, and service management. He has published in several international journals, including *Scandinavian Journal of Information Systems, Scandinavian Journal of Management, European Management Journal, European Journal of Marketing, International Journal of Retail & Distribution Management, The Service Industries Journal*, and *The International Journal of Service Industry Management*. Recently he has been coordinating an international research project on technology and market orientation in Nordic banks.

Frank Goethals completed his master's studies in economics (option informatics) at the Katholieke Universiteit Leuven, Belgium (2000). He is presently working on a PhD under the theme of dependencies in extended enterprise integration. This research is conducted at K.U. Leuven under the guidance of Prof. Jacque Vandenbulcke and is financed by SAP Belgium. Goethals has a strong interest in coordination and dependency theory and enterprise architecture.

Jaap Gordijn is an associate professor of e-business at the Free University Amsterdam. He previously was a consultant for Deloitte & Touche and Cisco. His research interests are networked business modeling, value-based requirements engineering, and innovative e-business applications, and he developed the e³-value ontology and related methodology and tools. He received his PhD in computer science from the Free University Amsterdam.

Viggo Høst is an associate professor with the Department of Economics, School of Economics and Management, University of Aarhus, Denmark. His research interests include applied statistics and structural equation modeling. He has published in journals such as *The Scandinavian Journal of Management* and *The Service Industries Journal*.

Philip Houle is an associate professor of information systems in the College of Business & Public Administration, Drake University. He received a PhD in computer and information control sciences from the University of Minnesota. Professor Houle teaches database management, data communications and networking, and introductory information systems.

He also served as the top information technology administrator at Drake University from 1999-2001, a time during which the university upgraded its campus network to improve campus security and network performance. Currently, he is working on issues involving e-mail address identity/mobility and e-commerce, including the use of spyware.

Gary Hunter is an assistant professor of marketing at Illinois State University. He received a PhD in 2000 from the University of Kentucky His research interests include technology adoption and the impact of information overload and automaticity theory. His work has been published in the *Journal of Consumer Research, Journal of Personal Selling and Sales Management, Journal of Consumer Satisfaction, Dissatisfaction, and Complaining Behavior, International Journal of Service Industry Management, International Journal of E-Business Research, and the Journal of Marketing Education.*

Wen-Jang (Kenny) Jih currently is a professor of computer information systems at the Jennings A. Jones College of Business, Middle Tennessee State University. He previously taught at Longwood University, University of Tennessee at Chattanooga, Auburn University, Da-Yeh University (Taiwan), and Chung-Yuan Christian University (Taiwan). He also served as the dean of the School of Management at Da-Yeh University (1997-2001). He has consulted for a number of companies in Taiwan, including a major automobile manufacturing company. He obtained his doctorate degree in information systems from the University of North Texas in 1985. His recent research interests include e-commerce, knowledge management, customer relationship management, and innovative instruction methods in information systems.

Irma Kikvidze is a graduate of Tbilisi State University and Institute of Public Affairs in Georgia, CIS. Currently pursuing an MBA from Purdue University, she has a background in the health care sector and wholesale business of pharmaceuticals. During the last several years she has worked in central and commercial bank accounting, internal auditing, and consulting in Georgia, CIS. She is a participant in the accounting reform for the implementation of international accounting standards in the Georgian banking sector.

Larry Korba is a principle research officer with the National Research Council of Canada. He is the leader of the information security group in the Institute for Information Technology (http://www.iit-iti.nrc-cnrc.gc.ca/) and involved in the research and development of security- and privacy-enhancing technologies for applications ranging from gaming to ad hoc wireless systems.

Jean-Pierre Kuilboer is an associate professor in information systems and chairman of the management science and information systems department at the University of Massachusetts Boston. Dr. Kuilboer's current interests are in the area of business strategic agility, electronic business, information security and privacy, and database management. He has published a book on e-business and e-commerce infrastructure and articles in such journals as the *Database for Advances in Information Systems, Journal of Database Management, Information & Management, Annals of Cases on Information Technology, Information and*

Software Technology, International Journal of E-business Research, and *ACM – Computers and Society.*

Wilfried Lemahieu holds a PhD from the Department of Applied Economic Sciences of the Katholieke Universiteit Leuven, Belgium (1999). At present, he is an associate professor with the Management Informatics Research Group of the Faculty of Economics and Applied Economics. His teaching includes database management, data storage architectures, and management informatics. His research interests are comprised of distributed object architectures and Web services, object-relational and object-oriented database systems, and hypermedia systems.

Zakaria Maamar received a PhD in computer sciences from Laval University (Canada) in 1998. Currently, he is an associate professor in the College of Information Systems at Zayed University, Dubai, UAE. His research interests are the areas of mobile computing, Web/mobile services, and software agents.

Qusay H. Mahmoud is an assistant professor in the department of computing and information science at the University of Guelph and also holds the associate chair of the distributed computing and wireless & telecommunications systems technology program at the University of Guelph-Humber in Toronto, Canada. He received his PhD in computer sciences from Middlesex University (UK) in 2002. His research interests include wireless computing, agent technology, and Web-based systems. He is a member of the ACM and the IEEE Computer Society.

Carleen Maitland is an assistant professor in the School of Information Sciences and Technology at the Pennsylvania State University (USA). She received a doctorate in 2001 from Delft University of Technology, The Netherlands, where she was an assistant professor prior to joining Penn State. Her research interests include the effects of new mobile and wireless technologies on organizations and industry structure, as well as the role of national policies in bringing about these effects. She has published in journals such as *Telecommunications Policy, Information Economics and Policy,* and *Communications and Strategies.*

Turan Melemez, from Turkey, has a master's degree in computer science from the University of Dortmund, Germany. He has worked in e-business consulting companies for the last seven years and is currently managing e-business implementations in the customer relationship management (CRM) area as a senior consultant for IBM Global Services in Sercon, Germany.

Niels Peter Mols is a professor of marketing with the Department of Management, School of Economics and Management, University of Aarhus, Denmark. His research interests include marketing channels, buyer-seller relationships, transaction cost economics, and e-commerce. He has published in journals such as *European Journal of Marketing, International Journal of Retail & Distribution Management, International Review of Retail, Distribution and*

Consumer Research, Journal of Euromarketing, Journal of Marketing Channels, Journal of Segmentation in Marketing, Journal of Targeting, Measurement and Analysis for Marketing, and *The International Journal of Service Industry Management.*

Andrei Morch is a researcher in the Energy Systems Department, SINTEF Energy Research. He received his Master of Science in energy management from the Norwegian School of Management (BI) in 1998. He obtained the previous academic grade, mechanical engineer, in 1992. Morch has been engaged in several research projects related to electricity trade and strategic planning in deregulated power markets.

Ghita Kouadri Mostéfaoui received a PhD in computer science from the University of Fribourg (Switzerland) and Paris VI Pierre et Marie Curie University (France) in 2004. Currently, she is a postdoctoral researcher with the Department of Computer Sciences and Operations Research at the University of Montreal, Canada. Her research interests include software engineering, Web services, security and context-aware computing. She is a member of the IEEE Computer society, ACM, and the Swiss Computer Scientists Society.

Soroya Kouadri Mostéfaoui is a PhD candidate in the Pervasive and Artificial Intelligence Research Group with the Computer Sciences Department of the University of Fribourg, Switzerland. Her research interests include ubiquitous computing, context-aware computing, Web services, and emergent behaviors.

Ravinder Nath is the associate dean for graduate programs and the holder of the Jack and Joan McGraw endowed chair of information technology management in the College of Business Administration, Creighton University. He has published numerous research papers in the area of electronic commerce and information systems in various national and international publications. Dr. Nath teaches and conducts research in information systems, electronic commerce, and data mining. Also, Dr. Nath serves on the boards of several for-profit and non-profit organizations. He holds a master's degree from Wichita State University and a PhD from Texas Tech University.

Chris Paslowski, from Canada, earned a Bachelor of Arts in economics from the University of Western Ontario and an MBA from Purdue University/German International School of Management and Administration. For three years, he has worked for the Forzani Group Limited in Calgary, Alberta, Canada, as a merchandise planner.

Mahesh Raisinghani is an associate professor at TWU's School of Management. He is also the president and CEO of Raisinghani and Associates International, Inc., a diversified global firm with interests in strategic information systems consulting and technology options trading. Dr. Raisinghani earned a PhD from the University of Texas at Arlington and is a certified e-commerce consultant (CEC). Dr. Raisinghani was the recipient of the 2005 TWU School of Management Award for most innovative teaching methods; the 1999 UD Presidential Award; the 2001 King/Haggar Award for excellence in teaching, research, and service; the

2002 research award; and a finalist at the 2002 Asian Chamber of Commerce awards. Dr. Raisinghani won the Organizational Service Award at GITM 2005 and IRMA 2002. As a global thought leader on e-business and global information systems, he serves as the vice president of the Global IT Management Association and the chairman of IRMA's Special Research Cluster on E-Business. He has also served as the local chair of the International Symposium on Research Methods in 2002 and the World Conference on Global Information Technology Management in 2001, and as the track chair for e-commerce technologies management at the Information Resources Management Association since 1999.

Sridhar Ramaswami is a professor of marketing in the College of Business at Iowa State University. Dr. Ramaswami received a BS in engineering from the University of Madras, India, and a PhD in marketing from the University of Texas-Austin. His research focuses on consumer behavior in online markets, marketing of financial services, sales management, and brand equity management.

Hanne Sæle received her Master of Science in electrical engineering at Norges Teknisk-Naturvitenskapelige Universitet (NTNU), Trondheim (1998). She is currently a research scientist at SINTEF Energy Research, Department of Energy Systems. Her main fields of competence are power market studies, demand-side bidding, demand-side management and load management, information and communication technology in the power market, and the aspects of customer's behavior concerning electricity consumption.

Klaus Simons, from Brazil, has an undergraduate degree in industrial engineering from the Polytechnic School of University of Sao Paulo (POLI-USP), Brazil, and an MBA from Purdue University at GISMA Business School, Germany. He has extensive work experience in the Brazilian financial markets, where he worked as a relationship manager at the Corporate Bank of Banco ItaÃ° SA, one of the largest private-sector banks in Brazil.

Monique Snoeck obtained her PhD in May 1995 from the Department of Computer Science of the Katholieke Universiteit Leuven with a thesis that lays the formal foundations for the object-oriented business modeling method MERODE. Since then, she has done further research in the area of formal methods for object-oriented conceptual modeling. She now is full professor with the Management Information Systems Group of the fFaculty of Economics and Applied Economics at the Katholieke Universiteit Leuven in Belgium. She has been involved in several industrial conceptual modeling projects. Her research interests are object-oriented conceptual modeling, software architecture, and software quality.

Thomas Stafford is an assistant professor of MIS at the Fogelman College of Business and Economics, University of Memphis (USA). With doctoral degrees from the University of Georgia and the University of Texas-Arlington, Stafford has published his research on Internet usage motivations and instant messaging use in *Decision Sciences*, *IEEE Transactions on Engineering Management*, and *Communications of the ACM*. He will be editing a special issue of *IEEE Transactions on Professional Communication* on the topic of instant messaging in 2008.

Troy Strader is an associate professor of information systems at the Drake University College of Business & Public Administration. He received his PhD in business administration (information systems) from the University of Illinois at Urbana-Champaign in 1997. Dr. Strader has co-edited two books on mobile commerce and electronic commerce and has published in *Communications of the ACM, the International Journal of Electronic Commerce, Decision Support Systems, the Journal of the AIS, Electronic Commerce Research, Electronic Markets,* and several other academic journals. His research interests include mobile commerce, online investment banking, consumer behavior in online markets, and communication technology adoption.

Susanne Taha, from Germany, has a master's degree in economics from the University of Cologne, Germany, and a master's degree in business administration from Purdue University. She worked in the financial services sector for two major banks over the course of seven years. Upon relocating to Germany, she worked as a consultant, where she managed an Intranet project and was a member of the committee that was responsible for the selection of a new CRM system for a large financial services and consulting firm.

Steven Taylor is a professor of marketing at Illinois State University. Dr. Taylor's studies have been published in numerous journals, including the *Journal of Marketing, Journal of Retailing, International Journal of Service Industry Management, Journal of Business Ethics,* and *Journal of Insurance Issues,* among numerous others. In addition to regularly serving as an ad hoc reviewer for numerous major marketing journals, Dr. Taylor also serves as a member of the editorial review boards of the *Journal of Service Research* and the *International Journal of Service Industry Management.* Most recently, he assumed the position of associate editor of the *Journal of Consumer Satisfaction/Dissatisfaction & Complaining Behavior* and is a founding member of SPSS' academic advisory board.

Els van de Kar is an assistant professor in the Faculty of Technology, Policy and Management (TPM) at Delft University of Technology, The Netherlands. She received a PhD in systems engineering for her research on a design approach for mobile information services in which the customer, technology and organizational issues are balanced. van de Kar has more than 10 years' working experience in industry at the Dutch telecommunication operator KPN Telecom and as independent consultant. van de Kar's research interests include service design, mobile service systems, and organizational design aspects of e-business.

Jacques Vandenbulcke is a professor with the Faculty of Economics and Applied Economics of the Katholieke Universiteit Leuven, Belgium. His main research interests are in database management, data modeling, and business information systems. He is co-ordinator of the Leuven Institute for Research on Information Systems (LIRIS) and holder of the SAP chair on extended enterprise infrastructures. He is president of Studiecentrum voor Automatische Informatieverwerking (SAI), the largest society for computer professionals in Belgium, and co-founder of the Production and Inventory Control Society (PICS) in Belgium.

Uta Wehn de Montalvo is senior researcher and advisor on information and communication technology (ICT) policy at Netherlands Organisation for Applied Scientific Research. Previously, she worked as a research officer in Science and Technology Policy Research and as a programmer for IBM UK Ltd. She holds a doctorate of philosophy in science and technology policy from the University of Sussex (UK). Her research focuses on new ICT services with a special interest in business models for location-based services and spatial data policy.

Michael Weiss is an assistant professor at Carleton University, which he joined in 2000 after a five-year stint in industry after receiving his PhD in computer science in 1993 (University of Mannheim, Germany). In particular, he led the advanced applications group within the strategic technology group of Mitel Corporation. His research interests include service-oriented architectures, patterns, business model design and evolution, and open source development.

Shu-Yeng Wong currently is a professor of statistics at Da-Yeh University, Taiwan. She obtained her doctoral degree in educational inquiry methodology from Indiana University in 1980. Her recent research interests include: e-commerce, customer relationship management, and user behavior for information technology.

Soushan Wu received his PhD in finance from the University of Florida in 1984. He is currently a chair professor and dean of the College of Management, Chang-Gung University, Taiwan. His research interests include management science, investment science, and information systems. He has published more than 100 articles in research in *Finance, Financial Management, Decision Support Systems, Decision and Negotiation, Journal of Safety Research, International Journal of Accounting and Information Systems*, and more. He is now the chief editor of the *Journal of Management* (in Taiwan) and an editor of several international journals, including *International Journal of E-Finance*.

George Yee (http://georgeyee.ca) is a senior research officer in the information security group, Institute for Information Technology, National Research Council Canada (NRC). Prior to joining the NRC in late 2001, he spent more than 20 years at Bell-Northern Research and Nortel Networks. He received his PhD in electrical engineering from Carleton University, Ottawa, Canada, where he is currently an adjunct research professor. He is a senior member of IEEE as well as a member of ACM and Professional Engineers Ontario. His research interests include security and privacy for e-services, using software agents to enhance reliability, security, and privacy, and engineering software for reliability, security, and performance.

Lijie Zou is a graduate of the Tianjin Foreign Language Institute in the People's Republic of China and holds an MBA from Purdue University. She has work experience in an import and export trading company, and overseeing international tenders and BOT projects financed by the World Bank, Asia Bank, and the Chinese Commerce Ministry.

Index

product data management 96
ProductExists 197
production rules 213, 215, 229
production system 213
property-based resource 70
property rights theory 6
proposal process 28
protocol 335
public policies 146
purchase good 168
purchasing 94
purchasing decisions 116

Q

qualitative (fuzzy) value 178
qualitative-interpretive 202
quality function deployment (QFD) 227
quality standard 153

R

R-context 237, 250
rational decision-making model 58
rebel phase 155, 156
REJ(demand, resource) 213
relational exchange theory 93
relations 227
relationship 73
renewal phase 155, 156
ReplenishTimer_timeout 197
RepositoryAvailable 197
requirement expression 210
requirements engineering (RE) 208, 228
resource 76, 238
resource-based literature 70
resource-based perspective 72
resource-based view (RBV) 71
resource dependence 73
resources 73, 204, 207, 227
RetailerService 188
right architecture 36
right solution 36
right strategy 36
risk-reduction measure 118
risk management 26, 152
role integrity 95

S

sacrifice 205, 221
SAP-systems 34
SARS 151
SARS crisis management 151
satisfaction 177
scenario definition 173
secure format 30
security 241
security strategy 246
SEL 216
selection policy 173
semi-automated 349
service-oriented architecture (SOA) 188
service bundle 199, 223
service dependency 207
service element 206
service innovation 45
service input 207
service marketing 206
service network 76
service ontology 215
service outcome 207
service property 206, 221
service provider 69
service provision 80
service quality 206
serviguration process 222, 223
severeness 218
siblings 220
Simonian approach information 146
simulation 202
skew distribution 136, 158
skew phenomena 141, 158
small and medium-sized firms 51
social network 147
software engineering 227
SomeItemsShipped 197
soundness 202
source goods 170
source trustworthiness 246
sourcing 94
spam 322
specialized Investment 48, 59
speed 27
spim 323